PRAISE FOR
DRED SCOTT AND THE PROBLEM OF CONSTITUTIONAL EVIL

"Here is one of the most provocative books on constitutional law you will ever read, about history's most reviled case. Bucking the tide, Graber argues the Supreme Court actually got it right in *Dred Scott*. Constitutions, Graber explains, often are compromises with the devil. Once made, there are no tricks of constitutional law or interpretation that can make the evil go away."

> – Barry Friedman, New York University School of Law

"Constitutional 'evil' is an unsettling idea. It is a wrenching and embarrassing part of American constitutional history, but it is often painted with a light brush. In this fascinating book, Mark Graber has brilliantly compelled us to do much more. No longer can we ignore evil in our own experience. The emphasis on the *Dred Scott* case is a superb choice to highlight within the many other examples that are also considered. It provokes us to think about evil in its many forms – from racial to institutional. It is a powerful solvent against the notion of American exceptionalism."

> – Thomas D. Morris, author of *Southern Slavery and the Law, 1619–1860*, and Cleveland-Marshall College of Law

"Mark Graber shows that, sadly, the *Dred Scott* decision's grim affirmation of slavery's constitutionality was an all-too-reasonable reading of American law. He then poses an even more painful question: whether the Civil War was the best route to eradicating that great constitutional evil. His sobering reflections will stimulate disagreements but also deeper understanding of monumental issues that are very much with us today."

> – Rogers M. Smith, University of Pennsylvania

CAMBRIDGE STUDIES ON THE AMERICAN CONSTITUTION

SERIES EDITORS

Maeva Marcus, *George Washington University*
Melvin Urofsky, *Virginia Commonwealth University*
Mark Tushnet, *Georgetown University Law Center*
Howard Gillman, *University of Southern California*

Cambridge Studies on the American Constitution publishes books that examine the American Constitution and offers a range of interpretations and approaches, from traditional topics of constitutional history and theory, case studies, and judicial biographies to more modern and often controversial issues dealing with gender and race. Although many estimable series have incorporated constitutional studies, none have done so exclusively. This series seeks to illuminate the implications – governmental, political, social, and economic – of the relationship between the American Constitution and the country it governs through a wide array of perspectives.

Dred Scott and the Problem of Constitutional Evil

MARK A. GRABER

University of Maryland

CAMBRIDGE UNIVERSITY PRESS
Cambridge, New York, Melbourne, Madrid, Cape Town, Singapore,
São Paulo, Delhi, Dubai, Tokyo

Cambridge University Press
32 Avenue of the Americas, New York, NY 10013-2473, USA

www.cambridge.org
Information on this title: www.cambridge.org/9780521728577

First published 2006
First paperback edition 2008
Reprinted 2009

A catalog record for this publication is available from the British Library

Library of Congress Cataloging in Publication data

Graber, Mark A.
Dred Scott and the problem of constitutional evil / Mark A. Graber.
  p. cm. – (Cambridge studies on the American Constitution)
Includes index.
ISBN 0-521-86165-9 (hardback)
1. Slavery – Law and legislation – United States – History.   2. Scott, Dred,
1809–1858 – Trials, litigation, etc.   3. Slavery – United States – Legal
status of slaves in free states.   4. Constitutional history – United States.
I. Title. II. Series.
KF4545.S5G73   2006
342.7308'7 – dc22   2006005050

ISBN 978-0-521-86165-6 Hardback
ISBN 978-0-521-72857-7 Paperback

Transferred to digital printing 2010

In memory of Julius W. Graber and Jerome D. Frank,
who were for every decent cause long before those causes
were known to be decent

I John Brown am now quite *certain* that the crimes of this *guilty land,* *will* never be purged *away,* but with Blood.

Shalom rav al yisra'el am'cha tasim l'olam

Grant abundant peace eternally for Israel, Your people

Contents

Acknowledgments

Communities write books. Individuals may type the words, see their name on the front cover, and collect the royalty check, but the ideas they express are derived from and depend upon the communities they inhabit. Although common courtesy requires an author to absolve friends and associates for any mistakes in his work, the strengths and weaknesses of our writings inevitably reflect the strengths and weaknesses of our communities. Whatever virtues and vices you may find in *Dred Scott and the Problem of Constitutional Evil* are virtues and vices that were fostered by the many communities I have been fortunate to inhabit. I am grateful beyond words for the way these communities have helped me discipline my intellectual quirkiness and even more grateful for their forbearance when this intellectual quirkiness manifested itself as neurosis.

Every paragraph in *Dred Scott* is indebted to the growing school of historical institutionalism in political science, history, and law. My ongoing conversations with the exceptionally gifted scholars in that community have enriched my academic and personal life to the point where I might seriously consider remaining in the academy even if offered the opportunity to play point guard for the New York Knicks. Keith Whittington, Mark Tushnet, Sandy Levinson, and Jeff Tulis continually teach me about the crucial importance of the Constitution outside of the courts. Mark Brandon and Howard Gillman continually teach me about the crucial role that constitutional failure plays in American political development. Rogers Smith, Julie Novkov, and Pamela Brandwein continually teach me about the crucial role that race and slavery play in American constitutional development. Ran Hirschl, Sandy Levinson, and Keith Whittington continually teach me about the crucial role constitutional structures play in constitutional development. Paul Frymer, Ron Kahn, Leslie Goldstein, John Brigham, Steve Griffin, Barry Friedman, Christine Harrington, Douglas Grob, Bruce Ackerman, Karen

Orren, Stephen Skowronek, Ken Kersch, George Lovell, Michael McCann, Gordon Silverstein, Jim Fleming, Linda McClain, Howard Schweber, Donald Downs, Gary Jacobsohn, Neal Devins, Steve Elkin, Scot Powe, Michael Klarman, Jack Balkin, H. W. Perry, Joel Grossman, Judy Baer, Sotirios Barber, and many others continually teach me to think about constitutionalism in ways that were alien to the young would-be scholar who once thought that the only purpose of constitutional argument was to persuade five justices on the Supreme Court. Every thought in this text was inspired by these wonderful and giving scholars. In the case of Sandy Levinson, Howard Gillman, Mark Tushnet, Ran Hirschl, and Keith Whittington, I can no longer tell the difference between my ideas and theirs. I am particularly grateful for the too many times they commented on this manuscript and to such younger scholars as Bradley Hays, Justin Wert, Steve Simon, and Rebecca Thorpe for challenging all of our ideas, for recognizing that their task is to build new paradigms for their generation. *Dred Scott* will be a success in my eyes if readers are convinced that they must read and read carefully the major works of all the scholars mentioned in this paragraph.

My communities at the University of Texas and the University of Maryland contributed greatly to *Dred Scott*. Jim Fishkin, Walter Dean Burnham, Sandy Levinson, and Scot Powe played vital roles in my formative years as a scholar, teaching me about the possibilities of American constitutional development, encouraging me to find my distinctive scholarly voice, and giving me a taste for barbecue at bizarre places. Jon Wilkenfeld, Mark Lichbach, and Steve Elkin of the University of Maryland, College Park, provided crucial guidance and support when we moved back to the East Coast. I am particularly grateful to Dean Karen Rothenberg at the University of Maryland School of Law for her encouragement and summer money, to Dean Richard Boldt for encouragement and ideas and for giving me a second home in Baltimore, and to Deborah Hellman, Jana Singer, Gordon Young, David Bogen, Peter Quint, Maxwell Stearns, David Super, and many other colleagues at the law school for ideas and stimulation. I was also made welcome at numerous other academic communities, whose faculty calmly listened to earlier versions of this book and made exceptionally helpful suggestions. These institutions include the UCLA Law School, Johns Hopkins University, Syracuse University, the University of Texas at Dallas, New York University School of Law, DePaul College of Law, and the University of North Carolina School of Law. The hospitality of these institutions merits mention for being responsible for whatever weight gain I experienced when writing *Dred Scott*. I am also grateful to *Constitutional Commentary* and the *University of North Carolina Law Review* for publishing earlier essays on themes discussed in this work and for their granting permission to republish parts of those essays here. Maeva Marcus and the Institute for Constitutional Studies deserve special thanks for supporting my scholarship.

The academic publishing community has supported and shaped *Dred Scott* for almost a decade. Malcolm Litchfield, Chuck Myers, and John Tyrneski have always fostered my ambitions and demonstrated the highest professional standards in all our interactions. Lewis Bateman and Cambridge University Press brought those ambitions to fruition. Lewis is a model editor. Under his guidance the reviewing and publication process was handled expeditiously, and more than 50,000 unnecessary words were cut from this manuscript. Both he and Ruth Homingras politely, but firmly, disciplined my writing excesses, allowing me to say the same thing twice and sometimes even thrice but not ten times. Maeva Marcus, Howard Gillman, Mark Tushnet, and Mel Urofsky kindly included this work in their series, "Cambridge Studies on the American Constitution." Given their reputations and the high standards they demand of authors and reviewers, I look forward to the marvelous works they will publish in the future. Matt Darnell and Vickie Darnell provided quick and first-rate copy-editing and typesetting, respectively. Cynthia Monroe did a wonderful job on the index.

My family is the most important community responsible for this book. For half a century I have been blessed with unbelievably loving and nurturing parents, Anita Wine Graber and Julius W. Graber. They were the first to foster my intellectual quirkiness and be amused by my innumerable neuroses. My spouse, Dr. Julia Bess Frank, who by marriage inherited the responsibility for putting up with both the quirkiness and neurosis, has for more than twenty years been a source of strength, an exceptional editor, and a model of human decency for our children, her students, and her communities. Our children – Naomi, Abigail, and Rebecca – provided much of the research for this book (along with their friends Rebecca Cole and Emily Sutton) and, to the great joy of their father, seem to have inherited a bit of that intellectual quirkiness (I am also to blame for whatever neuroses they exhibit). The last paragraph of this book is written in the hope that our future grandchildren will have the full opportunity to exhibit their intellectual quirkiness and neuroses.

Introduction

REHABILITATING *DRED SCOTT*

J. P. Morgan demanded that his attorneys make only those legal arguments that advanced his causes. When informed by counsel that his business plans violated federal law, Morgan bluntly replied: "I don't ... want a lawyer to tell me what I cannot do; I hire him to tell me how to do what I want to do."[1] Morgan's example seems to inspire contemporary constitutional rhetoric. Constitutional theorists of all political persuasions often display less interest in determining what is constitutional than in making arguments that they believe will help the social movements they favor achieve desired ends constitutionally. My claim that the result in *Dred Scott v. Sandford*[2] *may* have been constitutionally correct – and that Stephen Douglas understood the antebellum constitutional order better than Abraham Lincoln – is likely to startle, puzzle, and probably offend readers reared on a steady diet of constitutional advocacy. No decent person living at the dawn of the twenty-first century supports the proslavery and racist policies that Douglas and Chief Justice Roger Taney championed. Nevertheless, important normative, historical, and constitutional reasons exist for rehabilitating the *Dred Scott* decision.

Dred Scott and this book are about the problem of constitutional evil. The problem of constitutional evil concerns the practice and theory of sharing civic space with people committed to evil practices or pledging allegiance to a constitutional text and tradition saturated with concessions to evil. People pledge allegiance to constitutions they acknowledge are saturated with evil when they perceive compelling reasons to cooperate politically with the purveyors of injustice. Some Americans at the constitutional convention thought

---

[1] Ida M. Tarbell, *The Life of Elbert H. Gary: The Story of Steel* (Appleton: New York, 1925), p. 81.
[2] 60 U.S. 393 (1857).

1

slavery a "nefarious institution." Others regarded slavery as "justified by the example of all the world."[3] I believe the death penalty to be barbaric, discrimination against homosexuality to be bigotry, and the level of inequality in the United States to be outrageous. My neighbors claim that justice demands murderers be executed, that homosexuality is an abomination, and that economic redistribution is theft. The problem of constitutional evil is about why, how, and whether we form and sustain political communities despite these deep disagreements.

Constitutionalism, in this work, mediates the controversies that arise among citizens who hold clashing political aspirations. In regimes wracked with problems of constitutional evil, political actors must negotiate and renegotiate constitutional meanings with rivals whose positions they find morally abhorrent. The challenge of creating and preserving political relationships among people who hold conflicting conceptions of justice requires that compromises be forged in every dimension of political life. Bargaining occurs over constitutional rules, the structure of constitutional politics, and the practices for resolving constitutional silences and ambiguities. "Constitution perfecting theory,"[4] "justice-seeking constitutionalism,"[5] and other approaches that treat constitutional language primarily as pure expressions of agreed-upon normative aspirations play little role in this endeavor. The constitutional task is better described as finding settlements that everyone perceives as "not bad enough" to justify secession and civil war than as making the Constitution "the best it can be"[6] from some contestable normative perspective.

Much contemporary constitutional theory attempts vainly to adjudicate constitutional disputes. Practitioners employ some combination of textual, doctrinal, historical, and philosophical analysis to determine which party to a political conflict is constitutionally right. Deeply rooted constitutional evils, however, are immune to standard interpretive treatments. Past compromises cannot persuasively be confined to a few discrete constitutional rules. Previous accommodations typically provide champions of an alleged injustice with resources for fashioning reasonable legal arguments that interpret remaining constitutional ambiguities in their favor as well as the political

---

[3] Max Farrand, ed., *The Records of the Federal Convention of 1787*, vol. 2 (Yale University Press: New Haven, 1937), pp. 221 (Gouverneur Morris), 371 (Charles Pinckney).

[4] James E. Fleming, "Constructing the Substantive Constitution," 72 *Texas Law Review*, 211, 213 (1993).

[5] Christopher L. Eisgruber and Lawrence G. Sager, "Good Constitutions and Bad Choices," *Constitutional Stupidities, Constitutional Tragedies* (ed. William N. Eskridge and Sanford V. Levinson) (New York University Press: New York, 1998), p. 147.

[6] Ronald Dworkin, *Law's Empire* (Harvard University Press: Cambridge, 1986), p. 379.

power to ensure that such arguments are at least partly incorporated in any future official constitutional settlement. Past accommodations may also be understood as expressing the more general constitutional aspiration that disputes over the justice of a particular practice should not jeopardize national unity – that all constitutional controversies should be settled in ways satisfactory to both proponents and opponents of the contested practice.

Obsessive searches for "correct" answers to past and present contested questions of constitutional law are politically futile, even when possible jurisprudentially. Powerful social groups are unlikely to accept any constitutional arrangement, clear or ambiguous, that they believe undermines their vital interests and fundamental values. Constitutions settle political conflicts successfully in the short run by providing pre-existing answers to contested political questions. They successfully settle political conflicts in the long run by creating a constitutional politics that consistently resolves contested questions of constitutional law in ways that most crucial political actors find acceptable.

These ongoing struggles over constitutional meaning highlight how problems of constitutional evil are not simply about whether persons should respect explicit constitutional provisions that accommodate practices they believe unjust. Political orders in divided societies survive only when opposing factions compromise when constitutions are created and when they are interpreted. The price of constitutional cooperation and union is a willingness to abide by clear constitutional rules protecting evil that were laid down in the past and a willingness to make additional concessions to evil when resolving constitutional ambiguities and silences in the present. The problem of constitutional evil, in short, is primarily the problem of when and whether citizens should accommodate more injustice than constitutionally necessary by providing protections for heinous practices not clearly mandated by the constitutional text or history.

Slavery and *Dred Scott* present the stark reality of constitutional evil. Antebellum Americans did not have the luxury of peacefully affirming a constitution that all agreed was fundamentally hostile to human bondage. In order to form a "more perfect union" with slaveholders, citizens in the late eighteenth century fashioned a constitution that plainly compelled some injustices and was silent or ambiguous on other questions of fundamental rights. The constitutional relationships thus forged could survive only as long as a bisectional consensus was required to resolve all constitutional questions not settled in 1787. This commitment to bisectionalism meant that crucial (not all) political elites in both the free and slave states had to approve all constitutional settlements on slavery issues. Human bondage under these conditions could be eradicated quickly only by civil war, not by judicial decree or the election of an antislavery coalition. Given these bleak alternatives, *Dred Scott* challenges persons committed to human freedom to determine whether antislavery Northerners should have provided more accommodations for slavery than were constitutionally strictly necessary or risked the enormous destruction of life and property that preceded Lincoln's "new birth of freedom."

Theories of constitutional *interpretation* cannot successfully eradicate constitutional evil. When political controversies have long excited a constitutional community, the central legal claims of all prominent participants will be well grounded in institutional, historical, aspirational, or other constitutional logics. *Dred Scott* highlights the ways in which previous political accommodations provide all parties to subsequent constitutional disputes with legal justifications for their updated positions. From ratification until the Civil War, constitutional compromises accommodating slavery generated numerous precedents and principles that supported both racist and more egalitarian answers to contested constitutional questions. Heirs to an ambiguous and ambivalent constitutional text and tradition, proslavery and antislavery advocates before the Civil War relied heavily on half-truths about previous constitutional bargains that ignored the equal historical validity of rival assertions. As Part I details, although Chief Justice Taney and his judicial allies did not write flawless opinions, their conclusion that slavery could not be banned in the territories and that former slaves could not be American citizens was constitutionally as plausible as the contrary views detailed in the dissents to *Dred Scott*. Careful historical analysis belies the standard institutional, historical, and aspirational criticisms of that decision. The majority opinions in *Dred Scott*, while flawed, are consistent with claimed judicial obligations to respect the majority will, to follow the rules laid down by constitutional framers and previous precedents, or to be guided by fundamental constitutional values.

Ordinary constitutional *politics* cannot successfully eradicate constitutional evil. Constitutional bargains in divided societies typically guarantee proponents of alleged injustices the political power necessary to influence how political and constitutional issues that arise after ratification will be settled. The American experience with slavery illustrates the crucial role that power-sharing arrangements play in creating and sustaining constitutional regimes whose members dispute fundamental political norms. Part II develops the argument that the primary protections for human bondage in the original constitution were political institutions constructed to ensure a united South (and North) the representation necessary to veto any national measure deemed injurious to sectional interests. Confident that population was moving southwestward, the persons responsible for the Constitution assumed that representation by population, the electoral college, and the three-fifths clause would ensure Southern control over the House of Representatives, the presidency, and the federal judiciary. A detailed examination of constitutional politics in Jacksonian America reveals that the antebellum regime disintegrated when an unexpected northwestward population explosion undermined these power-sharing arrangements. The ensuing constitutional breakdown was ironically facilitated by the very constitutional practices originally designed to promote compromise. Americans elected an antislavery president in 1860 only because the electoral college, originally designed to magnify slaveholding influence on elections, inflated Republican popular support by more than 50 percent. Responding to the collapse of bisectionalism, slaveholders preferred secession to a polity where slavery would be no more protected than a free-state majority thought constitutionally necessary.

Theories of constitutional *authority* cannot successfully eradicate constitutional evil. The compromises that make constitutionalism possible in divided societies generate principles and precedents that may be invoked to support claims that compromise is the only legitimate means for settling constitutional controversies. As explored in Part III, Lincoln's attempts to justify the Republican Party's power to ban slavery in the territories were beset with the constitutional problems that confront all efforts to impose unilateral solutions on long-standing political disputes. The compromises that made American constitutionalism possible support slaveholding assertions that the Constitution was committed to bisectionalism: the view that constitutional settlements were legitimate only when endorsed by crucial elites in both the slave and free states. Antebellum Americans, Part III contends, lived in a consensus democracy. Their constitutional relationships could be maintained only when contested questions about slavery were settled in ways that enabled citizens from all sections of the United States to continue benefiting from constitutional cooperation.

Part IV revisits the election of 1860 as a vehicle for examining the tension between maintaining the constitutional peace and achieving constitutional justice. Virtually all contemporary constitutionalists vote for Abraham Lincoln, the candidate who promised to accommodate no more evil than constitutionally necessary. A good constitutional case can be made for John Bell, a candidate who promised bisectional solutions to contested constitutional questions. By seeking to maintain the union and avoid war with foreign nations, Bell hoped to preserve the conditions under which slavery *might* have been abandoned peacefully. Given the destructive capacities of modern weapons, present-day constitutional theorists have an even more pressing duty to explore whether constitutional peace should ever be sacrificed in the name of constitutional justice.

By erroneously presenting *Dred Scott* as an obvious constitutional mistake and ignoring the bloody consequences of Lincoln's election, constitutional theorists foster the dangerous illusion that the problems of constitutional evil that have plagued American constitutionalism from its inception could have been avoided had the Supreme Court interpreted the Constitution more justly. The American Constitution was a compromise between antislavery and proslavery forces. The continued existence of that constitutional regime depended on the continued satisfaction of each side with that constitutional bargain. When asking how much slavery the antebellum Constitution permitted, antislavery constitutional theorists in 1857 could not simply consult their constitutional aspirations; they had to consider how much slavery they would tolerate as the price for enjoying the continued benefits of their constitutional union.

Slavery is no longer a constitutional evil, but the legacy of *Dred Scott* remains. All political orders struggle with the problems of institutional design, political development, and constitutional evil that structured the antebellum American regime. A constitutionalism obsessed with constitutional law too often ignores how constitutional founders entrench political interests and values by designing institutions that privilege particular policies and political actors. A constitutionalism obsessed with originalism too often ignores how political changes inevitably frustrate the visions of constitutional designers. A constitutionalism obsessed with justice too often ignores how constitutions function best by creating the conditions under which political order can be preserved, enabling ordinary politics to be concerned with justice.

The American experience with slavery highlights the crucial role that constitutional institutions play in determining what legal definitions of government powers and individual rights are authoritative at a given time. Constitutional procedures bias political outcomes, advantaging some political interests and handicapping others. The electoral college in 1800 augmented slaveholding power but magnified the influence of free-state parties in 1860. Today, the Senate bestows more federal funds on the Rocky Mountain states than would have been the case had representatives to that branch of Congress been apportioned by population.[7] How constitutional silences and ambiguities are interpreted depends largely on who staffs the institutions responsible for settling constitutional controversies. Antebellum Americans

---

[7] See Frances E. Lee and Bruce I. Oppenheimer, *Sizing Up the Senate: The Unequal Consequences of Equal Representation* (University of Chicago Press: Chicago, 1999).

understood that governing institutions controlled by slaveholders protected human bondage more effectively than proslavery legal rules. At the dawn of the twenty-first century, many national judiciaries provide more protection for property and abortion rights than do national legislatures because the former are staffed by legal elites who are more inclined than the general public to favor property and abortion rights.[8] Parchment limits on government, both American and comparative constitutional history teach, are of little significance in the absence of political institutions capable of respecting those limits.

Problems caused by the failure of constitutional institutions to perform as expected have haunted American constitutionalism for more than two centuries. Unforeseen political and social changes continually wreak havoc with constitutional orders. Constitutional institutions broke down during the first decades of American national life.[9] The succeeding Jacksonian political order collapsed when crucial assumptions underlying the slavery compromises were falsified. The "Fourteenth Amendment's Constitution"[10] lasted but eight years.[11] During the Progressive Era, industrialization destroyed the original vision of a classless politics.[12] Unfortunately, the difficulties of passing formal constitutional amendments, combined with a tradition of constitutional obeisance that compels political actors to deny any allegation of constitutional flaw,[13] compound these failings. Americans too often propose restoring Madisonian institutions in their pristine form as solutions for political problems caused by flaws in Madisonian political science.

Problems of constitutional evil continue to challenge constitutional projects. Both newly formed constitutional regimes and ongoing constitutional enterprises must accommodate practices that numerous citizens find venal.

---

[8] See Ran Hirschl, *Towards Juristocracy: The Origins and Consequences of the New Constitutionalism* (Harvard University Press: Cambridge, 2004).

[9] See Gordon S. Wood, *The Radicalism of the American Revolution: How a Revolution Transformed a Monarchial Society into a Democratic One Unlike Any That Had Ever Existed* (Knopf: New York, 1992); Stanley Elkins and Eric McKitrick, *The Age of Federalism: The Early American Republic, 1788–1800* (Oxford University Press: New York, 1993); James Roger Sharp, *American Politics in the Early Republic: The New Nation in Crisis* (Yale University Press: New Haven, 1993); Elaine K. Swift, *The Making of an American Senate: Reconstitutive Change in Congress, 1787–1841* (University of Michigan Press: Ann Arbor, 1996); Stephen M. Griffin, *American Constitutionalism: From Theory to Politics* (Princeton University Press: Princeton, 1996).

[10] See Christopher L. Eisgruber, "The Fourteenth Amendment's Constitution," 69 *University of Southern California Law Review*, 47 (1995).

[11] See Mark A. Graber, "The Constitution as a Whole: A Partial Political Science Perspective," 33 *University of Richmond Law Review*, 343, 368–71 (1999).

[12] Howard Gillman, *The Constitution Besieged: The Rise and Demise of Lochner Era Police Powers Jurisprudence* (Duke University Press: Durham, 1993).

[13] Stephen M. Griffin, "The Nominee is … Article V," *Constitutional Stupidities*, p. 51 (noting how these practices require most constitutional changes to take place "off the books").

Because all constitutions remain compromises as long as citizens cannot agree on the qualities of the good society, most persons are likely to think their present constitution provides too much or too little protection for state and local interests, property, privacy, religion, racial equality, and other civil liberties or rights. When considering how much evil they would interpret their constitution as permitting, members of all constitutional communities must consult their constitutional aspirations and consider how much evil they will tolerate as the price for enjoying the continued benefits of constitutional union.

Dred Scott was wrong and Lincoln right only if insufficient reasons existed in 1861 for antislavery Americans to maintain a constitutional relationship with slaveholders. Both constitutionality and morality may support that conclusion. Many reasons advanced in 1787 for putting up with what appeared to be a dying practice were no longer valid by the middle of the nineteenth century. Fear of foreign invasion had lessened. Abolition by 1850 required positive government action, which the original Constitution abjured. Slaveholders no longer tolerated arguments that slavery was wrong. Nevertheless, the better case may be that debate over human bondage was sufficiently robust to justify the additional free-state accommodations necessary to preserve union. *Dred Scott* was wrong and Lincoln right only if John Brown was correct when he insisted that slavery was sufficiently evil to warrant political actions that "purge[d] this land in blood."[14]

THE PROBLEM OF CONSTITUTIONAL EVIL

Problems of constitutional evil arise in large, diverse polities. The constitutions of political orders where "one person's notion of justice is often perceived as manifest injustice by someone else"[15] contain provisions many people believe inefficient, stupid, or evil.[16] Government enjoys too much power to abridge some rights and too little power to protect others. Some

---

[14] See Stephen B. Oates, *To Purge This Land with Blood: A Biography of John Brown* (Harper & Row: New York, 1970), especially p. 351 (quoting John Brown).

[15] Sanford Levinson, *Constitutional Faith* (Princeton University Press: Princeton, 1989), p. 72.

[16] The Constitution's most prominent **supporters** believed that the final product was marred by these defects. Madison favored proportional representation in both houses of Congress and thought that the final constitution did not adequately limit state power to violate individual rights. Farrand, 1 *Records*, pp. 36–7, 164. See also "Madison Resolution: June 8, 1789," *Creating the Bill of Rights: The Documentary Record from the First Federal Congress* (ed. Helen E. Veit, Kenneth R. Bowling, and Charlene Bangs Bickford) (Johns Hopkins University Press: Baltimore, 1991), p. 11. Near the end of the constitutional convention, Hamilton asserted that he "meant to support the plan to be recommended [only] as better than nothing": Farrand, 2 *Records*, p. 524.

fundamental rights are missing from the national charter altogether. Other enumerated rights license socially reprehensible behavior. Providing uncontroversial examples of these constitutional infirmities is impossible. The crux of the problem of constitutional evil is that citizens do not agree on what practices are constitutionally evil. Constitutional provisions that everyone thinks evil (or stupid) are rejected by constitutional framers, formally abandoned by a textual amendment, or informally abandoned by some practice that may or may not constitute an amendment.[17] Alleged constitutional imperfections are ratified, maintained, or proposed only when many people regard those constitutional provisions or interpretations as necessary evils or positive goods.

The severe constitutional stupidities and evils that result from these compromises pervade every aspect of constitutionalism. Citizens who dispute basic regime questions engage in political struggles across all constitutional terrains. The framing debates over federal–state relations influenced the structure of the national government, the powers given to the national government, the Bill of Rights, and the fundamental principles underlying the Constitution. Parties to controversies over fundamental constitutional values may win small victories, but the more common outcomes are further compromises and vague provisions capable of being interpreted as supporting conflicting values.

Constitutional accommodations for evil beget constitutional accommodations for evil. Past compromises generate legal and political support for subsequent constitutional decisions mandating injustice. Congressional decisions after the Civil War that weakened the language in the Fourteenth and Fifteenth Amendments provided legal grounds for justifying judicial decisions sustaining Jim Crow. The Compromise of 1876, by fully incorporating former Confederate states in the Union, allowed Southern white supremacists to influence the interpretation of ambiguities in the post–Civil War Constitution.

These and related constitutional compromises are the means by which persons who share civic space agree to cooperate despite disagreeing over fundamental political principles. The various compromises reached in 1787 enabled Americans with diverse beliefs to form a state strong enough to forestall foreign invasion. Later constitutional compromises over the tariff enabled Jacksonian Democrats to promote bisectional cooperation on Native

[17] See William N. Eskridge, Jr., and Sanford Levinson, "Introduction: Constitutional Conversations," *Constitutional Stupidities*, p. 6. For debates over what constitutes an amendment, see Sanford Levinson, ed., *Responding to Imperfection: The Theory and Practice of Constitutional Amendment* (Princeton University Press: Princeton, 1995).

American removal, national banking, and expansion. Successful constitutional bargains and renegotiations preserve the peace and may indirectly reduce constitutional evil. The persons responsible for the American Constitution preferred government by "reflection and choice" to government by "accident and force" because they had more faith in republican institutions than military arms as vehicles for realizing justice in the long run.[18] Ongoing cooperation exposes proponents of an alleged evil to normatively superior practices. If persons have some tendency to recognize and act on better theories of justice, then agreements that form and preserve constitutional unions may be the best means for achieving a better political order over time.

Modern constitutional commentaries ritually proclaim the theoretical possibility of constitutional evil. Felix Frankfurter insisted that the "great enemy of liberalism" was making "constitutionality synonymous with wisdom."[19] His numerous followers play variations on that litany. "A neutral and durable principle may be a thing of beauty and a joy forever," John Hart Ely noted, "[b]ut if it lacks connection with any value the Constitution marks as special, it is not a constitutional principle and the Court has no business imposing it."[20] Constitutional commentators committed to this distinction between constitutionality and justice insist that constitutional authorities disdain mere outcomes. Robert Bork asserts: "Legal reasoning ... is rooted in a concern for legitimate process rather than preferred results."[21]

Despite these professed commitments to the distinction between constitutionality and justice, few constitutional theorists highlight any particular constitutional evil they believe contemporary constitutional authorities must maintain. Some prominent scholars, when asked to give an example of a constitutional tragedy, conclude that "[t]he range of permissible constitutional arguments now extends so far that a few workable ones are

---

[18] Alexander Hamilton, James Madison, and John Jay, *The Federalist Papers* (New American Library: New York, 1961), p. 33.

[19] *West Virginia State Board of Education v. Barnette*, 319 U.S. 624, 670 (1943) (Frankfurter, dissenting). See *Dennis v. United States*, 341 U.S. 494, 556 (1951) (Frankfurter, concurring).

[20] John Hart Ely, "The Wages of Crying Wolf: A Comment on Roe v. Wade," 82 *Yale Law Journal*, 920, 949 (1973). See Alexander M. Bickel, *The Morality of Consent* (Yale University Press: New Haven, 1975), p. 26; Ronald Dworkin, *Freedom's Law: The Moral Reading of the American Constitution* (Harvard University Press: Cambridge, 1996), pp. 10–11; Cass R. Sunstein, *The Partial Constitution* (Harvard University Press: Cambridge, 1993), pp. 7–8; Fleming, "Constructing the Substantive Constitution," pp. 218, 280, 290, 302; Sotirios Barber, *On What the Constitution Means* (Johns Hopkins University Press: Baltimore, 1984), pp. 45, 61–2, 75.

[21] Robert H. Bork, *The Tempting of America: The Political Seduction of the Law* (Simon & Schuster: New York, 1990), p. 264. See Hans A. Linde, "Due Process of Lawmaking," 55 *Nebraska Law Review*, 197, 255 (1976); Laurence H. Tribe, "Taking Text and Structure Seriously: Reflections on Free-Form Method in Constitutional Interpretation," 108 *Harvard Law Review*, 1223, 1302 (1995).

always available in a pinch." [22] Controversial cases in leading studies consistently come out "right," as "right" is defined by the theorist's political commitments.[23] Conservative constitutional commentators insist that principled justices sustain bans on abortion and strike down affirmative action policies; their liberal peers insist that principled justices strike down bans on abortion and sustain affirmative action policies.[24] When a contemporary consensus exists on the just policy, all constitutional commentators agree that the policy is constitutionally mandated. No prominent theorist admits that *Dred Scott* might have been a legitimate exercise of judicial review, nor would any have the judiciary overrule *Brown v. Board of Education*.[25]

This consensus that *Dred Scott* was wrong (and *Brown* was right) inhibits serious discussion of constitutional evils. If every present constitutional ambiguity can be resolved justly and no constitutional provision clearly entrenches practices remotely analogous to slavery, then few pressing political reasons exist for questioning constitutional authority. That inquiry might be more urgent were contemporary feminists to acknowledge that the constitutional case for abortion is contestable or if contemporary evangelicals were to conclude that important elements of the constitutional tradition require a high wall of separation between church and state. Some citizens might

[22] Pamela S. Karlan and Daniel R. Ortiz, "Constitutional Farce," *Constitutional Stupidities*, p. 180. Others responded with a disquisition on the inevitability of constitutional evil, without pointing to a specific evil that constitutional authorities are compelled to accommodate. See e.g. Larry Alexander, "Constitutional Tragedies and Giving Refuge to the Devil," *Constitutional Stupidities*. Only two or three of the seventeen essays in the section ostensibly devoted to constitutional tragedies discuss a specific evil the author believed presently sanctioned by the Constitution of the United States. See Gerard V. Bradley, "The Tragic Case of Capital Punishment," *Constitutional Stupidities* (capital punishment); Earl M. Maltz, "*Brown v. Board of Education*," *Constitutional Stupidities* (segregation); David A. Strauss, "Tragedies under the Common Law Constitution," *Constitutional Stupidities*, pp. 236–7 (precedent obligates justices to sometimes sustain death sentences and sometimes invalidate affirmative action measures).

[23] Mark Tushnet, "Policy Distortion and Democratic Debilitation: Comparative Illumination of the Countermajoritarian Difficulty," 94 *Michigan Law Review*, 245, 245 n.4 (1995).

[24] Compare Bork, *Tempting*, pp. 107–16, 359–61, with Sunstein, *The Partial Constitution*, pp. 149–50, 270–85, 331–2. Libertarians would have justices strike down bans on abortion and affirmative action policies. See Richard A. Posner, *Sex and Reason* (Harvard University Press: Cambridge, 1992); Richard A. Posner, "The *DeFunis* Case and the Constitutionality of Preferential Treatment of Racial Minorities," *1974 Supreme Court Review* (ed. Philip B. Kurland) (University of Chicago Press: Chicago, 1975). Democrats would have justices sustain both measures; see John Hart Ely, *Democracy and Distrust: A Theory of Judicial Review* (Harvard University Press: Cambridge, 1980), pp. 170–2; Ely, "The Wages of Crying Wolf."

[25] 374 U.S. 483 (1954). With the exception of Earl Maltz (see note 22), scholars who claim that *Brown* was wrongly decided in 1954 do not favor overruling in 2006. See Raoul Berger, *Government by Judiciary: The Transformation of the Fourteenth Amendment* (Harvard University Press: Cambridge, 1977), pp. 117–33, 412–13; Christopher Wolfe, *The Rise of Modern Judicial Review: From Constitutional Interpretation to Judge-Made Law* (Basic Books: New York, 1986), pp. 259–62, 380 n.52.

wonder why they should interpret a constitution that may sanction these evils. William Lloyd Garrison publicly burned the Constitution when he concluded that proslavery arguments had strong constitutional foundations.[26]

SLAVERY AS A CONSTITUTIONAL EVIL

Garrison recognized slavery as the quintessential constitutional evil. The original Constitution failed for numerous reasons to outlaw human bondage. Toleration of slavery was deemed necessary to secure the benefits of a more secure union. Most framers thought that the evil practice of slavery would soon disappear. Many believed states should be free to manage their purely domestic affairs; a few regarded slavery as a positive good. Constitutionalists writing two hundred years later may claim they would have bargained better, but historians generally agree that constitutional agreement would not have occurred had most Southerners perceived a genuine threat to their "peculiar institution."

Slavery ambiguously pervaded the antebellum constitutional order. Every government institution was structured with an eye to creating and maintaining a balance of sectional power. The powers various framers favored assigning to the national government depended on whether they believed constitutional majorities would be more inclined to protect or weaken human bondage. Neither the free nor the slave states emerged fully triumphant in 1787. The Constitution drafted in Philadelphia was interpreted as sufficiently proslavery to be ratified in the South and sufficiently antislavery to be ratified in the North. Subsequent developments did not clarify whether the Constitution was essentially proslavery or antislavery. Antebellum Americans cited the Missouri Compromise as demonstrating that Congress had the power to ban slavery in the territories,[27] that slavery in the territories could be banned only with Southern consent,[28] or that the free and slave states had a constitutional obligation to share the territories.[29]

The unforeseen population movements that gave free states the latent power to control the national government prevented the constitutional issues that slavery presented in 1857 from being resolved by reference to the compromises reached in 1787. The framers expected that contested constitutional questions would be settled by the bisectional coalitions they

---

[26] "The Meeting at Framingham," *The Liberator* (July 7, 1854), p. 106.
[27] See Abraham Lincoln, *The Collected Works of Abraham Lincoln*, vol. 2 (ed. Roy P. Basler) (Rutgers University Press: New Brunswick, 1953), p. 242.
[28] See *Congressional Globe*, 33rd Cong., 1st Sess., App., p. 413 (John Bell).
[29] See George Fisher, *The Law of the Territories* (C. Sherman: Philadelphia, 1859), p. 51.

anticipated would be elected under the rules laid down in Articles I, II, and III. During the 1850s, slaveholders emphasized the original intention that bisectional coalitions would resolve constitutional ambiguities. Antislavery advocates emphasized the original intention that a coalition in control of all branches of the national government would resolve constitutional ambiguities as that coalition thought best. The problem with both views is that the framers never considered how constitutional ambiguities should be resolved when the sectional coalitions elected following the letter of the constitutional rules subverted the bisectional constitutional purposes underlying those rules.

When *Dred Scott* was litigated, Americans were renegotiating the original constitutional bargain in a political environment where forces uninterested in accommodation had the power under the rules laid down in Article V to block any constitutional amendment from being passed. Although all parties to the slavery controversy claimed to be defending the old constitutional order, their real debate was over whether the original constitutional commitment to bisectionalism should be modified or abandoned. The national party leaders who foisted responsibility for slavery on the federal judiciary attempted to maintain bisectionalism by vesting veto power over slavery policies in the only remaining national institution with a Southern majority. In *Dred Scott*, the Supreme Court fostered sectional moderation by replacing the original Constitution's failing political protections for slavery with legally enforceable protections acceptable to Jacksonians in the free and slave states. Republicans spoke the language of constitutional preservation. Their refusal to acknowledge the constitutional commitment to bisectionalism, however, is best conceptualized as a de facto renunciation of the original constitutional understanding that slavery would never be left to the mercy of Northern majorities. Lincoln abandoned the original constitutional hope that conflicts over slavery would not disrupt union. His claim that the persons responsible for the Constitution intended to place slavery "in the course of ultimate extinction"[30] was faulty constitutional history. Taney was more faithful to the original Constitution when he championed policies that could be supported by Jacksonians throughout the nation.

We can understand and evaluate Lincoln's actions only when we acknowledge that *Dred Scott* highlights the possibility of severe conflict between constitutionality and justice. We celebrate Lincoln only by recognizing that in 1861 he chose justice over constitutionality, or at least that he refused to accommodate slavery to the extent necessary to maintain the old constitutional

---

[30] Lincoln, 3 *Collected Works*, p. 18.

order.[31] The devastation wrought by Union forces starkly demonstrates that the choice between constitutionality and justice rarely amounts to a simple decision between good and evil. Injustices deeply rooted, as slavery was in 1860, can be swiftly eradicated only by actions that kill, maim, and devastate millions of persons, many of whom bear little if any direct responsibility for the evil in question. The greater the evil, the greater the probable cost of abolition and the more likely the failure. No guarantee existed in 1861 that war would free the slaves. We take the problem of constitutional evil seriously only when we stop using *Dred Scott* to advance partisan positions and acknowledge that, in 1860, the alternative to *Dred Scott* was a civil war that – with different battlefield accidents – might have further entrenched and expanded human bondage.

---

[31] "The mystical cords of Union" cannot legitimate the carnage of 1861–1865; only the abolition of slavery can. See Sanford Levinson, *Written in Stone: Public Monuments in Changing Societies* (Duke University Press: Durham, 1998), p. 60; Mark E. Brandon, *Free in the World: American Slavery and Constitutional Failure* (Princeton University Press: Princeton, 1998), p. 186.

PART ONE

The Lessons of *Dred Scott*

Contemporary constitutional theory rests on three premises: *Brown v. Board of Education*[1] was correct, *Lochner v. New York*[2] was wrong, and *Dred Scott v. Sandford*[3] was wrong. A few intrepid souls question whether *Brown* was correctly decided.[4] Some proponents of law and economics favor reviving the freedom of contract and the *Lochner* decision.[5] No one wishes to rethink the universal condemnation of *Dred Scott*. "American legal and constitutional scholars," *The Oxford Companion to the Supreme Court* states, "consider the *Dred Scott* decision to be the worst ever rendered by the Supreme Court."[6] David Currie's encyclopedic *The Constitution in the Supreme Court* maintains that the decision was "bad policy," "bad judicial politics," and "bad law."[7] Other commentators describe *Dred Scott* as "the worst constitutional decision of the nineteenth century,"[8] "the worst atrocity in the Supreme

---

[1] 347 U.S. 484 (1954).

[2] 198 U.S. 45 (1905).

[3] 60 U.S. (19 Howard) 393 (1856).

[4] See Earl M. Maltz, *"Brown v. Board of Education," Constitutional Stupidities, Constitutional Tragedies* (ed. William N. Eskridge and Sanford V. Levinson) (New York University Press: New York, 1998); Raoul Berger, *Government by Judiciary: The Transformation of the Fourteenth Amendment* (Harvard University Press: Cambridge, 1977), pp. 117–33; Christopher Wolfe, *The Rise of Modern Judicial Review: From Constitutional Interpretation to Judge-Made Law* (Basic Books: New York, 1986), pp. 259–62.

[5] Richard A. Epstein, "Toward a Revitalization of the Contract Clause," 51 *University of Chicago Law Review,* 703, 734 (1984); Douglas Ginsburg, "Delegation Running Riot," 1995 *Regulation,* 83, 84 (1995).

[6] Walter Ehrlich, *"Scott v. Sandford," The Oxford Companion to the Supreme Court of the United States* (ed. Kermit L. Hall) (Oxford University Press: New York, 1992), p. 761.

[7] David P. Currie, *The Constitution in the Supreme Court: The First Hundred Years 1789–1888* (University of Chicago Press: Chicago, 1985), p. 264.

[8] Robert H. Bork, *The Tempting of America: The Political Seduction of the Law* (Simon & Schuster: New York, 1990), p. 28.

Court's history,"[9] "the most disastrous opinion the Supreme Court has ever issued,"[10] "the most odious action ever taken by a branch of the federal government,"[11] a "ghastly error,"[12] "a tragic failure to follow the terms of the Constitution,"[13] "a gross abuse of trust,"[14] "a lie before God,"[15] "an abomination,"[16] and "judicial review at its worst."[17] "Infamous" and "notorious" are the preferred contemporary adjectives.[18] In the words of former Chief Justice Charles Evans Hughes, the *Dred Scott* decision was a "self-inflicted wound" that almost destroyed the Supreme Court.[19]

---

[9]   Christopher L. Eisgruber, "*Dred* Again: Originalism's Forgotten Past," 10 *Constitutional Commentary*, 37, 41 (1993). See Paul Finkelman, "The Constitution and the Intentions of the Framers: The Limits of Historical Analysis," 50 *University of Pittsburgh Law Review*, 349, 391 (1989); Charles Fairman, *Reconstruction and Reunion*, pt. 1 (Macmillan: New York, 1971), p. 217; Cass R. Sunstein, "Foreword: Leaving Things Undecided," 110 *Harvard Law Review*, 6, 48 (1996); Robert A. Burt, "What Was Wrong with *Dred Scott*, What's Right about *Brown*," 42 *Washington and Lee Law Review*, 1 (1985).

[10] Robert G. McCloskey, *The American Supreme Court*, 4th ed. (rev. by Sanford Levinson) (University of Chicago Press: Chicago, 2005), p. 62. See Walter F. Murphy, *Congress and the Court: A Case Study in the American Political Process* (University of Chicago Press: Chicago, 1962), p. 31; David M. Potter, *The Impending Crisis: 1848–1861* (ed. Don E. Fehrenbacher) (Harper & Row: New York, 1976), pp. 290–1.

[11] Gary J. Jacobsohn, *The Supreme Court and the Decline of Constitutional Aspiration* (Rowman & Littlefield: Totowa, 1986), p. 44.

[12] Alexander M. Bickel, *The Supreme Court and the Idea of Progress* (Yale University Press: New Haven, 1978), p. 41.

[13] William Bradford Reynolds, "Another View: Our Magnificent Constitution," 40 *Vanderbilt Law Review*, 1343, 1348 (1987).

[14] Edward S. Corwin, "The *Dred Scott* Case in the Light of Contemporary Legal Doctrines," *Corwin on the Constitution*, vol. 2, *The Judiciary* (ed. Richard Loss) (Cornell University Press: Ithaca, 1987), p. 312. See Charles Warren, *The Supreme Court in United States History*, vol. 2 (Little, Brown: Boston, 1947), p. 316.

[15] Frederick Douglass, *The Frederick Douglass Papers: Series One: Speeches, Debates, and Interviews*, vol. 3, *1855–63* (Yale University Press: New Haven, 1985), p. 147. For other contemporaneous criticisms of *Dred Scott*, see *Congressional Globe*, 35th Cong., 1st Sess., pp. 616–17 (William P. Fessenden); *Congressional Globe*, 38th Cong., 2nd Sess., pp. 1012–17 (Charles Sumner, John P. Hale, Henry Wilson, and Benjamin F. Wade).

[16] Cass R. Sunstein, "*Dred Scott* and Its Legacy," *Great Cases in Constitutional Law* (ed. Robert P. George) (Princeton University Press: Princeton, 2000).

[17] Malcolm M. Feeley and Samuel Krislov, *Constitutional Law*, 2nd ed. (Scott, Foresman: Glenview, 1990), p. 34. See Don E. Fehrenbacher, *The Dred Scott Case: Its Significance in American Law and Politics* (Oxford University Press: New York, 1978), p. 573.

[18] Keith E. Whittington, "The Road Not Taken: *Dred Scott*, Judicial Authority, and Political Questions," 63 *Journal of Politics*, 365, 367 (2001); Paul W. Kahn, "Reason and Will in the Origins of American Constitutionalism," 98 *Yale Law Journal*, 449, 494 (1989); Lea VanderVelde and Sandhya Subramanian, "Mrs. Dred Scott," 106 *Yale Law Journal*, 1033, 1033 (1997); William N. Eskridge, Jr., "Public Law from the Bottom Up," 97 *West Virginia Law Review*, 141, 165 (1994); William W. Freehling, *The Reintegration of American History: Slavery and the Civil War* (Oxford University Press: New York, 1994), p. 208.

[19] Charles Evans Hughes, *The Supreme Court of the United States: Its Foundation, Methods and Achievements: An Appraisal* (Columbia University Press: New York, 1928), p. 50. Justice Scalia

This agreement that *Dred Scott* was a "national calamity"[20] masks a deeper disagreement over exactly what was wrong with the Supreme Court's decision in that case. Each school of contemporary constitutional thought claims *Dred Scott* embarrasses rival theories. Institutional theorists, who champion judicial restraint, maintain that Chief Justice Roger Taney's opinion for the Court demonstrates the evils that result when federal justices prevent the elected branches of government from resolving major social disputes. Historicists, who insist that judicial opinions rely exclusively on the original meaning of constitutional provisions and past legal precedents, argue that the Taney opinion demonstrates the evils that result when constitutional authorities fail to be tethered to the constitutional understandings of 1787 or subsequent judicial decisions. Aspirational theorists, who demand that constitutional provisions be interpreted in light of their broader animating principles, maintain that the Taney opinion demonstrates the evils that result when constitutional authorities are too tethered to precedent or the original meaning of the Constitution. Critics of *Dred Scott* agree, however, that Taney could not have reached that decision's proslavery and racist conclusions had he properly executed the correct theory of the judicial function.[21]

These contemporary uses of the *Dred Scott* decision to discredit rival theories are fruitless. No prominent approach to the judicial function compels any result in that case. Both the right to bring slaves into the territories and the claim that former slaves could not be American citizens may be supported (and opposed) by jurists sincerely committed to institutional, historical, and aspirational theories. The majority opinions in *Dred Scott* used many different constitutional arguments to reach their immoral conclusions. The dissents in that case similarly relied on various constitutional logics.

Constitutional law is almost always structurally incapable of generating the clear right answer that might resolve hotly disputed constitutional questions.[22] When a relatively enduring constitutional controversy divides a society, every position that enjoys substantial political support rests on plausible constitutional foundations. All major parties to ongoing constitutional conflicts win some skirmishes. These victories become precedents that support

---

similarly describes *Dred Scott* as a ruling that "covered [the Court] in dishonor and deprived [it] of legitimacy." *Planned Parenthood of Southeastern Pennsylvania v. Casey*, 505 U.S. 883, 998 (1992) (Scalia, concurring in part and dissenting in part).

[20] Hughes, *The Supreme Court*, p. 50.

[21] See more generally Robert M. Cover, *Justice Accused: Antislavery and the Judicial Process* (Yale University Press: New Haven, 1975), p. 257; Ronald Dworkin, "The Law of the Slave Catchers," *Times Literary Supplement*, 1437 (December 5, 1975).

[22] See Louis Michael Seidman, *Our Unsettled Constitution: A New Defense of Constitutionalism and Judicial Review* (Yale University Press: New Haven, 2001).

particular policies and broader constitutional visions. Decisions on controversial issues are often compromises or contain ambiguities that all sides
interpret as supporting their underlying positions. *Prigg v. Pennsylvania*[23]
stood for the proslavery principle that the Constitution mandated an efficient
rendition process and also for the antislavery principle that the federal government could not require free-state officials to help return fugitive slaves.

The better lesson of *Dred Scott* is that constitutional theory cannot mitigate or eradicate constitutional evil. Constitutional evils exist because, at
crucial constitutional moments, citizens agree to accommodate a practice
many think or come to think a substantial injustice. The reasons that originally suffice for accommodation become legitimate constitutional arguments
for ongoing accommodation. If, for example, the Constitution accommodated slavery partly because Virginians believed slavery could not yet be
abandoned, then descendants of those Virginians had a plausible constitutional argument that conditions were not yet constitutionally ripe for emancipation. Opponents of the alleged constitutional evil will find strands in
constitutional text and history that support their belief that the Constitution
is committed to the ultimate abolition of that injustice. Still, such evils as
slavery are not abolished simply because a plausible constitutional argument
exists for eradicating that injustice. Constitutional evils are eliminated only
by a constitutional politics that persuades or by a nonconstitutional politics
that compels crucial political actors to abandon an evil practice.

THE *DRED SCOTT* DECISION

Dred Scott was a Missouri slave who went with his master, John Emerson, to
a free state (Illinois) and a free territory (Minnesota) before he "voluntarily"
returned with Emerson to Missouri.[24] On April 6, 1846, Scott and his wife,
Harriet, sued their putative owner, who by 1853 was considered to be John
Sanford,[25] the executor of Emerson's will. The crux of the lawsuit was that
the time the Scotts spent on free soil made them free persons. Although
their suit was successful in the local trial court, that judgment was reversed
by the Supreme Court of Missouri. The Missouri justices held that, as a matter of Missouri law, slave status "reattached" whenever a slave voluntarily

---

[23] 41 U.S. 539 (1842).

[24] For more detailed accounts of the facts in *Dred Scott*, see *Dred Scott v. Sandford* at 397–9;
Fehrenbacher, *Dred Scott*, pp. 239–49.

[25] The Supreme Court reporter misspelled John Sanford's name in both *Dred Scott v. Sandford*
and *Willot v. Sandford*, 60 U.S. 79 (1856), a land law case decided nine weeks previously.

reentered a slave state from a free state or territory. Immediately following that defeat, Scott and his family brought a similar suit in federal court. The final result was no different. The local federal circuit court rejected their claims, and the United States Supreme Court dismissed the Scotts' appeal by a 7-2 vote. The first part of Chief Justice Taney's opinion ruled that, because former slaves were not American citizens or citizens of another country, Article III did not vest federal courts with the jurisdiction necessary to adjudicate their lawsuits. The second part of his opinion declared that Emerson's move to Minnesota was of no legal significance because the Missouri Compromise's ban on slavery north of the 36° 30′ line was unconstitutional. Justices Curtis and McLean dissented, insisting that free persons of color could be American citizens and that the Missouri Compromise was constitutional.[26]

The precise holding of *Dred Scott* is not entirely clear. All nine justices wrote opinions, and the seven justices in the majority gave different reasons for rejecting Scott's appeal. Conventionally, the case stands for the two central propositions in Chief Justice Taney's opinion: (1) no black could be a citizen of the United States; and (2) slavery could not be constitutionally prohibited in American territories.[27] Strictly speaking, this interpretation of *Dred Scott* is not entirely correct. Only three other justices explicitly endorsed Taney's analysis of black citizenship.[28] Some commentators argue that Taney's analysis of slavery in the territories is *obiter dictum* and thus of no legal significance. His initial ruling that federal courts could not adjudicate claims brought by persons of color, prominent Republicans in 1857 claimed, meant that the court had no jurisdiction to determine whether the Missouri Compromise was constitutional.[29] Still, Taney's opinion was,

---

[26] For a detailed account of the procedural history of *Dred Scott*, see Fehrenbacher, *Dred Scott*, pp. 250–83.

[27] See Fehrenbacher, *Dred Scott*, p. 2. Taney's opinion also ruled that the Supreme Court should apply Missouri law when determining whether slave status reattached to Scott after he returned to Missouri from a free state or a free territory: *Dred Scott* at 452. Justice Nelson's concurring opinion was devoted exclusively to this choice-of-law question: *Dred Scott* at 457–69 (Nelson, concurring).

[28] *Dred Scott* at 475–82 (Daniel, concurring); *Dred Scott* at 454 (Wayne, concurring); *Dred Scott* at 469 (Grier, concurring). The other justices in the majority – Campbell, Catron, and Nelson – did not believe the citizenship issue was properly before the Court: *Dred Scott* at 458 (Nelson, concurring); *Dred Scott* at 493 (Campbell, concurring); *Dred Scott* at 518 (Catron, concurring).

[29] See e.g. Laurence H. Tribe, *American Constitutional Law*, 2nd ed. (Foundation Press: Mineola, 1988), p. 549; Thomas Hart Benton, *Historical and Legal Examination of That Part of the Decision of the Supreme Court of the United States in the Dred Scott Case, Which Declares the Unconstitutionality of the Missouri Compromise Act, and the Self-Extension of the Constitution to Territories, Carrying Slavery along with It* (Appleton: New York, 1857), p. 10; John Lowell and Horace Gray, *A Legal Review of the Case of Dred Scott* (Crosby, Nichols: Boston, 1857), pp.

without apparent objection, designated the opinion of the Court.[30] Debate over *Dred Scott* consequently concentrates on the flaws in Taney's discussion of black citizenship and slavery in the territories.

Taney did not reject black citizenship per se. His opinion explicitly stated that black persons living in foreign countries were constitutionally eligible to become American citizens. Congress had the power, he wrote, to "authorize the naturalization of any one, *of any color,* who was born under allegiance to another Government" (emphasis added).[31] The only persons *Dred Scott* declared permanently ineligible for citizenship were slaves and free blacks born in the United States.[32] Taney's analysis of black citizenship asked whether "a negro, *whose ancestors were imported into this country, and sold as slaves,* [could] become a member of the political community formed and brought into existence by the Constitution of the United States" (emphasis added).[33] His answer was negative. The chief justice, however, left open the possibility that Congress could naturalize a former slave or descendant of a slave who at the time of naturalization was a citizen of a foreign country.[34] These broader issues about black citizenship were moot in *Dred Scott.* As Taney pointed out, Congress had consistently limited naturalization to white aliens.[35]

CRITIQUES OF *DRED SCOTT*

Modern-day critics of *Dred Scott* have presentist concerns. By yoking that ruling to a particular conception of constitutional interpretation or the judicial function, each school of contemporary constitutional thought hopes to discredit rival theories and the judicial opinions believed to rely on those

11–12, 26. Taney explicitly stated that his analysis of slavery in the territories provided an alternative ground for denying jurisdiction: *Dred Scott* at 430. See Corwin, "*Dred Scott* Case," p. 302. Justices Daniel and Wayne maintained that the Supreme Court could resolve the merits of Scott's appeal even though both justices thought the Court had no jurisdiction to hear the case: *Dred Scott* at 455–6 (Wayne, concurring); *Dred Scott* at 482 (Daniel, concurring).

[30] *Dred Scott* at 399. For lengthy analyses concluding that five justices supported Taney's claims on both the procedure and substance of the citizenship issue, see John S. Vishneski III, "What the Court Decided in *Dred Scott v. Sandford*," 32 *American Journal of Legal History,* 373 (1988); Fehrenbacher, *Dred Scott,* pp. 2, 325–34.

[31] *Dred Scott* at 419.

[32] *Dred Scott* at 417.

[33] *Dred Scott* at 403. See also *Dred Scott* at 573 (Curtis, dissenting).

[34] In a private memorandum written the year after *Dred Scott* was handed down, Taney denied that "a negro of the African race born in the United States whose ancestors had not been brought here as slaves, is a citizen of the United States within the meaning of the Constitution." Roger Brooke Taney, "Supplement to the *Dred Scott* Opinion," *Memoir of Roger Brooke Taney* (ed. Samuel Tyler) (John Murphy: Baltimore, 1872), p. 578.

[35] *Dred Scott* at 419.

theories. Don Fehrenbacher worries that commentators who support the Warren Court's expansion of individual liberties "have yet to comprehend the full meaning ... of the *Dred Scott* decision."[36] Lea VanderVelde and Sandhya Subramanian think "*Dred Scott* deprived modern commentators of an opportunity ... to recognize a new kind of freedom – a freedom of family continuity, cohesion, autonomy, and privacy."[37] The real target of historical and institutional critiques of *Dred Scott* is typically *Roe v. Wade*. According to many proponents of judicial restraint and originalism, that decision on abortion repeats Taney's most salient errors. "Who says *Roe*," Robert Bork proclaims, "must say ... *Scott*."[38] Aspirational theorists charge contemporary originalists with using the same methods that Taney employed in *Dred Scott*. Christopher Eisgruber suggests that such prominent opponents of *Roe* as Judge Bork and Justice Scalia "adhere ... to a professional credo that mimics Taney's indifference to injustice."[39]

Why contemporary scholars think analogies to *Dred Scott* undermine competing constitutional theories is not entirely clear. Proof that a particular constitutional theory performs better than its rivals when applied to antebellum slavery cases seems no more relevant to contemporary constitutional debates than proof that some other constitutional theory performs better than its rivals when applied to the constitutions of ancient Babylon or medieval France. American constitutionalists are interested in the theory that performs best with respect to the present Constitution of the United States. Performance with respect to other constitutions or previous versions of the Constitution may not be relevant to this inquiry. No one worries that a justice committed to the wrong theory of constitutional interpretation or the judicial function will presently conclude that *Dred Scott* remains good law, since the Thirteenth Amendment abolishes slavery and the Fourteenth Amendment declares all persons born in the United States to be citizens of the United States.[40]

---

[36] Fehrenbacher, *Dred Scott*, p. 595. See Alfred H. Kelly, "Clio and the Court: An Illicit Love Affair," 1965 *Supreme Court Review* (ed. Philip Kurland) (University of Chicago Press: Chicago, 1965), pp. 126, 158.

[37] VanderVelde and Subramanian, "Mrs. Dred Scott," p. 1036.

[38] Bork, *Tempting*, p. 32. See Michael W. McConnell, "A Moral Realist Defense of Constitutional Democracy," 64 *Chicago-Kent Law Review*, 89, 101 (1988); *Casey* at 998 (Scalia, concurring in part and dissenting in part).

[39] Eisgruber, "*Dred* Again," p. 64. For similar suggestions, see VanderVelde and Subramanian, "Mrs. Dred Scott," p. 1119; Sotirios A. Barber, "Whither Moral Realism in Constitutional Theory?: A Reply to Professor McConnell," 64 *Chicago-Kent Law Review*, 111, 126 (1988); Thurgood Marshall, "Reflections on the Bicentennial of the United States Constitution," 101 *Harvard Law Review*, 1, 5 (1987).

[40] For all practical purposes, *Dred Scott* was a dead letter after 1861. The Civil War Congress prohibited slavery in American territories, and Lincoln's attorney general ordered government officials

Still, *Dred Scott* matters very much to contemporary constitutional theorists. The Constitution derives its present authority in part from beliefs that the persons responsible for the original text were particularly wise and virtuous. Challenges to the integrity of the framers challenge the integrity of the Constitution.[41] "The historian who questions Jefferson," Paul Finkelman points out, "implicitly questions America."[42] Given how vulnerable the framers are on the issue of slavery, constitutional theorists help validate the Constitution of 1787 as a document still worthy of authoritative status by minimizing the extent to which the original Constitution accommodated that peculiar institution. By demonstrating that the influence of slavery on the original Constitution was confined to a very limited set of protections, contemporary constitutionalists make plausible claims that the surgeries of 1865 and 1868 successfully removed all traces of that constitutional wart from the body politic. In this view, no present constitutional institution, practice, or right was originally rooted even in part on the need to provide more security for human bondage or white supremacy.[43]

Debates over which constitutional theory was responsible for *Dred Scott* are relevant to the extent that many basic constitutional institutions and practices remain essentially unchanged from the time when Taney's infamous ruling was handed down. No Article V amendment has since altered the policy-making process in the United States.[44] Hence, some reason exists for thinking general theories of judicial review may function today in much the same way they functioned 150 years ago. If the judicial effort in 1857 to resolve a major political crisis caused the American political system to malfunction, then – barring substantial change in the structure of governing institutions – a judiciary that in 2006 engages in the same practice risks the same untoward consequences.[45]

to treat free blacks as American citizens: 12 Stat. 432 (1862); Edward A. Bates, "Citizenship," 10 Op. Atty. Gen. 382 (1862).

[41] Charles Beard thought that once Americans realized that the Constitution resulted from a struggle among different interests, they would more thoroughly investigate whether the Constitution of 1787 served their interests. Charles A. Beard, *An Economic Interpretation of the Constitution of the United States* (Free Press: New York, 1986), p. liii.

[42] Paul Finkelman, *Slavery and the Founders: Race and Liberty in the Age of Jefferson* (M.E. Sharpe: Armonk, 1996), p. 143.

[43] No better way exists to discredit the electoral college than to note its origins in proslavery politics. See Paul Finkelman, "The Proslavery Origins of the Electoral College," 23 *Cardozo Law Review*, 1145 (2002).

[44] Powerful arguments have been made that the unofficial constitutional rules of the game have changed dramatically. See Stephen M. Griffin, *American Constitutionalism: From Theory to Practice* (Princeton University Press: Princeton, 1996), pp. 72–87.

[45] See Sunstein, *"Dred Scott,"* pp. 78–87.

The Institutional Critique

Institutionalists use *Dred Scott* to illustrate the dubious results they believe occur whenever justices attempt to settle major policy disputes that such critics believe should be resolved by the elected branches of government. Justice Robert Jackson proffered the most frequently cited instance of this critique when he claimed that, by declaring the Missouri Compromise unconstitutional, the Supreme Court foreclosed any "hope that American forbearance and statesmanship would prove equal to finding some compromise between the angry forces that were being aroused by the slave issue." [46] Judicial restraint was necessary, institutionalists believe, because the Supreme Court was confronted with a politically explosive controversy over territorial policy that could only be aggravated by legal intrusion. Lino Graglia maintains that "the *Dred Scott* decision . . . , by denying national political power to deal with the slavery issue, seemed to make the Civil War inevitable." [47] Institutional critics of *Dred Scott* claim that judicial institutions lack and should lack the power necessary to resolve those controversies that divide the body politic. The Taney Court erred in *Dred Scott*, they argue, by "imagin[ing] that a flaming political issue could be quenched by calling it a 'legal' issue and deciding it judicially." "The great fundamental decisions that determine the course of society," Robert McCloskey argues, "must ultimately be made by society itself" and not by unelected judges. [48] Cass Sunstein declares, "we should understand *Dred Scott* to suggest that . . . the Supreme Court should avoid political thickets [and] . . . leave Great Questions to politics." [49]

Proponents of judicial restraint offer majoritarian, pragmatic, and accountability variations on their institutionalist critique of *Dred Scott*. Majoritarians condemn the Court for substituting judicial will for popular sentiment. By "mistaking its own views for the restrictions laid down in the Constitution," Chief Justice William Rehnquist maintains, the Taney Court violated "the

---

[46] Robert H. Jackson, *The Struggle for Judicial Supremacy: A Study of a Crisis in American Power Politics* (Vintage: New York, 1941), p. 327.

[47] Lino A. Graglia, "'Interpreting' the Constitution: Posner on Bork," 44 *Stanford Law Review*, 1019, 1036 (1992). See Bernard Schwartz, *A History of the Supreme Court* (Oxford University Press: New York, 1993), pp. 116, 125; Sunstein, "Leaving Things Undecided," p. 49; Alfred H. Kelly, "Clio and the Court," p. 126; Jenna Bednar and William N. Eskridge, Jr., "Steadying the Court's 'Unsteady Path': A Theory of Judicial Enforcement of Federalism," 69 *University of Southern California Law Review*, 1447, 1480 (1995); James W. Ely, "The Oxymoron Reconsidered: Myth and Reality in the Origins of Substantive Due Process," 16 *Constitutional Commentary*, 315, 318 (1999); Eskridge, "Public Law," p. 166.

[48] McCloskey, *American Supreme Court*, pp. 62, 60. See Fehrenbacher, *Dred Scott*, pp. 5–6.

[49] Sunstein, "*Dred Scott*," p. 66.

principle of majority rule."[50] Pragmatists insist that the judiciary is the governing institution *least* capable of forging acceptable compromises when intense controversies create bitter political divisions. Alexander Bickel describes *Dred Scott* as "a futile and misguided effort, by way of a legalism ..., to resolve the controversy over the spread of slavery."[51] Bednar and Eskridge regard the case as a "melodramatic example" of how judicial efforts to resolve national issues have historically "undermined the ability of the political system to achieve a compromised equilibrium."[52] Proponents of political accountability condemn the Court's decision in *Dred Scott* for abandoning the fundamental democratic principle that policy decisions should be made by the elected officials subject to popular recall. Arthur Bestor complains: "Policy would be made *for* the nation, but not *by* the nation. Power would be neatly divorced from accountability, action from deliberation" (emphasis in original).[53]

The Historical Critique

Commentators who favor historicist methods of constitutional interpretation condemn the actual ruling the justices made. While Bork and others support the Taney Court's decision to decide whether slavery could be prohibited in the territories, they maintain that *Dred Scott* was inconsistent with the intentions of the framers and previous legal precedents. The majority opinions, historicists insist, were "result-oriented" and "as blatant a distortion of the original understanding of the constitution as we can find."[54] The Missouri Compromise was clearly constitutional and the Court should have said so.[55]

Institutionalist and historicist critics agree that the flawed judicial crafting of *Dred Scott* can be detected and exposed without reference to the evils sanctioned by the Court's decision. Robert Burt, a prominent institutionalist, asserts that *Dred Scott* was "wrongly decided ... because it followed

---

[50] William H. Rehnquist, *The Supreme Court: How It Was, How It Is* (Morrow: New York, 1987), p. 313.

[51] Alexander M. Bickel, *The Morality of Consent* (Yale University Press: New Haven, 1975), pp. 36–7.

[52] Bednar and Eskridge, "Steadying," p. 1480; Eskridge, "Public Law," p. 166. See Sunstein, "*Dred Scott*," p. 76; Whittington, "Road Not Taken," p. 389.

[53] Arthur Bestor, "State Sovereignty and Slavery: A Reinterpretation of Proslavery Constitutional Doctrine, 1846–1860," 54 *Illinois State Historical Society Journal*, 117, 167 (1961).

[54] Reynolds, "Another View," p. 1348; Bork, *Tempting*, p. 30. See Corwin, "*Dred Scott* Case," p. 313; Currie, *The Constitution*, p. 272.

[55] See e.g. Bork, *Tempting*, pp. 29–34; Currie, *The Constitution*, pp. 267–73; McConnell, "Moral Realist Defense," p. 101.

from an incorrect view of the judicial role in our society" and not primarily "because it rested on a view of black people that [he] find[s] morally repugnant." "The fault," he insists, was "in the Court's decision to answer the question as posed, in its decision to decide."[56] "Speaking only of the constitutional legitimacy of the decision, and not of its morality," Bork, a leading historicist, similarly contends that "the case remained unchallenged as the worst in our history until the twentieth century provided rivals for that title."[57] Historicists do not say so explicitly, but their criticisms clearly imply that a decision prohibiting Congress from establishing slavery in the territories would have been (almost) as much a judicial outrage as the actual *Dred Scott* decision.

Bork focuses his fire on Taney's claim that the Constitution protected the right to bring slaves into American territories.[58] He declares that the judicial decision denying congressional power to ban slavery in those regions was based "upon reasons purely political."[59] Chief Justice Taney reached such a "dishonest" conclusion only "by changing the plain meaning of the due process clause of the Fifth Amendment." The *Dred Scott* Court's "transformation of the due process clause from a procedural to a substantive requirement," Bork argues, is "an obvious" and "a momentous sham."[60] Worse, he continues, many contemporary justices perpetuate this "obvious sham." The "concept" of substantive due process that Taney invented out of thin constitutional air, Bork maintains, "has been used countless times since by judges who want to write their personal beliefs into a document that, most inconveniently, does not contain those beliefs."[61]

Currie proclaims: "Taney's arguments against the citizenship of blacks ... left a good deal to be desired."[62] He regards as constitutionally irrelevant the chief justice's long list of legal disabilities that black persons suffered at the time of the framing and immediately before the Civil War.[63] Any

---

[56] Burt, "What Was Wrong," pp. 3, 11.

[57] Bork, *Tempting*, p. 28. See Currie, *The Constitution*, p. 264; *Casey* at 998, 1003 (Scalia, concurring in part and dissenting in part).

[58] *Dred Scott* at 450–1. For similar arguments that did not explicitly refer to the Fifth Amendment, see *Dred Scott* at 488–90 (Daniel, concurring); *Dred Scott* at 515–17 (Campbell, concurring); *Dred Scott* at 526–7 (Catron, concurring).

[59] *Dred Scott* at 620 (Curtis, dissenting); Bork, *Tempting*, p. 33. See Currie, *The Constitution*, p. 273.

[60] Bork, *Tempting*, pp. 31–2. For a similar criticism, see Corwin, "*Dred Scott* Case," pp. 307–11.

[61] Bork, *Tempting*, p. 32. For similar objections to *Dred Scott*, see *Casey* at 998 (Scalia, concurring in part and dissenting in part); McConnell, "Moral Realist Defense," p. 101; Wolfe, *Modern Judicial Review*, pp. 69–70.

[62] Currie, *The Constitution*, p. 266.

[63] *Dred Scott* at 412–16.

competent jurist, Currie writes, would have realized that "mere citizenship would not entitle anyone to privileges for which he lacked other requisite qualifications such as age, sex or race." [64] Currie observes that many citizens during the mid-nineteenth century, women in particular, were similarly saddled with numerous legal disabilities. Such policies demonstrate that "laws discriminating against blacks no more disproved citizenship than did those laws disadvantaging married women." [65]

In sharp contrast to the rough treatment they give Taney's analysis, Currie and other historicists celebrate the Curtis dissent in *Dred Scott* as "one of the great masterpieces of constitutional opinion-writing." [66] Curtis (and McLean), Fehrenbacher contends, were "sound constitutional conservatives" who "follow[ed] established precedent along a well beaten path to their conclusions." [67] Bork asserts that Curtis "destroyed Taney's reasoning, and rested his own conclusions upon the original understanding of those who made the Constitution." [68] Currie maintains that Curtis "demolished" Taney's arguments against black citizenship by noting that citizenship did not entitle a person to any particular rights and by pointing to a North Carolina case that explicitly declared free black inhabitants to be citizens of that state.[69] Whittington, who has developed a fascinating theory that combines institutional and historical values, proudly proclaims that Justice Curtis anticipated that approach to the judicial function. Curtis "would have had the Court avoid making th[e] mistake[n]" decision in *Dred Scott,* Whittington writes, "not because he happened to be on the right side of history, but because he had a better understanding of the judicial role." [70]

The Aspirational Critique

Proponents of aspirational methods of constitutional interpretation find the historicist critique of *Dred Scott* perverse. The true problem with Taney's opinion, they argue, is the chief justice's exclusive reliance on the specific intentions of the framers. Christopher Eisgruber contends that "an originalism more contemptuous of fundamental values is scarcely more imaginable"

---

[64] Currie, *The Constitution,* p. 265.

[65] Currie, *The Constitution,* p. 266.

[66] Currie, *The Constitution,* pp. 265–6, 273. For more general endorsements of the Curtis dissent, see *Casey* at 984 (Scalia, concurring in part and dissenting in part); McConnell, "Moral Realist Defense," pp. 101–2; Corwin, "*Dred Scott* Case," p. 311.

[67] Fehrenbacher, *Dred Scott,* p. 403.

[68] Bork, *Tempting,* p. 33.

[69] *Dred Scott* at 573–82 (Curtis, dissenting); Currie, *The Constitution,* pp. 265–6. The state court decision is *State v. Manuel,* 20 N.C. 114 (1838).

[70] Whittington, "Road Not Taken," p. 389.

than Taney's opinion in *Dred Scott*.[71] William Wiecek condemns Taney (and Garrisonian proslavery constitutionalists) for regarding "a constitution [as] a rigid, static, concrete instrument, rather than a plastic, fluid, and growing one."[72] Aspirational critics are outraged by the immorality of *Dred Scott*'s holdings. Taney's originalism, writes Eisgruber, was "indifferent to the justice or injustice of the Framers' intentions."[73] Gary Jacobsohn criticizes the chief justice for "fail[ing] to acknowledge the moral dimension of American constitutionalism."[74] Taney "is justly condemned," Milner Ball concludes, "for refusing the responsibility to create with us a future of human flourishing."[75] Aspirationalists celebrate the dissents in *Dred Scott* as transcending originalist modes of constitutional interpretation. In sharp contrast to Taney's opinion for the Court, Eisgruber contends, the Curtis dissent rests on the principle that "to study the constitutional text, one must study justice."[76]

Despite their anti-originalist rhetoric, no aspirationalist would have federal justices ignore the text and history of the Constitution. Taney's originalism was wrong, aspirationalist critics contend, because judicial decisions should be animated by the general values that structure the constitutional order rather than by the precise policies the framers favored. The broad antislavery principles underlying the Constitution should have trumped whatever specific protections for slavery the framers reluctantly accepted. Ronald Dworkin asserts, "the general structure of the American Constitution presupposed a conception of individual freedom antagonistic to slavery." This concept of liberty, he maintains, was "more central to the law than were the particular and transitory policies of the slavery compromise."[77] Sotirios Barber declares that, because "the Constitution had put slavery 'in the course of ultimate extinction,' … asking the Court to overrule *Dred Scott* can be

---

[71] Eisgruber, "*Dred* Again," p. 47. See Richard A. Posner, *Overcoming Law* (Harvard University Press: Cambridge, 1995), p. 251; Barber, "Whither Moral Realism," p. 126; Finkelman, "The Constitution," pp. 390–1, 395; Kahn, "Reason and Will," pp. 494–500; Erwin Chemerinksy, "The Price of Asking the Wrong Question: An Essay on Constitutional Scholarship and Judicial Review," 62 *Texas Law Review*, 1207, 1249 (1984).

[72] William M. Wiecek, *The Sources of Antislavery Constitutionalism in America* (Cornell University Press: Ithaca, 1977), p. 247.

[73] Eisgruber, "*Dred* Again," p. 49.

[74] Jacobsohn, *The Supreme Court*, p. 8.

[75] Milner S. Ball, "A Letter to Professor Burt," 42 *Washington and Lee Law Review*, 27, 35 (1985).

[76] Eisgruber, "*Dred* Again," p. 57; see also Kahn, "Reason and Will," pp. 502–4. Aspirationalists and originalists dispute the merits of the McLean dissent, which rests more clearly on general principles of justice. Eisgruber praises McLean for "insist[ing] that we should interpret the Framers' intentions in the way most consistent with justice": Eisgruber, "*Dred* Again," p. 49. Historicists barely acknowledge the existence of the McLean dissent. See Currie, *The Constitution*, p. 273 n.271; Fehrenbacher, *Dred Scott*, p. 403.

[77] Dworkin, "Slave Catchers," p. 1437.

construed as asking the Court to play its part in achieving a constitutional aspiration to rise above conditions responsible for the initial protection of slavery."[78]

Different aspirational theorists offer different sources for this perceived constitutional hostility to slavery. Jacobsohn sees the Jeffersonian claim that "all persons are created equal" as the fundamental constitutional commitment that should have compelled a judicial ruling in favor of Scott. He praises "Lincoln's opposition to the *Dred Scott* decision" because that opposition was "rooted in natural rights principles, specifically those of the Declaration of Independence."[79] Barber and Eisgruber condemn the *Dred Scott* majority for ignoring the more basic principles of natural law that they find at the foundation of the American constitutional order. Taney's positivism, Barber states, "furthered the degradation of both law and the community by denying that the Constitution is what it says it is: an instrument of justice."[80]

This aspirational demand that justices rely on transcendent standards of justice when deciding constitutional cases is what historicists find objectionable about *Dred Scott*. Originalists claim Taney read his racist and proslavery principles into the Constitution. Aspirational theorists cannot escape this criticism by responding that *Dred Scott* is aspirationalism done badly. Many agree that Taney's historical arguments were flawed.[81] If, as Eisgruber nevertheless claims, originalism done badly discredits originalism,[82] then aspirationalism done badly discredits aspirationalism. The issue in *Dred Scott* seems to be whether Taney was, as aspirationalists claim, a bad historicist or, as historicists claim, a bad aspirationalist. In fact, he was at times both and at other times neither.

CRITIQUING THE CRITIQUES

Taney's constitutional claims in *Dred Scott* were well within the mainstream of antebellum constitutional thought. The judicial denial of black citizenship reflected beliefs held by the overwhelming majority of antebellum jurists in

---

[78] Barber, "Whither Moral Realism," p. 118. See Christopher L. M. Eisgruber, "Justice Story, Slavery, and the Natural Law Foundations of American Constitutionalism," 55 *University of Chicago Law Review*, 273, 296 (1988).

[79] Jacobsohn, *The Supreme Court*, p. 8.

[80] Barber, "Whither Moral Realism," p. 127. See Eisgruber, "*Dred* Again," pp. 41, 49, 56–7, 61–2; Randy E. Barnett, "Was Slavery Unconstitutional Before the Thirteenth Amendment?: Lysander Spooner's Theory of Interpretation," 28 *Pacific Law Journal*, 977, 1013 (1997).

[81] Eisgruber, "*Dred* Again," p. 48. See H. Jefferson Powell, *The Moral Tradition of American Constitutionalism: A Theological Interpretation* (Duke University Press: Durham, 1993), p. 121.

[82] Eisgruber, "*Dred* Again," p. 48.

both the North and the South. Virtually every state court that ruled on black citizenship before 1857 concluded that free persons of color were neither state nor American citizens.[83] Four attorneys general of the United States rejected black citizenship.[84] Their view was endorsed by the leading Northern treatise on jurisprudence, James Kent's *Commentaries on American Law*,[85] and by Chief Justice John Marshall. "It is cause of real gratification," Marshall wrote in 1834, "that in the Northern and middle States, the opinion of

---

[83] *Leech v. Cooley*, 14 Miss. (6 Smedes & Marshall) 93, 99 (Miss. 1846); *Bryan v. Walton*, 14 Ga. 185, 198–207; *Cooper and Worsham v. The Mayor and Alderman of Savannah*, 4 Ga. 68 (1848); *State v. Morris*, 2 Harr. 537 (Del. 1837); *White v. Tax Collector*, 3 Rich. 136 (S.C. 1846); *Hobbs and Others v. Fogg*, 6 Watts 553, 556–9 (Pa. 1837); *Amy v. Smith*, 11 Ken. 326, 333–4 (1822); *People v. Hall*, 4 Cal. 399, 404–5 (1854); *Pendleton v. The State*, 6 Ark. 509, 511–12 (1843); *Aldridge v. The Commonwealth*, 2 Va. Cas. 447, 449 (1824); *Heirs of Jacob Bryan v. Dennis, Mary, and Others*, 4 Fla. 445, 454 (1852); *Benton v. Williams*, 1 Dallam's Decisions 496, 497 (Tex. 1843). See also *Cory et al. v. Carter*, 48 Ind. 327, 338–42 (1874) (finding that free blacks were not considered to be citizens of Indiana before the Civil War); *Stoner v. State*, 4 Mo. 614, 616 (1837) (possibly rejecting black citizenship). The chief justice of Connecticut ruled that free blacks were not citizens in a constitutional sense – *Crandall v. The State*, 10 Conn. 339, 345–7 (1834) – though a later Connecticut opinion maintained that his view was not shared by the rest of his brethren: *Opinion of the Judges of the Supreme Court*, 32 Conn. 565, 565–6 (1865). The Supreme Court of North Carolina in 1838 claimed that "slaves manumitted here become free-men – and therefore if born within North Carolina are citizens of North Carolina": *State v. Manuel*, 20 N.C. 114 (1838). Six years later that court significantly narrowed *Manuel*, holding that "free people of color" were "a separate and distinct class" and "cannot be considered as citizens in the largest sense of the term": *State v. Newsom*, 27 N.C. 181, 183, 185 (1844); see also *Cox v. Williams*, 39 N.C. 11, 13 (1845). Louisiana law is unclear. A majority opinion in 1860 concluded that "the African race are strangers to our Constitution": *The African Methodist Episcopal Church v. City of New Orleans*, 15 La. Ann. 441, 443 (1860). The concurrence maintained that "free persons of color are regarded as persons under our law": *African Methodist Episcopal Church* at 445 (Merrick, concurring). The weight of Louisiana cases seems to support the latter view. See *State v. Harrison*, 11 La. Ann. 722, 724 (1856); *State v. Levy and Dreyfous*, 5 La. Ann. 64 (1850); see also *Walsh v. Lallande*, 25 La. Ann. 188, 189 (1873) (claiming that free blacks were considered citizens before the Civil War). The Supreme Court of Massachusetts was the only bench that, before *Dred Scott*, clearly indicated that free blacks were state citizens. That tribunal did so in an opinion that sustained segregated schools in Boston: *Roberts v. City of Boston*, 59 Mass. 198, 206 (1849).

[84] Caleb Cushing, "Right of Expatriation," 8 Op. Atty. Gen. 139 (1856); Caleb Cushing, "Relation of Indians to Citizenship," 7 Op. Atty. Gen. 746 (1856); John MacPherson Berrien, "Validity of South Carolina Police Bill," 2 Op. Atty. Gen. 426 (1831); Carl Brent Swisher, *Roger B. Taney* (Macmillan: New York, 1935), p. 154 (discussing a memo Taney wrote in 1832); William Wirt, "Rights of Free Virginia Negroes," 1 Op. Atty. Gen. 506 (1821). Attorney General Hugh Legare in 1843 ruled that free persons of color were among the citizens eligible to purchase land under federal law. Legare reached this conclusion because he "conceive[d] the purpose of the lawgiver to be only to exclude aliens, … men born and living under the ligeance of a foreign power – from the enjoyment of the contemplated privilege." Hugh S. Legare, "Pre-emption Rights of Colored Persons," 4 Op. Atty. Gen. 147, 147 (1843). He explicitly refused to consider whether free blacks were citizens in a political sense: Legare, "Pre-emption," p. 147.

[85] James Kent, *Commentaries on American Law*, vol. 2, 8th ed. (William Kent: New York, 1854), p. 282.

the intelligent on this delicate subject, on which the Slave-holding States are so sensitive, accords so entirely with that of the South." [86] Taney's claim that the federal government had no power to ban slavery in the territories did not enjoy this degree of bisectional support. Nevertheless, the general principles advanced by the *Dred Scott* majority concerning the constitutional limits on federal power in the territories and the rights protected by the due process clause better reflect the main lines of antebellum jurisprudence than those advanced by many prominent contemporary critics of *Dred Scott*. Viewed from within a polity whose leading jurists, with rare exceptions, believed the Constitution protected the right to bring personal property to the territories, *Dred Scott* had much stronger historical and aspirational foundations than scholars reared on post–New Deal jurisprudence realize.

The Institutional Critique

The Majoritarian Critique

The Taney Court's rulings on black citizenship and the constitutional status of slavery in the territories were, if not perfectly majoritarian, certainly consistent with the policy preferences of the dominant national coalition before the Civil War. Jacksonian leaders in the legislative and executive branches of the national government actively procured a judicial ruling on the constitutional status of slavery in the territories. If the Court had decided *Dred Scott* on narrow grounds, then that ruling, in the famous words of Alexander Bickel, would have "thwart[ed] the will of the representatives of the actual people of the here and now." [87]

The Decision on the Merits. Dred Scott sustained policies favored by the dominant Jacksonian coalition. The slavery and citizenship prongs of the Taney Court's ruling were anticipated in the early 1850s by opinions issued by the attorney general of the United States.[88] The Taney Court's conclusion that Congress could not ban slavery in the territories mirrored the victorious Democratic Party's platform of 1856. That platform stated that "under the

---

[86] John F. Denny, *An Enquiry into the Political Grade of the Free Coloured Population under the Constitution of the United States, and the Constitution of Pennsylvania* (Hickok & Blood: Chambersburg, 1836) (reprinting J. Marshall to John Denny, October 24, 1834). Joseph Story may have privately informed Charles Sumner that free persons of color could be American citizens. Carl Brent Swisher, *The Taney Period, 1836–1864* (Macmillan: New York, 1974), p. 531 (quoting Charles Sumner to Robert C. Winthrop, February 3, 1843).

[87] Alexander M. Bickel, *The Least Dangerous Branch: The Supreme Court at the Bar of Politics* (Bobbs-Merrill: Indianapolis, 1962), p. 16.

[88] See note 84.

Constitution" the federal government was obligated to follow the policy of "non-interference ... with Slavery in State and Territory."[89] Both President Buchanan and his attorney general, Jeremiah Black, vigorously endorsed the most Southern understanding of *Dred Scott*, one that required territories to take affirmative steps to protect slave holdings.[90] Democrats in power consistently regarded free blacks as outsiders. Taney, when attorney general in 1832, explicitly declared that free blacks were not and could not become American citizens. This view was generally adopted by later Jacksonians in the executive branch of the national government.[91] James Buchanan, when Secretary of State, publicly denied that persons of color could receive passports indicating that they were American citizens. This policy was maintained during his presidential administration.[92]

The Taney Court ruling on citizenship captured the dominant "herrenvolk egalitarianism" of the middle nineteenth century. Slavery was local, but racism was national. Equality, Jacksonians in both the free and slave states agreed, was equality for white males. Persons of color were regarded as biologically inferior, perhaps even a different species.[93] Fehrenbacher maintains

[89] "Democratic Platform of 1856," *National Party Platforms*, vol. 1 (compiled by Donald Bruce Johnson) (University of Illinois Press: Urbana, 1956), p. 25.

[90] Caleb Cushing, "Eminent Domain of the States. – Equality of the States," 7 Op. Atty. Gen. 571 (1855); Cushing, "Right of Expatriation"; James Buchanan, "Third Annual Message," *A Compilation of the Messages and Papers of the Presidents*, vol. 5 (ed. James D. Richardson) (Government Printing Office: Washington, D.C., 1897), pp. 554–5; Jeremiah Black, *Observations on Senator Douglas's Views of Popular Sovereignty as Expressed in Harper's Magazine for September, 1859* (Thomas McGill: Washington, D.C., 1859). Franklin Pierce, in his last annual message to Congress, also denied federal power to prohibit slavery in the territories. Franklin Pierce, "Fourth Annual Message," 5 *Messages and Papers*, pp. 400–4.

[91] Swisher, *Taney*, p. 154; Fehrenbacher, *Dred Scott*, p. 361; Wiecek, *Antislavery*, pp. 164–5. Justice William Johnson and the Monroe administration objected to a South Carolina law imprisoning any free black sailor whose ship was docked in a state port, but they did so because they regarded such commercial measures as the exclusive preserve of the federal government: *Elkison v. Deliesseline*, 8 Fed. Cas. 493, 494–6 (C.C.D. S.C. 1823); William Wirt, "Validity of South Carolina Police Bill," 1 Op. Atty. Gen. 659 (1824); John Quincy Adams to Stratford Canning, June 17, 1823, quoted in "Free Colored Seaman – Majority and Minority Reports," H.R. Report, 27th Cong., 3rd Sess., no. 80 (1843). See *The Cynosure*, 6 Fed Cas. 1102 (D.C.D. Mass. 1844) (declaring a similar Louisiana law an unconstitutional interference with interstate commerce); *Roberts v. Yates*, 20 Fed. Cas. 937 (C.C.D. S.C. 1853) (holding such laws constitutional). That federal policy was overruled by Jackson's first attorney general, John MacPherson Berrien, "Validity of South Carolina Police Bill." Taney, as attorney general, maintained Berrien's policy: Swisher, *Taney Period*, pp. 380–1. A House committee in 1843 concluded that similar laws imprisoning free seamen of color violated the privileges and immunities clause of Article IV: "Free Colored Seaman," pp. 2–4; that report was never acted upon. For a general account of the debates of the negro seaman's acts, see Swisher, *Taney Period*, pp. 378–82, 393–4.

[92] Leon F. Litwack, *North of Slavery: The Negro in the Free States, 1790–1860* (University of Chicago Press: Chicago, 1961), pp. 31–2, 53–6.

[93] See Finkelman, *Slavery*, p. 109.

that "the *Dred Scott* decision, as it applied to free Negroes, had a majoritarian ring that transcended sectional lines." "A national poll," Rogers Smith concurs, "would have shown that a majority of [white males] approved of the *Dred Scott* decision and its racist vision of American citizenship."[94] Virtually every community in antebellum America disdained free persons of color. "[I]n the United States," Tocqueville observed, "the prejudice which repels the Negroes seems to increase in proportion as they are emancipated."[95] Prominent political leaders from Henry Clay to Governor Washington Hunt of New York denied that free persons of color were American citizens.[96] Free black males were routinely denied rights commonly identified with citizenship. "Only five states, all in New England," Foner states, "allowed the black man equal suffrage, and there he was confined to menial occupations and subjected to constant discrimination." "In the West," Foner adds, "Negroes were often excluded from public schools, and four [actually five] states – Indiana, Illinois, Iowa, [Missouri,] and Oregon, even barred them [from] entering their territory."[97] These political practices played a significant role in Taney's argument that slaves and their descendants could not become American citizens.[98]

Mainstream Republicans, who shared the racial prejudices of the time, were reluctant to criticize Taney's ruling on black citizenship. Abraham Lincoln, during his debates with Stephen Douglas, made clear that he "never ha[d] complained *especially* of the *Dred Scott* decision because it held that a negro could not be a citizen" (emphasis added). Lincoln opposed making free blacks citizens of Illinois[99] and had previously condemned Van Buren Democrats for permitting limited black suffrage in New York.[100] William Seward, Lincoln's main party rival for the presidential nomination in 1860, regarded members of "[t]he African race" as "being incapable of . . . assimilation

---

[94] Fehrenbacher, *Dred Scott*, p. 430; Rogers M. Smith, *Civic Ideals: Conflicting Visions of Citizenship in U.S. History* (Yale University Press: New Haven, 1997), p. 271. See Harry V. Jaffa, *Crisis of the House Divided: An Interpretation of the Issues in the Lincoln–Douglas Debate* (Doubleday: Garden City, 1959), p. 380.

[95] Alexis de Tocqueville, *Democracy in America*, vol. 1 (ed. Phillips Bradley) (Vintage: New York, 1945 [1835]), pp. 373–4. See Eric Foner, *Free Soil, Free Labor, Free Men: The Ideology of the Republican Party before the Civil War* (Oxford University Press: London, 1970), p. 261.

[96] Litwack, *North of Slavery*, pp. 84, 158, 252–3.

[97] Foner, *Free Soil*, p. 261; Glover Moore, *The Missouri Controversy 1819–1821* (Smith: Gloucester, 1967), pp. 238, 273. See Smith, *Civic Ideals*, p. 293; Litwack, *North of Slavery*, pp. vii–viii, 3–112.

[98] *Dred Scott* at 407–16.

[99] Abraham Lincoln, *The Collected Works of Abraham Lincoln*, vol. 3 (ed. Roy P. Basler) (Rutgers University Press: New Brunswick, 1953), pp. 299, 179.

[100] See Robert W. Johannsen, *Stephen A. Douglas* (Oxford University Press: New York, 1973), p. 78.

and absorption," to "be regarded as accidental, if not disturbing political forces."[101] Those Republican legislators in New York and Ohio who supported black citizenship in the wake of *Dred Scott* were voted out of office.[102]

Members of the dominant Jacksonian coalition from all regions of the country praised the Court's handiwork on the status of slavery in the territories as well as on black citizenship. Southern Democrats asserted: "The decision is right and the argument unanswerable." Their Northern brethren agreed. The *New Hampshire Patriot* declared that "resistance to that decision is ... resistance to the constitution – to the government – to the Union itself."[103] Both Southern and Northern Democrats were pleased that the justices had, "at a single blow, shiver[ed] the anti-slavery platform of the late great Northern Republican party into atoms." The official newspaper of the Buchanan administration celebrated the "salutary influence" of the Taney Court's ruling, predicting that slavery would "cease to be a dangerous element in our political contests."[104] Even committed antislavery advocates ruefully admitted that no aspect of *Dred Scott* was countermajoritarian. "Judge Taney's decision, infamous as it is," Susan B. Anthony acknowledged, "is but the reflection of the spirit and practice of the American people, North as well as South."[105] Lincoln, too, recognized that the Taney Court merely followed the most recent voting returns. "[T]he *Dred Scott* decision," he observed, "would never have been made in its present form if that party that made it had not been sustained previously by the election."[106]

The Decision to Decide. The Taney Court's decision to determine the constitutional status of slavery in the territories enjoyed the same majoritarian support in 1857 as did the substance of the decision the justices made. *Dred Scott* was "undertaken only upon the explicit invitation of Congress" and the president.[107] Prominent Jacksonians (and moderate Whigs) in all regions of

---

[101] *Congressional Globe,* 31st Cong., 1st Sess., App., p. 261.

[102] Fehrenbacher, *Dred Scott,* pp. 432–6.

[103] Fehrenbacher, *Dred Scott,* pp. 418–19 (quoting the *Louisville Democrat,* March 8, 1857, and the *New Hampshire Patriot,* March 18, 1857). See Fehrenbacher, *Dred Scott,* pp. 427–8; Warren, 2 *Supreme Court,* pp. 312–15; Smith, *Civic Ideals,* p. 199.

[104] Fehrenbacher, *Dred Scott,* pp. 419–20 (quoting the *New York Herald,* March 8, 1857, and the *Washington Union,* March 6, 11, 12, 1857).

[105] Fehrenbacher, *Dred Scott,* p. 430 (quoting Susan B. Anthony).

[106] Lincoln, 3 *Collected Works,* p. 232. See Lincoln, 3 *Collected Works,* p. 20.

[107] Wallace Mendelson, "Dred Scott's Case – Reconsidered," 38 *Minnesota Law Review,* 16 (1953). For detailed accounts of legislative efforts to have the judiciary resolve contested issues over slavery, see Fehrenbacher, *Dred Scott,* pp. 152–208; Mendelson, "Dred Scott's Case"; Mark A. Graber, "The Nonmajoritarian Difficulty: Legislative Deference to the Judiciary," 7 *Studies in American Political Development,* 35, 46–50 (1993).

the country during the late 1840s and early 1850s publicly declared that the federal judiciary was the institution responsible for determining the extent to which slavery could be regulated in the territories. President James K. Polk, Stephen Douglas, Jefferson Davis, and Henry Clay were among the numerous antebellum political leaders who urged Congress "to leave the question of slavery or no slavery to be declared by the only competent authority that can definitely settle it forever, the authority of the Supreme Court."[108] President James Buchanan's inaugural address declared that the status of slavery in the territories was "a judicial question, which legitimately belongs to the Supreme Court of the United States."[109] Lest jurisdictional problems bar judicial review, Congress after the Mexican War routinely inserted provisions facilitating judicial action in all statutes concerned with status of slavery in the territories.[110] Dissenting voices were limited to abolitionists and antislavery advocates, who correctly predicted that the Southern-dominated judiciary would hand down decisions consistent with Southern understandings of slavery and race.[111] The justices in the *Dred Scott* majority responded to and encouraged these political demands for legal action. Justice Wayne thought "the peace and harmony of the country required the settlement" of the status of slavery in the territories "by judicial decision." Justice Campbell maintained that "the Court would not fulfil public expectations or discharge its duties by maintaining silence upon [the] questio[n]."[112] Justice Catron inspired President Buchanan's declaration in his first inaugural that elected officials should allow the justices to determine whether slaveholders had a right to take their human property into the territories.[113]

---

[108] *Congressional Globe*, 31st Cong., 1st Sess., pp. 1154–5 (Henry Clay). See James K. Polk, "Fourth Annual Message," 4 *Messages and Papers*, p. 642; *Congressional Globe*, 31st Cong., 1st Sess., App., p. 154 (Jefferson Davis); *Congressional Globe*, 34th Cong., 1st Sess., App., p. 797 (Stephen Douglas). See also *Congressional Globe*, 33rd Cong., 1st Sess., App., p. 232 (Andrew P. Butler); *Congressional Globe*, 31st Cong., 1st Sess., App., p. 95 (Samuel Phelps). Leading Know-Nothings insisted that the federal judiciary could best resolve conflicts over slavery. See Tyler Anbinder, *Nativism and Slavery: The Northern Know Nothings and the Politics of the 1850s* (Oxford University Press: New York, 1992), p. 207. Even Abraham Lincoln may have claimed that the "Supreme Court of the United States is the tribunal to decide such questions": Lincoln, 2 *Collected Works*, p. 355; but see Fehrenbacher, *Dred Scott*, p. 645 n.39 (disputing the authenticity of that statement).

[109] James Buchanan, "Inaugural Address," 5 *Messages and Papers*, p. 431.

[110] 9 Stat. 450 (1850); 9 Stat. 455–6 (1850); 10 Stat. 280, 287 (1854).

[111] See *Congressional Globe*, 31st Cong., 1st Sess., App., pp. 473–4 (Salmon Chase); 30th Cong., 2nd Sess., p. 610 (Horace Greeley).

[112] *Dred Scott* at 493 (Wayne, concurring); *Memoir of Taney*, p. 384 (quoting J. A. Campbell to Samuel Tyler, November 24, 1870).

[113] Philip Auchampaugh, "James Buchanan, the Court, and the *Dred Scott* Case," 9 *Tennessee Historical Magazine*, 231, 236 (1929).

Northern Democrats, who some modern commentators claim were the "victims"[114] of *Dred Scott*, applauded the Taney Court's decision to issue a broad ruling. "If the case had been disposed on narrow grounds," Stephen Douglas asked three months after the judicial decision had been handed down, "who can doubt ... the character of the denunciations which would have been hurled upon the elevated heads of those illustrious judges, with much more plausibility and show of fairness than they are now acknowledged for having decided the case ... upon its merits?"[115] Free-state Jacksonians wanted the Court to decide *Dred Scott,* endorsed the resulting judicial decision, and continued calling for judicial decisions on the most controversial issues of the day. When, after the defeat of Kansas statehood in 1858, slave-holders emphatically rejected Stephen Douglas's claim that *Dred Scott* did not undermine popular sovereignty,[116] Northern Democrats responded by overwhelmingly supporting a resolution that the Supreme Court determine whether the federal government was constitutionally obligated to establish slave codes in the territories.[117] These frequent Jacksonian efforts to foster judicial policy making – combined with strong Jacksonian support for the policies the justice made – demonstrate that Taney did not impose a judicial solution to the question of black citizenship or slavery in the territories on a hostile Congress or nation. The *Dred Scott* decision was as majoritarian as any other race or slavery policy made during the 1850s.

The Compromise Critique

Institutionalist claims that *Dred Scott* inhibited a possible legislative compromise are no more convincing than claims that *Dred Scott* was counter-majoritarian. The legislative decision to foist responsibility onto the courts for deciding the constitutional status of slavery was "the last great territorial compromise[] of the antebellum era."[118] The self-conscious efforts of prominent antebellum elected officials to procure a judicial decision on the constitutional status of slavery in the territories was wiser than they knew or contemporary critics acknowledge. Jacksonians foisted slavery on the Supreme Court partly to take that issue out of electoral politics and partly because they thought that public policy with a judicial imprimatur might command broader respect than mere legislation. This legislative invitation is commonly criticized by scholars who believe the "evaluation and balancing

---

[114] Schwartz, *History,* p. 124.
[115] Schwartz, *History,* p. 124 (quoting Stephen Douglas).
[116] See Whittington, "Road Not Taken," pp. 380, 388–9.
[117] Fehrenbacher, *Dred Scott,* pp. 537–8.
[118] Whittington, "Road Not Taken," p. 378.

of fundamental principles and interests [are] resolved most appropriately in the political branches."[119] The very structure of the national legislature during the 1850s, however, practically guaranteed that Congress would be the worst imaginable site for securing a broad-based agreement on slavery policies. When public opinion on any bitterly contested issue is geographically concentrated, an institution staffed exclusively by persons elected by local constituencies is unlikely to be capable of reaching a middle ground. Moderation is particularly unlikely when the decision-making process includes numerous veto points that enable sizable minorities to defeat centrist proposals. The institution most likely to fashion a workable compromise is one whose members are selected by a national political process that favors political moderates and whose decision rules empower the median member. The Taney Court was such an institution.

The Forum of Compromise. The Supreme Court of the 1850s is better described as the forum of compromise (or principled moderation) than the forum of principle. From 1837 until 1857, the justices consistently found the political center on issues of national importance. Judicial rulings on the commerce clause and the contracts clause regularly took "a middle – and generally popular ground."[120] For example, when faced with competing constitutional claims that, in the absence of federal regulation, states had either no power or absolute freedom to regulate interstate commerce, the judicial majority creatively concluded in 1851 that states could regulate interstate commerce in the absence of federal legislation on matters of more local concern but not on matters of more national concern.[121] The Taney Court refused to use the contracts clause to police state regulation as aggressively as most Whigs wished and refused to abandon contract clause scrutiny as more radical Jacksonians desired.[122]

The Court's moderation was rooted in the judicial selection process, which – then as now – favors persons with ambivalent, unknown, or centrist views on the hotly contested constitutional issues of the day. Supreme Court justices are nominated by the president, the only elected official in the national government chosen by a national electorate. Judicial nominees must then be confirmed by a Senate composed of two representatives from each state. During times of sectional strife, successful nominees need strong

---

[119] Whittington, "Road Not Taken," p. 387.
[120] McCloskey, *American Supreme Court*, p. 56.
[121] See *Cooley v. Board of Wardens*, 53 U.S. 299 (1851).
[122] See *Dodge v. Woolsey*, 59 U.S. 331 (1855); *Proprietors of Charles River Bridge v. Proprietors of Warren Bridge*, 36 U.S. 420 (1837).

transsectional support, strong bipartisan support, or near-unanimous support from politically moderate senators. Persons with known militant views on such issues as abortion or slavery need not apply unless their faction has supermajoritarian control of the national government or their vote is not likely to be decisive on any crucial issue.

This structural bias toward moderation explains the remarkable centrism of the Taney Court. The tribunal that decided *Dred Scott* was dominated by Southern unionists and conservative Northerners. Only one member, Justice Daniel, is fairly characterized as a Southern extremist.[123] Justice Campbell was a reluctant secessionist.[124] Justices Catron and Wayne were the two highest-ranking national officials from seceding states who did not resign their positions after secession.[125] Justices Grier and Nelson were conservative Northern Democrats.[126] Chief Justice Taney was a conservative border-state Democrat.[127] Justice Curtis was a cotton Whig who, after 1857, sided more often with Democrats than Republicans.[128] Justice McLean was a conservative Republican.[129] On the issues that most clearly divided the radicals from the moderates within each section of the United States, Taney Court justices aggressively championed the moderate position. Justices Grier, Curtis, and Nelson, despite their lifelong Northern residence, distinguished themselves by defending national power to recapture fugitive slaves.[130] Southern justices Campbell and Wayne, conversely, distinguished themselves by defending national power to ban the importation of slaves.[131]

---

[123] See John P. Frank, *Justice Daniel Dissenting: A Biography of Peter V. Daniel* (Harvard University Press. Cambridge, 1964).

[124] See Swisher, *Taney Period*, pp. 739–40; Robert Saunders, Jr., *John Archibald Campbell: Southern Moderate 1811–1889* (University of Alabama Press: Tuscaloosa, 1997), pp. 138–45.

[125] See Alexander A. Lawrence, *James Moore Wayne: Southern Unionist* (University of North Carolina Press, Chapel Hill, 1943).

[126] See Frank Otto Gatell, "Samuel Nelson," *The Justices of the United States Supreme Court 1789–1978: Their Lives and Major Opinions*, vol. 2 (ed. Leon Friedman and Fred L. Israel) (Chelsea House: New York, 1980); Gatell, "Robert C. Grier," ibid.

[127] See Swisher, *Taney*.

[128] See George Ticknor Curtis, *Memoir of Benjamin Robbins Curtis, LL.D.*, vol. 1 (ed. Benjamin R. Curtis) (Little, Brown: Boston, 1879).

[129] See Francis P. Weisenburger, *The Life of John McLean: A Politician on the United States Supreme Court* (Da Capo: New York, 1971).

[130] For Grier, see *Ex parte Jenkins*, 13 F. Cas. 445 (C.C.E.D. Pa. 1853); *Von Metre v. Mitchell*, 28 F. Cas. 1036 (C.C.W.D. Pa. 1853). For Curtis, see *Charge to Grand Jury*, 30 F. Cas. 983 (C.C.D. Mass. 1854); *United States v. Morris*, 26 F. Cas. 1323 (C.C.D. Mass. 1851). For Nelson, see *Charge to Grand Jury*, 30 F. Cas. 1013 (C.C.N.D. N.Y. 1851); *Charge to Grand Jury*, 30 F. Cas. 1007 (C.C.S.D. N.Y. 1851).

[131] See *United States v. Haun*, 26 F. Cas. 227 (C.C.S.D. Ala. 1860) (Campbell); *Charge to Grand Jury*, 30 F. Cas. 1026 (C.C.D. Ga. 1859) (Wayne).

The Taney Court appears as a bastion of moderation particularly when compared to the national legislature of the time. Approximately one third of all members of Congress in 1857 could be counted on to support militant proslavery positions, and another third were as reliably strong antislavery voters. Of the nine justices on the Supreme Court, only one identified with Southern fire-eaters and only one identified with the antislavery movement. If all persons in the legislative, executive, and judicial branches of the national government in 1857 were placed into quintiles on the basis of opinions about slavery, a five-person judicial majority composed of Wayne, Catron, Curtis, Nelson, and Grier would belong in the middle quintile. Two justices, Taney and Campbell, are best placed at the more moderate end of the less extreme proslavery quintile. One, McLean, is best placed in the middle of the less extreme antislavery quintile. Daniel aside, the two most extreme quintiles would be populated exclusively by those elected officials whom institutional theory naïvely expects would have reached a compromise on slavery had the Supreme Court not interfered.

The national institution staffed by the greatest percentage of political moderates is the national institution whose decision rules most privilege the center. Judicial rules vest far more power in the median justice than legislative practices vest in the median representative. Many veto points exist in both the contemporary and antebellum legislative process.[132] The Supreme Court eschews practices analogous to the committee system, the open debate rule in the Senate, and the presidential veto. Votes are taken one case – often one issue – at a time. Justices do not trade votes, gaining support for some proposals by sacrificing other constitutional values. With rare exceptions,[133] these decision rules empower median justices on all issues before the Court. Justice Lewis Powell, for example, "rarely negotiated over opinions, in part because his position at the Court's center meant that his colleagues had to move to meet him."[134] These judicial decision rules guaranteed that Justices Catron, Grier, Wayne, Curtis, and Nelson effectively controlled any decision the Supreme Court made on slavery. Northern Republicans and Southern disunionists in the antebellum Congress could wield weapons against border-state accommodationists not possessed by their counterparts in the judiciary. Chief Justice Taney had no veto power. Justices Daniel and McLean could not trade votes so as to forge an alliance of the judicial extremes against

---

[132] See Keith Krehbiel, *Pivotal Politics: A Theory of U. S. Lawmaking* (University of Chicago Press: Chicago, 1998), p. 230.
[133] See Maxwell L. Stearns, *Constitutional Process: A Social Choice Analysis of Supreme Court Decision Making* (University of Michigan Press: Ann Arbor, 2002), pp. 3–39, 215–301.
[134] Mark Tushnet, "Justice Lewis F. Powell and the Jurisprudence of Centrism," 93 *Michigan Law Review*, 1854, 1856 (1995).

the judicial middle. If three or four of the five centrist justices on the Taney Court reached a common position on any sectional issue, they had the power to ensure that their agreement became the constitutional law of the land.

Dred Scott as a Compromise. The best candidate for being the forum of compromise in the 1850s produced what may have been the most politically acceptable compromise on slavery. Judicial rulings recognizing a constitutional right to bring slaves into the territories enjoyed enough support to maintain the antebellum constitutional order. *Dred Scott* did aggravate some tensions responsible for the Civil War.[135] Antislavery advocates in the North were outraged by what they feared was a conspiracy to make slavery a national institution.[136] Southerners were offended by Northern refusals to accept the judicial ruling.[137] Still, the historical evidence suggests that *Dred Scott* did not further destabilize, and may have temporarily preserved, the antebellum political regime. The decisions most responsible for the Civil War were made by those political actors whom institutionalist dogma entrusts with the authority to reach compromises on divisive political issues.

In 1857, compromise was needed only to enable the Democratic Party to maintain its majority status.[138] With Jacksonians gaining enough free-state votes in 1856 to maintain control over the national government, the Supreme Court did not have to make decisions in 1857 that appealed to existing Republicans as long as judicial decisions did not create new Republicans. Besides, no institution could have fashioned a slavery compromise that would have satisfied all Americans (even if persons of color are excluded). Southern disunionists were actively weaning their electorate from the Jacksonian coalition in order to pave the way for secession.[139] Northern Republicans were more interested in putting slavery on the road to extinction than in preserving the Union.[140] Whether *Dred Scott* was a reasonable compromise

---

[135] See Fehrenbacher, *Dred Scott*, p. 562; Potter, *Impending Crisis*, p. 291.

[136] See Lincoln, 2 *Collected Works*, pp. 452–3, 461–7, 521–3, 525–6, 539–40, 550–3; Lincoln, 3 *Collected Works*, pp. 20–30, 45–8, 73–6, 78, 89–90, 95, 99–101, 230–4, 349, 368–9, 424–30, 443–4, 484, 548–50, 553; Lincoln, 4 *Collected Works*, p. 29. See also Foner, *Free Soil*, pp. 97–8, 101; Fehrenbacher, *Dred Scott*, pp. 437–8, 451–3, 457, 464, 487–8, 493.

[137] Fehrenbacher, *Dred Scott*, pp. 450, 562.

[138] Disputes over slavery had already finished off the Whigs as a national political party and prevented the Know-Nothings from developing any cross-sectional coalitions. See Potter, *Impending Crisis*, p. 254; Anbinder, *Nativism*, pp. 18, 100–1.

[139] See John C. Calhoun, *The Works of John C. Calhoun*, vol. 4 (ed. Richard K. Cralle) (Appleton: New York, 1856), p. 576. See also William W. Freehling, *The Road to Disunion: Secessionists at Bay, 1776–1854* (Oxford University Press: New York, 1990), pp. 4–5, 316–19, 337–8, 479–86, 519–35.

[140] See e.g. Lincoln, 3 *Collected Works*, pp. 454–5, 502, 542–3; *Congressional Globe*, 31st Cong., 1st Sess., App., p. 479 (Salmon Chase).

must be judged in light of that decision's impact on those forces previously committed to peaceful union, not on the reactions from partisans committed to either secession or a set of policies that risked secession.

Dred Scott did not immediately weaken the capacity of the Democratic Party to serve as a vehicle for statesmen interested in compromising on the slavery issue. Fehrenbacher observes that "reaction to the *Dred Scott* decision does not appear to have produced ... any significant number of new adherents for the Republican party."[141] The Taney Court ruling did not sap Democratic strength in any region of the country or immediately increase enmity between Northern and Southern Jacksonians. Stephen Douglas made no enemies in the South when, in the spring of 1857, he proclaimed that territories retained the practical power to exclude slavery by not passing proslavery legislation.[142] Jefferson Davis endorsed that view of territorial power during the summer of 1857.[143] At that time, Southerners wanted Kansas as a slave state, not territorial slave codes for territories without slaves.

Dred Scott, if anything, improved Democratic electoral prospects in the North. Jacksonians had suffered massive defections in the 1854 congressional and 1856 presidential elections as a result of the Kansas–Nebraska Act.[144] Democrats regained some legislative seats in 1856 that they had lost in 1854. This legislative trend continued in the immediate wake of *Dred Scott*. Northern Democrats in state elections held during the spring and fall of 1857 recovered more offices previously lost to Republicans.[145] Fehrenbacher's study of the voting returns finds "no evidence that *Dred Scott* manufactured votes for Republicans anywhere"; he concludes: "it is difficult to escape the impression that the decision, if it helped anyone, helped the Democrats."[146]

President Buchanan's decision in the late fall of 1857 to demand that Kansas be admitted as a slave state "brought on a genuine uprising of Northern rank-and-file Democrats" and ruined the party of accommodation.[147] Led by Stephen Douglas, Northern Democrats who had accepted the *Dred Scott* decision bitterly attacked the fraudulent proslavery Lecompton constitution. The resulting struggle between the Buchanan administration and anti-Lecompton Democrats destroyed the fragile union between Northern and Southern Jacksonians, severely weakened Democratic Party strength in

---

[141] Fehrenbacher, *Dred Scott*, p. 437. See Kenneth M. Stampp, *America in 1857: A Nation on the Brink* (Oxford University Press: New York, 1990), p. 109.

[142] Fehrenbacher, *Dred Scott*, pp. 456–7.

[143] See Fehrenbacher, *Dred Scott*, p. 499.

[144] See Potter, *Impending Crisis*, p. 239; Foner, *Free Soil*, pp. 155–68.

[145] See Stampp, *America in 1857*, pp. 102–4, 109; Fehrenbacher, *Dred Scott*, pp. 565–6.

[146] Fehrenbacher, *Dred Scott*, p. 566.

[147] Stampp, *America in 1857*, p. 330; Fehrenbacher, *Dred Scott*, pp. 468, 563.

the North, and paved the way for the Lincoln victory in 1860.[148] The bitter debates over Kansas inspired the Southern demand for territorial slave codes that caused the Jacksonian split at the Democratic national convention in 1860. Before Douglas broke with the South on Kansas, leading slave-state spokespersons had publicly agreed that territories had no affirmative obligation to protect slavery. Southerners demanded a territorial slave code after Douglas refused to support the admission of Kansas as a slave state, not after Douglas first declared that territories could still effectively exclude slavery by not passing a slave code. Fehrenbacher correctly notes that, although "[h]istorians have often said that the Freeport doctrine made Douglas unacceptable in the South, ... it would be more accurate to turn the statement around and say that Douglas made the Freeport doctrine unacceptable in the South."[149] Douglas did not improve his standing in the South by promising to support slave codes when judicially obligated to do so.[150] Southern rejection of his proposal to have the judiciary mediate this sectional dispute, given the likely favorable judicial decision, suggests that slave-state hostility to Douglas in 1860 stemmed almost entirely from his opposition to Lecompton, not from his interpretation of *Dred Scott*.

In sharp contrast to contemporary commentators who think *Dred Scott* made compromise over slavery nearly impossible, many Republicans living at the time thought that, had Buchanan compromised and allowed a fair election in Kansas on the Lecompton constitution, he and the Taney Court would have destroyed the nascent Republican Party.[151] Lincoln was quite concerned that Republicans would support Douglas for the Senate in 1858, despite the latter's defense of *Dred Scott*, as a reward for successfully opposing the Buchanan administration on Lecompton.[152] Prominent Eastern Republicans were making significant overtures to Douglas in 1858. Lincoln used *Dred Scott* in the debates less to convert Democrats into Republicans than to remind Republicans why Douglas was unacceptable.[153]

The Reason Why. *Dred Scott* was a political compromise even though most members of the Taney Court did not attempt to fashion a political compromise. Except for Justice Grier and perhaps Justice Nelson,[154] no Taney

---

[148] See Stampp, *America in 1857,* pp. 309–16, 322–4, 329–30; Fehrenbacher, *Dred Scott,* p. 566.

[149] Fehrenbacher, *Dred Scott,* p. 501.

[150] See Fehrenbacher, *Dred Scott,* pp. 537–8.

[151] Stampp, *America in 1857,* pp. 309–10.

[152] See Lincoln, 2 *Collected Works,* pp. 443–4, 446–51, 455–7, 459, 467–9, 497–8, 509–11.

[153] See Fehrenbacher, *Dred Scott,* pp. 486–8; Robert W. Johannsen, "Introduction," *The Lincoln–Douglas Debates* (ed. Robert W. Johannsen) (Oxford University Press: New York, 1965), p. 10.

[154] Grier does appear to have joined the *Dred Scott* majority in part because he thought having a Northern justice support the result would make the decision more acceptable to that region. See

Court justice self-consciously sought to resolve slavery issues in the way they thought most likely to accommodate those political actors crucial to the continued maintenance of the Union. Although the Southern Jacksonians on the bench took proslavery positions they believed to be most consistent with constitutional history and principle, the compromise lay in having the judiciary make the decision, in the centrist character of the justices making the decision, and in the belief that a judicial decision might gain more support than an identical legislative decision. Most important, compromise was more possible than many subsequent commentators have recognized because important changes in territorial settlement patterns made the central holding of *Dred Scott* largely irrelevant to the swing free-state voters.

All parties to political debates over the status of slavery in the territories were primarily concerned with the eventual status of slavery in the states fashioned from those territories. Northerners of all political persuasions wanted free territories because they wanted free states. Additional free states facilitated Northern control of the national government and allowed free white labor to avoid competing against slave black labor. "We are fighting for a majority of free states," William Sewart declared.[155] Governor Alexander Randall of Wisconsin spoke for most Northerners when he insisted that "[f]ree labor languishes and becomes degraded when put in competition with slave labor."[156] All parties to antebellum debates also initially perceived a close connection between territorial and state policy. "To opponents and defenders of slavery alike," Arthur Bestor points out, "it seemed clear that the first decisions made in the territories would be the determining ones." Antebellum Americans feared that "[l]ong before a state attained full standing, its social system could have been irrevocably fixed by decisions irrevocably made." Lincoln asserted: "The first few may get slavery IN, and the subsequent many cannot easily get it OUT." As another antislavery advocate observed, "if we are wrong on the subject of slavery, it can never be righted."[157]

Fehrenbacher, *Dred Scott*, pp. 311–12 (quoting Grier to Buchanan, February 23, 1857). Nelson simply refused to address the larger issues discussed by the other justices. See note 27.

[155] *Congressional Globe*, 35th Cong., 1st Sess., p. 521. See Parke Godwin, *Political Essays* (Dix, Edwards: New York, 1856), p. 286; Foner, *Free Soil*, pp. 58, 222, 236.

[156] Foner, *Free Soil*, p. 57 (quoting Alexander W. Randall). See Henry Ruffner, *Address to the People of West Virginia* (R.C. Noel: Lexington, 1847); Jesse Burton Harrison, *Review of the Slave Question* (T.W. White: Richmond, 1833), p. 10. See also W. Freehling, *Disunion*, pp. 148, 203; Foner, *Free Soil*, pp. 11–72; Alison Goodyear Freehling, *Drift toward Dissolution: The Virginia Slavery Debate of 1831–32* (Louisiana State University Press: Baton Rouge, 1982), pp. 145–7, 174–7, 211, 222–3, 243–5.

[157] Bestor, "State Sovereignty and Slavery," p. 150; Lincoln, 2 *Collected Works*, p. 268; Foner, *Free Soil*, p. 55 (quoting General James Nye). See also Lincoln, 3 *Collected Works*, pp. 483, 485–6, 499; Foner, *Free Soil*, pp. 54, 56; Godwin, *Political Essays*, pp. 286–9.

Antislavery fears about slave territories were warranted during the first half of the nineteenth century, when every territory that allowed slavery became a slave state. Illinois almost became a slave state despite the Northwest Ordinance. Both Illinois senators consistently took Southern positions during the Missouri controversy, and more than 40 percent of state voters in 1824 supported a referendum that legalized human bondage. "Only law," Freehling concludes, "stopped slavery from entering midwestern latitudes."[158] When the Kansas–Nebraska law was enacted, most Northerners had good reason to believe that, by permitting slavery in Kansas and other territories, Congress had ensured that those regions would maintain that institution upon admission to the Union. Lincoln thought it an "already settled question" in 1855 that Kansas would join the Union as a slave state.[159]

Developments immediately after the Kansas–Nebraska Act challenged this axiom of American territorial politics, apparently confirming Stephen Douglas's repeated assertions that popular sovereignty was the least controversial means for obtaining free states.[160] By the time *Dred Scott* was decided, a majority of Kansans seemed committed to banning slavery upon admission to the Union. Slavery was not taking hold in Nebraska and in other territories where that practice was permitted by legislation or judicial decree. Slavery was legal in the New Mexico and Utah territories, but fewer than a hundred slaves could be found in both jurisdictions.[161] "The whole controversy over the Territories," cooler heads began claiming, "related to an imaginary negro in an impossible place."[162] Slavery may not have reached its natural limits by the 1850s,[163] but assertions that slavery

---

[158] W. Freehling, *Disunion*, p. 139. See Moore, *Missouri Controversy*, pp. 53–4, 85, 97, 108–9; Peter S. Onuf, *Statehood and Union: A History of the Northwest Ordinance* (Indiana University Press: Bloomington, 1987), pp. 123–30; Finkelman, *Slavery*, pp. 36, 77–8; David Brion Davis, "The Significance of Excluding Slavery from the Old Northwest in 1787," 84 *Indiana Magazine of History*, 75, 78, 87–8 (1988). For Southern concerns that no territory where slavery was banned would become a slave state, see *Congressional Globe*, 36th Cong., 1st Sess,. App., p. 77 (James Green); Jaffa, *House Divided*, p. 125.

[159] Lincoln, 2 *Collected Works*, p. 321.

[160] Stephen A. Douglas, *The Letters of Stephen A. Douglas* (ed. Robert W. Johannsen) (University of Illinois Press: Urbana, 1961), pp. 182, 289. See Robert W. Johannsen, *The Frontier, the Union, and Stephen A. Douglas* (University of Illinois Press: Urbana, 1989), p. 194; Jaffa, *House Divided*, p. 64. Henry Clay and Daniel Webster had similarly maintained that slavery would not thrive in territories west of Texas. See *Congressional Globe*, 31st Cong., 1st Sess., App., p. 1408; *Congressional Globe*, 31st Cong. 1st Sess., App., p. 274.

[161] Fehrenbacher, *Dred Scott*, pp. 175–7.

[162] James G. Blaine, *Twenty Years of Congress from Lincoln to Garfield*, vol. 1 (Henry Bill: Norwich, 1884), p. 272. See Earl M. Maltz, "The Unlikely Hero of *Dred Scott*: Benjamin Robbins Curtis and the Constitutional Law of Slavery," 17 *Cardozo Law Review*, 1995, 2014–15 (1996).

[163] See Jaffa, *House Divided*, pp. 299, 392–3; Don E. Fehrenbacher, *Prelude to Greatness: Lincoln in the 1850s* (Stanford University Press: Stanford, 1962), p. 22.

necessarily flourished where not forbidden no longer seemed self-evident to most Northern voters.

These changes in territorial settlement patterns explain why a party almost destroyed by the legislative decision in 1854 to repeal a ban on slavery in territories north of the Missouri Compromise line could accept with some grace the judicial decision three years later requiring slavery in those territories. The increased strength of free-soil interests in territories where slavery was nominally permitted influenced voting decisions during the years between Kansas–Nebraska and Lecompton. Democrats had abandoned the party of Douglas when they believed making Kansas a slave territory guaranteed that Kansas would be a slave state. They began returning when many perceived that Kansas would become a free state despite being a slave territory. Confident that other remaining slave territories would be future free states, a number of Northerners sufficient to maintain Democratic hegemony in national politics could accept Southern demands that slavery be allowed in the territories. Even Republicans, upon taking power in 1860, expressed little interest in regulating human bondage in territories where the institution was not thriving. Some even endorsed popular sovereignty where that policy was known to privilege antislavery policies.[164]

Popular support for the Supreme Court helped *Dred Scott* unite the Democratic Party.[165] Judicial decisions often provide cover for political actors who cannot advocate certain policies directly.[166] Just as many politicians who do not vote to repeal bans on abortion nevertheless insist that the Supreme Court's decision in *Roe v. Wade* be obeyed,[167] so Northern Democrats who might not have been able to vote for measures repealing the Missouri Compromise or making slavery legal in all territories nevertheless supported a Supreme Court decision to that effect. Northern Democrats could accept Southern pretensions in the territories as long as they could do so indirectly by supporting a judicial decision rather than by expressing direct support for the policy.

Lecompton was an abomination to Democrats who tolerated *Dred Scott*. Northerners could not accept Southern demands that Kansas become a slave state despite what seemed to be the presence of a clear antislavery majority. Democrats could concede this issue, Stephen Douglas and his political allies realized, only at the cost of becoming the permanent minority party in the North. Fighting Lecompton, the Little Giant and others knew, was "the

---

[164]   Fehrenbacher, *Dred Scott*, p. 548.

[165]   See Warren, 2 *Supreme Court*, p. 206.

[166]   Graber, "Nonmajoritarian Difficulty," pp. 42–3; Gerald N. Rosenberg, *The Hollow Hope: Can Courts Bring About Social Change?* (University of Chicago Press: Chicago, 1991), pp. 33–6.

[167]   Graber, "Nonmajoritarian Difficulty," pp. 56–9.

only course that could save the Northern Democracy from annihilation at the next election."[168]

Whatever one thinks of *Dred Scott* as an example of judicial statesmanship, that alleged political miscalculation was dwarfed by the legislative and executive blunders committed during the 1850s. The decisions that destroyed the Jacksonian coalition and then the nation were made by a Jacksonian president, Jacksonians in Congress, and Jacksonian party activists, not by Jacksonian justices. The Kansas–Nebraska Act and President Buchanan's effort to pass the Lecompton constitution, in particular, did far more than the entire corpus of judicial decisions to destroy the Democratic Party and bring about the Civil War.[169] Nevertheless, no contemporary constitutional theorist claims Kansas–Nebraska or Lecompton demonstrates that the elected branches of government are not institutionally capable of resolving hotly disputed issues through compromise.

The Accountability Critique

The accountability critique of *Dred Scott* rests on no better foundations than the majoritarian or compromise critiques. The political decision to seek judicial resolution of slavery issues was reached in a manner that promoted political accountability to the degree politically feasible before the Civil War. Democrats throughout the United States loudly proclaimed that their political coalition was committed to seeking a judicial decision on the constitutional status of slavery in the territories. When the justices decided *Dred Scott*, these same Democrats loudly proclaimed their support for that ruling. No politically astute voter in 1856 or 1860 could have voted for the Democratic Party under any misapprehension about what Jacksonians had done or intended to do about slavery in the territories.

The Jacksonian effort to foist on the judiciary the responsibility for making slavery policy was part of a broader political effort to maximize political accountability. Free-state Democrats and their Republican rivals recognized that issues consistently compete against each other for space on political agendas. Political coalitions must convince the public both that they are right about some issue and that the public should vote on that issue.[170] Politics before the Civil War was structured by a political competition between sectional and transsectional issues. Northern Democrats and Republicans spent as much energy disputing what issues politics should be about as they did

---

[168] Fehrenbacher, *Dred Scott,* p. 466 (quoting C. Goody to Douglas, December 20, 1857). See Douglas, *Letters,* p. 404; Johannsen, *The Frontier,* pp. 152, 197, 239.

[169] See Anbinder, *Nativism,* p. 18.

[170] See especially E. E. Schattschneider, *The Semisovereign People: A Realist's View of Democracy in America* (Dryden: Hinsdale, 1975), pp. 60–74.

debating slavery policy. Douglas began his debates with Lincoln by extolling at great length the virtues of transsectional parties that took clear positions on the national bank, tariffs, and internal improvements. He repeatedly condemned a politics that focused on such sectional issues as slavery.[171] The Republican response was not a demand for political accountability on all the issues of the day: Lincoln urged his coalition partners to *avoid* discussing issues (such as the tariff) that might weaken Republican capacity to take clear positions on slavery.[172] Northern voters were given a clear choice between the party that publicly endorsed a politics about the national political economy or the party that publicly endorsed a politics about slavery.

The accountability critique of *Dred Scott* makes the impossible demand that elected officials make all substantive policy decisions, no matter what. This standard is utopian and antidemocratic. Institutional theory does not explain why a democratic polity cannot decide by election that some issues are more important than others, that some issues should be resolved by elected officials and that other issues should be resolved by the judiciary. Serious issues of democratic accountability arise when elected officials deny or obscure their complicity with judicial decisions.[173] Jacksonians did nothing of the sort. Prominent members of that political coalition publicly called for judicial policy making and then publicly supported the policy that the justices made. Given the limits politics places on mass political coalitions, a realistic theory of political accountability should demand no more than Jacksonians did when confronted with slavery issues that threatened the capacity of their coalition to take coherent positions on the other pressing national issues of the day.

The Historical Critique

The Supreme Court majority in *Dred Scott* would not have reached different, more antislavery, conclusions had Taney and his fellow justices faithfully applied historicist methods of constitutional interpretation. Taney declared that his arguments were rooted in the original intentions of the framers and in judicial precedent. Much historical evidence supports his conclusions that freed slaves could not become American citizens and that slavery could not be banned in the territories west of the Mississippi. Significant problems

---

[171] See e.g. Stephen Douglas, "Mr. Douglas's Speech, First Joint Debate," *Lincoln–Douglas Debates*, pp. 37–48.

[172] Lincoln, 3 *Collected Works*, p. 487.

[173] See Mark A. Graber, "Constructing Judicial Review," 8 *Annual Reviews in Political Science*, 425, 447 (2005).

exist with important historical claims made in the majority opinions, but the Curtis and McLean dissents also relied on historically questionable propositions. Contemporary commentators ought to hesitate before damning on originalist grounds the judicial opinions that quote extensively from a letter James Madison wrote in 1819, asserting that the framers had not vested Congress with any power to ban slavery in the territories.[174]

The opinion of the Court in *Dred Scott* was "a riot of originalism."[175] Taney declared that the Constitution "must be construed now as it was understood at the time of its adoption." The Constitution, he wrote, "speaks not only in the same words, but with the same meaning and intent with which it spoke when it came from the hands of its framers, and was voted on and adopted by the people of the United States."[176] Other justices in the majority relied on originalist premises and discussed constitutional history at length. Justice Campbell concluded that a congressional right to ban slavery in the territories "is not supported by the historical evidence drawn from the Revolution, the Confederation, or the deliberations which preceded the ratification of the Federal Constitution."[177]

Citizenship

Contemporary historicists are correct to point out flaws in Taney's attack on black citizenship. The chief justice was wrong when he asserted that free blacks had "*never* been regarded as a part of the people or citizens of the State" according to "the public opinion and laws which *universally* pervaded in the Colonies when the Declaration of Independence was framed and when the Constitution was adopted" (emphasis added).[178] The Curtis dissent demonstrated that some black residents of Northern states were treated as citizens after the Revolution. A Massachusetts court decision in 1783 apparently affirmed the citizenship of free blacks in that commonwealth.[179] If, as Taney asserted, all persons "who at the time of the adoption of the constitution recognized as citizens in the several States, became citizens of this

---

[174] *Dred Scott* at 491–2 (opinion of Daniel) (quoting Madison to Robert Walsh, November 27, 1819).

[175] Eisgruber, "*Dred* Again," p. 46.

[176] *Dred Scott* at 426. See *Dred Scott* at 405; Taney, "Supplement," p. 602. In Taney's view, the critics of his opinion were the parties guilty of "act[ing] upon the principle that the end will justify the means": Taney, "Supplement," p. 608.

[177] *Dred Scott* at 512 (opinion of Campbell). See *Dred Scott* at 502–7, 510–12 (opinion of Campbell); *Dred Scott* at 519–22, 526 (opinion of Catron).

[178] *Dred Scott* at 412; Taney, "Supplement," p. 602. See *Dred Scott* at 407–9.

[179] *Dred Scott* at 572–6 (Curtis, dissenting); James H. Kettner, *The Development of American Citizenship, 1608–1870* (University of North Carolina Press: Chapel Hill, 1978), p. 315 (discussing *Commonwealth v. Jennison* [Mass. 1783]). See also Lowell and Gray, *Legal Review*, pp. 15–16.

new political body,"[180] then at least some persons of color were citizens of the United States when the Constitution was ratified.

Taney need not have made such a strong historical assertion. The historical foundations of *Dred Scott* survive mere demonstrations that at least one person of color was a citizen of a state when the Constitution was ratified. The chief justice was more prudent when he declared that free blacks "were not even in the minds of the framers of the Constitution";[181] this claim provides support for his analysis of citizenship no matter what version of originalism historicists rely on. Original **understandings** concern the extent to which the persons responsible for the Constitution were aware of and intended to sanction black citizenship. Original **meanings** concern how language was commonly understood at the time of ratification. If the vast majority of framers and ratifiers thought free blacks were everywhere in the United States regarded as unfit for citizenship and adopted no provision that might suggest otherwise to the average constitutional reader, then the actual existence in 1787 of a few black citizens in one or two states hardly clinches the historical case for national citizenship. The *Dred Scott* holding on black citizenship meets historicist standards if, as Taney noted in 1858, "[t]he few persons who, in certain localities, have endeavored to obliterate the line of division, and to amalgamate the races, are hardly sufficient in number or in weight of character to be noticed as an exception to the overwhelming current [or even majority] of public opinion and feeling upon this subject."[182]

The dissents in *Dred Scott* made a more fundamental historical error when deriving black citizenship from black voting rights. Conventional wisdom maintains that McLean and Curtis devastated Taney's denial of black citizenship by pointing out that some blacks voted in 1787 and thus must have been citizens of the states where they resided. "Several of the States have admitted persons of color to the right of suffrage," the Ohio justice stated, "and in this view have recognized them as citizens."[183] The chief justice, however, pointed out that the franchise in many jurisdictions had historically not been restricted to citizens. "A person," Taney stated,

> may be entitled to vote by the law of the State, who is not a citizen even of the State itself. And in some of the States of the Union foreigners not naturalized are allowed to vote. And the State may give the right to free

[180] *Dred Scott* at 406.
[181] *Dred Scott* at 411–12.
[182] Taney, "Supplement," p. 601.
[183] *Dred Scott* at 533 (McLean, dissenting). See *Dred Scott* at 531, 537 (McLean, dissenting); *Dred Scott* at 572–6, 581–2 (Curtis, dissenting).

negroes and mulattoes, but that does not make them citizens of the State, and still less of the United States.[184]

A leading contemporary study strongly supports this point. "Noncitizen suffrage," Alexander Keyssar documents, was "commonplace in Jacksonian America and supported by the decision of the Supreme Court of Illinois.[185] If there was a knockdown blow in this exchange between the majority opinions and the dissents, the punch appears to have been thrown by Chief Justice Taney.

Mainstream antebellum politicians anticipated or endorsed Taney's claim that suffrage did not entail citizenship. Both Stephen Douglas and Abraham Lincoln claimed states could grant voting rights to noncitizens. Long before *Dred Scott* was decided, Douglas supported state laws granting aliens the right to vote while rejecting state power to make aliens citizens.[186] Lincoln described as "a grave error" the belief that "none but a citizen of the United States can vote" in a presidential election. His attorney general, Edward Bates, declared: "Suffrage and eligibility have no necessary connection with citizenship." In his experience, "the one may, and often does, exist without the other."[187]

Taney, Douglas, and Lincoln agreed that suffrage was not an exclusive prerogative of citizenship because the citizens of every state were legally free to grant that and other privileges to noncitizens. Prominent politicians and judges who asserted that free blacks had no constitutional rights that white citizens were obligated to respect recognized that white majorities had the power to grant free blacks various statutory liberties.[188] Persons of color, an influential Virginian noted, "had many *legal* rights and privileges in Virginia, but no *constitutional* ones" (emphasis in original).[189] The Supreme Court of Mississippi declared, "the negro or African race have no status, civil or

---

[184] *Dred Scott* at 422. See *Dred Scott* at 405 ("each State may still confer [rights and privileges] upon an alien, or any one it thinks proper . . . ; yet he would not be a citizen in the sense in which that word is used in the Constitution of the United States").

[185] Alexander Keyssar, *The Right to Vote: The Contested History of Democracy in America* (Basic Books: New York, 2000), p. 32. See *Spragins v. Houghton*, 3 Ill. 377 (1840); Kettner, *American Citizenship*, p. 121; Gerald L. Neuman, *Strangers to the Constitution: Immigrants, Borders, and Fundamental Law* (Princeton University Press: Princeton, 1996), pp. 63–7. The difference between Taney and Curtis on alien voting was partisan, not historical. Jacksonians were inclined to favor alien voting; Whigs were opposed. Keyssar, *Right to Vote*, p. 40.

[186] Johannsen, *Douglas*, p. 74.

[187] Lincoln, 2 *Collected Works*, p. 355; Bates, "Citizenship," p. 408.

[188] *Dred Scott* at 405, 412–13, 426; *Dred Scott* at 482 (Daniel, concurring); Douglas, "Speech of Douglas, Chicago, July 9," *Lincoln–Douglas Debates*, p. 33. See Douglas, "Mr. Douglas's Speech, First Joint Debate," pp. 46–8; *Leech v. Cooley* at 99; *Real Estate of Hardcastle v. Porcher*, 16 S.C.L. (Harp.) 495 (1826).

[189] A. Freehling, *Drift*, p. 180 (quoting William Henry Brodnax).

political, in this country, save such as each State may choose to confer by special legislation in its own jurisdiction."[190]

Antislavery framers routinely distinguished the basic rights that free blacks enjoyed as human beings from the distinctive rights of American citizens. Jefferson and other prominent antebellum politicians, Herbert Storing notes, understood that "[t]o concede the Negro's right to freedom is not to concede his right to U.S. citizenship."[191] The author of the Declaration of Independence firmly believed both that black and white persons were created equal and that members of different races could not inhabit the same civic space.[192] These common distinctions between human, statutory, and citizenship rights – unacknowledged by the *Dred Scott* dissents – explain why the mere existence of free blacks with certain statutory liberties in many states at the time the Constitution was ratified did not provide historical proof that the persons responsible for the Constitution would have thought Dred Scott an American citizen. The historical issue before the justices was whether the liberties enjoyed by persons of color in 1787 and afterward were then conceptualized as the rights of citizens or as mere exercises of communal grace.

The claim that slaves and their descendants did not enjoy distinctive citizenship rights in 1787 and immediately afterward rests on strong historical foundations. The severe legal disabilities that free blacks suffered in every region of the United States at the time of ratification and afterward indicate that no community considered black residents to be equal citizens.[193] Taney observed that in New Hampshire, the most antislavery state in the Union at the time of ratification, only "free white citizens" could be "enrolled in the militia of the State." He might have added that, by the 1790s, all Northern states forbade persons of color from joining state militias.[194] The reason members of "the African race, born in the State [were] not permitted to share in one of the highest duties of the citizen" seemed "obvious" to Taney: "he forms no part of the sovereignty of the State, and is not therefore called on to uphold and defend it."[195] In the eighteenth century, Northern states granted free blacks rights only when persons of color were too few in number

---

[190] *Heirn v. Bridault*, 37 Miss. 209, 224 (1859).

[191] Herbert J. Storing, "Slavery and the Moral Foundations of the American Republic," *Slavery and Its Consequences: The Constitution, Equality, and Race* (ed. Robert A. Goldwin and Art Kaufman) (American Enterprise Institute for Public Policy Research: Washington, D.C., 1988), p. 59. See Lincoln, 3 *Collected Works*, p. 328; St. George Tucker, *A Dissertation on Slavery: With a Proposal for the Gradual Abolition of It, in the State of Virginia* (M. Carey: Philadelphia, 1796), pp. 86–7.

[192] See Storing, "Slavery," pp. 50–1, 58; see also notes 355–357 and the relevant text.

[193] *Dred Scott* at 412–16.

[194] *Dred Scott* at 415; Smith, *Civic Ideals*, p. 143.

[195] *Dred Scott* at 415. Taney may have misstated New Hampshire law, at least during the 1780s. See "An Act for Forming and Regulating the Militia within the State of New Hampshire" (1784),

to be of any consequence. When the number of free blacks increased, their statutory rights decreased. During the Massachusetts ratification debates, "Mark Anthony" opposed incorporating more antislavery provisions into the Constitution because "great numbers of slaves becoming citizens, might be burdensome and dangerous to the Public." Fearful of black political power, the New York legislature combined a proposal to emancipate slaves with a measure to disenfranchise free blacks in 1785.[196]

Claims that the disabilities suffered by women (whom everyone recognized to be citizens) were analogous to those of free blacks[197] fail to grasp fundamental differences in the perceived basis of gender and race distinctions. In 1787 and 1857, women belonged to America in ways that persons of color did not. Antebellum women lacked basic political rights, but republican theory at the founding maintained that females were virtually and adequately represented by the males in their family. "It is true," the Kentucky Supreme Court noted in an opinion denying black citizenship,

> that females and infants do not personally possess those rights and privileges [of citizenship], in any state of the Union; but they are generally dependent upon adult males through whom they enjoy the benefits of those rights and privileges; and it is a rule of common law, as well as of common sense, that females and infants should, in this respect, partake of the quality of those adult males who belong to the same class and condition in society.[198]

No claim was made that anyone virtually represented free blacks or that public policy should promote their interests. The prevalent doctrine of separate spheres assigned women important civic duties in private life, namely the bearing and rearing of offspring. Rogers Smith notes that women "lack[ed] any power to participate politically themselves, but [were] charged with conveying political morality to children in the domestic sphere." "As republican mothers," he continues, "women were indeed citizens and moral equals."[199]

Early American Reprints, Microcard, Evans #20547 (not listing race as a disability). Special thanks to Stephen Siegel for sharing his sources on New Hampshire law with me.

[196] John P. Kaminski and Gaspare Saladino, eds., *The Documentary History of the Ratification of the Constitution*, vol. 5, *Ratification of the Constitution by the States: Massachusetts [2]* (State Historical Society of Wisconsin: Madison, 1998), pp. 676–7 ("Mark Anthony"); "Objections of the Council of Revision of the Gradual Abolition Bill," March 21, 1785, in *A Necessary Evil?: Slavery and the Debate over the Constitution* (ed. John Kaminski) (Madison House: Madison, 1995), p. 31. The New York bill was vetoed by the Council of Revision on the ground that free blacks were citizens: "Objections," pp. 31–2. As a result, New York had no clear law during ratification as to whether free blacks were citizens.

[197] See *Dred Scott* at 583 (Curtis, dissenting).

[198] *Amy v. Smith* at 333–4.

[199] Rogers M. Smith, "'One United People': Second-Class Female Citizenship and the American Quest for Community," 1 *Yale Journal of Law & the Humanities*, 229, 255 (1989); Smith, *Civic Ideals*, p. 112.

Persons of color had no distinctive civic responsibilities that might explain their legal disabilities. Free blacks were denied the opportunity to exercise most civic duties because they were thought unfit to be citizens, not because they were regarded as making some special contribution to the polity that was inconsistent with their exercising basic political rights.[200] Gender determined the role of a citizen; race determined membership in the political community.

The surviving records of the framing and ratification debates contain no information on whether the persons responsible for the Constitution intended to sanction black citizenship. The framers neither textually defined nor specifically discussed the status of free blacks. Participants in the constitutional convention, when drafting what would become the privileges and immunities clause of Article IV, did drop specific references to "white and other free citizens." No record exists whether the reference to "white" or "other free" was the offending expression.[201] More general citizenship issues that might cast some light on the status of Dred Scott attracted little or no attention during the framing and ratification debates. No solid historical evidence exists on the original understanding of national citizenship or on the relationship between state and national citizenship.[202] Most important, no clause in the original Constitution sets out any criteria for American citizenship. Thus, whether interpreted consistently with the "original understanding" or "original meaning" strands of historicism,[203] the Constitution of 1787 provides no clear grounds for determining whether free persons of color could be citizens of the United States.

Framers from different regions held different opinions about black citizenship that were neither aired nor resolved.[204] Pierce Butler's private notes taken at the constitutional convention equated white with free and black with slave.[205] The famous passage in Virginia's Declaration of Rights – "all men are by nature equally free and independent, and have certain inherent rights" – was followed by a proviso that was commonly understood as

---

[200] See *Dred Scott* at 416.
[201] See Max Farrand, ed., *The Records of the Federal Convention*, vol. 1 (Yale University Press: New Haven, 1937), pp. 193, 201, 229, 243, 444 (references to "white citizens"); Farrand, 2 *Records*, pp. 154, 168, 182–3 (same); Farrand, 2 *Records*, pp. 566, 571 (references to "white" omitted); Smith, *Civic Ideals*, pp. 115, 124.
[202] Smith, *Civic Ideals*, p. 115.
[203] For the distinctions between various originalisms, see Randy E. Barnett, *Restoring the Lost Constitution: The Presumption of Liberty* (Princeton University Press: Princeton, 2004), pp. 92–4; Jack N. Rakove, *Original Meanings: Politics and Ideas in the Making of the Constitution* (Vintage: New York, 1996), pp. 7–10.
[204] Finkelman, "The Constitution," pp. 385, 392; Kettner, *American Citizenship*, pp. 231–2.
[205] Farrand, 4 *Records*, p. 161.

excluding persons of color from the liberties enjoyed by Virginia citizens.[206] Charles Pinckney, a surviving member of the framing convention, claimed during the debates over the Missouri Compromise that in 1787 "there did not then exist such a thing in the Union as a black or colored citizen."[207] Some Northerners in 1787 implied that free blacks were citizens. "Mark Anthony" worried about emancipation because he thought freed slaves automatically became citizens.[208] Most Northern framers probably had no conscious intentions about black citizenship.[209] The only inference clearly supported by the historical record is that no meeting of the minds took place during the 1780s that might justify confident assertions about the constitutional conditions under which Dred Scott might have become a citizen of the United States.

The limited federal case law on citizenship that existed when *Dred Scott* was decided supports the Taney Court's conclusion that former slaves could not become American citizens. No previous case explicitly discussed who was eligible for American citizenship,[210] but the Court in *Moore v. Illinois* indicated that states had the power to prohibit liberated slaves from entering their territory.[211] This decision implies that such persons were not constitutional citizens. The citizens of each state would hardly be entitled to "the privileges and immunities of the citizens of the several states" if states were entitled to bar some citizens entirely.[212] Should previous executive and state court opinions count as valid constitutional precedents, a common practice in Jacksonian America,[213] the historical support for the Taney

---

[206] A. E. Dick Howard, *Commentaries on the Constitution of Virginia*, vol. 1 (University Press of Virginia: Charlottesville, 1974), p. 62. See *Aldridge v. The Commonwealth*, 4 Va. (2 Va. Cas.) 447, 449 (1824).

[207] *Annals of Congress*, 16th Cong., 2nd Sess., p. 1134 (Charles Pinckney). See William Wiecek, "'The Blessings of Liberty': Slavery in the American Constitutional Order," *Slavery and Its Consequences*, p. 28. See also Storing, "Slavery," pp. 57–60; Paul Finkelman, "The Color of Law," 87 *Northwestern University Law Review*, 937, 964 (1992).

[208] 5 *Documentary History*, p. 676. See John P. Kaminski and Gaspare Saladino, eds., *The Documentary History of the Ratification of the Constitution*, vol. 6, *Ratification of the Constitution by the States: Massachusetts [3]* (State Historical Society of Wisconsin: Madison, 2000), p. 1244 (speech of Thomas Dawes).

[209] Elected officials in New York at the time of ratification could not decide whether free blacks were citizens. See note 196 and the relevant text.

[210] Previous decisions did support the Taney Court's conclusion that the naturalization power was exclusive. See notes 223–225 and the relevant text.

[211] *Moore v. Illinois*, 55 U.S. 13, 18 (1852).

[212] The *Moore* opinion indicated that states could bar paupers; see *Moore* at 18. Paupers could qualify for entry by becoming self-sufficient, but persons of color could never possess the qualities necessary for citizenship. See *Amy v. Smith* at 333–4.

[213] See Mark A. Graber, "Antebellum Perspectives on Free Speech," 10 *William & Mary Bill of Rights Journal*, 779, 804–10 (2002).

Court's ruling on citizenship becomes overwhelming. Virtually every state court and attorney general of the United States who considered the issue before 1857 concluded that free blacks were not citizens.[214] Lincoln offered no response in the sixth debate when Douglas asked: "What court or judge ever held that a negro was a citizen?" "The State courts had decided that question over and over again," Douglas continued, "and the *Dred Scott* decision on that point only affirmed what every court in the land knew to be the law." [215]

The central problem with both the Taney opinion and the Curtis dissent is that "free negroes appeared to occupy a middle ground in terms of the rights they were allowed to claim in practice, a status that could not be described in the traditional language of slave, alien, or citizen." [216] Forced to fit free blacks into one of these traditional categories, both Curtis and Taney suppressed part of the historical record. Curtis was on strong ground when he noted that some states had explicitly declared free blacks to be citizens.[217] Nevertheless, in order to explain away the disabilities that those free blacks suffered, Curtis took the position that "naked citizenship" conferred no rights whatsoever.[218] This conclusion is flatly inconsistent with the American law of citizenship at the time.[219] Taney's claim that free blacks were best regarded as "subjects" [220] seems a more accurate, if still imperfect, description of the actual legal status free persons of color enjoyed at most times and places in antebellum America.

Taney and Daniel presented a historical argument that supports the more modest claim that Dred Scott, any person enslaved after 1787, or any person descended from a person enslaved after 1787 could not be or become a citizen of the United States no matter what their status in state law. Both justices declared that the naturalization power granted to Congress in Article I, Section 8 was exclusive. Persons who were not citizens of the United States in 1787 or descended from such citizens could become United States citizens only pursuant to an act of Congress. Masters could not create American citizens by freeing their slaves. States could not create American citizens by granting state citizenship to free blacks. "No state can, by any act or law of its own," Taney wrote, "introduce a new member into the political community

---

[214] See notes 83–84.

[215] Stephen A. Douglas, "Mr. Douglas's Speech, Sixth Joint Debate," *Lincoln–Douglas Debates,* p. 268.

[216] Kettner, *American Citizenship,* p. 319.

[217] See note 179.

[218] *Dred Scott* at 583–4 (Curtis, dissenting).

[219] See Kettner, *American Citizenship,* pp. 235, 260, 311–12, 319.

[220] Taney, "Supplement," pp. 605–6. See *Shaw v. Brown,* 35 Miss. 246, 315 (1858); Kent, 2 *Commentaries,* p. 282.

created by the Constitution of the United States." [221] Only Congress could make Dred Scott a citizen of the United States. Congress plainly had not done so. [222]

This interpretation of Article I, Section 8 rests on strong historical foundations. Both Alexander Hamilton in *Federalist* 32 and Madison at the constitutional convention stated that the federal naturalization power was exclusive. Subsequent Supreme Court decisions adopted this position. [223] By 1857, American constitutional law clearly denied states the power to grant national citizenship to persons who did not enjoy citizenship by birth. [224] Justices Curtis and McLean conceded the exclusivity of the naturalization power in their dissents. [225]

Federal exclusivity did not prevent freed slaves from becoming citizens, the dissents in *Dred Scott* maintained, because the naturalization power did not encompass persons born on American soil. McLean declared that native-born slaves became United States citizens immediately upon gaining their freedom, but he cited no historical evidence or legal precedent that supported his position. [226] Curtis insisted that persons born in the United States were United States citizens if they were recognized as citizens by the state of their birth. [227] "The Constitution," he asserted, "has recognized the general principle of public law, that allegiance and citizenship depend on the place of birth." [228] No other state or the federal government, in his view, could grant American citizenship to persons who were not citizens at birth. [229] Curtis fairly observed that previous discussions of exclusivity had focused on aliens. Given the principle that the federal government had limited powers, he reasoned, the absence of historical evidence that naturalization was intended to encompass the native born meant that states retained the constitutional power to determine whether persons born within their jurisdictions enjoyed national citizenship. [230]

Curtis was right to note that the Constitution did not expressly declare that the naturalization power encompassed persons born without and within

[221] *Dred Scott* at 406. See *Dred Scott* at 405–6, 417–20; *Dred Scott* at 481–2 (Daniel, concurring). See Tucker, *A Dissertation on Slavery,* p. 73; *Heirn v. Bridault* at 233; *Bryan v. Walton* at 201–2.

[222] *Dred Scott* at 482 (Daniel, dissenting).

[223] Alexander Hamilton, James Madison, and John Jay, *The Federalist Papers* (New American Library: New York, 1961), p. 199; Farrand, 1 *Records,* p. 245: *Thurlow v. Massachusetts,* 46 U.S. 504, 585 (1847); *Chirac v. Chirac,* 15 U.S. 259 (1817).

[224] See Corwin, "*Dred Scott* Case," pp. 312–13; Kettner, *American Citizenship,* pp. 225, 249–50.

[225] *Dred Scott* at 578 (Curtis, dissenting); *Dred Scott* at 533 (McLean, dissenting).

[226] *Dred Scott* at 531 (McLean, dissenting).

[227] *Dred Scott* at 582–6 (Curtis, dissenting). See Maltz, "Unlikely Hero," pp. 2009–11 (1996).

[228] *Dred Scott* at 581 (Curtis, dissenting). See *Dred Scott* at 531 (McLean, dissenting).

[229] *Dred Scott* at 585–6 (Curtis, dissenting).

[230] *Dred Scott* at 579 (Curtis, dissenting).

the United States, but good reason exists for thinking that those constitutional framers who favored exclusivity wished to deny states any power over national citizenship. Proponents of federal exclusivity feared that individual states, in the absence of uniform rules, might adopt citizenship policies that would result in other states being flooded with unwanted residents. *Federalist* 42 observed:

> By the laws of several States, certain descriptions of aliens who had rendered themselves obnoxious, were laid under interdicts inconsistent, not only with the rights of citizenship, but with the privilege of residence. What would have been the consequence, if such persons, by residence or otherwise, had acquired the character of citizens under the laws of another State and then asserted their rights as such, both to residence and citizenship within the State proscribing them?[231]

Free blacks and former slaves were the least desired residents in antebellum America. If the primary purpose of uniform rules of naturalization was to allow states to fence out persons generally thought to be unfit for citizenship, then federal exclusivity must have been understood to apply to "undesirables" born in the United States as well as to "undesirables" born abroad.

Even if constitutionally sound, the Curtis position "was hardly a triumph of antislavery ideology."[232] For all practical purposes, Curtis denied citizenship to all persons of color not born in New England. His celebrated dissent on citizenship was based entirely on a technicality. Curtis maintained that the case had previously been pleaded in such a way as to allow the Supreme Court to take jurisdiction if any person "of African descent, whose ancestors were sold as slaves in the United States, can be a citizen of the United States."[233] Had Sanford claimed when challenging federal jurisdiction that Dred Scott was not an American citizen, Curtis would have voted with the *Dred Scott* majority.

Daniel and Taney overreached when they claimed that "the African race never have been acknowledged as belonging to the family of nations."[234] Many Americans living in 1787, Jefferson in particular, believed that black persons "were created equal" and were "endowed by their Creator with certain inalienable rights."[235] The denial of black citizenship in *Dred Scott*

---

[231] Hamilton, Madison, and Jay, *Federalist Papers*, p. 270. See Joseph Story, *Commentaries on the Constitution of the United States*, vol. 2, 3rd ed. (Little, Brown: Boston, 1858), pp. 51–3.

[232] Maltz, "Unlikely Hero," p. 2016; Smith, *Civic Ideals*, pp. 269–71.

[233] *Dred Scott* at 571 (Curtis, dissenting). See *Dred Scott* at 588 (Curtis, dissenting).

[234] *Dred Scott* at 475 (opinion of Daniel). See *Dred Scott* at 404–8.

[235] See e.g. Thomas Jefferson, *The Portable Thomas Jefferson* (ed. Merrill D. Peterson) (Penguin: New York, 1975), p. 215.

does not, however, depend on Taney's ahistorical reading of the Declaration of Independence. The Taney–Daniel argument is true to the framers and subsequent legal doctrine as long as "the African race [had not] been acknowledged as belonging to the [American] family."[236] This claim that people of different races could not occupy the same civic space was frequently made during the founding era and was accepted by most white Americans during the 1850s.[237] When combined with federal naturalization policies that had always excluded black persons, and in the absence of any provision plainly setting out qualifications for American citizenship,[238] the persistent strand of white nationalism in American politics provides strong support for Taney's claim that most persons responsible for the Constitution thought that Dred Scott was not and could not become a citizen of the United States.

Slavery in the Territories

The Taney Court's ruling that federal bans on slavery in the territories were inconsistent with the original understanding of the Constitution and subsequent doctrinal developments was as historically defensible as its ruling that former slaves could not be American citizens. As was the case with the citizenship issue, every major opinion in *Dred Scott* made questionable assertions when trying to document an understanding that never existed. Chief Justice Taney strained history by confidently proclaiming that the territorial clause sanctioned congressional power only over territories claimed by the United States in 1787. Justice Curtis strained history by confidently proclaiming that Article IV, Section 3 sanctioned congressional power over all territories acquired by the United States after 1787. The majority opinions in *Dred Scott* were on stronger historical grounds when they noted the absence of Southern opposition to the alleged constitutional power to prohibit slavery throughout a substantially expanded national domain. Neither Justice Curtis nor Justice McLean explained why slaveholders deeply concerned with their status in the Union consciously empowered the national government to allow free-state settlers to monopolize the West.

The chief justice's analysis of slavery in the territories relied heavily on two premises that in 1857 enjoyed broad, transsectional support. The first,

---

[236] See Eisgruber, "*Dred* Again," p. 48.

[237] See Jefferson, *The Portable Jefferson*, p. 186; Reginald Horsman, *Race and Manifest Destiny: The Origins of American Racial Anglo-Saxonism* (Harvard University Press: Cambridge, 1981); George M. Fredrickson, *The Black Image in the White Mind: The Debate on Afro-American Character and Destiny, 1817–1914* (Harper & Row: New York, 1971), pp. 1–164. See also notes 355–372 and the relevant text.

[238] *Dred Scott* at 419. See *Dred Scott* at 482 (Daniel, dissenting); 1 U.S. Stat. 103 (1790); 1 U.S. Stat. 414 (1795).

that persons did not lose constitutional rights by moving to the territories, was far more controversial in 1803 than in 1857 or 2003; the second, that the due process clause protected the right to bring personal property into the territories, is far more controversial in 2003 than it was in 1803 or 1857. Once one concedes, as antebellum Republicans did, that the Fifth Amendment to the Constitution protected the right to bring personal property into the territories, the historical case for *Dred Scott* becomes quite persuasive.

Constitutional Rights in the Territories. Chief Justice Taney began the argument for the constitutional right to bring slaves into the territories by asserting that constitutional restrictions on federal power were not limited by geography. The national government, he declared, "cannot, when it enters a Territory of the United States, put off its character, and assume discretionary or despotic powers which the Constitution has denied to it." [239] The other Southern Jacksonians on the Taney Court agreed that Congress could not rule the territories by fiat. Given the framers' commitment to limited government, these justices reasoned, the Constitution could not have been intended to vest Congress with "supreme and irresponsible power ... over boundless territories." After surveying at length the founders' hostility to absolutism of any kind, Justice Campbell declared that he sought "in vain for an annunciation that a consolidated power had been inaugurated which had no restriction but the discretion of Congress." [240]

Taney pointed to differences between Article I and Article IV that provide plausible textual bases for thinking the language in the latter was not understood or intended to vest Congress with "general powers of government" over the territories.[241] Article I states: "Congress shall have the power to exercise exclusive legislation in all cases" concerning the District of Columbia. This language plainly entails a power to ban slavery. Article IV merely enables Congress to make "needful rules and regulations respecting the Territory or other Property belonging to the United States." This language is plainly more restrictive and was interpreted as such by the *Dred Scott* majority. Taney concluded that Article IV's more limited power to make "needful rules and regulations respecting the Territory" – when read in conjunction with Article I's "exclusive legislation" – implies a grant only of

---

[239] *Dred Scott* at 449. See *Dred Scott* at 447 ("citizens of the United States who migrate to a Territory cannot be ruled as mere colonists, dependent upon the will of the General Government, and to be governed by any laws it may think proper to impose").

[240] *Dred Scott* at 505, 511 (opinion of Campbell). See *Dred Scott* at 510–11 (opinion of Campbell).

[241] *Dred Scott* at 440.

"some particular specified power," not the general "power of sovereignty" necessary to prohibit slavery.[242]

The Bill of Rights provided specific constitutional limits on federal power in the territories. Taney declared: "No one will contend that Congress can make any law in a Territory respecting that establishment of religion, or the free exercise thereof, abridging the freedom of speech or of the press." "Nor can Congress deny to the people" in territories, he added, "the right to keep and bear arms, nor the right to trial by jury, nor compel any one to be a witness against himself in a criminal proceeding."[243] These constitutional limits on national power bound all governmental institutions established by national power. No Southern Jacksonian defended the Northern version of popular sovereignty, which interpreted the Constitution as vesting territorial governments with the exclusive power to ban slavery within their jurisdictions. "Congress could confer no power on any local Government," Taney wrote, "established by its authority, to violate the provisions of the constitution."[244] If Congress could not ban slavery when governing the territories, then Congress could not vest a territorial government with the power to ban slavery. The dissents in *Dred Scott* endorsed this restriction on territorial power. "In organizing the Government of a Territory," McLean wrote, "[n]o powers can be exercised which are prohibited by the Constitution." Curtis declared that federal power over the territories was limited by "the express prohibitions on Congress not to do certain things."[245]

American constitutional law throughout the nineteenth and early twentieth centuries echoed the *Dred Scott* consensus that persons lost no constitutional rights by moving to the territories. A unanimous Taney Court decision in 1850 held or implied that territorial governments could not violate the first eight amendments to the Constitution.[246] Republican justices after *Dred Scott* treated Taney Court doctrine on the territorial reach of the Bill of Rights as sound constitutional law.[247] The justices in the *Insular Cases*, a series of decisions on federal power over territories acquired after the Spanish-American War, agreed that Congress was bound by the Bill of Rights in any territory being prepared for statehood, although they disputed

---

[242] *Dred Scott* at 440.

[243] *Dred Scott* at 450.

[244] *Dred Scott* at 451.

[245] *Dred Scott* at 542 (McLean, dissenting); *Dred Scott* at 614 (Curtis, dissenting). See Neuman, *Strangers to the Constitution*, p. 80.

[246] *Webster v. Reid*, 52 U.S. 437, 460 (1850). See 5 Stat. 235 (1838).

[247] See *Thompson v. Utah*, 170 U.S. 343 (1898).

whether the Constitution limited national power in possessions acquired for other reasons.[248]

This judicial agreement masks the intense controversy over the territorial reach of the Constitution during the first fifty years of the nineteenth century. A strong strand of antebellum thought advocated a "membership" theory of national power. On this view, the Constitution was a contract between existing states or the people of existing states. That bargain gave no rights to persons who, residing in the territories, were not parties to the constitutional agreement.[249] Federalists during the debates over Louisiana insisted that new territories could be governed however Congress thought fit.[250] Daniel Webster maintained that persons in the territories were not protected by the Bill of Rights.[251] Many early American constitutionalists challenged this claim, asserting that Congress was bound by constitutional limitations in all areas subject to federal jurisdiction. John Marshall declared that constitutional references to the "United States" encompassed "states and territories."[252] Given that the persons responsible for the Bill of Rights had no conscious intentions on questions associated with new territories and included no constitutional language delineating the geographical scope of those amendments, the Taney–Marshall position that the Constitution follows the flag is not as historically uncontroversial as the absence of historicist criticism in 1857 or 2003 suggests. The claim that persons in territories being prepared for statehood retain all constitutional rights is the only conclusion Taney reached that enjoyed more support after 1857 than before.

The Right to Bring Personal Property into the Territories. Taney's argument that the first eight amendments constrained national power in the territories concluded by asserting that the Fifth Amendment protected the right to bring personal property into the territories. His opinion declared that "an act of Congress which deprives a citizen of the United States of his liberty or

---

[248] See *Balzac v. Porto Rico*, 258 U.S. 298, 304–5 (1922); Neuman, *Strangers to the Constitution*, pp. 81–9.

[249] See Neuman, *Strangers to the Constitution*, pp. 73–9. This paragraph relies heavily on Neuman's excellent analysis.

[250] *Annals of Congress*, 8th Cong., 1st Sess., p. 45 (Timothy Pickering); Neuman, *Strangers to the Constitution*, p. 74.

[251] See *American Insurance Company v. 356 Bales of Cotton*, 26 U.S. 511, 538 (1828) (argument of Mr. Webster).

[252] *Loughborough v. Blake*, 18 U.S. 317, 319 (1820). See Neuman, *Strangers to the Constitution*, p. 75.

property, merely because he came himself or brought his property into a particular Territory of the United States, ... could hardly be dignified with the name due process of law."[253] Campbell claimed that, when regulating the territories, the national government could not "disturb the legitimate distribution of property ... among ... individuals."[254] Neither Taney nor Campbell elaborated on the historical pedigree of this asserted right. The Taney opinion reads as if the chief justice thought the right to bring property into the territories followed as naturally as the right to practice religion in the territories from the premise that the Bill of Rights protected persons in the territories.

Contemporary commentators either dismiss or deride this argument about property rights. Some believe the Fifth Amendment largely irrelevant to Taney's broader claims. James Ely asserts, "due process received only passing attention."[255] Other commentators claim that the *Dred Scott* opinion is "the birthplace of the controversial idea of 'substantive due process,'"[256] the claim that the due process clause protects fundamental liberties as well as fair procedures; they then condemn the argument. No contemporary critic of *Dred Scott* takes seriously a constitutional right to bring property into the territories. Cass Sunstein declares: "If California says that people may not own lions, and if a citizen from Arizona takes a lion into California, there is no constitutional problem if the lion is taken from the owner and even freed in California."[257]

What is clear to present commentators was not clear before the Civil War. The two dissents in *Dred Scott* disputed whether persons had a constitutional right to bring personal property into the territories. Justice Curtis took the modern position. He rejected the claim that the "power to make all needful rules and regulations respecting the territory of the United States is subject to an exception of the allowance or prohibition of slavery therein."[258] His analysis did not explicitly discuss the extent to which the due process clause might protect various property rights. Instead, Curtis implicitly denied the constitutional right to bring personal property into the territories by treating persons seeking to bring slaves into the territories as demanding a special "exception." Justice McLean was more sympathetic. His opinion endorsed

---

[253] *Dred Scott* at 450.
[254] *Dred Scott* at 516 (Campbell, concurring).
[255] Ely, "The Oxymoron Reconsidered," p. 317. See Fehrenbacher, *Dred Scott*, p. 382.
[256] Sunstein, "*Dred Scott*," p. 65. See Bork, *Tempting*, p. 31.
[257] Sunstein, "*Dred Scott*," p. 73.
[258] *Dred Scott* at 623 (Curtis, dissenting).

Taney's claim that all Americans had the constitutional right to bring their personal property into the territories. Because "the Territories are common property of the States," McLean declared, "every man has a right to go there with his property." [259] McLean disputed Taney's conclusion only because the Ohio justice maintained that "a slave is not a mere chattel." Following abolitionist logic, McLean refused to regard "a slave [as] property beyond the local operation of the local law which makes him such." [260]

McLean's understanding of due process reflected mainstream Republican thought. Prominent Republicans during the 1850s supported "substantive due process" [261] and asserted that persons had a constitutional right to bring property into the territories. Historicists who claim that Taney's reading of the due process clause is a "momentous sham" [262] seem unaware that Abraham Lincoln and his antislavery supporters promulgated the same and related constitutional "abominations." Proslavery and antislavery advocates agreed that the due process clause of the Fifth Amendment limited national power to regulate and define property in the territories. They disputed the substance of those limits, not their existence. The antislavery Fifth Amendment, the antebellum Republican Party believed, forbade federal laws permitting human bondage in the territories. "[T]he [due process] clause," Salmon Chase and other prominent abolitionists asserted, "prohibits the General Government from sanctioning slaveholding, and renders the continuance of slavery, as a legal relation, in any place of exclusive national jurisdiction, impossible." [263] The Republican Party platforms of 1856 and 1860 declared that federal laws establishing slavery in the territories deprived enslaved blacks of their liberty without due process of law.[264]

Prominent Republicans believed that the due process clause protected the property of white settlers moving westward as well as the liberty of their

---

[259] *Dred Scott* at 549 (McLean, dissenting).

[260] *Dred Scott* at 549–50 (McLean, dissenting).

[261] James Ely properly notes that "the phrase 'substantive due process' is anachronistic when used to describe decisions rendered during the nineteenth and early twentieth centuries," that "courts did not differentiate between procedural and substantive due process until the New Deal era": "The Oxymoron Revisited," p. 319.

[262] Bork, *Tempting*, pp. 31–2.

[263] Samuel Portland Chase and Charles Dexter Cleveland, *Anti-Slavery Addresses of 1844 and 1845* (J.A. Bancroft: Philadelphia, 1867), p. 86. See Chase and Cleveland, *Anti-Slavery*, pp. 17, 101; "Liberty Party Platform of 1844," 1 *National Party Platforms*, p. 5; Theodore Dwight Weld, *The Power of Congress over the District of Columbia* (J.F. Trow: New York, 1838), p. 40. See also Foner, *Free Soil*, pp. 76–7, 83; Wiecek, *Antislavery*, pp. 155–6, 190, 198, 209–10, 252–5, 265–6, 274–5.

[264] "Republican Platform of 1856," 1 *National Party Platforms*, p. 27; "Republican Platform of 1860," 1 *National Party Platforms*, p. 32.

would-be slaves. Abraham Lincoln supported Taney's claim that persons had a right to bring their possessions into the territories. "[T]he slaveholder [would have] the same [political][265] right to take his negroes to Kansas that a freeman has to take his hogs or his horses," he informed his fellow citizens, "if negroes were property in the same sense that hogs and horses are."[266] As late as 1901, Republican justices on the Supreme Court treated the Taney–Lincoln–McLean position as good constitutional law. Justice Homer Billings Brown in *Downes v. Bidwell* declared, "if … slaves were indistinguishable from other property, the inference from the *Dred Scott* case is irresistible that Congress had no power to prohibit their introduction into a territory." "It would scarcely be insisted," Brown continued,

> that Congress could with one hand invite settlers to locate in the territories of the United States, and with the other deny them the right to take their property and belongings with them. The two are so inseparable from each other that one could scarcely be granted and the other withheld without an exercise of arbitrary power inconsistent with the underlying principles of a free government. It might indeed be claimed with great plausibility that such a law would amount to a deprivation of property within the Fourteenth Amendment. The difficulty with the *Dred Scott* case was that the court refused to make a distinction between property in general, and a wholly exceptional class of property.[267]

Whether Taney and the Republican Party were right to claim that due process had a substantive component is a subject of an ongoing historical debate. The accepted view throughout most of the twentieth century was that due process rights were strictly procedural. "[D]ue process," Raoul Berger and others contend, "did not comprehend judicial power to override legislation on substantive or policy grounds."[268] This view has recently been challenged by constitutionalists of all political persuasions. James Ely and others find numerous state cases from the late eighteenth and early nineteenth centuries holding that the due process clause, the law of the land clause, or a related state constitutional provision forbade legislatures from

---

[265] Lincoln apparently did not use the word "political"; that term was inserted in brackets by the newspaper reporting his speech. See Lincoln, 2 *Collected Works*, p. 247.

[266] Lincoln, 2 *Collected Works*, p. 245. See Lincoln, 2 *Collected Works*, p. 264; *Congressional Globe*, 31st Cong., 1st Sess., App., p. 479 (Salmon Chase).

[267] *Downes v. Bidwell*, 182 U.S. 244, 274–5 (1901) (opinion of Brown).

[268] Berger, *Government by Judiciary*, p. 194. See Louis B. Boudin, *Government by Judiciary*, vol. 2 (Godwin: New York, 1932), p. 374; John Hart Ely, *Democracy and Distrust: A Theory of Judicial Review* (Harvard University Press: Cambridge, 1980), pp. 14–18; Edward S. Corwin, *Court over Constitution: A Study of Judicial Review as an Instrument of Popular Government* (Princeton University Press: Princeton, 1938).

divesting persons (who had not committed crimes) of their vested property rights.[269] "[I]t is clearly unwarrantable," the Supreme Court of New Hampshire proclaimed, "to take from any citizen, a vested right; a right 'to do certain actions or possess certain things,' which he has already begun to exercise, or to the exercise of which no obstacle exists in the present law of the land."[270] By 1857, property owners could cite a substantial body of state constitutional law decisions as providing precedential support for claims that due process or analogous constitutional provisions forbade legislatures from confiscating property, restricting traditional uses of property, or transferring ownership of property from one person to another.[271]

Federal constitutional law provided additional precedential support for the constitutional right not to be divested of property rights. The Taney Court declared several private bills unconstitutional on the ground that Congress had unconstitutionally given to one person land that already belonged to another person.[272] A judicial majority in a patent case decided four years before *Dred Scott* concluded that the due process clause of the Fifth Amendment forbade Congress from passing a law redistributing existing property rights. Chief Justice Taney declared that the national government had no power to "authorize an inventor to recall rights which he had granted to others; or reinvest in him rights of property which he had conveyed for a valuable and fair consideration." "[I]t can hardly be maintained," his opinion in *Bloomer v. McQuewan* continued, that "Congress could lawfully deprive a citizen of the use of his property after he had purchased the absolute and unlimited right from the inventor."[273] The two dissenting justices, Nelson and McLean, did not challenge the due process analysis in the majority opinion.

---

[269] See Ely, "The Oxymoron Revisited"; Robert E. Riggs, "Substantive Due Process in 1791," 1990 *Wisconsin Law Review*, 941 (1990).

[270] *Merrill v. Sherburne*, 1 N.H. 199, 214 (1818); See *Den ex dem. Trustees of University v. Foy*, 5 N.C. 58, 87–9 (1805); *Lindsay v. Commissioners*, 2 Bay 38, 59–60, 61–2 (S.C. 1796); *Bowman v. Middleton*, 1 Bay 252, 254–5 (S.C. 1792).

[271] See *Hoke v. Henderson*, 15 N.C. 1, 11–17 (1833); *Taylor v. Porter & Ford*, 4 Hill 140, 145–7 (N.Y. 1843) (due process and law of the land clauses); *Jones's Heirs v. Perry*, 18 Tenn. 59, 71, 78 (1836) (law of the land); *Regents of University of Maryland v. Williams*, 9 G. & J. 365, 408–13 (law of the land and due process); *Reed v. Wright*, 2 Greene 15, 22–8 (Iowa 1849) (law of the land); *In re Dorsey*, 7 Port. 293, 381–2 (1838) (opinion of Ormond) (due course of law). See also Stephen A. Siegal, "Lochner Era Jurisprudence and the American Constitutional Tradition," 70 *North Carolina Law Review*, 1, 54–62 (1991).

[272] *Willot v. Sandford*, 60 U.S. 79, 82 (1856); *Delauriere v. Emison*, 56 U.S. 525, 538 (1854); *Chouteau v. Eckhart*, 43 U.S. 344 (1844). See *United States v. Covilland*, 66 U.S. 339, 341 (1862); *Landes v. Brant*, 51 U.S. 348, 370 (1851); *Marsh v. Brooks*, 49 U.S. 223, 233–4 (1850); *Les Bois v. Bramell*, 45 U.S. 449, 463 (1846); *Stoddard v. Chambers*, 43 U.S. 284, 317 (1844). See more generally Mark A. Graber, "Naked Land Transfers and American Constitutional Development," 53 *Vanderbilt Law Review*, 73 (2000).

[273] *Bloomer v. McQuewan*, 55 U.S. 539, 553–4 (1852).

This substantial body of state and federal constitutional law may explain the cursory treatment Taney gave to substantive due process when defending the right to bring property into the territories. Alfred Hill notes that, before the Civil War, "courts thought it obvious that a statute they deemed confiscatory was not a law of the land within the meaning of the clause of that name (or for the purposes of the due process clause)."[274] If the chief justice's old adversary, Daniel Webster, was a reliable guide, then the challenge in *Dred Scott* was getting the Constitution into the territories, not establishing constitutional protection for private property. Webster and his constitutional successors could be counted on to give enthusiastic support for judicial decisions protecting vested rights. "Taney's ... unsupported assertions in *Bloomer* and *Dred Scott* of a substantive scope for the due process clause," Hill observes after detailing the relevant precedents, "are less plausibly explained by an assumption of uncharacteristic slovenliness on so important an issue, than by his probable awareness that, on the state level, such a scope for the clause ... in protection of 'vested rights' had long been taken for granted."[275]

It is impossible to determine whether the persons responsible for the Constitution thought the right not to be divested of property included the right not to be divested of property when moving into the territories. Little discussion took place in 1787 over the precise meaning of the territorial clause; less debate took place in 1791 over the precise meaning of the due process clause.[276] No record exists of any debate in 1787 or 1791 over the extent to which the Bill of Rights or Article I limited federal power in the territories. All that can be said with some certainty is that mainstream thinkers in both the free and slave states at the time *Dred Scott* was decided concluded that persons had a constitutional right not to be divested of property rights and that bans on slavery, a common form of property, in the territories divested persons who moved into them of their property rights. Moving to the territories was legal, and persons could be divested of existing property rights only if they had committed a crime. A law banning slavery in the territories, Taney might have stated, took a property right from A (the master) and gave it to B (the slave). This was the quintessential constitutional wrong in antebellum America.[277] If Taney was wrong when insisting that the due process

---

[274] Alfred Hill, "The Political Dimension of Constitutional Adjudication," 63 *University of Southern California Law Review*, 1237, 1317 (1990). See John Harrison, "Substantive Due Process and the Constitutional Text," 83 *Virginia Law Review*, 493, 553 (1997).

[275] Hill, "Political Dimension," p. 1317.

[276] See Riggs, "Substantive Due Process," pp. 947–8 ("the legislative history of the due process clause is especially sterile").

[277] John V. Orth, "Taking from A and Giving to B: Substantive Due Process and the Case of the Shifting Paradigm," 14 *Constitutional Commentary*, 337 (1997).

clause protected property rights, then so was Lincoln and the platform of
the Republican Party.

The Right to Bring Slaves into the Territories. The bone of contention between Taney and most antebellum Northerners was whether the generally
understood right to bring property into the territories entailed a right to
bring *human* property into the territories. Free- and slave-state constitutionalists disputed whether slavery enjoyed less protection than other forms
of property – not, as Curtis suggested, whether slavery enjoyed more protection than other forms of property. Taney correctly set out the issue between
Republicans and Southerners when he asked whether "there is a difference
between property in a slave and other property, and that different rules may
be applied to it in expounding the Constitution of the United States."[278] As
a Northern federal court asked in another context: "How is it possible ...
to regard slave property as less effectively secured by the provisions of [the
Constitution] than any other property which is recognized as such by the law
of the owner's domicil?"[279]

Whether the persons responsible for the Constitution thought constitutional protections for property encompassed property in human beings
is unclear. The framers deliberately chose language that neither affirmed
nor denied the legality of slavery.[280] Taney maintained that the twenty-year
moratorium on federal laws banning the international slave trade proved the
framers recognized that a slave could be bought and sold "like an ordinary
article of merchandise."[281] Curtis and McLean thought the felt need for the
fugitive slave clause demonstrated that slaves were "not property beyond the
operation of ... local law."[282] Both are plausible interpretations of the Constitution of 1787. Thirty years after ratification, all living Southern framers
maintained that they had not intended to vest Congress with the power to
ban slavery in the territories,[283] while the surviving Northern framers uniformly maintained they *had* intended to vest Congress with the power to
ban slavery in the territories.[284]

---

[278] *Dred Scott* at 451.
[279] *United States ex rel. Wheeler v. Williamson,* 28 Fed. Cas. 686, 693 (1855).
[280] See Part II.
[281] *Dred Scott* at 451.
[282] *Dred Scott* at 549 (McLean, dissenting). See *Dred Scott* at 524 (Curtis, dissenting).
[283] James Madison, *Letters and Other Writings of James Madison,* vol. 3 (R. Worthington: New
       York, 1884), pp. 150–2; *Annals of Congress,* 16th Cong., 1st Sess., pp. 1312, 1315–22, 1326–7
       (Charles Pinckney). See Richard H. Brown, "The Missouri Crisis, Slavery, and the Politics of
       Jacksonianism," 65 *South Atlantic Quarterly,* 55, 59 (1965).
[284] John Jay, *The Correspondence and Public Papers of John Jay,* vol. 4 (ed. Henry P. Johnston)
       (Putnam's: New York, 1893), pp. 430–1; Rufus King, *The Life and Correspondence of Rufus*

Justices Curtis and McLean relied on international law when asserting that the persons responsible for the Constitution thought slavery constitutionally different from other forms of property. In their view, established legal principles required sovereignties to recognize ordinary property rights validly obtained under foreign laws. Citizens of Mississippi could bring their hogs into the territories because the law of nations required the United States to give extraterritorial effect to state property laws. However, the law of nations at the time of the framing held that "[s]lavery, being contrary to natural right, is created only by municipal law."[285] This meant that the law of slavery had no extraterritorial effect unless specifically embodied in a treaty or some other agreement between sovereignties. Persons could hold property in other persons only when and to the extent that local law declared slavery legal. Interpreted consistently with this principle of international law, the United States properly denied extraterritorial effect to state or foreign laws sanctioning human bondage. "[T]hey who framed and adopted the Constitution were aware that persons held to service under the laws of a State are property only to the extent and under the condition fixed by those laws," Curtis wrote, and "they must cease to be available as property, when their owners voluntarily place them permanently within another jurisdiction, where no municipal laws on the subject of slavery exist."[286]

Taney briefly dismissed this claim by noting that the law of nations did not provide appropriate rules for the relationship between the federal government and the states.[287] Had he a greater gift for whimsy, he might have noted that the very statutes the dissents cited as evidence for the federal power to ban slavery in the territories were evidence against the claim that the framers recognized slavery as constitutionally different from other forms of property. The federal statutes organizing the territories suggest, if anything, that the framers believed slaves and other chattel were lawful unless prohibited by positive national law. Congress included provisions explicitly banning slavery when organizing free territories. The statutes organizing slave territories simply omitted that statutory ban.[288]

When claiming that slaveholders moving to the territories enjoyed the same due process rights as other property holders, Taney focused on the constitutional text. No constitutional provision asserts a slavery exception to any constitutional property right. As the chief justice stated, "no word can

---

King: Comprising His Letters, Private and Official, His Public Documents, and His Speeches, vol. 6 (ed. Charles R. King) (Da Capo: New York, 1971), pp. 690–703.

[285] *Dred Scott* at 524 (Curtis, dissenting). See *Dred Scott* at 547–9 (McLean, dissenting).

[286] *Dred Scott* at 625 (Curtis, dissenting). See *Dred Scott* at 548 (McLean, dissenting).

[287] *Dred Scott* at 451.

[288] Fehrenbacher, *Dred Scott,* pp. 86–7, 137–8.

be found in the Constitution which gives Congress a greater power over slave property, or which entitles property of that kind to less protection than property of any other description."[289] Taney overreached when he claimed "the right of property in a slave is distinctly and expressly affirmed in the Constitution."[290] Still, constitutional practice and constitutional understandings in 1787 accepted as legitimate those state laws that made some human beings the owners of other human beings. "[T]he Constitution," Taney reasonably wrote, "recognizes the right of property of the master in a slave, and makes no distinction between that description of property and other property owned by a citizen." Hence, he continued, "no tribunal acting under the authority of the United States ... has a right to draw such a distinction, or deny to [slavery] the benefit of the provisions and guarantees which have been provided for the protection of private property against the encroachments of the Government."[291]

Taney Court justices supplemented this appeal to text with more general constitutional principles. Although the national government had been given extensive power to protect property, the Southern Jacksonians on the Supreme Court maintained that the framers vested Congress with no power to define property. Property was defined by state law. Campbell declared that "whatever [state] Constitutions and laws validly determine to be property, the Federal Government [had] to recognize to be property."[292] Laws banning slavery in the territories, justices in the *Dred Scott* majority further insisted, violated the original understanding of constitutional equality by unconstitutionally giving one class of citizens the right to the exclusive use of jointly owned American possessions. Territories, Taney asserted, were "acquired by the General Government, as the representative and trustee of the people of the United States, and ... must therefore be held in that character for their common and equal benefit." Justice Daniel maintained that Congress could not, by banning slavery in the territories, "bestow upon a portion of the citizens of this nation that which is the common property and privilege of all."[293]

This "right to enjoy the territory as equals"[294] was derived from the more general animus against class legislation central to early American constitutional thinking. The framers of the Constitution and antebellum jurists

---

[289] *Dred Scott* at 452.
[290] *Dred Scott* at 451. See *Dred Scott* at 490 (Daniel, concurring).
[291] *Dred Scott* at 451.
[292] *Dred Scott* at 515 (Campbell, concurring).
[293] *Dred Scott* at 448; *Dred Scott* at 488 (Daniel, concurring).
[294] *Dred Scott* at 527 (opinion of Catron).

believed that "equality ... ought to be the basis of every law," that government should not pass laws that "subject 'some to peculiar burdens' or grant 'to others peculiar exemptions.'" [295] The notion that unequal laws violated due process was articulated by Daniel Webster in the *Dartmouth College* case and became a staple of Jacksonian-era state judicial rhetoric.[296] Long before he sat on the Supreme Court, Justice Catron defined "the law of the land" as "a general public law, equally binding upon every member of the community." [297] From the perspective of the Southern Jacksonians on the Supreme Court, laws banning slavery in the territories looked suspiciously like the special privileges that state court precedent and their inherited tradition claimed violated the first principle of due process.[298] Sidney George Fisher, a leading Philadelphia jurist, endorsed this sentiment in a monograph published shortly after *Dred Scott* was handed down. "Should [Congress] make a distinction between [the Southern people] and the North in regard to the national domain," he declared, "then the great principle of equality before the law would be violated." [299] Justice McLean's claim that bans on slavery would encourage persons from free states to populate the territories[300] probably strengthened the Taney Court's resolve that such policies were unconstitutional instances of the partial legislation that the Fifth Amendment was intended to ban.

James Madison, by both his arguments and his status as the "Father of the Constitution," provided the *Dred Scott* majority with more evidence that the persons responsible for the Constitution intended to protect the right to bring slaves into the territories. In an 1819 letter that Justice Daniel quoted at length,[301] Madison informed a correspondent that "nothing in the proceedings of the State Conventions" evinced an intention to give Congress "a power over the migration or removal of individuals, whether freemen or

---

[295] James Madison, *The Mind of the Founder: Sources of the Political Thought of James Madison* (ed. Marvin Meyers) (Bobbs-Merrill: Indianapolis, 1973), pp. 10–11; Howard Gillman, *The Constitution Besieged: The Rise and Demise of Lochner Era Police Powers Jurisprudence* (Duke University Press: Durham, 1993), p. 29.

[296] *Dartmouth College v. Woodward*, 17 U.S. 518, 581 (1819) (argument of Daniel Webster). See *Clapp & Albright v. Administrator of Reynolds*, 2 Texas Reports 250, 252 (1851); *Vanzant v. Waddell*, 2 Yerg. 260, 271 (Tenn. 1829) (Catron, concurring); *State Bank v. Cooper*, 2 Yerg. 599 (Tenn. 1831). For a general discussion of class legislation before the Civil War, see Rodney L. Mott, *Due Process of Law* (Bobbs-Merrill: Indianapolis, 1926), pp. 259–66; Gillman, *The Constitution Besieged*, pp. 50–5, 59–60.

[297] *Wally's Heir v. Kennedy*, 10 Tenn. 554, 555–6 (1831).

[298] See Corwin, "*Dred Scott* Case," p. 306.

[299] Sidney George Fisher, *The Law of the Territories* (C. Sherman: Philadelphia, 1859), p. 51.

[300] *Dred Scott* at 543 (McLean, dissenting).

[301] *Dred Scott* at 491–2 (Daniel, concurring).

slaves, from one State to another, whether new or old." "Had such been the construction," Madison added, the Constitution might not have been ratified. Yet, he noted, "among the objections to the Constitution, and among the numerous amendments to it proposed by the State Conventions, not one of which amendments refers to the [territorial] clause."[302] Madison further observed how political practice from 1787 until 1819 strengthened the constitutional right to bring slaves into American territories. In language that recalled his objections to John Marshall's opinion in *McCulloch v. Maryland*,[303] Madison declared that the territorial clause merely gave Congress "a power to make the provisions really needful or necessary for the government of settlers." "The interdict of slavery in the territories" could hardly be regarded as "among the needful regulations contemplated by the Constitution," he concluded, "since in none of the territorial governments created by Congress is such an interdict found."[304]

McCulloch and the Northwest Ordinance. Madison's constitutional argument against bans on slavery in the territories hardly clinches the historical case for *Dred Scott*. The former president "forgot" that the First Congress had voted almost unanimously to prohibit slavery in the Northwest Territories.[305] This exercise of legislative power played a major role in both *Dred Scott* dissents.[306] The *Dred Scott* dissents also cited an important Marshall Court precedent for their view of federal power in the territories. Chief Justice John Marshall declared in *American Insurance Company v. 356 Bales of Cotton* that, when "legislating for [the territories], Congress exercises the combined powers of the general, and of a state government."[307] The precise issue in *American Insurance Company*, Taney correctly observed, was whether Congress could create territorial courts staffed by justices holding

---

[302]　Madison, 3 *Letters*, pp. 150–2.

[303]　17 U.S. 316 (1819).

[304]　Madison, 3 *Letters*, pp. 152–3. See Madison, 3 *Letters*, p. 168. For Madison's restrictive interpretation of "necessary" in the "necessary and proper" clause, see Madison, *Mind of the Founder*, pp. 391–4.

[305]　1 Stat. 50 (1789).

[306]　See *Dred Scott* at 539–40, 547 (McLean, dissenting); *Dred Scott* at 617 (Curtis, dissenting). See also Lincoln, 3 *Collected Works*, pp. 527–35. General agreement existed that the ban on slavery in the Northwest Ordinance was void because Congress under the Articles of Confederation lacked the power to govern the territories: *Dred Scott* at 608, 617 (Curtis, dissenting); *Dred Scott* at 490 (Daniel, concurring); *Dred Scott* at 503–4 (Campbell, concurring); Hamilton, Madison, and Jay, *Federalist Papers*, p. 239; John Quincy Adams, *Memoirs of John Quincy Adams, Comprising Portions of His Diary from 1795 to 1848* (ed. Charles Francis Adams) (Books for Libraries Press: Freeport, 1969), p. 7.

[307]　26 U.S. 511, 546 (1828). See *Dred Scott* at 540 (McLean, dissenting); *Dred Scott* at 613 (Curtis, dissenting).

office for a term of years.[308] Still, as Fehrenbacher notes, "no one questioned the power of a state to prohibit slavery."[309]

The *Dred Scott* dissents are particularly congenial to the contemporary
constitutional mind when they discuss the general powers of the national
government. A crucial passage in the Curtis dissent claims: "Regulations
must be needful, but it is necessarily left to the legislative discretion to determine whether a law be needful."[310] Most contemporary constitutionalists
agree, endorsing twentieth-century Supreme Court decisions holding that
elected officials have the power to regulate property in any way that might
plausibly be regarded as a rational means to a legitimate government end.[311]
Committed to post–New Deal understandings of federal power, contemporary critics of *Dred Scott* never doubt that McLean was on solid historical ground when the Ohio justice cited *McCulloch* for the proposition that
Congress was the sole judge of "needful regulations." "[T]he degree of its
necessity," both Curtis and McLean insisted, "is a question of legislative discretion, not of judicial cognizance."[312]

However, imputing the modern embrace and interpretation of *McCulloch*
to pre–Civil War constitutionalism is problematic. Many framers sharply
disputed John Marshall's claim that "necessary ... means no more than ...
conducive to."[313] Madison claimed with respect to *McCulloch* that "it was
anticipated ... by few, if any, of the friends of the Constitution, that a rule
of construction would be introduced as broad and pliant as what has occurred."[314] Prominent constitutional historians now recognize that most
antebellum Americans had a far narrower conception of national power than
is presently the case.[315] *McCulloch* survived the Taney Court only because
Jacksonian presidents vetoed on constitutional grounds every measure that
might have given the justices an opportunity to overrule or narrow Marshall's

---

[308] *Dred Scott* at 442–5.

[309] Fehrenbacher, *Dred Scott*, p. 373.

[310] *Dred Scott* at 616 (Curtis, dissenting).

[311] See e.g. *United States v. Carolene Products Co.*, 304 U.S. 144 (1938); *Wickard v. Filburn*, 317
U.S. 111 (1942); Fehrenbacher, *Dred Scott*, p. 369.

[312] *Dred Scott* at 542 (McLean, dissenting) (quoting *McCulloch* at 423). See *Dred Scott* at 616
(Curtis, dissenting).

[313] *McCulloch* at 413.

[314] Madison, 3 *Letters*, p. 145. See Madison, *Mind of the Founder*, p. 392; Jefferson, *The Portable
Jefferson*, pp. 264–7.

[315] See Howard Gillman, "More on the Origins of the Fuller Court's Jurisprudence: Reexamin-
ing the Scope of Federal Power over Commerce and Manufacturing in Nineteenth-Century
Constitutional Law," 49 *Political Research Quarterly*, 415 (1996); Stephen M. Griffin, "Constitutional Theory Transformed," 108 *Yale Law Journal*, 2115, 2124–9 (1999); Randy E. Barnett,
"The Original Meaning of the Commerce Clause," 68 *University of Chicago Law Review*, 101
(2001).

broad conception of national power.[316] In 1858, Lincoln considered *McCulloch* to be overturned by this political practice.[317] Given the sparse historical record on the original meaning of "necessary" in the Constitution,[318] the narrower Jacksonian interpretation underlying the Daniel concurrence in *Dred Scott*[319] has as good a historical pedigree as the Hamiltonian interpretation that animated the Curtis and McLean dissents.

Contemporary historicists make similarly anachronistic claims when interpreting the Northwest Ordinance as demonstrating the powerful antislavery sentiments of the framers, since that measure acquired a strong antislavery gloss only after enactment.[320] If the persons responsible for the Constitution intended that Congress have the power to ban slavery in every territory, then this was the best-kept secret in American politics during the late 1780s. Northern proponents of ratification, who boasted that Congress would ban the importation of slaves after twenty years,[321] failed to highlight the alleged legislative power to ban slavery immediately in all territories. Only James Wilson mentioned that possibility, and he did so very briefly.[322] Southern opponents of ratification failed to include bans on slavery in the territories when cataloging potential constitutional horrors. Patrick Henry and William Grayson warned that free-state representatives would prevent settlement in

---

[316] No justice in the *Dred Scott* majority ever cited *McCulloch* as supporting broad federal power. Several Taney Court justices were previously on record as being opposed to the Marshall Court's interpretation of "necessary." Taney helped write Jackson's message vetoing the national bank, which opposed broad constructions of federal power: Swisher, *Taney*, pp. 194–7. Justice Daniel's dissent in *Searight v. Stokes* clearly indicated that he would overrule *McCulloch* when given the appropriate case: *Searight v. Stokes*, 44 U.S. 151, 180–1 (1845) (Daniel, dissenting). For evidence that the Taney Court was prepared to declare the national bank unconstitutional, see Graber, "Antebellum Perspectives," pp. 779, 808–9 n.161.

For presidential vetoes clearly rejecting Marshall's interpretation of "necessary," see James Madison, "Veto Message," 1 *Messages and Papers*, pp. 584–5; James Monroe, "Veto Message," 5 *Messages and Papers*, pp. 142–3; Andrew Jackson, "Veto Message," 2 *Messages and Papers*, pp. 483–93, 576–91; John Tyler, "Veto Messages," 4 *Messages and Papers*, pp. 63–72, 330–3; James K. Polk, "Veto Messages," 4 *Messages and Papers*, pp. 460–6, 610–26; Franklin Pierce, "Veto Messages," 5 *Messages and Papers*, pp. 247–71, 386–8; James Buchanan, "Veto Messages," 5 *Messages and Papers*, pp. 543–50, 601–14.

[317] Lincoln, 3 *Collected Works*, p. 278.

[318] See Mark A. Graber, "Unnecessary and Unintelligible," 12 *Constitutional Commentary*, 167 (1995).

[319] *Dred Scott* at 491–2 (Daniel, concurring).

[320] Davis, "Significance of Excluding Slavery," pp. 88–9.

[321] See Kaminsky, *A Necessary Evil*: pp. 87 (Thomas Dawes); 91 (statement of Isaac Backus); 114 (statement of Simeon Baldwin); 115, 117 (statement of Dr. Benjamin Rush); 137, 138, 140–1, 146–7; "Plain Truth" to Timothy Meanwell, p. 121. See also Hamilton, Madison, and Jay, *Federalist Papers*, p. 266.

[322] Merrill Jensen, ed., *The Documentary History of the Ratification of the Constitution*, vol. 2, *Ratification of the Constitution by the States: Pennsylvania* (State Historical Society of Wisconsin: Madison, 1976), p. 463.

the Southwest Territories by failing to contest Spanish control over the Mississippi, not by prohibiting slavery in those regions.[323]

The persons who framed the Constitution and banned slavery in the Northwest Territories had no conscious intentions with respect to the status of slavery in new territories acquired by the United States and incorporated no language into the Constitution that plainly delineated federal territorial practice. These matters were unresolved in 1787 largely because the framers had no conscious intentions about the possibility of acquiring new territories. The subject received no sustained attention during the framing and ratification debates.[324] Those framers who anticipated westward expansion kept their thoughts to themselves. Thomas Paine informed Jefferson that "the framers of the Constitution probably did not think much about 'the acquisition of new territory, and even if they did it was prudent to say nothing about it.'"[325]

Subsequent legal doctrine provided no better guide to the constitutional problems presented by new territories. Antebellum constitutional law did not clarify the scope of Article IV. Justice Johnson on circuit claimed that the territorial clause was intended to sanction congressional power only in territories possessed by the United States at the time of ratification. The Marshall Court left the issue undecided.[326] Agreement existed by 1857 that the national government could acquire and govern new territories. What Americans disputed was whether the constitutional rules for governing territories acquired from foreign countries during the nineteenth century were the same as the constitutional rules for governing territories ceded by existing states during the eighteenth century.

Taney distorted the historical record when he claimed that the framers consciously intended to limit the territorial clause to "territory ... then known or claimed as territory of the United States."[327] His opinion demonstrated that the persons who framed the territorial clause were thinking only about existing territories[328] but cited no historical evidence that the framers specifically rejected using the territorial clause for acquiring and governing new

[323] John P. Kaminski and Gaspare Saladino, eds., *The Documentary History of the Ratification of the Constitution*, vol. 10, *Ratification of the Constitution by the States: Virginia [3]* (State Historical Society of Wisconsin: Madison, 1993), pp. 1192 (Grayson), 1245 (Henry).

[324] Wiecek, *Antislavery*, p. 114. See Lincoln, 3 *Collected Works*, pp. 525–6.

[325] Alexander DeConde, *The Affair of Louisiana* (Scribner's: New York, 1976), p. 185 (quoting Thomas Paine to Thomas Jefferson, September 23, 1803).

[326] *American Insurance Company* at 515–22 (republishing the opinion of Johnson); *American Insurance Company* at 542–3.

[327] *Dred Scott* at 436.

[328] *Dred Scott* at 432–6.

possessions. Taney claimed that the first paragraph of Article IV, Section 3 – which set out rules for admitting new states – authorized the federal government to acquire new territories.[329] No constitutional provision, he continued, "defined the power which the General Government may exercise over the person or property of a citizen in a Territory thus acquired."[330] Taney never explained why, even though no clause in Section 3 contained any language about scope, the framers understood that the first paragraph on statehood applied to both existing and new territories while the second paragraph was limited to existing territories. Nor did he explain why Section 3 authorized the national government to acquire new territories and provided rules for governing existing territories but did not provide rules for governing acquired territories.

Curtis similarly distorted the historical record when he claimed that the framers consciously intended the territorial clause to apply to new acquisitions. His dissent cited the Louisiana Purchase as evidence that members of the framing generation anticipated national expansion. The justice from Massachusetts would not "imput[e] to those who negotiated and ratified the [Louisiana] treaty, and passed the laws necessary to carry it into execution, a deliberate and known violation of their oaths to support the Constitution."[331] This claim is well-known nonsense. Justice Campbell's dissent pointed out that leading supporters of national expansion in 1803 acknowledged that their actions were constitutionally suspect.[332] President Jefferson declared: "The constitution has made no provision for our holding foreign territories, still less for incorporating foreign nations into our Union." His decision to purchase Louisiana was "an act beyond the Constitution" that had to be ratified by a constitutional amendment.[333] No consensus emerged during the first decade of the nineteenth century on the constitutionality of national expansion. Most Federalists and some Republicans thought the Constitution could not cross the Mississippi; others disagreed.[334] Given the vigorous dispute among persons responsible for the Constitution who were still living in 1803 over the constitutional rules for acquiring new territories, the claim that the framers agreed on the constitutional rules for governing new territories seems preposterous.

---

[329] *Dred Scott* at 447.

[330] *Dred Scott* at 447.

[331] *Dred Scott* at 613 (Curtis, dissenting).

[332] *Dred Scott* at 512 (Campbell, concurring).

[333] Thomas Jefferson, *The Writings of Thomas Jefferson* (ed. Merrill D. Peterson) (Library of America: New York, 1984), p. 1139. See also ibid., p. 1140.

[334] See Neuman, *Strangers to the Constitution*, p. 74.

The Northwest Ordinance is best interpreted in conjunction with the Southwest Ordinance and the Missouri Compromise. For much of antebellum history, moderates in both sections of the United States agreed to share the territories. The Congress that banned slavery in the Northwest Territories permitted slavery in the Southwest Territories.[335] The Missouri Compromise was brokered by free- and slave-state representatives who agreed to divide the Louisiana Purchase between the North and South.[336] These agreements were thought to have constitutional significance. Lincoln declared in 1854: "All the evidences of public opinion at that day seemed to indicate that this Compromise had become canonized in the hearts of the American people as a sacred thing, which no ruthless hand should attempt to disturb."[337] The general constitutional principle that guided these settlements was that no section should monopolize the territories, that national policy should serve the interests of free- and slave-state settlers. Sidney Fisher offered a variation on this theme when he declared that the Northwest Ordinance and the Missouri Compromise were constitutional because those measures were secured "with the consent and co-operation of the Southern States."[338]

Fisher's claim that "to exclude the people of the slave States . . . , *without their consent*, would be unequal and opposed to the spirit and intent of the constitution" (emphasis in original)[339] is the most plausible historical understanding of federal power in the territories.[340] Unlike any opinion in *Dred Scott*, Fisher could explain Southern consent to a document that permitted Congress to pass the Northwest Ordinance and the Missouri Compromise. If Fisher was right, then both Taney and Curtis were wrong. Congress could, contrary to the Taney opinion, ban slavery in some territories. Congress could not, contrary to the Curtis opinion, do so on a sectional vote. Both justices erred by trying to translate into constitutional law an original understanding about the structure of constitutional politics. The national government could constitutionally ban slavery in the territories, but only by a process that secured consent from both free- and slave-state representatives.

---

[335] See Staughton Lynd, *Class Conflict, Slavery, and the United States Constitution* (Bobbs-Merrill: Indianapolis, 1967), pp. 186, 190–3, 199; Donald L. Robinson, *Slavery in the Structure of American Politics 1765–1820* (Harcourt Brace Jovanovich: New York, 1971), pp. 382–5.

[336] See Merrill D. Peterson, *The Great Triumvirate: Webster, Clay, and Calhoun* (Oxford University Press: New York, 1987), p. 65; Robinson, *Slavery*, p. 416; Lincoln, 3 *Collected Works*, pp. 529–30.

[337] Lincoln, 2 *Collected Works*, p. 236.

[338] Fisher, *Law*, p. 50. See Fisher, *Law*, pp. 44, 65.

[339] Fisher, *Law*, p. 52. See Fisher, *Law*, pp. 50–2, 63.

[340] This point will be detailed in Part II.

The Taney Court decision came closer than the dissents to the original understanding that national slavery policy be made in ways that accommodated crucial elites in both North and South. The practical difference between *Dred Scott* and Fisher's claim that slavery could be banned only with Southern consent did not amount to much after 1850. Southerners were unlikely to accept any future federal ban on slavery in the territories that aggravated the increasing imbalance of political power between free and slave states. The Republican Party platform and the *Dred Scott* dissents abandoned these implicit constitutional restrictions on federal power over slavery.[341] Curtis, McLean, and Lincoln would sanction the feared sectional monopoly in the West by vesting Northern congressional majorities with the absolute power to fashion the remaining territories in the image of the free states.

The Aspirational Critique

The aspirational critique of *Dred Scott* ignores the references to fundamental constitutional principles in the Taney Court opinions and the powerful racist currents in antebellum constitutionalism. The justices in the *Dred Scott* majority relied at crucial junctures on the general principles of justice they believed were at the core of the constitutional regime. The racist and proslavery principles they relied on had strong roots in both the Constitution and the American political tradition. That present-day Americans regard those principles as pernicious is beside the point. Justices who make aspirational arguments will base their rulings on the values that they think place the constitutional order in its best light.[342] For Southern Jacksonian jurists during the mid-nineteenth century, those values included both slavery and white supremacy.

The dissents in *Dred Scott* provide reasons for questioning the aspirational claim that constitutional injustices are best prevented when justices interpret the framers' specific policy intentions and legal precedent in light of those general principles of justice underlying the constitutional order. Justices McLean and Curtis apparently believed that historicist arguments were the means for challenging Taney's racist and proslavery conclusions. Justice McLean offered a detailed history of the territorial clause, the Northwest Ordinance, and John Marshall's opinion in *American Insurance Company* when claiming that Congress had the power to prohibit slavery in American

---

[341] See Fisher, *Law*, pp. 79–80.
[342] See Ronald Dworkin, *Law's Empire* (Harvard University Press: Cambridge, 1986), pp. 45–86, 355–99.

territories.[343] Justice Curtis referred at length to the history of the privileges and immunities clause of Article IV, which he declared "clear[ly]" demonstrated that, "at the time of the adoption of the Constitution, free colored persons of African descent might be, and, by reason of their citizenship in certain States, were entitled to the privileges and immunities of general citizenship of the United States."[344] Many prominent contemporary aspirationalists think that those dissents had the better of the historical argument on several points.[345]

Justice Curtis rejected aspirational reasoning emphatically. "General considerations concerning the social and moral evils of slavery," he bluntly declared, are "reasons purely political" that render "judicial interpretation impossible – because judicial tribunals cannot decide upon political considerations."[346] The justice from Massachusetts was a white supremacist who would have voted with the *Dred Scott* majority on the citizenship issue had constitutional aspirations been his primary guide. Curtis opposed granting rights to persons of color in Massachusetts. Such persons, he said, were "foreigners as to us."[347] His polity was for white persons only. "Whatever natural rights they have," Curtis declared when defending the rendition of fugitive slaves, "*this* is not the *soil* on which to vindicate them. This is *our* soil, sacred to *our* peace, on which we intend to perform *our* promises, and work out, for the benefit of ourselves and our posterity and the world, the destiny which our Creator has assigned to *us*" (emphases in original).[348] Curtis, with the exception of *Dred Scott*, consistently adopted the anti-egalitarian, racist positions typical of Cotton Whigs in the free states. In *Commonwealth v. Aves*,[349] he unsuccessfully defended the right of Southerners to bring slaves into free territories for short visits.[350] Curtis scorned abolitionists, vigorously defended the Fugitive Slave Act, urged that state personal liberty laws be repealed, favored laws restricting antislavery activity in the free states, opposed

---

[343] *Dred Scott* at 535–41 (McLean, dissenting).

[344] *Dred Scott* at 575–6 (Curtis, dissenting).

[345] See Eisgruber, "*Dred* Again," p. 48; Sunstein, "*Dred Scott*," pp. 74–5.

[346] *Dred Scott* at 620 (Curtis, dissenting). The noted abolitionist Lysander Spooner outdid Taney in public zeal for originalism when, at the close of an argument declaring human bondage unconstitutional, he asserted: "Such was the character of the constitution when it was offered to the people, and before it was adopted. And if such was its character then, such is its character still. It cannot have been changed by all the errors and perversions, intentional or unintentional, of which the government may have since been guilty." Lysander Spooner, *The Unconstitutionality of Slavery* (Burt Franklin: New York, 1967) p. 124.

[347] Curtis, 1 *Memoir of Curtis*, p. 133. See Curtis, 1 *Memoir of Curtis*, p. 135.

[348] Curtis, 1 *Memoir of Curtis*, p. 136.

[349] 35 Mass. 195 (1836).

[350] Curtis, 1 *Memoir of Curtis*, pp. 69–92; Swisher, *Taney Period*, pp. 554–5.

the Emancipation Proclamation, sought to have declared unconstitutional various Reconstruction measures aimed at improving the lot of former slaves, and was horrified by proposals to have the national government impose black suffrage on the states.[351] Given his general outlook on racial matters, abolitionists were far better-off making technical legal appeals when before Justice Curtis than seeking decisions based on more general constitutional visions.

The example of Justice Curtis highlights how aspirational arguments in societies as deeply racist as the antebellum United States are not vehicles for justice. Racist and other ascriptive ideologies are as rooted in the American political tradition as liberal, democratic, and republican ideals. Americans cherished white supremacy. Policies preserving racial hegemony were means to valued ends, not temporary expedients. "Publius" took "pleasure" observing "that Providence has been pleased to give this one connected country to one united people – a people descended from the same ancestors, speaking the same language, professing the same religion."[352] This founding vision expressed a more general national commitment to a racially homogenous polity. "Through most of U.S. history," Rogers Smith details at great length, "lawmakers pervasively and unapologetically structured U.S. citizenship in terms of illiberal and undemocratic racial, ethnic, and gender hierarchies."[353]

Racism was well grounded in American political thought from the very beginning. Although most framers believed that slavery was wrong and inconsistent with the ideals expressed by the Declaration of Independence,[354] the vast majority of the persons responsible for the Constitution did not believe as a matter of political principle or prudence that a multiracial society was desirable. "Nothing is more certainly written in the book of fate," Jefferson asserted, "than that these two people are to be free; nor is it less certain that the two races, equally free, cannot live in the same government."[355] The third president insisted on a provision vesting citizenship on "white inhabitants" in the constitutional amendment he thought necessary to sanction the Louisiana Purchase.[356] Jefferson and his fellow framers "tie[d]

---

[351] Curtis, 1 *Memoir of Curtis*, pp. 72, 123–36, 161–2, 329–35, 345–8, 354, 390–7; Curtis, 2 *Memoir of Curtis*, pp. 184, 306–55.

[352] Hamilton, Madison, and Jay, *Federalist Papers*, p. 38.

[353] Smith, *Civic Ideals*, p. 1. See Frederickson, *The Black Image*, pp. 130–1.

[354] See Diamond, "No Call to Glory," p. 104; William W. Freehling, "The Founding Fathers and Slavery," 77 *American Historical Review*, 81, 82 (1992).

[355] Thomas Jefferson, *The Life and Selected Writings of Thomas Jefferson* (ed. Adrienne Koch and William Peden) (Modern Library: New York, 1944), p. 51.

[356] Thomas Jefferson, *The Writings of Thomas Jefferson*, vol. 10 (Thomas Jefferson Memorial Association: Washington, D.C., 1903), pp. 415–17.

American emancipation to African colonization."[357] "It is impossible for us to be happy," a delegate to the North Carolina ratification debate declared, "if, after manumission, they are to stay among us."[358] In 1775, Northerners proposed to free slaves who fought for American independence and then reward them with land in Canada.[359]

Americans who opposed slavery during the nineteenth century believed white supremacy the higher constitutional value. Slaves could be freed only when doing so furthered or at least did not weaken white racial hegemony. Emancipation proposals after the Revolution were hostile to integration and almost always included mandatory colonization for blacks. Madison described colonization as "the only mode presenting a chance of effecting" emancipation. Jefferson emphasized the importance of "provid[ing] an asylum to which we can, by degrees, send the whole of that population from among us."[360] "[C]olonization," free-state citizens agreed, must be "the next step after emancipation."[361] Prominent opponents of human bondage repeatedly criticized slaveholders for increasing the number of black persons in the United States. Hinton Helper, whose call for emancipation during the 1850s resulted in his works being suppressed in the South,[362] insisted that the United States was a white republic and demanded that free blacks be removed to Africa.[363] Even during Reconstruction, one border-state senator declared that the Constitution could not be amended to grant citizenship to free persons of color. America, Garrett Davis maintained, was "a close white corporation." Article VII granted a power "simply to amend;... not a power to revolutionize."[364]

---

[357] W. Freehling, *Disunion*, p. 83.

[358] "North Carolina Ratifying Convention Debates," *A Necessary Evil?*, p. 199 (James Galloway).

[359] "A Proposal to Free the Slaves," *A Necessary Evil?*, pp. 4–5. See Jonathan Dickinson Sergeant, "A Plan to Free the Slaves," ibid., p. 11.

[360] Madison, *Mind of the Founder*, p. 425; Thomas Jefferson, *The Works of Thomas Jefferson*, vol. 12 (ed. Paul Leicester Ford) (Putnam's: New York, 1905), p. 335. See Madison, *Mind of the Founder*, p. 399; James Madison, *The Writings of James Madison*, vol. 8 (ed. Gaillard Hunt) (Putnam's: New York, 1905), pp. 440–1; Jefferson, *The Portable Jefferson*, pp. 186, 546, 568.

[361] Michael Kent Curtis, "The 1859 Crisis over Hinton Helper's Book, *The Impending Crisis*: Free Speech, Slavery, and Some Light on the Meaning of the First Section of the Fourteenth Amendment," 68 *Chicago-Kent Law Review*, 1125 (1993). See W. Freehling, *Reintegration*, p. 191.

[362] See Curtis, "1859 Crisis."

[363] Hinton Rowan Helper, *The Impending Crisis of the South: How to Meet It* (ed. George M. Frederickson) (Harvard University Press: Cambridge, 1968), p. 182. For similar claims, see Henry Ruffner, *Address*, pp. 39–40; Harrison, *Review of the Slave Question*, pp. 25, 34–48; Tucker, *A Dissertation on Slavery*, p. 92; King, 6 *King*, p. 702. See also Litwack, *North of Slavery*, pp. 20–4; Finkelman, *Slavery*, pp. 118–19, 126–8, 150–1; W. Freehling, *Disunion*, pp. 126, 156–61; 181–96, 202–7; George M. Fredrickson, "A Man but Not a Brother: Abraham Lincoln and Racial Equality," 41 *Journal of Southern History*, 39, 43 (1975).

[364] *Congressional Globe*, 39th Cong., 1st Sess., pp. 529, 530.

Conservative and moderate Republicans shared this racist vision of America. "The idea of liberating the slaves and allowing them to remain in this country," Lincoln's confidant Frank Blair declared, "is one that will never be tolerated." [365] Lincoln repeatedly denied that a multiracial society was desirable. Until the last year of his life, he insisted that colonization was the proper solution to the potential race problems that would result after emancipation. [366] Following Jefferson, the sixteenth president sharply distinguished between the human right not to be a slave and matters of legislative grace, such as citizenship, which in his opinion should not be extended to persons of color. [367]

Outside of a few abolitionists, hardly any antebellum Americans thought the Constitution aspired to a multiracial society. Republicans routinely described their coalition as a "white man's party" and proposed "to settle the Territories with free, white men." [368] The "main impulse" of many Republicans, the *New York Tribune* admitted, "is a desire to secure the new territories for Free White Labor, with little or no regard for the interests of negroes, free or slave." [369] Another Republican newspaper, the *Cincinnati Commercial*, declared that "the question is not whether the negroes shall be set free ... but whether poor white men are to be kept out of territories of the United States." David Wilmot, the author of the Wilmot Proviso, was "more antiblack than John C. Calhoun." [370] The congressman from Pennsylvania wanted slaves out of the territories to "preserve to free white labor a fair country, a rich country, where the sons of toil, of my own race and color, can live without the disgrace which association with negro slavery brings upon

---

[365] Foner, *Free Soil*, p. 270 (quoting Frank Blair). See *Congressional Globe*, 36th Cong., 1st Sess., p. 60 (Lyman Trumbull); *Congressional Globe*, 31st Cong., 1st Sess., App., p. 276 (Daniel Webster); Williard L. King, *Lincoln's Manager, David Davis* (Harvard University Press: Cambridge, 1960), p. 51; John Niven, *Salmon P. Chase: A Biography* (Oxford University Press: New York, 1995), p. 45. See also Foner, *Free Soil*, pp. 267–79; Litwack, *North of Slavery*, pp. 29, 62–3, 277–8.

[366] See e.g. Lincoln, 2 *Collected Works*, pp. 131–2, 409. See also David Herbert Donald, *Lincoln* (Jonathan Cape: London, 1995), pp. 165–7, 343–6, 396, 469; Frederickson, "A Man," pp. 48–52, 55–7.

[367] Lincoln, 2 *Collected Works*, pp. 256, 328, 405–6, 520; Lincoln, 3 *Collected Works*, pp. 16, 328.

[368] *Congressional Globe*, 34th Cong., 3rd Sess., App., p. 91 (William Cumback); Lyman Trumbull, *Great Speech of Senator Trumbull on the Issues of the Day* (Lost Cause Press: Louisville, 1966), p. 12. John Quincy Adams referred to free states as "white States." J. Q. Adams, 5 *Memoirs*, p. 4.

[369] Foner, *Free Soil*, p. 61 (quoting the *New York Tribune*, October 15, 1856); William E. Gienapp, *The Origins of the Republican Party: 1852–1856* (Oxford University Press: New York, 1987), p. 373 (quoting the *Cincinnati Commercial*, November 2, 1856). See William Henry Seward, *The Works of William H. Seward*, vol. 4 (ed. George E. Baker) (Houghton, Mifflin: New York, 1884), p. 312; Lincoln, 2 *Collected Works*, pp. 268, 363; Lincoln, 3 *Collected Works*, pp. 312, 437; Lincoln, 4 *Collected Works*, pp. 8, 9, 12, 16.

[370] W. Freehling, *Disunion*, p. 459; Litwack, *North of Slavery*, pp. 267–9.

free labor." [371] The antislavery settlers of Kansas expressed their racist aspirations by adopting a constitution that forbade free blacks from entering the state. [372]

Proslavery aspirationalism was similarly grounded in the original Constitution, although the initial roots were geographically narrow. Some framers, particularly those from South Carolina, believed that a commercial republic would aspire to slavery. Northern mercantile interests would become more sympathetic to the South's peculiar institution, one contributor to a Columbia newspaper suggested, once New Englanders realized that "the more rice we make, the more business will be for their shipping." [373] Those Southern framers who did not cherish slavery cherished practices they thought intrinsically linked to slavery. Edmund Morgan commented that "racism made it possible for white Virginians to develop a devotion to the equality that English republicans had declared to be the soul of liberty." "American economic opportunity and political freedom," he concluded, "rest[ed] on Virginia's slaves." [374]

Homilies to the virtues of slavery were staples in Southern judicial opinions when *Dred Scott* was decided. [375] Members of the Georgia Supreme Court made extensive use of aspirational arguments in opinions that limited manumission and the rights of free negroes. Slavery, the judges opined in 1854, "was wisely ordained by a forecast high as heaven above man's, for the good of both races." [376] Four years later, that bench implored "women and old men, and persons of weak and infirm minds, [to] be disabused of the false and unfounded notion that slavery is sinful, and that they will peril their souls if they do not disinherit their offspring by emancipating their slaves!" [377] While on the Tennessee bench, Catron spoke out against

---

[371] *Congressional Globe*, 29th Cong., 2nd Sess., App., pp. 314–18 (David Wilmot).

[372] Potter, *Impending Crisis*, pp. 203, 207.

[373] Robert M. Weir, "South Carolina: Slavery and the Structure of the Union," *Ratifying the Constitution* (ed. Michael Allen Gillespie and Michael Lienesch) (University Press of Kansas: Lawrence, 1989), p. 216.

[374] Edmund S. Morgan, *American Slavery – American Freedom: The Ordeal of Colonial Virginia* (Norton: New York, 1975), p. 386. See Derrick Bell, *And We Are Not Saved: The Elusive Quest for Racial Justice* (Basic Books: New York, 1987), pp. 26–50; Eugene D. Genovese, *The Slaveholders' Dilemma: Freedom and Progress in Southern Conservative Thought, 1820–1860* (University of South Carolina Press: Columbia, 1992), pp. 18, 26.

[375] See *Mitchell v. Wells*, 37 Miss. 235, 238 (1859); *American Colonization Society v. Gartrell*, 23 Ga. 448 (1857); *Vance v. Crawford*, 4 Ga. 445, 459 (1848); *Bryan v. Walton*, 14 Ga. 185, 205–6 (1853).

[376] *Cleland v. Waters*, 16 Ga. 496, 514 (1854).

[377] *American Colonization Society v. Gartrell* at 465. For similar proslavery aspirations, see *Pendleton v. State*, 6 Ark. 509, 511–12 (1843); *Fisher's Negroes v. Dabbs*, 14 Tenn. 119, 125–32 (1834).

manumission, asking: "How can we then, as honest men, thrust our freed negroes on our neighbors?"[378]

The *Dred Scott* opinions articulated these constitutional aspirations. Black persons, Taney declared, were "regarded as beings of an inferior order, and altogether unfit to associate with the white race, either in social or political relations; and so far inferior, that they had no rights which the white man was bound to respect."[379] Justice Daniel relied on general principles of constitutional justice when he asserted that slavery enjoyed special constitutional status as "the only private property which the Constitution has *specifically recognized*, and has imposed it as a direct obligation both on the States and the Federal Government to protect and *enforce*" (emphases in original).[380] Although his feelings on slavery, particularly as a young man, were somewhat ambivalent, Taney was committed throughout his life to white rule and Southern culture.[381] He informed a correspondent that he thought the Court's ruling in *Dred Scott* would promote the interests of both races.[382]

That no twenty-first–century aspirationalist overtly endorses racism or slavery does not absolve aspirationalism of responsibility for *Dred Scott*. Controversies over slavery and racism occur only in societies where they are contested values. "Both sides" in the *Dred Scott* case, Mark Brandon aptly observes, "saw themselves as engaged in an activity with unquestionably moral consequences." Constitutionalists who take an antebellum perspective must remember that "the connection between morality and interpretation can have consequences both desirable and despicable."[383] For every William Seward who declared in service of antislavery positions that there was "a higher law than the Constitution," there was a William Yancey who in defense of slavery asserted that "laws of nature in their majesty stand

---

[378] *Fisher's Negroes* at 129. See Swisher, *Taney Period*, pp. 378–9.

[379] *Dred Scott* at 407. See *Dred Scott* at 475 (Daniel, concurring).

[380] *Dred Scott* at 490 (Daniel, concurring). Daniel regarded natural law as a legitimate source for constitutional interpretation. "The natural society of nations," he declared, "can not subsist unless the natural rights of all be respected": *Dred Scott* at 483 (Daniel, concurring). See Earl M. Maltz, "Fourteenth Amendment Concepts in the Antebellum Era," 32 *American Journal of Legal History*, 305, 309, 315–16 (1988); *Congressional Globe*, 35th Cong., 1st Sess., pp. 1065–9 (Judah Benjamin).

[381] See Swisher, *Taney*, pp. 586–8; Fehrenbacher, *Dred Scott*, pp. 552–5, 557–61. The chief justice regarded slavery "as normal and right" and thought that free blacks were "better off" enslaved. Swisher, *Taney*, pp. 93, 159.

[382] Swisher, *Taney*, pp. 516–18 (quoting Taney to Rev. Samuel Nott, August 19, 1857). See Fehrenbacher, *Dred Scott*, pp. 554–5 (discussing a long proslavery memorandum that Taney wrote in 1860 but never made public). Justice Wayne also had a lifelong commitment to racial supremacy; see Lawrence, *Wayne*, p. 143.

[383] Mark E. Brandon, *Free in the World: American Slavery and Constitutional Failure* (Princeton University Press: Princeton, 1998), pp. 150, 157.

out from the issue more imperative than the obligations due to ... Constitutions." [384] Southern extremists frequently invoked higher law to justify violating statutes banning the African slave trade. [385]

The aspirational critique of *Dred Scott* is at bottom based on the silly proposition that Southerners fought to the death to preserve what they knew in their hearts was a necessary evil. Slavery was embedded in a way of life that most Southerners and some Northerners thought intrinsically valuable and expressive of the highest constitutional aspirations. Southerners who retained some qualms about human bondage had little doubt about the political culture that slavery fostered. The political crisis of the 1850s was about the survival of this political culture, which depended so heavily on slavery – not about the precise timing of an emancipation that all allegedly agreed was desirable in the long run.

INJUSTICE AND CONSTITUTIONAL LAW

The American experience with slavery demonstrates how, in the wrong hands or in the wrong circumstances, all constitutional theories yield unjust conclusions. Taney could employ numerous constitutional modalities to promote proslavery and racist policies because all forms of constitutional logic are capable of yielding evil results. [386] Institutional arguments yield evil results whenever elected officials and popular majorities support evil laws. Historical arguments yield evil results whenever constitutional framers and ratifiers constitutionalize evil practices. Aspirational arguments yield evil results whenever constitutional framers and ratifiers have evil constitutional values.

The Tyranny of Examples

Institutionalism is uniquely vulnerable to evil outcomes when applied to the Fugitive Slave Acts that Congress passed in 1793 and 1850. [387] Historical and

---

[384] John Witherspoon DuBose, *The Life and Times of William Lowndes Yancey*, vol. 1 (Peter Smith: New York, 1942). See Ronald T. Takaki, *A Pro-Slavery Crusade: The Agitation to Reopen the African Slave Trade* (Free Press: New York, 1971), pp. 221–2.

[385] See Takaki, *Pro-Slavery Crusade*, pp. 202, 220–2.

[386] Stephen Douglas similarly combined historical, institutional, and aspirational appeals when maintaining that the Constitution required inhabitants of particular territories to decide for themselves whether to permit slavery. Popular sovereignty, he declared, was endorsed by "the founders of our system of government" and followed from "[t]he principle ... that every distinct political Community ... is entitled to all the rights, privileges, and immunities of self-government in respect to their local concerns and internal policy." Stephen A. Douglas, *The Dividing Line between Federal and Local Authority: Popular Sovereignty in the Territories* (Harper: New York, 1859), p. 40.

[387] 1 Stat. 302 (1793); 9 Stat. 462 (1850).

aspirational theories provide strong grounds for declaring these statutes unconstitutional. Historicists point out that the language used by the fugitive slave clause[388] and its placement in Article IV rather than Article I (which lists national powers) of the Constitution indicates that the framers vested Congress with no power over fugitive slaves. The fugitive slave clause merely established state obligations.[389] Antislavery aspirationalists argue that the fugitive slave clause was a constitutional contradiction that courts should have either ignored or interpreted as narrowly as possible.[390] Institutionalists are more prone to sustain the Fugitive Slave Acts. Reasonable persons debated whether those measures were constitutional, and institutionalists believe that courts should strike down only those laws that are clearly unconstitutional. Moreover, according to institutionalist dogma, if popular majorities believed that the federal government should assist slave catchers in the rendition process or give slave catchers immunities from hostile state laws, then judges should let the people have their way.

Historicism is uniquely vulnerable to evil outcomes when applied to a federal law that required states to keep manumission legal. Institutional and aspirational theories provide strong reasons for sustaining all federal efforts to promote emancipation. Proponents of judicial restraint would argue that judges should not second-guess whatever slavery policies the people's national representatives think best. Antislavery aspirationalists would see such measures as fulfilling the antislavery aspirations of the Constitution. Historicists would be more inclined to declare such antislavery measures unconstitutional on the ground that, in 1857 at least, a clear consensus existed that the persons responsible for the Constitution had vested Congress with "no power to interfere with slavery as it exists in the States."[391]

The vulnerability of aspirational theories to unique proslavery outcomes is complicated. Antislavery aspirationalists reach every antislavery result that

---

[388] "No Person held to Service or Labour in one State, under the Laws thereof, escaping into another, shall, in Consequence of any Law or Regulation therein, be discharged from such Service or Labour, but shall be delivered up on Claim of the Party to whom such Service or Labour may be due."

[389] See Salmon Portland Chase, *Speech of Salmon P. Chase in the Case of the Colored Woman, Matilda* (Pugh & Dodd: Cincinnati, 1837), pp. 17–27; Salmon Portland Chase, *Reclamation of Fugitives from Service* (B.P. Donogh: Cincinnati, 1847), pp. 75, 96–106; *Congressional Globe*, 31st Cong., 1st Sess., App., p. 263 (William Seward).

[390] Sotirios A. Barber, *On What the Constitution Means* (Johns Hopkins University Press: Baltimore, 1984), pp. 199–201.

[391] *Dred Scott* at 536–7 (McLean, dissenting). See *Dred Scott* at 500 (Campbell, concurring); Lincoln, 2 *Collected Works*, pp. 230–1, 492; Lincoln, 3 *Collected Works*, pp. 77–8, 96, 327, 329, 334, 402, 404, 435, 439–40, 460; Lincoln, 4 *Collected Works*, pp. 5, 162, 258, 263, 270. See also Chase and Cleveland, *Anti-Slavery*, p. 45; *Congressional Globe*, 31st Cong., 1st Sess., App., pp. 268 (William Seward), 476, 480 (Salmon Chase).

institutionalists or historicists reach and sometimes reach antislavery results unattainable by alternative approaches to the judicial function. Proslavery aspirationalists reach every proslavery result that institutionalists or historicists reach and sometimes reach proslavery results unattainable by alternative approaches. Consider the result of *Dred Scott* had Scott sued for his freedom in Illinois. Both institutional and historical theories support a judicial decision favoring freedom. An institutionalist would, absent national legislation, defer to the state's judgment that slaves became free when voluntarily taken to Illinois. A historicist would defer to the framers' judgment that Illinois should have the authority to determine the status of slavery in Illinois. A proslavery aspirationalist could, by citing the comity clause[392] or perhaps a more general constitutional right to travel,[393] insist that slave-owners had a right to bring their slaves along when they journeyed or temporarily resided in free states.[394]

Contemporaneous critics of *Dred Scott* recognized that their dispute with the Taney Court was not over general principles that transcended the constitutional status of slavery. They objected to the decision the justices made, not the general theory of the judicial function underlying that decision. Frederick Douglass thought the justices "laid down rules of interpretation ... in harmony with the true idea and object of law and liberty." The first of these rules was historical. "[T]he intention of legal instruments must prevail," Douglass declared, and "this must be collected from its words." The second rule was aspirational. The famed abolitionist insisted that "language must be construed strictly in favor of liberty and justice."[395] Douglass's quarrel with the Court was not over basic questions of constitutional exegesis. He and Taney disputed results.

From Constitutional Law to Constitutional Politics

No prominent constitutional theory could have ensured perfectly just outcomes during the 1850s. Slavery concerns were sufficiently accommodated throughout antebellum American history to provide committed proponents of human bondage with the evidence necessary to make plausible arguments for the result in *Dred Scott* using any constitutional logic. *Dred Scott* was

---

[392] "The Citizens of each State shall be entitled to all Privileges and Immunities of Citizens in the several States."

[393] See *Saenz v. Roe*, 526 U.S. 489 (1999); *Shapiro v. Thompson*, 394 U.S. 618 (1969).

[394] See *Congressional Globe*, 35th Cong., 1st Sess., App., pp. 199–200 (Charles E. Stuart) (quoting the *Washington Union*, November 11, 1857). See also Maltz, "Fourteenth Amendment Concepts," pp. 342–6.

[395] Douglass, 3 *Papers*, p. 175.

constitutionally permissible because American popular majorities supported racist practices, the framers in 1787 provided some degree of protection for that racist institution, many framers had racist aspirations, and proponents of slavery had established additional precedents supporting their practice during the years between ratification and the Civil War. General constitutional principles that sanctioned antislavery behavior in some instances also sanctioned proslavery behavior in others. Northern proponents of jury nullification refused to convict persons who violated fugitive slave laws; Southern proponents of jury nullification refused to convict persons who violated bans on the African slave trade.[396] The rare general constitutional principle that privileged antislavery concerns before the Civil War later privileged racial injustice. Assertions that Supreme Court decisions bind only parties to the particular case[397] licensed antislavery resistance to proslavery judicial decisions during the 1850s as well as prosegregation resistance to antisegregation judicial decisions during the 1950s.[398] The view that the Constitution follows the flag had racist implications before the Civil War but antiracist implications after the Spanish-American War.[399]

In 1857, constitutional law was structurally incapable of persuading people who did not think human bondage an injustice that Americans were constitutionally committed to emancipation and racial equality. Proslavery and antislavery forces mutually influenced the genesis and development of the American constitutional tradition. Their struggles created a constitutional grammar in which both "human bondage belongs on the road to ultimate extinction" and "human bondage is an enduring feature of the political regime" were legitimate constitutional sentences. The various materials for making constitutional arguments before the Civil War were, unsurprisingly, as conflicted about slavery as was the general polity. What Americans needed – and what constitutional law had no capacity to provide – was the political consensus necessary for a decisive choice to be made between the more egalitarian and more racist strands of the antebellum American constitutional tradition.

Constitutional law remains structurally incapable of yielding consensually just or consensually right answers to constitutional controversies. The very factors that generate social movements generate reasonable constitutional arguments for that movement's foundational visions. The preconditions of

---

[396] Takaki, *Pro-Slavery Crusade*, pp. 210, 216–19.

[397] See e.g. Edwin Meese III, "The Law of the Constitution," 61 *Tulane Law Review*, 979 (1987); Sanford Levinson, "Could Meese Be Right This Time," 61 *Tulane Law Review*, 1071 (1987).

[398] See Lincoln, 2 *Collected Works*, pp. 400–4, 494–6, 516–18; 3 *Collected Works*, p. 255; 4 *Collected Works*, p. 268; "Southern Manifesto," 1 *Race Relations Law Reporter*, 435, 436 (1956).

[399] See *Downes v. Bidwell*, 182 U.S. 244, 352–75 (1901) (Fuller, dissenting).

political struggle practically guarantee that, when constitutional controversies have excited a society for any period of time, historicists will find particular framers or past judicial precedents that support their policy prescriptions, aspirationalists will find political traditions indicating that their cherished values are also fundamental constitutional principles, and institutionalists will find evidence that favorable judicial review satisfies basic democratic standards. Demands that proponents of a particular policy place more weight on a particular constitutional logic will usually change only the balance of citations in legal arguments, not the general policy prescriptions. Antebellum controversies were particularly fierce because persons mining for traditions in a society historically ambivalent about human bondage naturally found rich lodes of proslavery and antislavery ore. Subsequent constitutional controversies that inspired similar passions were similarly rooted in an ambiguous constitutional heritage.

School segregation was fervently attacked and defended because powerful racist and egalitarian traditions coexisted for more than a century in the United States. Opponents of *Brown* with a historicist bent could cite *Plessy v. Ferguson* [400] and evidence Raoul Berger later claimed proved that the framers of the equal protection clause did not intend to mandate school desegregation. [401] Proponents of *Brown* could cite *Sweatt v. Painter* [402] and evidence Michael McConnell later claimed proved that the framers of the equal protection clause intended to prohibit school segregation. [403] Prosegregation aspirationalists could highlight the "rampant racism in the North of 1866" and the powerful influence of racist ideologies throughout American history. [404] Antisegregationists could note the traditional American antipathy to any form of caste. [405]

Abortion is controversial because "[t]he foundational values of pro-choice, pro-life, and anti-*Roe* positions all enjoy broad popular support and all are deeply rooted in the American political and constitutional tradition." [406]

---

[400] 163 U.S. 537 (1896). See *Gong Lum v. Rice*, 275 U.S. 78 (1927); *Berea College v. Kentucky*, 211 U.S. 45 (1908); *Cumming v. Richmond Board of Education*, 175 U.S. 528 (1899).

[401] Berger, *Government by Judiciary*, pp. 117–28. See Michael J. Klarman, "Brown, Originalism, and Constitutional Theory: A Response to Professor McConnell," 81 *Virginia Law Review*, 1881 (1995).

[402] 339 U.S. 629 (1950). See *Strauder v. West Virginia*, 100 U.S. 303, 308 (1880); *Buchanan v. Wardley*, 245 U.S. 60 (1917); *McLaurin v. Oklahoma State Regents*, 339 U.S. 637 (1950).

[403] Michael W. McConnell, "Originalism and the Desegregation Decisions," 81 *Virginia Law Review*, 947 (1995). See Bork, *Tempting*, pp. 76, 82–3.

[404] Berger, *Government by Judiciary*, p. 118; Smith, *Civic Ideals*.

[405] See Cass R. Sunstein, *The Partial Constitution* (Harvard University Press: Cambridge, 1993), pp. 156–7.

[406] Mark A. Graber, *Rethinking Abortion: Equal Choice, the Constitution and Reproductive Politics* (Princeton University Press: Princeton, 1996), pp. 37–8.

Pro-life constitutionalists turn to Robert Bork for historical arguments,[407] to John Noonan for aspirational arguments,[408] and to John Hart Ely for institutional arguments.[409] Pro-choice constitutionalists turn to the historian's briefs submitted in recent Supreme Court cases for historical arguments,[410] to Ronald Dworkin for aspirational arguments,[411] and to Guido Calabresi for institutional arguments.[412] Anti-*Roe* advocates highlight the de jure tradition of bans on abortion,[413] pro-*Roe* advocates the de facto tradition of permitting abortion.[414]

No approach to constitutional law is practically vulnerable to producing consensually evil outcomes. Americans need not worry that the Supreme Court, gripped by some bizarre constitutional fad, will sustain legislation mandating that babies be thrown into the river or declare that elected officials are constitutionally obligated to throw babies into the river. Elected officials do not pass laws that everyone recognizes as unjust. Statutory relics now universally regarded as unjust (or stupid) are either repealed, not enforced, or struck down by courts. Constitutional authorities and commentators demonstrate great skill in avoiding consensually unjust conclusions. Faced with evidence that the post–Civil War amendments were unconstitutionally ratified[415] and that those responsible for the equal protection clause did not intend to ban segregation,[416] no respectable scholar concludes that slavery is presently constitutional, and only one thinks *Brown* should be overruled.[417] American constitutionalists either reject the factual bases for constitutional arguments that might lead to consensually unjust conclusions or declare those arguments outweighed by other constitutional considerations.

---

[407] Bork, *Tempting*, pp. 110–16.

[408] John T. Noonan, Jr., *A Private Choice: Abortion in America in the Seventies* (Free Press: New York, 1979).

[409] John Hart Ely, "The Wages of Crying Wolf: A Comment on *Roe v. Wade*," 82 *Yale Law Journal*, 920 (1973).

[410] Clyde Spillenger, Jane E. Larson, and Sylvia A. Law, "Brief of 281 American Historians as Amici Curiae Supporting Appellees," *Webster v. Reproductive Health Services*, 492 U.S. 490 (1989).

[411] Ronald Dworkin, *Life's Dominion: An Argument about Abortion, Euthanasia, and Individual Freedom* (Knopf: New York, 1993).

[412] Guido Calabresi, "Foreword: Antidiscrimination and Constitutional Accountability (What the Bork–Brennan Debate Ignores)," 105 *Harvard Law Review*, 80 (1991).

[413] See *Casey* at 980 (1992) (Scalia, concurring in part and dissenting in part).

[414] Graber, *Rethinking Abortion*.

[415] Bruce Ackerman, *We the People*, vol. 2, *Transformations* (Harvard University Press: Cambridge, 1998), pp. 99–252.

[416] See Klarman, "*Brown*"; Rogers M. Smith, "The Inherent Deceptiveness of Constitutional Discourse: A Diagnosis and Prescription," *NOMOS XL: Integrity and Conscience* (ed. Ian Shapiro and Robert Adams) (New York University Press: New York, 1998), pp. 242–9.

[417] See Maltz, "*Brown v. Board of Education*."

Particular constitutional commentators have candidates for contemporary decisions analogous to *Dred Scott*, where the Supreme Court has misinterpreted the Constitution and protected an evil practice. Some view *Roe v. Wade* in this light.[418] My choice is *McCleskey v. Kemp*,[419] the decision upholding death penalty procedures that result in murderers of white persons being significantly more likely to receive the death penalty than those who murder persons of color. If *Roe* and *McCleskey* are evil, however, the underlying reason is that too many Americans believe abortion a fundamental right, do not believe the death penalty is barbaric, or do not believe the imposition of capital punishment is racist. Perhaps a consensus will develop in the future that both abortion and the death penalty are moral wrongs. Should that consensus develop, *Roe* and *McCleskey* will be overruled or abandoned in some other way. Until that or the opposite consensus develops, conventional constitutional theories will continue to generate plausible arguments supporting all sides to the debates over abortion and the death penalty. An ambivalent polity generates ambivalent constitutional arguments.

The persons responsible for the Constitution of 1787 recognized that the survival of the national government depended on constitutional politics and not on the constitutional law of slavery. They designed representative institutions in ways they believed would permanently ensure that all national decisions on slavery enjoyed broad transsectional support. The framers did not intend that there be a predetermined solution to most constitutional controversies about slavery independent from what the constitutional politics of slavery yielded. By pretending otherwise, all the major opinions in *Dred Scott* were forced to strain history and mislead subsequent commentary. The central constitutional problem that gave rise to *Dred Scott* was what could be constitutionally done – under changing political circumstances – to maintain the original constitutional politics of slavery, a politics designed to generate slavery policies that crucial elites in both sections of the country could support. The lessons of that case cannot be learned by looking for imaginary right answers to questions the persons responsible for the Constitution never asked.

---

[418] See note 38.
[419] 481 U.S. 279 (1987). See Graber, *Rethinking Abortion*, pp. 94–5.

PART TWO

The Constitutional Politics
of Slavery

The Civil War is commonly explained as the consequence of an "irrepressible conflict" between the sections over slavery.[1] "Lincoln's election," Michael Morrison insists, "genuinely reflected irreconcilable divisions in the American electorate."[2] Mark Brandon maintains that the antebellum constitutional order broke down when "an interpretive schism between Northern and Southern states ... deepened and widened to such an extent that the two regions adopted distinctive interpretive paradigms that could not accommodate each other."[3] Kenneth Stampp agrees. "[T]here was no basis for sectional harmony," he writes, "as long as Negro slavery survived and as long as Northerners used their overwhelming political power to advance their special interests at the expense of the South."[4]

This emphasis on "irreconcilable differences," "interpretive schisms," and "irrepressible conflicts" overlooks how flawed constitutional institutions and practices were as vital to Republican success as bloody Kansas. For example, had the framers mandated electoral rules of the type adopted by most contemporary democracies, Stephen Douglas or John Bell would have delivered the inaugural address in March 1861. Secession would have been postponed until a free-state coalition gained a majority of the popular vote. Differences between the slave and free states were irreconcilable in 1860

---

[1] William Henry Seward, *The Works of William H. Seward*, vol. 4 (ed. George E. Baker) (Houghton, Mifflin: New York, 1884), pp. 289–302.

[2] Michael A. Morrison, *Slavery and the American West: The Eclipse of Manifest Destiny and the Coming of the Civil War* (University of North Carolina Press: Chapel Hill, 1997), p. 251.

[3] Mark E. Brandon, *Free in the World: American Slavery and Constitutional Failure* (Princeton University Press: Princeton, 1998), p. 7. See Avery Odelle Craven, *The Growth of Southern Nationalism: 1848–1861* (Louisiana State University Press: Baton Rouge, 1953), p. 397.

[4] Kenneth M. Stampp, *And the War Came: The North and the Secession Crisis* (Louisiana State University Press: Baton Rouge, 1950), p. vii.

only because the constitutional system of elections did not permit moderates in both sections to effect a reconciliation.

The Constitution of 1787 sought to secure a balance of sectional power by establishing institutions thought to give both the free and slave states a practical veto on national policy. Convinced that population was moving southwestward, framers from both North and South assumed that allocating representation by population in the House of Representatives, the electoral college, and the three-fifths clause would guarantee slave states the political power necessary to protect their distinctive concerns. Federalist assumptions about political geography obviated the need for explicit legal restrictions on national power over slavery that would forever bind legislative majorities. The framers understood that slavery might be restrained or even abolished under the constitutional arrangements agreed upon in 1787, but they believed that would happen only when many Southerners thought such policies desirable.

The constitutional causes of the Civil War lie in the reasons these constitutional institutions, which were intended to secure bisectional agreements, failed to work. A severe constitutional crisis developed when the Northwest unexpectedly proved more attractive to settlers than the Southwest. As the number and population of free states grew, the same republican principles that the framers thought would help legitimate proslavery policies increasingly provided effective grounds for condemning human bondage and its slave-power promoters. By the time *Dred Scott v. Sandford*[5] was handed down, demographic trends placed antislavery Northerners on the verge of gaining the total control of the national government that was necessary to dictate slavery policy to the South.

National parties became the primary vehicle for preserving the original constitutional commitment to bisectionalism. The constitutional institutions designed in 1787 could yield slavery policies acceptable to the South even when a united free-state majority was capable of controlling the national government – as long as many Northerners either did not care about slavery or tolerated proslavery policies to secure other interests. The Jacksonian party system, however, was undermined by constitutional practices originally thought to promote the bisectional veto and sectional moderation. The constitutional system for electing national officials in states encouraged losing politicians to emphasize sectional issues. The electoral college, originally understood as a boon to the South, enabled Republicans to gain constitutional majorities in presidential campaigns without making any effort to win

[5] 60 U.S. 393 (1856).

popular majorities. Had Articles I and II provided for truly national elections, the apparently irreconcilable differences between the sections might
have been reconciled for another generation.

THE SLAVERY COMPROMISES REVISITED

The American Constitution was a product of many compromises, the most
important of which were those between the states committed to maintaining slavery in the near future and the states that had either abolished human
bondage or were in the process of doing so. James Madison noted at the constitutional convention that "the real difference of interests lay, not between
the large & small but between the N. & Southn. States." "The institution
of slavery & its consequences," he observed, "formed the line of discrimination."[6] Most major constitutional provisions were debated with slavery
in mind, and the influence of that practice permeates the convention's final
product. "Slavery," studies consistently find, "was an ever-present incubus,
dominating some very explicit debates and affecting questions in which the
words 'slave' and 'slavery' were never mentioned."[7]

Most accounts of the constitutional bargaining over slavery emphasize constitutional law. Slaveholders, in this view, sought legal protections for their
human property. Standard histories tell how Southern framers yielded various commercial benefits to the North in return for the fugitive slave clause,
the twenty-year moratorium on federal legislation banning the international
slave trade, and the provisions counting every slave as three fifths of a person
when allocating representation.[8] Other constitutional provisions, such as the
national power to suppress local insurrections (which presumably included

---

[6] Max Farrand, ed., *The Records of the Federal Convention of 1787*, vol. 2 (Yale University Press:
New Haven, 1937), p. 10 (James Madison). See Farrand, 1 *Records*, pp. 146 (Alexander Hamilton), 486–7 (Madison), 566 (Rufus King); Farrand, 2 *Records*, p. 362 (George Mason).

[7] Robert M. Weir, "South Carolina: Slavery and the Structure of the Union," *Ratifying the Constitution* (ed. Michael Allen Gillespie and Michael Lienesch) (University Press of Kansas: Lawrence,
1989), p. 208. See Donald L. Robinson, *Slavery in the Structure of American Politics 1765–1820*
(Harcourt Brace Jovanovich: New York, 1971), pp. 178–9, 223–4; Staughton Lynd, *Class Conflict, Slavery, and the United States Constitution* (Bobbs-Merrill: Indianapolis, 1967); William
M. Wiecek, *The Sources of Antislavery Constitutionalism in America* (Cornell University Press:
Ithaca, 1977), pp. 63–4; Paul Finkelman, "Slavery and the Constitutional Convention: Making
a Covenant with Death," *Beyond Confederation: Origins of the Constitution and American Na-
tional Identity* (ed. Richard Beeman, Stephen Botein, and Edward C. Carter II) (University of
North Carolina Press: Chapel Hill, 1987), pp. 194, 199–201.

[8] See Farrand, 2 *Records*, pp. 449–51 (Charles Coteworth Pinckney and Pierce Butler); Finkelman, "Slavery," pp. 194–223; Weir, "South Carolina," pp. 210–14; Rogers M. Smith, *Civic Ideals:
Conflicting Visions of Citizenship in U. S. History* (Yale University Press: New Haven, 1997), pp.
133–4; Peter Kolchin, *American Slavery, 1619–1877* (Hill & Wang: New York, 1993), p. 80.

the power to suppress local slave insurrections), may also have played roles in the slavery compromises.[9] Most commentators agree that the federal government was granted no power to regulate slavery within a state.[10] Several assert that Southerners favored a very limited national government to ensure that national powers would not be used to free slaves.[11]

This legal view of the original constitutional bargain over slavery ignores numerous instances when prominent slaveholders at the framing convention championed broad national powers that seemingly could be used to abolish human bondage. The Virginia Plan enabled the national government to "legislate in all cases to which the separate states are incompetent."[12] Charles Pinckney of South Carolina proposed giving the federal government the power to appoint state governors and insisted "the States must be kept in due subordination to the nation."[13] Madison and Pinckney repeatedly asserted that "the national government skid. have the authority to negative all [state] Laws which they [should] judge to be improper."[14] This proposal, which would have given Congress the power to emancipate all slaves, was described by Pinckney as "indispensably necessary" and by Madison as "absolutely necessary."[15] Even if Madison thought the veto would "provide an entering wedge to weaken the hold of slavery and its evil effects,"[16] the rabidly proslavery Pinckney was hardly guilty of this subterfuge. Fears of a strong national government may explain why some Southerners supported more limited national powers and helped defeat the national veto.[17] Nevertheless,

---

[9] Finkelman, "Slavery," pp. 190–2; Wiecek, *Antislavery*, pp. 62–3, 81–2. See Paul Finkelman, *Slavery and the Founders: Race and Liberty in the Age of Jefferson* (M.E. Sharpe: Armonk, 1996), pp. 3–6.

[10] See Weir, "South Carolina," p. 214.

[11] See Richard H. Brown, "The Missouri Crisis, Slavery and the Politics of Jacksonianism," 65 *South Atlantic Quarterly*, 55, 56 (1965); Finkelman, *Slavery*, p. 6.

[12] Farrand, 1 *Records*, p. 21.

[13] Farrand, 2 *Records*, p. 391; Farrand, 1 *Records*, p. 164.

[14] Farrand, 1 *Records*, p. 164. See Farrand, 1 *Records*, pp. 131, 162–4; Farrand, 2 *Records*, p. 28.

[15] James H. Hutson, ed., *Supplement to Max Farrand's The Records of the Federal Convention of 1787* (Yale University Press: New Haven, 1987), p. 60; Farrand, 1 *Records*, p. 164. See Madison to Washington, April 16, 1787, in James Madison, *The Papers of James Madison*, vol. 9 (ed. Charles F. Hobson and Robert A. Rutland) (University Press of Virginia: Charlottesville, 1979), pp. 383–4. See also 9 *Papers of Madison*, 368, 370, 318; John P. Kaminski and Gaspare J. Saladino, eds., *The Documentary History of the Ratification of the Constitution*, vol. 8, *Ratification of the Constitution by the States: Virginia [1]* (State Historical Society of Wisconsin: Madison, 1988), pp. 97, 102 (Madison); Jack N. Rakove, *Original Meanings: Politics and Ideas in the Making of the Constitution* (Knopf: New York, 1996), pp. 51–3, 62; Larry D. Kramer, "Madison's Audience," 112 *Harvard Law Review*, 611, 627–8, 634–5, 641, 649 (1999).

[16] Rakove, *Original Meanings*, p. 337.

[17] See Farrand, 1 *Records*, p. 53 (Pierce Butler and John Rutledge); Farrand, 2 *Records*, p. 17 (Butler and Rutledge). See also Joseph M. Lynch, *Negotiating the Constitution: The Earliest Debates over Original Intent* (Cornell University Press: Ithaca, 1999), p. 15.

the voting alignment when questions of national authority were decided suggests no Southern tendency to favor limiting federal power.[18]

The constitutional text also provides little support for subsequent claims that Congress had no power to emancipate slaves. Anti-Federalists maintained that such provisions as the necessary and proper clause gave the national government near absolute power to regulate any subject.[19] Patrick Henry and George Mason emphasized how various constitutional clauses could plausibly be interpreted as authorizing extensive federal interference with Southern property. The federal government would use the "power to provide for the general defense and welfare," Henry insisted, to "pronounce all slaves free." [20] Southern anti-Federalists easily refuted one standard Federalist response to charges of unlimited power: that representatives would not pass oppressive laws because such measures would prevent their reelection and burden their close associates.[21] Northern politicians who passed antislavery measures would benefit professionally and personally, they pointed out. Henry reminded Virginians that citizens from free states "have not the ties of sympathy and fellow-feeling for those whose interest would be affected by their emancipation." William Grayson suggested that representatives from "Delaware will assist in laying a tax on our slaves, of which they will pay no part whatever." [22]

Read as a legal text, the constitutional bargain over slavery was remarkably indifferent to numerous issues that divided North from South.[23] The

[18] See Farrand, 2 Records, pp. 21–4; William J. Cooper, Jr., Liberty and Slavery: Southern Politics to 1860 (Knopf: New York, 1983), p. 61.
[19] See Hutson, Supplement, pp. 292, 294 (Luther Martin); Merrill Jensen, ed., The Documentary History of the Ratification of the Constitution, vol. 2, Ratification of the Constitution by the States: Pennsylvania (State Historical Society of Wisconsin: Madison, 1976), pp. 310, 392, 395–6, 399, 408–10, 426, 453, 627; John P. Kaminski and Gaspare Saladino, eds., The Documentary History of the Ratification of the Constitution, vol. 4, Ratification of the Constitution by the States: Massachusetts [1] (State Historical Society of Wisconsin: Madison, 1997), pp. 368–9; 8 Documentary History, pp. 32–3, 45, 62, 233, 324, 393–4, 462, 470; John P. Kaminski and Gaspare Saladino, eds., The Documentary History of the Ratification of the Constitution, vol. 9, Ratification of the Constitution by the States: Virginia [2] (State Historical Society of Wisconsin: Madison, 1990), pp. 1111–12; John P. Kaminski and Gaspare Saladino, eds., The Documentary History of the Ratification of the Constitution, vol. 10, Ratification of the Constitution by the States: Virginia [3] (State Historical Society of Wisconsin: Madison, 1993), pp. 1284, 1299, 1326, 1340, 1602.
[20] 10 Documentary History, pp. 1186, 1341, 1476–7. See 10 Documentary History, pp. 1338, 1504.
[21] Merrill Jensen, ed., The Documentary History of the Ratification of the Constitution, vol. 3, Ratification of the Constitution by the States: Delaware, New Jersey, Georgia, and Connecticut (State Historical Society of Wisconsin: Madison, 1978), p. 468; 8 Documentary History, pp. 295, 497; 9 Documentary History, pp. 996, 998, 1122–3; 10 Documentary History, pp. 1282, 1308, 1327, 1533.
[22] 10 Documentary History, p. 1477; 10 Documentary History, p. 1186.
[23] Don E. Fehrenbacher, The Slaveholding Republic: An Account of the United States Government's Relations to Slavery (ed. Ward M. McAfee) (Oxford University Press: New York, 2001), pp. 44, 47.

Constitution did not clarify national power over slavery in the territories, determine when and whether persons of color could become American citizens, or set out the procedures required for recapturing fugitive slaves. Westward expansion was an ongoing Southern concern. Virginians debated at length whether Northern representatives would take all possible steps to prevent new slave states from forming in the Southwest.[24] No party to these debates displayed any overt interest in whether the congressional power to make needful rules for the territories authorized congressional bans on slavery. Claims that these omissions reflect a deeper, entirely tacit, compromise not to establish any fixed legal rules[25] fail to explain why a very clear agreement was reached on federal power to ban the international slave trade or why a vaguer solution to the fugitive slave problem was placed in the text.

The relative absence of legal rules was not an oversight, a consequence of any failure to reach more specific agreements, or the result of a conscious decision not to decide. The persons responsible for drafting the Constitution did not establish legal rules governing slavery because they did not see fundamental constitutional arrangements as laying down rules of constitutional law. Federalists were more concerned with devising institutions that would facilitate bisectional agreements on slavery policy than with determining the substance of those agreements in advance. The more perfect union crafted in Philadelphia primarily relied on a constitutional politics constructed to yield policies that moderates in both the North and the South would support.

The Original Constitutional Politics of Slavery

The Political Constitution

Participants in the framing convention focused almost entirely on determining the processes for electing national officials and making national laws. One looks in vain through various notes taken at Philadelphia for specific legal definitions of interstate commerce or the freedom of speech. The most famous struggle at the convention was fought over the structure of the national legislature.[26] Once the convention agreed that senators would be elected by state legislatures – a political arrangement that all thought protected state interests – many leading proponents of state rights endorsed broad national

---

[24] See especially 10 *Documentary History*, pp. 1192, 1237–8, 1245, 1259; John P. Kaminski and Gaspare Saladino, eds., *The Documentary History of the Ratification of the Constitution*, vol. 16, *Commentaries on the Constitution: Public and Private [4]* (State Historical Society of Wisconsin: Madison, 1986), pp. 153, 262.

[25] See e.g. Brandon, *Free in the World*, pp. 29–30.

[26] See Kramer, "Madison's Audience," p. 653.

powers. "From the day when every doubt of the right of the smaller states to an equal vote in the senate was quieted," Madison remembered, "they ... exceeded all others in zeal for granting powers to the general government."[27]

Leading Federalists scorned legal limits on national power. The *Federalist Papers* assert that crucial government powers should not be legally defined or restricted by constitutional rules. *Federalist* 31 declares, "there ought to be no limitation of a power destined to effect a purpose which is itself incapable of limitation."[28] *Federalist* 23 insists that the powers "essential to the common defense ought to exist without limitation *because it is impossible to foresee or to define the extent and variety of national exigencies, and the correspondent extent and variety of the means which may be necessary to satisfy them*" (emphasis in original).[29] Delineating the precise scope of national authority, the framers felt, was not only unwise but also impossible. Edmund Randolph and Madison informed delegates at Philadelphia that "defining ... the limits and powers of the federal legislature ... could not be done." "Is it, indeed, possible," Jasper Yeates challenged members of the Pennsylvania ratifying convention, "to define any power so accurately, that it shall reach the particular object for which it was given, and yet not be liable to perversion and abuse?"[30]

Prominent Federalists insisted that legal restrictions on federal power were dangerous, useless, and confusing. Government officials committed to the public good would sometimes face irresistible pressures to ignore textual limits on their powers, and such officials would not be deterred by clear constitutional guidelines.[31] Clear constitutional guidelines would not restrain officials bent on unconstitutional usurpations. *Federalist* 48 comments, "a mere demarcation on parchment of the constitutional departments is not a sufficient guard against those encroachments which lead to a tyrannical concentration of all the powers of government in the same hand."[32] Rights could not be defined in ways that adequately identified government

---

[27] Huston, *Supplement*, p. 322. See Farrand, 1 *Records*, p. 255 (Pinckney); Rakove, *Original Meanings*, pp. 63–5; Lynch, *Negotiating the Constitution*, pp. 18–19.

[28] Alexander Hamilton, James Madison, and John Jay, *The Federalist Papers* (New American Library: New York, 1961), p. 193.

[29] Hamilton, Madison, and Jay, *Federalist Papers*, p. 153. See Hamilton, Madison, and Jay, *Federalist Papers*, p. 257. See also 2 *Documentary History*, p. 417; 8 *Documentary History*, p. 395; 9 *Documentary History*, pp. 999, 1011, 1016, 1134–5, 1144; 10 *Documentary History*, pp. 1197, 1396.

[30] Farrand, 1 *Records*, p. 60; 2 *Documentary History*, p. 438. See 8 *Documentary History*, pp. 101–2; 10 *Documentary History*, p. 1501.

[31] See Hamilton, Madison, and Jay, *Federalist Papers*, pp. 160, 167, 257; James Madison, *Letters and Other Writings of James Madison*, vol. 1 (R. Worthington: New York, 1884), pp. 424–5.

[32] Hamilton, Madison, and Jay, *Federalist Papers*, p. 313. See Hamilton, Madison, and Jay, *Federalist Papers*, p. 442.

oppression. "What signifies a declaration that 'the liberty of the press shall be inviolably preserved'?" Hamilton asked. "What is the liberty of the press? Who can give it any definition which would not leave the utmost latitude for evasion?"[33]

This hostility to "parchment barriers"[34] explains why the Constitution of 1787 did not contain an extensive list of legal limits on government powers. As Roger Sherman informed New Englanders: "No bill of rights ever yet bound the supreme power longer than the *honey moon* of a new married couple, unless the *rulers were interested* in preserving the rights" (emphasis in original).[35] Mere legal recognition could not secure fundamental liberties in the long run, other Federalists declared, because parchment declarations could be ignored or rescinded. "Neither would a general declaration of rights be any security," Civic Rusticus wrote, "for the sovereign who made it could repeal it."[36]

Federalists believed the best way to limit government power was by careful design of government institutions. "[A]ll observations founded upon the danger of usurpation," Hamilton wrote, "ought to be referred to *the composition and structure of the government, not to the nature or extent of its powers*" (emphasis added).[37] The key to maintaining the separation of powers was the manner in which each branch of government was elected and compensated. The Constitution prevented all powers from being centralized in a single institution "by so contriving the interior structure of the government as that its several constituent parts may, by their mutual relations, be the means of keeping each other in their proper places."[38] The national government could be vested with substantial powers because the design of that regime guaranteed such authority would not be abused. "[T]he delegating of power to a government in which the people have so many checks," James Bowdoin Dalton asserted, "will be perfectly safe, and consistent with the preservation of their liberties."[39] The Constitution protects religious

---

[33] Hamilton, Madison, and Jay, *Federalist Papers*, p. 514.

[34] Hamilton, Madison, and Jay, *Federalist Papers*, pp. 308–9.

[35] 2 *Documentary History*, p. 433. See 8 *Documentary History*, pp. 308, 438; 9 *Documentary History*, p. 975; 10 *Documentary History*, pp. 1196–7, 1333–4.

[36] 8 *Documentary History*, p. 334. See 8 *Documentary History*, p. 337.

[37] Hamilton, Madison, and Jay, *Federalist Papers*, p. 196. See Hamilton, Madison, and Jay, *Federalist Papers*, pp. 196, 255–6. See also Farrand, 1 *Records*, pp. 108, 169 (Madison); Farrand, 2 *Records*, pp. 25 (Gouverneur Morris), 77 (Madison), 252 (Mason); John P. Kaminski and Gaspare Saladino, eds., *The Documentary History of the Ratification of the Constitution*, vol. 14, *Commentaries on the Constitution: Public and Private [2]* (State Historical Society of Wisconsin: Madison, 1983), p. 173; 2 *Documentary History*, p. 400.

[38] Hamilton, Madison, and Jay, *Federalist Papers*, p. 320.

[39] Jonathan Elliot, ed., *The Debates in the Several State Conventions on the Adoption of the Federal Constitution as Recommended by the General Convention at Philadelphia in 1787,*

freedom and private property, the framers thought, by establishing a constitutional politics that privileges policies favorable to religious exercise and property holders, not by placing legal limits on government power to establish a church and confiscate land. When, at the drafting convention, Madison emphasized the need to "introduce the checks ... for the safety of a minority in danger of oppression from an unjust and interested majority," he proposed a national veto on state legislation.[40] Forty years after ratification, Madison reminded delegates to the Virginia State Constitutional Convention that "the only effectual safeguard to the rights of the minority, must be laid in such a basis and structure of the Government itself."[41]

Federalists maintained that republican institutions provided the most important protection against tyranny. They repeatedly declared that making officials "dependent on the suffrage of the people for their appointment to, and continuance in office" was "a much greater security than a declaration of rights, or restraining clauses upon paper."[42] The framing generation's experience with state practices under rudimentary republican constitutions had fostered careful consideration of the republican institutions most likely to yield particularly desirable policies. The separation of powers was thought vital for "produc[ing] wise and mature deliberation."[43] The Constitution established relatively large election districts and relatively long terms of office because the framers thought these practices would "obtain for rulers men who possess most wisdom to discern, and most virtue to pursue, the common good of society."[44] The six-year Senate term encouraged "men of integrity and abilities."[45] Recognizing that "[e]nlightened statesmen will not always

vol. 2 (Lippincott: Philadelphia, 1836), p. 103. See 9 *Documentary History*, pp. 987–8; Farrand, 1 *Records*, p. 34 (Butler); Herbert J. Storing, "The 'Other' Federalist Papers: A Preliminary Sketch," *Friends of the Constitution: Writings of the "Other" Federalists, 1787–1788* (ed. Colleen A. Sheehan and Gary L. McDowell) (Liberty Fund: Indianapolis, 1998), pp. xxxvi, xxxix, xli.

[40] Farrand, 1 *Records*, p. 108.

[41] Charles A. Syndor, *The Development of Southern Sectionalism: 1819–1848* (Louisiana State University Press: Baton Rouge, 1968), p. 279 (quoting Madison).

[42] 14 *Documentary History*, p. 387 (Roger Sherman). Huston, *Supplement*, p. 286 (Roger Sherman); 2 *Documentary History*, p. 433. See Farrand, 1 *Records*, p. 359 (Mason); 2 *Documentary History*, pp. 387, 412, 420, 436; 8 *Documentary History*, pp. 213, 216, 406, 512–13; 9 *Documentary History*, pp. 1024, 1122–3; 10 *Documentary History*, pp. 1196–7; "Fabius" (John Dickinson), "The Letters," *Friends of the Constitution*, p. 62.

[43] Storing, "'Other' Federalist Papers," p. xli (quoting "A Citizen").

[44] Hamilton, Madison, and Jay, *Federalist Papers*, p. 350. See 9 *Documentary History*, pp. 661, 915, 1006, 1016, 1023, 1025, 1150; John P. Kaminski and Gaspare J. Saladino, eds., *The Documentary History of the Ratification of the Constitution*, vol. 13, *Commentaries on the Constitution: Public and Private [1]* (Madison: State Historical Society of Wisconsin, 1981), p. 372; Elliot, 1 *Debates*, pp. 256–7. See also Mark A. Graber, "Conflicting Representations: Guinier and Madison on Electoral Systems," 13 *Constitutional Commentary*, 291, 299–304 (1996).

[45] "A Federalist", "Essay," p. 41.

be at the helm," [46] the framers structured government institutions so that less virtuous officeholders had the combination of interests necessary to privilege desired results. The Constitution, Madison wrote, adopted "the policy of supplying, by opposite and rival interests, the defect of better motives." [47]

State interests were protected by government institutions that required all national decisions to be made by officials dependent for their offices on local governments or local electorates. [48] "The construction of the Senate," Tench Coxe asserted, "affords an absolute certainty, that the states will not lose their present separate powers." [49] Legal boundaries were ruled out. Madison noted that "[n]o line can be drawn between the State Governments and the General Government." [50] Constitutional interests are secure when such decisions as whether local officials should enforce national laws are made by officials who have a strong bias toward protecting local interests. If constitutional institutions function according to design and if local officials are ordered to enforce national policies, then the reason must be that states either do not consider such measures threatening or regard the justifications for federal action as sufficiently compelling to warrant some intrusion into state sovereignty.

Rather than legally specify in advance and for all time what various interests were, the Constitution of 1787 enabled states, government officers, various religious sects, and other important political groups to determine and protect their interests. Whether governing institutions are functioning as originally designed depends on the extent to which the officers making decisions have the requisite abilities and interests, not on the precise decisions they make. Americans were protected from injustice and stupidity by well-constructed democratic institutions that would neither restrict liberty nor encroach on state rights unless nationally necessary. Herbert Storing's influential analysis of framing thought aptly concludes, "the substance [of the Constitution] is a design of government with powers to act and a structure arranged to make it act wisely and responsibly." "It is in that design, not in its preamble or its epilogue," he emphasizes, "that the security of American civil and political liberties lies." [51]

[46] Hamilton, Madison, and Jay, *Federalist Papers*, p. 80.

[47] Hamilton, Madison, and Jay, *Federalist Papers*, p. 322.

[48] See 2 *Documentary History*, pp. 437, 570; 3 *Documentary History*, pp. 531–2, 556; 8 *Documentary History*, pp. 101, 177–8, 439. See also Herbert Wechsler, *Principles, Politics, and Fundamental Law: Selected Essays* (Harvard University Press: Cambridge, 1961), pp. 78–81.

[49] 16 *Documentary History*, p. 50.

[50] Huston, *Supplement*, p. 61 (Madison). See Farrand, 1 *Records*, p. 323 (Hamilton); 2 *Documentary History*, p. 344.

[51] Herbert J. Storing, "The Constitution and the Bill of Rights," *How Does the Constitution Secure Rights?* (American Enterprise Institute for Public Policy Research: Washington, D.C., 1985),

Protecting Slavery Politically

The framers placed similar emphasis on government structure when determining the place of slavery in the political order. Rather than bind government in advance to a specific set of policies, Federalists designed governing
institutions they thought would always be exquisitely sensitive to Southern
concerns. The fundamental compromise on slavery reached by the framers
in 1787 was that their Constitution would neither sanction human bondage
nor give the national government the power to regulate that institution in any
way without Southern consent. Slavery was never explicitly mentioned or
acknowledged by the Constitution. The framers thought it "wrong to admit
in the Constitution the idea that there could be property in men."[52] They
rewrote the fugitive slave clause to avoid any implication that human bondage
was legal.[53] Slavery was protected by political arrangements thought to guarantee to a united coalition of slaveholders the ability to prevent any national
measure from becoming law that most Southerners believed inconsistent
with their mutual interests.

Southerners at the framing convention were concerned with the future
division of political power between the free and slave states. Proslavery advocates expressed their most vociferous defenses of human bondage when
the staffing of the national government was under consideration.[54] Pierce
Butler's notorious assertion – "the security the Southn. States want is that
their negroes may not be taken from them"[55] – was uttered during the debates over how representatives to the Congress should be apportioned. The
"security" he wanted was power. Butler favored "abolishing the State Legislatures" should representation "proceed[] on a principle favorable to wealth
as well as numbers of free inhabitants,"[56] a scheme that all thought was in
the South's interests.

Delegates from all regions shared Butler's concern with the future balance
of sectional power. Leading slaveholders "did not expect the S. States to be
raised [immediately] to a majority of representatives, but wished them to
have something like an equality." "The Southn. Interest must be extremely
endangered," HughWilliamson of North Carolina declared, if "[t]he Northn.

---

p. 35. See Walter Berns, "The Constitution as Bill of Rights," *How Does the Constitution Secure
Rights?*, especially pp. 51, 59–65.

[52] Farrand 2 *Records*, p. 417 (Madison). See Farrand, 1 *Records*, p. 561 (William Paterson); Far-
rand, 2 *Records*, pp. 408–9, 415 (James Madison and Roger Sherman); Luther Martin, "Genuine
Information," in Farrand, 3 *Records*, p. 210; Huston, *Supplement*, p. 158 (John Dickinson); 14
Documentary History, p. 262 (Benjamin Rush).

[53] Farrand, 2 *Records*, p. 628.

[54] Fehrenbacher, *Slaveholding Republic*, p. 33.

[55] Farrand, 1 *Records*, p. 605.

[56] Farrand, 1 *Records*, p. 144. See Farrand, 1 *Records*, p. 562 (Butler).

States are to have a majority in the first instance and the means of perpetrating it."[57] William Davie insisted that the slave states "would never confederate on any terms that did not rate [slaves] at least as 3/5."[58] Compromise was reached in 1787 when Northern framers proved sympathetic to this Southern fear of free-state hegemony. Rufus King of New York was one of many antislavery delegates who proved "ready to yield something in the proportion of representation for the security of the Southern" states.[59]

When considering how this "proportion of representation" could be maintained for the foreseeable future, constitutional framers from all regions of the country assumed that population increases would be greatest in the South and Southwest. Most believed that the New England states were fully settled and that the best available farming land was located in the colonies and territories where slavery was legal. George Mason expected that "the Southern & Western population should predominate in a few years."[60] Morris noted, "N.C., S.C., and Georgia only will in a little time have a majority of the people of America."[61] A population explosion, many thought, was already taking place in slaveholding regions. "The people & strength of America," Butler declared, "are evidently bearing Southwardly & S. westwardly." Madison agreed that "the people are constantly swarming ... from the Northn & middle parts of the U.S. to the Southern and Western."[62] Western territories were universally regarded as probable bastions for slavery.[63] Anticipating that expansion would empower slaveholders, New Englanders proposed a measure limiting the number of representatives from new states that was narrowly defeated by a united coalition of the states most committed to slavery.[64]

Sectional concerns permeated the debates over the structure of every national institution. Expecting that population growth would be greatest in the

---

[57] Farrand, 1 *Records*, p. 567 (Charles Cotesworth Pinckney and Hugh Williamson). See Finkelman, *Slavery*, p. 14.

[58] Farrand, 1 *Records*, p. 593.

[59] Farrand, 1 *Records*, p. 566. See Farrand, 1 *Records*, p. 562 (Charles Pinckney); Farrand, 2 *Records*, p. 10 (James Madison).

[60] Farrand, 1 *Records*, p. 586 (George Mason). See Farrand, 1 *Records*, pp. 561, 604–5 (Gouverneur Morris), 585–6 (James Madison), 595 (Rufus King); Farrand, 2 *Records*, pp. 111 (Hugh Williamson), 305 (Mason); Huston, *Supplement*, p. 83 (Alexander Hamilton); James Madison, *The Writings of James Madison*, vol. 2 (ed. Gaillant Hunt) (Putnam's: New York, 1901), p. 327.

[61] Farrand, 1 *Records*, pp. 604–5. King similarly stated "whenever the Southern States shall be more numerous than the Northern." Farrand, 1 *Records*, p. 595.

[62] Farrand, 1 *Records*, p. 605; Farrand, 1 *Records*, pp. 585–6 (Madison).

[63] Cooper, *Liberty and Slavery*, pp. 53–4.

[64] Farrand, 2 *Records*, p. 2. Massachusetts, Connecticut, Delaware, and Maryland supported the measure; New Jersey, Virginia, North Carolina, South Carolina, and Georgia voted against it. The Pennsylvania delegation was divided.

South, the more northern states almost uniformly favored representation by states. Massachusetts was the only state north of Pennsylvania "that would listen to a proposition for excluding the States as equal political Societies."[65] Southerners favored representation by population. Madison steadfastly opposed representing states in the Senate because of the "perpetuity it would give to the preponderance of the Northn, agst. the Southn." Slave-state representatives insisted the electoral college was necessary to ensure "influence on the election on the score of Negroes."[66] Hugh Williamson objected to a popular vote for the presidency because "slaves will have no suffrage."[67] Confident that a local population explosion was imminent, representatives from relatively unpopulated North Carolina and Georgia supported representation by population and the electoral college.[68] The final structure of Congress and the presidential election system was a compromise between free and slave states that secured a balance of sectional power in the national government. Southerners could not prevent the Senate from representing small/free-state interests, but proportional representation in the lower house of Congress and the electoral college – both augmented by the three-fifths clause – seemed to guarantee to the slave states the control of the House of Representatives and executive branch necessary to secure slave-holding interests.[69] After agreement was reached on the electoral college and state representation in the Senate, Virginians successfully moved the judicial appointment power from the upper house of Congress to the more Southern-tilting executive branch. Allowing the Senate to select federal justices, Madison declared, would "throw the appointments entirely into the hands of ye Nthern States."[70]

Having agreed upon these institutional means for balancing control of the government between the North and the South, the framers self-consciously

---

[65] Farrand, 1 *Records*, p. 469 (Madison). See Farrand, 1 *Records*, p. 503 (James Wilson).

[66] Farrand, 2 *Records*, pp. 9, 57. See Farrand, 1 *Records*, pp. 510, 516, 534, 536–7, 542; Farrand, 2 *Records*, pp. 501, 511. See also Paul Finkelman, "The Proslavery Origins of the Electoral College," 23 *Cardozo Law Review*, 1145, 1154–5 (2002).

[67] Farrand, 2 *Records*, p. 32.

[68] See Farrand, 2 *Records*, pp. 491, 500, 510.

[69] Rakove, *Original Meanings*, p. 75. See "North Carolina Ratifying Convention Debates," *A Necessary Evil?: Slavery and the Debate over the Constitution* (ed. John Kaminski) (Madison House: Madison, 1995), p. 197 (William R. Davie); Farrand, 2 *Records*, p. 356. See also Raymond T. Diamond, "No Call to Glory: Thurgood Marshall's Thesis on the Intent of a Pro-Slavery Constitution," 42 *Vanderbilt Law Review*, 93, 107–8 (1989); Rakove, *Original Meanings*, pp. 54, 72, 259; David Brion Davis, *The Problem of Slavery in the Age of Revolution, 1770–1823* (Cornell University Press: Ithaca, 1975), pp. 104–5. The analysis in this section borrows heavily from Raymond Diamond's insightful analysis of the slavery compromises.

[70] Farrand, 2 *Records*, p. 81. See Lynch, *Negotiating the Constitution*, pp. 28, 30.

rejected more explicit textual restraints on federal power over slavery. Every delegate from the major slaveholding states opposed Roger Sherman's proposal to limit the amending power set out in Article V so that "no state shall without its consent be affected in its internal police."[71] Southerners had also unanimously voted against an earlier motion declaring that the federal government was "not to interfere with the government of the individual states in any matter of internal police which respect the government of such States only."[72] When the First Congress proposed the Bill of Rights, no slave state's representatives demanded a ban on federal laws interfering with slavery. The failure to adopt such provisions meant that the antebellum Constitution would not plainly prohibit national laws emancipating slaves. Moreover, the surviving records of the framing convention belie subsequent claims made at ratifying conventions that the federal government was given no constitutional power to abolish slavery.[73] More specific assurances may have been privately communicated, but only three delegates – Oliver Ellsworth (Connecticut), Elbridge Gerry (Massachusetts), and Abraham Baldwin (Georgia) – publicly declared that "the morality or wisdom of slavery are considerations belonging to the States themselves."[74] Another delegate, George Mason, articulated a rival position. In his opinion, "it [was] essential in every point of view, that the Genl. Govt. should have the power to prevent the increase of slavery."[75] Established late eighteenth-century practice supported laws freeing slaves when abolition secured vital public interests. Virginia, Maryland, and other states emancipated thousands of slaves who fought during the Revolution. The Continental Congress approved a more national program of compensated emancipation for military service.[76] Madison stated in the First Congress that the federal government could pass antislavery measures concerning "a local affair" that "involve[d] national expense or safety."[77] Thus slavery was protected from unnecessary abolition schemes not by explicit constitutional limits on federal power but instead by a system of representation designed to ensure that slaves would be emancipated and slavery banned only when prominent slaveholders supported such policies.

Specific legal protections for slavery were necessary only with respect to the international slave trade, an issue on which slaveholders were internally

---

[71] Farrand, 2 *Records*, pp. 629–30.

[72] Farrand, 2 *Records*, pp. 21, 24.

[73] See note 105 and the relevant text.

[74] Farrand, 2 *Records*, p. 364 (Ellsworth). See Farrand, 2 *Records*, p. 372 (Baldwin and Gerry).

[75] Farrand, 2 *Records*, p. 370.

[76] See 10 *Documentary History*, p. 1508; Philip A. Klinkner and Rogers M. Smith, *The Unsteady March: The Rise and Decline of Racial Equality in America* (University of Chicago Press: Chicago, 1999), pp. 18–19; Fehrenbacher, *Slaveholding Republic*, pp. 19–20.

[77] *Annals of Congress*, 1st Cong., 1st Sess., p. 354.

divided, and the rendition of fugitive slaves, a matter that would otherwise be determined by antislavery majorities in Northern states.[78] The Deep South representatives who proposed the fugitive slave clause were not making an antislavery effort "to bring the fugitive slave problem within the ambit of national political discourse so as to facilitate a national solution to the slavery problem."[79] Rather, the clause was a proslavery effort to prevent the fugitive slave problem from being resolved by antislavery local authorities.[80] From the beginning, proponents of slavery were nationalists whenever they thought uniform federal legislation more likely than diverse state laws to serve Southern interests.

The confidence with which the most fervent supporters of human bondage believed population was flowing southward explains their willingness to accept a mere twenty-year moratorium on federal laws banning the international slave trade. That provision was added to the Constitution after Charles Cotesworth Pinckney bluntly stated that South Carolina would not ratify unless some specific protection for slavery was included.[81] His sine qua non for his state joining the union, remarkably, was a constitutional provision that explicitly empowered Congress to ban the international slave trade after 1808 and might also be interpreted as implying legislative power to regulate the domestic slave trade. Federalists in some Northern states and in Virginia declared that this clause doomed slavery, which required continuous importation.[82] Twenty years was probably the best South Carolina could have bargained for. Nevertheless, that delay was thought sufficient to serve vital slaveholding interests. Deep South representatives expected their political strength in 1808 would render unnecessary the legal protection for slavery demanded in 1787. South Carolinians, Rakove suggests, "assumed . . . that another two decades of slave importation and the southwestern movement of population should place slavery beyond the reach of the amendment process."[83]

Slavery was not placed "in the course of ultimate extinction" in 1787. Instead, emancipation was yoked to the sectional veto. The framers drafted

---

[78] See Finkelman, "Slavery," pp. 214–18; *A Necessary Evil?*, p. 200 (James Iredell); Cooper, *Liberty and Slavery*, pp. 60–1.

[79] Christopher L. M. Eisgruber, "Justice Story, Slavery, and the Natural Law Foundations of American Constitutionalism," 55 *University of Chicago Law Review*, 273, 323 (1988).

[80] Farrand, 2 *Records*, pp. 453–4; Farrand, 3 *Records*, p. 254 (Charles Cotesworth Pinckney); Huston, *Supplement*, p. 246.

[81] Farrand, 2 *Records*, p. 95. See Farrand, 2 *Records*, pp. 301, 373, 378.

[82] See Hamilton, Madison, and Jay, *Federalist Papers*, pp. 266–7; 3 *Documentary History*, p. 490; 4 *Documentary History*, p. 53; 10 *Documentary History*, pp. 1339, 1341. See also James Oakes, "The Compromising Expedient: Justifying a Proslavery Constitution," 17 *Cardozo Law Review*, 2023, 2025, 2044 (1996).

[83] Rakove, *Original Meanings*, p. 91.

and ratified a constitution that they hoped would prevent potentially irrec-
oncilable sectional differences from disrupting national union, their most
valued constitutional commitment.[84] When the national government was
functioning as originally intended, national policy would be approved by a
Southern-tilting House of Representatives and a Northern-tilting Senate.
In firm control of the presidency, the federal judiciary, and the House of
Representatives, a united South would veto any legislation too hostile to
Southern interests. What constituted "too hostile" was for future slavehold-
ers to decide.

Accommodating Evil in 1787

Late eighteenth-century Americans gave several reasons for endorsing constitutional arrangements that protected the South's peculiar institution. Most
framers spoke of "the necessity of compromise."[85] Benjamin Franklin decided not to present a petition urging the convention to outlaw the slave trade
because he "thought it advisable to let them lie over for the present."[86] Some
tolerance was thought the necessary price to avoid social disorder or military
catastrophe. Many nationalists feared civil war, foreign invasion, or commercial disaster should the Union not be immediately strengthened. "If we
do not agree on this middle & moderate ground," Oliver Ellsworth warned,
"we should lose two States, with such others as may be disposed to stand
aloof, should fly into a variety of shapes & directions, and most probably into
several confederations and not without bloodshed."[87] Madison informed
Virginians that "[t]he Southern States would not have entered the Union of
America, without temporary permission of [the slave] trade." "And if they
were excluded from the Union," he continued, "the consequences might be
dreadful to them and to us."[88] Many opponents of slavery worried that granting freedom to all slaves in the near future would have hazardous side effects.
"An immediate abolition of slavery," Noah Webster predicted, "would bring

---

[84] See Oakes, "Compromising Expedient," pp. 2047–8.

[85] Farrand, 1 *Records*, p. 587 (James Wilson).

[86] Huston, *Supplement*, p. 44. See Fehrenbacher, *Slaveholding Republic*, p. 28. Franklin presented
      similar petitions to the First Congress; see H. W. Brands, *The First American: The Life and Times
      of Benjamin Franklin* (Anchor: New York, 2000), pp. 708–9.

[87] Farrand, 2 *Records*, p. 375. See 10 *Documentary History*, p. 1341; Farrand, 3 *Records*, p. 325
      (quoting Madison); "Plain Truth" to Timothy Meanwell, *Philadelphia Independent Gazetteer*,
      October 30, 1787, in *A Necessary Evil?*, p. 122. See also Paul Finkelman, "The Constitution and
      the Intention of the Framers: The Limits of Historical Analysis," 50 *University of Pittsburgh Law
      Review*, 349, 382–3 (1989); Robinson, *Slavery*, pp. 172–3; Wiecek, *Antislavery*, p. 73; Oakes,
      "Compromising Expedient," pp. 2025, 2047; Klinkner and Smith, *Unsteady March*, p. 25.

[88] 10 *Documentary History*, pp. 1338–9.

ruin upon the whites and misery upon the blacks, in the southern states."
Franklin feared that emancipation, "if not performed with solicitous care,
may sometimes open a source of serious evils."[89]

Federalists from the (becoming) free states asserted that slavery would
gradually be abandoned if left alone. Roger Sherman was not concerned
about constitutional protections for human bondage because "the abolition
of slavery seemed to be going on in the U.S. & that the good sense of the
several states would probably by degrees compleat it." "Let us not inter-
meddle," Ellsworth agreed. "As population increases," he claimed, "poor
laborers will be so plenty as to render slavery useless. Slavery in time will
not be a speck in our Country."[90] Given that breaking up the constitutional
convention or refusing to ratify over slavery would not have alleviated the
present condition of black slaves, many antislavery delegates thought that
tolerating a decaying institution was a reasonable price to pay for union.

The notion that slavery would gradually wither away was not mere rational-
ization from the perspective of 1787. Antislavery forces had made remarkable progress from 1750 to 1775 both in public opinion and politically.[91] By
the time of the Revolution, slavery was being attacked "with a vehemence
that was inconceivable earlier."[92] A "general consensus" was emerging in the
United States and Europe that government need not act to weaken human
bondage. "[B]lack slavery," conventional wisdom maintained, "was an historical anomaly that could survive for a time only in the plantation societies
where it had become the dominant mode of production."[93] The American
experience was confirming this conjecture. Slavery was moribund in Northern states, even though human bondage had been at least as well established
in New York City and Massachusetts at the beginning of the eighteenth century as in Virginia or North Carolina.[94] These developments gave antislavery

[89] Noah Webster, "An Examination into the Leading Principles of the Federal Government," *A Necessary Evil?*, p. 118; Davis, *Problem of Slavery*, p. 84. See Noah Webster, *The Effects of Slavery
on Morals and Industry* (Hudson & Goodwin: Hartford, 1793), pp. 34–7; David Brion Davis,
Slavery and Human Progress (Oxford University Press: New York, 1984), p. 159.

[90] Farrand, 2 *Records*, pp. 369–71 (quoting Sherman and Ellsworth). See Webster, *Effects of Slavery*, pp. 34–7. See also Wiecek, *Antislavery*, pp. 63, 65; Finkelman, "Slavery," p. 215; Davis,
Human Progress, p. 159; Oakes, "Compromising Expedient," pp. 2044–9; Fehrenbacher, *Slaveholding Republic*, p. 29.

[91] Davis, *Problem of Slavery*, p. 41.

[92] Gordon S. Wood, *The Radicalism of the American Revolution* (Knopf: New York, 1992), p. 186.

[93] Davis, *Human Progress*, p. 81. See Wood, *Radicalism*, p. 186; Klinkner and Smith, *Unsteady
March*, pp. 12–23.

[94] Davis observes that "the proportion of slaves in New York City in the mid-eighteenth century
was higher than the comparable figure for Jamaica and Antigua in 1660, for South Carolina in
1680, for North Carolina in 1730, and for Georgia in 1750." Davis, *Human Progress*, pp. 75–6.

advocates reasons for believing that universal emancipation could be realized within a century without active government intervention.

Slavery politics in the Upper South buttressed antislavery optimism. Slave-state leaders north of South Carolina proudly burnished their humanitarian convictions. George Washington proclaimed, "there is not a man living who wishes more sincerely than I do, to see a plan adopted for the abolition of [slavery]." James Iredell of North Carolina asserted: "When the entire abolition of slavery takes place, it will be an event which must be pleasing to every generous mind, and every friend of human nature."[95] Many slaveholders fought harder against slavery during the framing convention than did some delegates from the North. Virginia's battle against the international slave trade failed only when New England allied with the Deep South in return for commercial concessions.[96] While free-state representatives were largely silent, George Mason attacked the "infernal traffic," and Luther Martin declared the slave trade "dishonorable to the American character."[97] No one was under the illusion that South Carolina or Georgia was moving toward emancipation.[98] Even so, antislavery advocates had reason to believe that, once Virginia joined the ranks of free states, the few remaining slave states could not hold out for long. South Carolina shared this conviction.[99]

Whether framers who were more antislavery or better bargainers could have done better by persons of color is nearly impossible to determine. Once the decision was made to accommodate South Carolina, any serious antislavery commitment was ruled out. Madison did not exaggerate when he informed Jefferson that "S. Carolina & Georgia were inflexible on the point of slaves."[100] Deep South slaveholders asserted from the month the

---

[95] George Washington, *George Washington: A Collection* (ed. W. B. Allen) (Liberty Classics: Indianapolis, 1988), p. 319; *A Necessary Evil?*, pp. 198–9 (James Iredell). See Thomas Jefferson, *The Portable Thomas Jefferson* (ed. Merrill D. Peterson) (Penguin: New York, 1975), pp. 185–6; James Madison, *The Papers of James Madison*, vol. 12 (ed. Charles F. Hobson and Robert A. Rutland) (University Press of Virginia: Charlottesville, 1979), p. 437; 10 *Documentary History*, pp. 1476–7 (Patrick Henry).

[96] Fehrenbacher, *Slaveholding Republic*, p. 34. For other border-state attacks on the slave trade see Huston, *Supplement*, p. 158 (John Dickenson).

[97] Farrand, 2 *Records*, pp. 370, 364.

[98] See Paul Finkelman, "Slavery, The Pennsylvania Delegation and the Constitutional Convention: The Two Faces of the Keystone State," 112 *Pennsylvania Magazine of History and Biography*, 49, 70 (1988).

[99] Deep South elites for the next seventy years obsessively monitored any hint of conditional termination in the Upper South. See William W. Freehling, *The Road to Disunion: Secessionists at Bay, 1776–1854* (Oxford University Press: New York, 1990), pp. viii, 6–7, 17–19, 23–4, 121–3, 134; Alison Goodyear Freehling, *Drift toward Dissolution: The Virginia Slavery Debate of 1831–32* (Louisiana State University Press: Baton Rouge, 1982), pp. 249, 252–3.

[100] 8 *Documentary History*, p. 105.

Declaration of Independence was signed that, "if it is debated whether these slaves are their property, there is an end of the confederation."[101]

Retrospective evaluation of the constitutional bargaining over slavery is particularly difficult because the framers failed to foresee the future. Under the erroneous impression that population increases would be greatest in the South, all parties to the constitutional compact sought institutions that subsequently did not serve their interests. Slaveholders at the constitutional convention fought to secure representation by population in the House of Representatives. So constructed, the House became the most antislavery branch of the national government in the years immediately before the Civil War. The free states in 1787 secured the state representation in the Senate that inflated Southern political power during the 1850s. Had antislavery advocates obtained what was thought in 1787 to be a better constitutional bargain, proslavery policies would have had more political support when *Dred Scott* was decided.

Cracks in the Constitutional Consensus

Providing political protections for the South's peculiar institution helped nationalists at the framing convention agree on constitutional language that could be ratified in all regions of the United States. Northerners were assuaged by the paucity of explicit textual protections for slavery, Southerners by their expected control of the national government. Federalists achieved national consensus that constitutional protections for slavery were acceptable without, however, forging a national consensus on the nature of those constitutional accommodations. The ratification process fostered largely unrecognized sectional differences in how the constitutional status of slavery was conceptualized. South Carolina, Virginia, and the Northern states ratified slightly different constitutions.

The practical requirement that the Constitution be ratified by each state encouraged sectionally biased accounts of constitutional arrangements. Federalists in every state ratification convention fought to gain support for the Constitution among persons who by and large held similar views about slavery. New Englanders agreed slavery was evil, South Carolinians thought the practice justified, and Virginians were ambivalent. Local Federalists helped secure ratification by characterizing the constitutional bargain over slavery in terms most favorable to their state's distinctive values and interests.[102]

---

[101] 6 *Journal of the Continental Congress*, 1080 (1776) (Thomas Lynch).
[102] See Fehrenbacher, *Slaveholding Republic*, p. 37; Cooper, *Liberty and Slavery*, p. 71.

Proponents of ratification in New Hampshire highlighted antislavery aspects of the Constitution;[103] their counterparts in South Carolina stressed constitutional protections for human bondage.[104] Poor communication between different regions prevented most participants in state ratification conventions from fully realizing the different interpretations of the constitutional compromises over slavery being advanced during the ratification processes in noncontiguous states.

South Carolina ratified a proslavery constitution that provided substantial legal and political protections for human bondage. "We have a security that the general government can never emancipate them," Charles Cotesworth Pinckney proudly informed the state ratifying convention, "for no such authority is vested."[105] Population growth guaranteed national support for Southern interests. Edward Rutledge declared, "we should, in the course of a few years rise high in our representation, whilst other states would keep their present position."[106] "In fifty years," David Ramsay agreed, "it is probable that the Southern states will have a great ascendancy over the Eastern."[107] South Carolinians regarded slavery as a positive good[108] and believed other Americans would become constitutionally committed to human bondage.[109] The constitutional failure to mention slavery reflected Northern squeamishness, according to Southern advocates of ratification, rather than more fundamental antislavery aspirations.[110]

Virginia ratified a constitution that guaranteed Southern control over slavery policy. Upper South elites agreed with South Carolinians on the legal and political protections for slavery. "No power," Madison bluntly declared, "is given to the General Government to interpose with respect to the property in slaves now held by the States."[111] Virginians also agreed with South Carolinians that population trends ensured Southern control of the national

---

[103] Jean Yarborough, "New Hampshire: Puritanism and the Moral Foundations of America," *Ratifying the Constitution*, pp. 245–9.

[104] Weir, "South Carolina," pp. 215–27.

[105] Elliot, 4 *Debates*, p. 268.

[106] Elliot, 4 *Debates*, pp. 276–7. See Cooper, *Liberty and Slavery*, pp. 66–7.

[107] 16 *Documentary History*, p. 23.

[108] See Farrand, 2 *Records*, p. 364; 16 *Documentary History*, p. 538.

[109] See Farrand, 2 *Records*, 371; 16 *Documentary History*, p. 25; *A Necessary Evil?*, pp. 167, 171–2 (Rawlins Lowndes); Weir, "South Carolina," pp. 207–10, 215–17, 220–2.

[110] James Iredell informed members of the North Carolina ratification convention that "[t]he northern delegates, owing to their particular scruples on the subject of slavery, did not choose the word slave to be mentioned": "North Carolina Ratifying Convention Debates," *A Necessary Evil?*, p. 200.

[111] 10 *Documentary History*, p. 1483. See Farrand, 3 *Records*, p. 334 (Randolph); 8 *Documentary History*, pp. 371–2 (George Nicholas); 10 *Documentary History*, pp. 1339 (James Madison), 1341–2 (George Nicholas), 1503–4 (Madison).

government. "We shall soon outnumber them in as great a degree as they do us at this time," George Nicholas confidently declared. "Therefore," he concluded, "this Government will be very shortly to our favor."[112] Unlike South Carolinians, however, Virginians and other Upper South elites were committed to abolishing the slave trade as soon as constitutionally permitted. "It ought to be considered as a great point gained in favor of humanity," Madison declared, "that a period of twenty years may terminate forever, within these States, a traffic which has so long and so loudly upbraided the barbarism of modern policy." Madison regarded the explicit omission of slavery in the constitutional text as reflecting a general national antipathy to human bondage.[113] He and other Virginia Federalists simply thought that, with the exception of the international slave trade, states bore the primary constitutional responsibility for determining when emancipation was appropriate.

Most Northerners ratified a constitution more concerned with commerce than slavery. While Southerners debated sectional issues during their ratification debates,[114] Northern framers debated whether the proposed constitution would exacerbate class differences among Americans. Outside of New Hampshire,[115] slavery was hardly ever mentioned and almost never discussed in any detail during Northern ratification debates. Although Madison spoke of population trends when addressing Virginians, he made no reference to the balance of sectional power when addressing New Yorkers. The *Federalist Papers* touched on slavery only during a short discussion of the three-fifths clause[116] and a briefer discussion of the moratorium on federal laws banning the international slave trade.[117] No prominent pamphleteer or representative at a Northern ratification convention was much concerned with which region would dominate national politics.[118]

---

[112] 9 *Documentary History*, pp. 1002–3. See 2 *Documentary History*, pp. 244–5; 8 *Documentary History*, p. 346; 9 *Documentary History*, pp. 648, 688, 962; 10 *Documentary History*, p. 1251. Some Southern anti-Federalists insisted that the free states would control the national government, at least during the first years of constitutional life. See 3 *Documentary History*, pp. 237–8, 260–1; 8 *Documentary History*, 45, 63, 151, 158, 386; 9 *Documentary History*, p. 1159; 10 *Documentary History*, pp. 1222, 1315–16, 1374, 1471, 1667.

[113] Farrand, 2 *Records*, p. 417.

[114] In addition to slavery, Virginians debated at length whether the Constitution would permit Northern states to pass oppressive commercial regulations and sacrifice Southern concerns respecting the Mississippi River; see 10 *Documentary History*, pp. 1229–56.

[115] Yarborough, "New Hampshire," pp. 245–9.

[116] Hamilton, Madison, and Jay, *Federalist Papers*, pp. 336–9.

[117] Hamilton, Madison, and Jay, *Federalist Papers*, pp. 266–7, 279.

[118] 3 *Documentary History*, p. 384. See 4 *Documentary History*, p. 419 ("[t]he northern antifederalists pretend that in the new constitution, the southern states will predominate"). For Northern anti-Federalist claims that Southerners would soon control the national government, see 3 *Documentary History*, pp. 376, 423.

Although some Northerners did ratify an antislavery constitution, many others were indifferent. Several Federalists regarded the federal power to ban the international slave trade as a great improvement on the Articles of Confederation[119] and as the foundation for eventual emancipation. A Quaker urged ratification because, after twenty years, "the new federal government, if established, would eagerly embrace the opportunity not only of putting an end to the importation of slaves, but of abolishing slavery forever."[120] James Wilson asserted that Congress could and would ban slavery in the territories.[121] This claim, however, was not repeated or well publicized. Most Northern federalists thought the federal government lacked any substantial power to interfere with slavery. Tench Coxe indicated that no authority to emancipate slaves could be found in the Constitution.[122] John Sherman informed Connecticut citizens that "each State retains its sovereignty in what respects its own internal government."[123] General William Heath stated the most common Northern belief when he pointed to the Constitution's seeming neutrality toward slavery. "[I]f we ratify the Constitution," Heath asked, "shall we do any thing by our act to hold the blacks in slavery – or shall we become partakers of other men's sins. I think neither."[124] This attitude hardly fostered detailed investigation into the extent to which the federal government could regulate domestic slavery.

Conflicting Federalist justifications for their decision to omit a bill of rights promised further confusion about federal power to emancipate slaves. Madison and Hamilton claimed that the structure of governing institutions provided better protection than parchment declarations for fundamental

---

[119] See *Providence United States Chronicle*, in *A Necessary Evil?*, p. 114; 2 *Documentary History*, p. 222; *A Necessary Evil?*, pp. 187 (statement of James Madison), 198–9 (statement of James Iredell). A few Northern anti-Federalists complained that the Constitution supported slavery. See "Letters from a Countryman from Dutchess County," *The Complete Anti-Federalist*, vol. 6 (ed. Herbert J. Storing) (University of Chicago Press: Chicago, 1981), p. 62; 2 *Documentary History*, pp. 212, 462; 3 *Documentary History*, pp. 379, 423–5; 8 *Documentary History*, pp. 45, 233, 367, 415, 450–1; 9 *Documentary History*, pp. 774, 776, 778.

[120] 8 *Documentary History*, p. 482. See John P. Kaminski and Gaspare Saladino, eds., *The Documentary History of the Ratification of the Constitution*, vol. 6, *Ratification of the Constitution by the States: Massachusetts [3]* (State Historical Society of Wisconsin: Madison, 2000), p. 1245; 4 *Documentary History*, pp. 1421–2 (Isaac Backus). See also *A Necessary Evil?*, pp. 114 (statement of Simeon Baldwin), 115, 117 (statement of Dr. Benjamin Rush); 2 *Documentary History*, p. 499 (James Wilson); Hamilton, Madison, and Jay, *Federalist Papers*, p. 266. But see Finkelman, "Pennsylvania Delegation," pp. 69–70 (claiming that Wilson was being disingenuous).

[121] 2 *Documentary History*, p. 463.

[122] 9 *Documentary History*, p. 836. See Howard A. Ohline, "Slavery, Economics, and Congressional Politics, 1790," 46 *Journal of Southern History*, 335, 338 (1980).

[123] Huston, *Supplement*, p. 287.

[124] 6 *Documentary History*, p. 1371. See William Lee Miller, *Arguing about Slavery: The Great Battle in the United States Congress* (Knopf: New York, 1996), pp. 14–15.

rights and interests.[125] Many local Federalists agreed, insisting that republican governments protected basic liberties politically by giving people the power to cashier representatives who violated their electoral trust. Francis Corbin asked,

> will the people re-elect the same men to repeat oppressive legislation? Will the people commit suicide against themselves, and discard all those maxims and principles of self-preservation which actuate mankind in all of their transactions?[126]

Other prominent Federalists asserted during the ratification debates that the Constitution already provided legal protections for fundamental rights and interests, making a bill of rights unnecessary. James Wilson claimed: "Constitutional authority is to be collected ... from positive grant expressed in the instrument of the union." Hence, "[e]verything which is not given is reserved."[127] "If I have one thousand acres of land, and I grant five hundred acres of it," George Nicholas asked, "must I declare that I retain the other five hundred?"[128]

This confusion over the extent to which constitutional protections for fundamental rights were political or legal had important implications for the constitutional status of slavery. The ratification debates did not clarify whether slavery was constitutionally protected by a system of representation thought to guarantee a united South the power to influence public policy or rather by a series of legal restrictions on national power. The Madisonian perspective suggested that those holding office under the Constitution would not interfere with slavery in existing states; the Wilsonian perspective suggested that such persons had no legal power to do so in any case. Uncertain as to the nature of constitutional protections and confident that the South would always have the population necessary to influence national policy, Southern Federalists did not determine precisely what would count as an unconstitutional interference with slavery. Most slaveholders thought Southerners in the national majority had some leeway on this matter. No one considered whether

---

[125] See notes 37–41 and the relevant text. See also 10 *Documentary History*, p. 1352; 2 *Documentary History*, pp. 436–7; 3 *Documentary History*, pp. 569–71; 4 *Documentary History*, pp. 49, 298; 9 *Documentary History*, pp. 1012, 1119.

[126] 9 *Documentary History*, p. 1024. See sources cited in note 42.

[127] 2 *Documentary History*, pp. 167–8.

[128] 10 *Documentary History*, p. 1038. See 2 *Documentary History*, pp. 190, 384, 430, 471, 542, 570; 3 *Documentary History*, pp. 154, 247, 489–90, 525; 4 *Documentary History*, p. 331; 8 *Documentary History*, pp. 213, 311, 369; 9 *Documentary History*, pp. 661, 715, 767, 996, 1012, 1080, 1099–1100, 1135; 10 *Documentary History*, pp. 1223–4, 1350, 1502.

an unexpected free-state majority could constitutionally exercise the same discretion.

Toward the Future

Bisectionalism could have survived these disparate understandings of federal power over slavery. As long as anticipated southwestward population movements enabled Southern moderates to influence national policy, citizens in neither section would have cause for constitutional complaint. Virginia slaveholders would prevent the federal government from adopting policies Virginians thought unconstitutionally interfered with domestic slavery. South Carolinians might grumble about bans on the international slave trade, but they would not find Upper South slave policies cause for secession. Northerners might grumble about the three-fifths clause, but they would not disrupt union as long as accommodating Virginians was necessary in order to secure national majorities on matters of more pressing commercial concern.

Nevertheless, the original constitutional order was unstable. Agreement was reached at the constitutional convention partly because prominent framers held inconsistent assumptions about the future. New Englanders accepted the compromises of 1787 because they were confident that antislavery trends would continue. South Carolinians endorsed the same bargain because they were confident that antislavery trends had crested. Sectional frustrations were bound to increase unless one section converted the other. A crisis would result should Virginia abolish slavery and join a New England crusade to impose emancipation on South Carolina. South Carolina extremists willing to be governed by proslavery Virginia moderates might not have accepted rule by antislavery Virginians or Virginians who traded emancipation for commercial concessions.

Divisions over federal power to regulate slavery would also remain latent only as long as slave states maintained at least partial control of the national government. Whether the federal government could constitutionally ban slavery in all territories was merely of theoretical interest while Southern moderates retained the power to influence, if not dictate, territorial policy. Demographics thus contained the seeds of a second constitutional crisis. Should free states prove more attractive to new settlers than slave states, the national government would cease to be staffed by officials whose interests and beliefs assured adequate protection for slavery. Even if favorable legal rules could be teased out of the original constitutional text, the *Federalist Papers* reminded slaveholders that perceived parchment guarantees for human bondage would not restrain a Northern majority committed to abolishing slavery.

THE COMPROMISES AND CONSTITUTIONAL DEVELOPMENT

The constitutional system of elections and lawmaking created in 1787 could yield policies acceptable to Southern moderates under four conditions:

1. if (as anticipated by the framers) population trends enabled the slave states to control the House of Representatives and presidency;
2. if (as anticipated by John C. Calhoun) free-state representatives backed down when faced with Southern constitutional demands;
3. if (as anticipated by some proponents of the Missouri Compromise) sectional balance in the Senate enabled a united South to reject anti-slavery proposals; or
4. if (as anticipated by the Jacksonian founders of the national party system) crucial Northerners supported proslavery policies in return for other political benefits, most notably political power.

These means for preserving the original constitutional commitment to bi-sectionalism either never worked out or soon broke down. Population shifts that began shortly after ratification gave a united North the potential to control both the House of Representatives and the presidency. Free-state majorities never acceded to Southern demands without various inducements. Divisions among slave-state representatives doomed the balance rule as a protection for slavery long before that rule was officially abandoned. Although national political parties proved the most enduring means for obtaining proslavery policies, the Jacksonian party system could not survive a constitutional system that facilitated sectionalism and sectional appeals. As population moved northwestward and attitudes toward slavery hardened, a constitution designed to promote bisectional compromise proved a better vehicle for promoting candidates and parties with sectionally divisive platforms.

The Original Constitutional Order in Action

The constitutional compromise over slavery functioned fairly smoothly during the early years of the republic.[129] Relative population balance between the sections, Southern political organization, and Federalist political blunders enabled slaveholders to occupy crucial government positions. Aided by the three-fifths clause,[130] Virginia moderates controlled the presidency for all

---

[129] Northerners fared well during the Washington and Adams administrations, leading Jefferson to complain that "we are completely under the saddle of Massachusetts and Connecticut": Thomas Jefferson, *The Works of Thomas Jefferson*, vol. 12 (ed. Paul Leicester Ford) (Putnam's: New York, 1905), p. 263.

[130] Had Southern states not obtained a bonus from the three-fifths clause, John Adams would have won the 1800 presidential election. See Finkelman, "Proslavery," pp. 1154–5.

but four of the first thirty-six years of constitutional rule. Jefferson, Madison, and Monroe were slaveholders who, while thinking human bondage an evil in the abstract, made clear by deed and word that "the Constitution has not empowered the federal legislature to touch in the remotest degree the question respecting the condition of property of slaves in any of the States."[131] The Jeffersonian Republican party that dominated American politics during the first two decades of the nineteenth century had a "special relationship" with the South. Slaveholders played leading roles in both houses of Congress. Twenty of the first thirty-five Supreme Court justices hailed from slave states.[132] Public policy so favored Southern interests during the Jefferson and Madison administrations that prominent New Englanders seriously considered secession. Members of the Hartford Convention demanded as the price of continued union that slave states forgo the extra representation that the three-fifths clause provided for their peculiar institution.[133]

The First Congress formally recognized Southern constitutional understandings when declaring that the national legislature had "no authority to interfere in the emancipation of slaves, or in the treatment of them within any of the States."[134] This limit on federal power had not clearly been established at Philadelphia or during the ratification process.[135] Nevertheless, most Northerners endorsed the "federal consensus," as the prohibition on federal interference with domestic slavery became known.[136] Some were partly influenced "by their desire to win southern support for Hamilton's report on Public Credit."[137] Many probably regarded the resolution as a constitutional truism.

Southerners in firm control of the national government favored national power, scorning the state-rights dogma coming out of New England. Such future stalwarts of limited federal power as John Taylor and John Randolph of Virginia endorsed broad conceptions of national authority in 1803 when the issue was whether the Louisiana Purchase was constitutional.[138] Some Old

---

[131] Cooper, *Liberty and Slavery*, pp. 97–8 (quoting Thomas Jefferson).

[132] Cooper, *Liberty and Slavery*, pp. 85, 87, 96, 100, 123, 148.

[133] "Report and Resolutions of the Hartford Convention," *Documents of American History*, vol. 1 (ed. Henry Steele Commager) (Appleton-Century-Crofts: New York, 1963), p. 211.

[134] *Annals of the Congress of the United States*, 1st Cong., 2nd Sess., p. 1474. See Richard S. Newman, "Prelude to the Gag Rule: Southern Reaction to Antislavery Petitions in the First Federal Congress," 16 *Journal of the Early American Republic*, 571 (1996).

[135] See notes 71–77 and the relevant text. See also Ohline, "Slavery," p. 336.

[136] See Miller, *Arguing about Slavery*, p. 35.

[137] Ohline, "Slavery," p. 336. See Ohline, "Slavery," pp. 349–50, 355, 358–9.

[138] See *Annals of Congress*, 8th Cong., 1st Sess., pp. 50–4, 435–8; Everett Somerville Brown, *The Constitutional History of the Louisiana Purchase, 1803–1812* (University of California Press: Berkeley, 1920), p. 63; Cooper, *Liberty and Slavery*, pp. 120–30.

Republicans from Virginia maintained after 1805 that constitutional powers had to be narrowly construed in order to avoid granting Congress the authority to emancipate slaves.[139] Most prominent early nineteenth-century representatives from slave states discounted that possibility. Two distinguished representatives from slave states, Henry Clay of Kentucky and John C. Calhoun of South Carolina, championed broad constructions of national power when leading legislative fights for internal improvements.[140] Indeed, when Southerners controlled the national government, slave states were bastions of unionist sentiment.[141] Calhoun entered the national stage as a nationalist. John Quincy Adams, when Secretary of State under President Monroe, regarded Calhoun as "above all sectional and factious prejudices more than any other statesman of this Union."[142] The lower house of the South Carolina legislature championed the nationalistic Marshall Court in 1824 as the ultimate authority on all national questions.[143] Some Southern historians suggest that "[i]t is anachronistic to speak of Southerners" before 1820.[144]

Southern moderates did not find the ban on human bondage in the Northwest Territories, which had been passed under the Articles of Confederation and was reaffirmed by the First Congress, to be constitutionally problematic or even controversial. Slaveholders favored prohibitions on slavery north of the Ohio River, sometimes with enthusiasm. Many believed the Northwest Territories would be settled by Southerners who would support Southern interests upon being admitted to statehood. Others thought that "Yankees without slaves would not grow Southern staples and thereby flood [the] slaveholders' market."[145] Moreover, an antislavery ban limited to the Northwest Territories implied the legality of slavery in other territories.[146] Southern concerns about uncompensated emancipation were assuaged when the first governor of the Northwest Territories ruled that the congressional ban on

---

[139] *Annals of Congress*, 8th Cong., 1st Sess., p. 1308 (John Randolph). See Syndor, *Development*, p. 139; Cooper, *Liberty and Slavery*, p. 109.

[140] Cooper, *Liberty and Slavery*, p. 120.

[141] Glover Moore, *The Missouri Controversy, 1819–1821* (Peter Smith: Gloucester, 1953), p. 10.

[142] John Quincy Adams, *Memoirs of John Quincy Adams, Comprising Portions of His Diary from 1795 to 1848*, vol. 5 (ed. Charles Francis Adams) (Books for Libraries Press: Freeport, 1969), p. 361. See Moore, *Missouri Controversy*, pp. 119, 246; Syndor, *Development*, p. 162.

[143] Cooper, *Liberty and Slavery*, p. 152.

[144] Syndor, *Development*, p. 95.

[145] W. Freehling, *Disunion*, p. 138.

[146] Fehrenbacher, *Slaveholding Republic*, p. 259. See generally Lynd, *Class Conflict*, pp. 186, 190–3, 199; David Brion Davis, "The Significance of Excluding Slavery from the Old Northwest in 1787," 84 *Indiana Magazine of History*, 75, 76–7 (1988); Robinson, *Slavery*, pp. 382–5. The ban was also apparently in part a reflection of the antislavery idealism of the Revolutionary period; see Denis P. Duffey, "The Northwest Ordinance as a Constitutional Document," 95 *Columbia Law Review*, 929, 963–5 (1995).

slavery did not apply to persons held as slaves prior to the passage of the ban or to their offspring.[147]

The federal government enjoyed nearly unanimous Southern support when moving against the international slave trade.[148] Three slaveholding states, hoping to reduce the black population of the United States and increase the value of their excess slaves, called on Congress to repeal the twenty-year moratorium on federal prohibitions. Slaveholders were more successful when they championed federal bans on importing foreign slaves into the territories and states where importation was illegal.[149] As soon as constitutionally permitted, prominent Southerners drafted legislation abolishing that human commerce, and the resulting law accommodated slaveholders by not freeing illegally imported slaves. Northerners later secured a ban on the coastal slave trade only with the support of some slave-state representatives.[150]

The Louisiana Purchase

The Louisiana Purchase was considered a major Southern victory in the struggle for control of the national government.[151] Convinced that slaveholders would rapidly settle the Louisiana territories, New England representatives "fought tooth and nail" against the bill authorizing the required payment to France.[152] New Englanders raised constitutional concerns about expansion and the constitutional rules for admitting new states[153] that were animated by fears that the balance of sectional power was threatened. Uriah Tracy of Connecticut insisted that "the relative strength which this admission gives to a Southern and Western interest, is contradictory to the principles of our original Union."[154] Josiah Quincy declared that the "proportion of political power" established in the original Constitution was "an inalienable,

---

[147] Fehrenbacher, *Slaveholding Republic*, pp. 255–9.

[148] Fehrenbacher, *Slaveholding Republic*, p. 136.

[149] Fehrenbacher, *Slaveholding Republic*, pp. 141–2; Cooper, *Liberty and Slavery*, p. 99.

[150] Fehrenbacher, *Slaveholding Republic*, pp. 144–7; Cooper, *Liberty and Slavery*, p. 99.

[151] Cooper, *Liberty and Slavery*, pp. 101–4.

[152] David P. Currie, "Jefferson and the West, 1801–1809," 39 *William and Mary Law Review*, 1441, 1462 (1998). See Robert Knowles, "The Balance of Forces and the Empire of Liberty: States' Rights and the Louisiana Purchase," 88 *Iowa Law Review*, 343, 347–9, 373–6, 380–2 (2003); Brown, *Louisiana Purchase*, pp. 32–3, 44–5, 69.

[153] See *Annals of Congress*, 8th Cong., 1st Sess., pp. 44–5, 54–7, 67, 432–4, 461–3; *Annals of Congress*, 11th Cong., 3rd Sess., pp. 108, 493–5, 528–39, 570–1.

[154] *Annals of Congress*, 8th Cong. 1st Sess., p. 56. See William Plumer, *William Plumer's Memorandum of Proceedings in the United States Senate, 1803–1807* (Macmillan: New York, 1923), p. 9; *Annals of Congress*, 8th Cong., 1st Sess., pp. 462, 465; *Annals of Congress*, 11th Cong., 3rd Sess., pp. 529–30, 537–42; J. Q. Adams, 1 *Memoirs*, p. 287.

essential, intangible right" that would be violated by the admission of any state formed out of territory not part of the United States in 1787. Quincy came within three votes of being declared out of order when he informed Congress that, if Louisiana were granted statehood, "the bonds of this Union are virtually dissolved."[155] A bare modicum of sectional parity might be maintained, opponents of expansion declared, only if the three-fifths clause was not applied to new states carved out of the Louisiana Territories.[156]

Southerners brushed these constitutional doubts aside, with only Jefferson expressing substantial private qualms.[157] John Randolph, Nathaniel Macon, George Nicholson, and John Taylor publicly declared that the national government had substantial power to acquire territories, govern territories, and grant statehood to territories.[158] The balance of sectional power was not, they felt, a constitutional concern. A delegate from the Mississippi Territory bluntly informed New Englanders that "political influence fluctuates in proportion to the augmentation or diminution of population, in the various sections of the country." Claims that Northerners were entitled to a proportional share of political power, he continued, were "inconsistent with the genius of a free Government."[159] Southerners similarly found no constitutional problems with the purchase of Florida from Spain in 1819. Expansion during the early republic was a Southern interest that enjoyed substantial Southern support.[160]

New England fussing aside, sectional politics during the early republic were relatively muted. Lines between the free and slave states had not yet hardened. The embryonic parties of the early nineteenth century had sectional bases and biases, but each had prominent adherents and enjoyed some electoral successes in the other section.[161] Sectional disputes over expansion, trade with Europe, and the Mississippi River pitted the South and West against the Northeast.[162] New Englanders who opposed national expansion worried about the "balance ... between Eastern and the Western

---

[155] *Annals of Congress*, 11th Cong., 3rd Sess., pp. 537, 525.

[156] Simpson, "Slave Representation," pp. 335–41; Rufus King, *The Life and Correspondence of Rufus King: Comprising His Letters, Private and Official, His Public Documents, and His Speeches*, vol. 6 (ed. Charles R. King) (Da Capo: New York, 1971), pp. 698–9; *Annals of Congress*, 16th Cong., 1st Sess., p. 124 (Jonathan Roberts); *Annals of Congress*, 16th Cong., 1st Sess., p. 184 (Prentiss Mellen).

[157] See Part I.

[158] See *Annals of Congress*, 8th Cong., 1st Sess., pp. 49–50, 435–7, 467–71; *Annals of Congress*, 11th Cong., 3rd Sess., pp. 503–5.

[159] *Annals of Congress*, 11th Cong., 3rd Sess., pp. 566–7.

[160] See Cooper, *Liberty and Slavery*, pp. 104, 132.

[161] Cooper, *Liberty and Slavery*, pp. 79, 85, 91, 94.

[162] Moore, *Missouri Controversy*, pp. 3–6.

State[s]"[163] rather than between North and South or free and slave states. Initial divisions over slavery were not always sectional. When prominent slave-state senators championed bans on slavery in Louisiana, Senator Dayton from New Jersey declared that such policies prevented Western settlement.[164] A few proslavery and antislavery representatives sought amendments to the Fugitive Slave Act of 1793, but most representatives from each section remained content with the political status quo.[165]

The Missouri Compromise

Disputes over federal power to regulate slavery first disrupted national unity in 1819, when Representative James Tallmadge of New York proposed that Missouri be admitted to the Union only on the condition that the state gradually emancipate all slaves.[166] Several days later, Representative John Taylor of New York proposed banning slavery in the Arkansas Territory.[167] Northern proponents of these measures insisted that the federal consensus applied only to existing states. Thomas Morril of New Hampshire concluded: "Congress have a right and power to prohibit slavery in every territory within its dominion, and in every State, formed of territory acquired without the limits of the original States."[168] The three-fifths clause, representatives from free states added, was intended to benefit only those states in the union at the time of ratification. Tallmadge declared that "an extension of that clause in the Constitution" to new territories "would be unjust in its operations, unequal in its results, and a violation of its original intentions."[169] Several New Englanders continued to assert that Congress had no power to admit states west of the Mississippi under any condition.[170]

---

[163] *Annals of Congress*, 8th Cong., 1st Sess., p. 465. See *Annals of Congress*, 11th Cong., 3rd Sess., pp. 539–40.

[164] See Brown, *Louisiana Purchase*, pp. 108–15.

[165] Eisgruber, "Justice Story," p. 277. Thomas D. Morris, *Free Men All: The Personal Liberty Laws of the North, 1780–1861* (Johns Hopkins University Press: Baltimore, 1974), p. 41.

[166] *Annals of Congress*, 15th Cong., 2nd Sess., pp. 1166, 1170.

[167] *Annals of Congress*, 15th Cong., 2nd Sess., p. 1222.

[168] *Annals of Congress*, 16th Cong., 1st Sess., p. 137. For similar arguments, see J. Q. Adams, 5 *Memoirs*, pp. 5–8; King, 6 *King*, pp. 690–1; *Annals of Congress*, 15th Cong., 2nd Sess., pp. 1171–4, 1179–84, 1207–9; *Annals of Congress*, 16th Cong., 1st Sess., pp. 71–2, 137–50, 202–6, 211–37, 279–86, 338–40, 1038–40, 1093, 1105, 1115–1200, 1248–53, 1413–18, 1440–4, 1468–70; *Annals of Congress*, 16th Cong., 1st Sess., App., pp. 2457, 2458, 2460–1. Only two Northern representatives spoke against congressional power to condition admission on emancipation: *Annals of Congress*, 16th Cong., 1st Sess., pp. 804, 897, 1489.

[169] *Annals of Congress*, 15th Cong., 2nd Sess., p. 1213. See *Annals of Congress*, 16th Cong., 1st Sess., pp. 153–4, 217, 965, 1192.

[170] *Annals of Congress*, 16th Cong., 1st Sess., pp. 1421, 1476 (speeches of Fuller and Plumer).

Slave-state representatives condemned the proposed Missouri and Arkansas restrictions. Every Southerner who spoke out agreed that Congress could not constitutionally require emancipation as a condition for statehood.[171] The overwhelming majority of Southerners in the national legislature either declared that Congress had no power to ban slavery in any territory or relied heavily on arguments later used to deny that power.[172] Prominent Southern notables, including former president James Madison, asserted that slaveholders were constitutionally authorized to bring their human property into the Western regions. All agreed that such measures as had been proposed

[171] For representative speeches, see *Annals of Congress*, 15th Cong., 2nd Sess., pp. 1184–8, 1195–1202, 1228–35; *Annals of Congress*, 16th Cong., 1st Sess., pp. 130–2, 166–70, 307–10, 315–26, 352–9, 1078–83, 1151–7, 1224–35, 1254–61, 1265–75, 1333–9, 1493–1505. See also Brown, "Missouri Crisis," pp. 58–9 (quoting Nathaniel Macon and Thomas Ritchie).

[172] Twenty-one slave-state representatives either asserted that Congress could not constitutionally ban slavery in the territories or advanced arguments in the debate over Missouri statehood that clearly entailed a lack of such Congressional power. See *Annals of Congress*: 15th Cong., 2nd Sess., pp. 1226 (Walker, N.C.), 1229 (McLane); 16th Cong., 1st Sess., pp. 131–2 (Elliot), 164 (Walker, Ga.), 198–9 (Leake), 222 (Macon), 262–3 (Smith), 320 (Barbour), 405 (Pinckney), 992–1009 (Smyth), 1026, 1031 (Reid), 1082 (Hardin), 1167 (McLane), 1236 (Cobb), 1281 (Barbour), 1318–19, 1326–7 (Pinckney), 1337–8 (Rankin), 1364–7 (Johnson, Va.), 1383–91 (Tyler), 1455 (Rhea), 1459–60 (Jones), 1405 (Scott). See also Cooper, *Liberty and Slavery*, p. 140 (quoting Nathaniel Macon); Moore, *Missouri Controversy*, pp. 63–4, 101–2, 121–2, 220, 260; Syndor, *Development*, p. 123. Ninian Edwards from Illinois and John Holmes from Massachusetts also hinted that Congress may have lacked power to ban slavery in the territories: *Annals of Congress*, 16th Cong., 1st Sess., pp. 189, 983–4. Several Southern representatives who spoke did not have their words recorded in the *Annals*, although the evidence indicates that John Randolph in particular attacked the constitutionality of any restriction on slavery. See *Annals of Congress*, 16th Cong., 1st Sess., pp. 1092, 1111, 1453–4. Several free-state representatives acknowledged Southern claims that slavery could not constitutionally be banned in the territories: *Annals of Congress*, 15th Cong., 2nd Sess., pp. 1175–6, 16th Cong., 1st Sess., pp. 337, 340, 1379, 1475. Three slave-state representatives clearly asserted Congressional power: *Annals of Congress*, 16th Cong., 1st Sess., pp. 736 (Mercer), 941 (Smith, Md.), 1561 (Clay). Robert Goodloe Harper, a prominent slaveholder not in Congress at the time, also publicly acknowledged the national power to ban slavery in American territories: H. Niles, "General Harper's Speech," 17 *Niles' Weekly Register*, 434, 435 (February 19, 1820). Three other Southern representatives indicated ambivalence: *Annals of Congress*, 16th Cong., 1st Sess., pp. 1262–3 (Anderson), 1274, 1283–6 (Pindall), 302–7 (Van Dyke). John Quincy Adams recalled that John C. Calhoun and other Southern members of the Monroe cabinet did maintain that Congress had the constitutional authority to ban slavery in the territories: J. Q. Adams, 5 *Memoirs*, pp. 5, 14–15. Adams pointed out, however, that no Southern member of the cabinet "could find any express power to that effect given in the Constitution," and all explicitly rejected claims that the power was located in the territorial clause. Anticipating Taney's position in *Dred Scott*, Calhoun and others insisted that the congressional "power to dispose of and make all needful rules and regulations respecting the territories … of the United States, had reference to land … and that a prohibition of slavery was not needful." Thus, the basic elements of Calhoun's later views were already in place by 1820. As Adams noted, the South Carolinian's claim that Congress could ban slavery in the territories was "in direct opposition to [his] premises": J. Q. Adams, 5 *Memoirs*, p. 5. See also Moore, *Missouri Controversy*, p. 124. Adams was the only cabinet member who thought Congress could make a ban on slavery a condition for statehood: J. Q. Adams, 5 *Memoirs*, p. 9.

would severely compromise the South's status in the Union. Some prominent Southerners threatened secession should their legal understandings not
be recognized as the fundamental law of the land.[173]

Slaveholders in Congress during the Missouri debates anticipated the
central themes of *Dred Scott*. The Northwest Ordinance was pronounced
"void," unconstitutional, or limited to the Northwest Territories.[174] Ten representatives asserted that the territorial clause in Article IV vested Congress
only with power over land or that bans on slavery were not "needful." John
Scott of Missouri declared: "The whole amount of authority Congress could
claim under this clause of the Constitution, was, to make rules and regulations for the surveying and disposing of the public lands, to regulate the
quantities in which it should be sold, the price, and the credit." "By what
principle, or by what rule," William Smith of South Carolina asked, "do you
apply the power over slaves, that is given over the territory only?"[175] Nine
Congressmen from slave states asserted that bans on slavery in the territories
violated the right of Southerners as joint owners to bring their property into
the territories. "I have an equal right with my worthy friend from Pennsylvania," Richard Johnson of Kentucky declared, "to remove with my property
(slaves and all) to Missouri – a common property, purchased with the money
of the whole people."[176] Several slaveholders suggested that federal bans violated the due process clause of the Fifth Amendment.[177] Numerous Southern representatives, anticipating Justice Catron's opinion in *Dred Scott*,[178]
insisted that the Louisiana Purchase treaty guaranteed that slavery would be
legal in territories acquired from France.[179]

---

[173] *Annals of Congress,* 16th Cong., 1st Sess., pp. 1013–14, 1220–1 (Smyth), 1091 (Hardin), 1372
(Johnson). See J. Q. Adams, 5 *Memoirs,* pp. 13–14; Moore, *Missouri Controversy,* pp. 92–3, 260
(quoting the *St. Louis Enquirer,* May 5, 1819).

[174] *Annals of Congress,* 15th Cong., 2nd Sess., p. 1187 (Barbour). See *Annals of Congress,* 16th
Cong., 1st Sess., pp. 164 (Walker, Ga.) (unconstitutional), 983–4 (Holmes) (limited to Northwest Territories), 1000–2 (Smyth) (unconstitutional), 1029 (Reid) (invalid), 1158–9 (McLane)
(limited to Northwest Territories), 1222 (Barbour) ("usurpation"), 1322–3 (Pinckney) ("usurpation"), 1455 (Rhea), 1460 (Jones) (limited to Northwest Territories); 1507 (Scott) (limited to
Northwest Territories).

[175] *Annals of Congress,* 16th Cong., 1st Sess., pp. 1501–2, 262–3. See *Annals of Congress,* 16th
Cong., 1st Sess., pp. 169 (Walker, Ga.), 198–9 (Leake), 230 (Macon), 1003 (Smyth), 1160
(McLane), 1337–8 (Rankin), 1364 (Johnson, Va.), 1386 (Tyler).

[176] *Annals of Congress,* 16th Cong., 1st Sess., p. 351. See *Annals of Congress:* 15th Cong., 2nd Sess.,
p. 1188 (Barbour); 16th Cong., 1st Sess., pp. 189 (Edwards), 222 (Macon), 315 (Barbour), 1009
(Smyth), 1031 (Reid), 1154 (McLane), 1228 (Barbour), 1342 (Rankin), 1390 (Tyler).

[177] *Annals of Congress,* 16th Cong., 1st Sess., pp. 998 (Smyth), 1083 (Hardin), 1261 (Anderson),
1521–2 (Scott).

[178] *Dred Scott v. Sandford,* 60 U.S. 393, 524–9 (1856) (Catron, dissenting).

[179] *Annals of Congress,* 16th Cong., 1st Sess., 1006–8 (Smyth), 1030–1 (Reid), 1078–83 (Hardin),
1143–9 (McLane), 1278 (Pindall), 1364 (Johnson, Va.), 1461–2 (Jones), 1508–13 (Scott).

Concerns with the balance of sectional power played obvious and significant roles in the Missouri and Arkansas debates. The *Charleston Southern Patriot* described the contest as "nakedly a question of political power and management."[180] John Quincy Adams acerbically noted: "The struggle for political power and geographical jealousy ... operated equally on both sides."[181] Northerners regarded slavery in Missouri as the means by which the slave states would control the national government. Should the South triumph, Rufus King predicted, "we shall be lost in political power or influence in the union."[182] The Pennsylvania legislature agreed that the admission of Missouri would "impair the political relations of the several states."[183] Southerners regarded proposed bans as free-state efforts to control the national government. "The true motive for all this dreadful clamor throughout the Union," Pinckney declared, "is, to gain a fixed ascendancy in the representation in Congress." "They want more presidential votes," William Smith bluntly stated.[184] These concerns with the balance of power transformed sectional divisions in the United States. The Louisiana Purchase in 1803 united the South and West against the Northeast. Representatives in 1820 identified themselves (and were identified) by the status of human bondage in their home districts. Harrison Gray Otis of Massachusetts spoke of the contrast between "white peopled States" and "slaveholding States."[185] Benjamin Hardin of Kentucky claimed that proposed bans on slavery were "intended to give to this Union a majority of non-slaveholding states."[186]

The original Constitution successfully survived the first intense sectional debate between North and South. Every antislavery measure passed in 1820 and 1821 enjoyed substantial Southern support. Southern representatives overwhelmingly approved the Missouri Compromise, a legislative package that admitted Missouri as a slave state, admitted Maine as a free state, and

---

[180] Moore, *Missouri Controversy*, p. 300.

[181] J. Q. Adams, 5 *Memoirs*, p. 15. See Moore, *Missouri Controversy*, pp. 126–8, 160–2, 298–9, 328–9, 332, 336; Simpson, "Slave Representation," pp. 335–9; Syndor, *Development*, pp. 126–8.

[182] Moore, *Missouri Controversy*, pp. 180, 299–300; King, 6 *King*, 501. See King, 6 *King*, 267, 282, 289–90, 697–700; *Annals of Congress,* 15th Cong., 2nd Sess., p. 1213 (Tallmadge); Moore, *Missouri Controversy*, pp. 160–2, 298–300, 328–9, 332, 336.

[183] *Annals of Congress,* 16th Cong., 1st Sess., p. 70. See *Annals of Congress:* 15th Cong., 2nd Sess., p. 1134 (Hemphill); 16th Cong., 1st Sess., pp. 153–4 (Morril), 1111 (Cook), 1203 (Sergeant), 337 (Roberts).

[184] *Annals of Congress,* 16th Cong., 1st. Sess., pp. 1314, 383. See *Annals of Congress,* 16th Cong., 1st Sess., pp. 94 (Lloyd), 220 (Macon), 1015 (Smyth), 1089 (Hardin).

[185] *Annals of Congress,* 16th Cong., 1st Sess., p. 254. See *Annals of Congress,* 16th Cong., 1st Sess., pp. 110, 241 (Otis), 337 (Roberts), 1192 (Sergeant), 1398 (Rich), 1438 (Plumer).

[186] *Annals of Congress,* 16th Cong., 1st Sess., p. 1089. See *Annals of Congress,* 16th Cong., 1st Sess., p. 383.

prohibited slavery in all territories north of the 36° 30′ line.[187] Even when the provisions of the Missouri Compromise were voted on separately, a Southern majority supported the ban on slavery above the compromise line. Virginians and, to a lesser extent, Georgians opposed that prohibition. Other Southerners, including South Carolinians, gave the Missouri Compromise line strong support.[188]

Many Southern representatives perceived the Missouri Compromise as a boon for slave states. Most of the area off-limits to slavery was considered to be uninhabitable. Charles Pinckney of South Carolina boasted that the compromise would yield as many as eight slave states while surrendering territory "inhabited by savages and wild beasts, in which not a foot of the Indian claim to soil is extinguished."[189] Hardin thought the region "a wilderness, [with] no inhabitants, citizens of the United States, living thereon."[190] Southern confidence was bolstered by previous experience demonstrating that slave states were fashioned out of slave territories far more rapidly than free states were fashioned out of free territories. Conventional wisdom in 1820 held that "slaveholders were able to clear land far more rapidly than farmers dependent on free labor."[191] Many free-state legislators agreed with their Southern colleagues that the Missouri Compromise would leave Northern states a permanent minority in the national government. "We shall have five more slave states," Rufus King mourned, while only "one state may be formed in the course of half a century on the Mississippi & north of the line 36 30′ N. Lat."[192] Otis thought this assessment too cheerful. "After Maine shall be incorporated," he moaned, "the prospect of another State, with an entirely white population, will be at an end."[193] Some Northerners were more optimistic about the future of free labor in the territories.[194] Still, Fehrenbacher observes, "most southerners and northerners alike seemed convinced that

---

[187] Moore, *Missouri Controversy*, p. 107; Don E. Fehrenbacher, *Sectional Crisis and Southern Constitutionalism* (Louisiana State University Press: Baton Rouge, 1980), p. 18. See Moore, *Missouri Controversy*, pp. 88–9, 107–8, 156, 158, 244; Simpson, "Slave Representation," p. 339.

[188] See Brown, "Missouri Crisis," p. 60. Moore, *Missouri Controversy*, pp. 244–5; Cooper, *Liberty and Slavery*, p. 139.

[189] Moore, *Missouri Controversy*, pp. 114–15 (quoting Charles Pinckney).

[190] *Annals of Congress*, 16th Cong., 1st Sess., p. 1091.

[191] Finkelman, *Slavery*, p. 74. See Harry V. Jaffa, *Crisis of the House Divided: An Interpretation of the Issues in the Lincoln–Douglas Debate* (Doubleday: Garden City, 1959), pp. 140–1; Moore, *Missouri Controversy*, pp. 56–7, 114–15.

[192] King, 6 *King*, p. 289. See King, 6 *King*, pp. 287–8; Moore, *Missouri Controversy*, pp. 200–1.

[193] *Annals of Congress*, 16th Cong., 1st Sess., p. 110.

[194] *Annals of Congress*, 16th Cong., 1st Sess., pp. 1209 (Sergeant), 1279 (Whitman). See Moore, *Missouri Controversy*, pp. 115–18, 202.

the Missouri bird in the hand was worth more than several territorial birds in the bush."[195]

In 1820, the sectional veto trumped constitutional law. The Southern demand for equality in the Union did not encompass the demand that Southern constitutional claims be fully honored. Constitutional rights were "waived" when many Southern representatives supported abandoning claimed Southern rights, and the resulting compromise preserved the balance of sectional power. At the end of the Missouri debates, prominent slave-state congressmen willingly surrendered the right to carry slaves into all American territory in exchange for Missouri statehood and better security for the right to carry slaves into some American territories.[196] Secession was not an issue when Southerners could not agree among themselves whether a bargain over slavery was desirable and when compromises on territorial and other issues were not thought to undermine Southern political power.

Several factors induced Northern support for the Missouri Compromise. Some free-state representatives were cowed by disunion talk emanating from the slave states. Prominent New Yorkers warned that efforts to ban slavery in the West would "terminate in a Severance of Empire."[197] Equal state voting in the Senate, once thought a concession to the North, gave the South enough strength to prevent House proposals for gradual emancipation in Missouri from becoming law. The resulting legislative deadlock compelled sectional compromise in order for any legislation to pass. Other free-state Jeffersonians supported the compromise, suspecting that proposals to ban slavery were a Federalist plot to regain political control of Northern states and the national government. Party stalwarts preferred the spoils of office to a free Missouri.[198]

Although the Missouri Compromise excited Congress more than the nation and had limited immediate electoral consequences,[199] the long-term impact of the legislative debate and resulting legislative practices undermined the original solution to the problem of constitutional evil. For Southerners, the Missouri Compromise highlighted the increasing need to gain free-state votes to secure proslavery policies. Sectional balance in the Senate, national political parties, and constitutional demands combined with secession threats made their debut as means for protecting Southern interests. All

---

[195] Fehrenbacher, *Sectional Crisis*, p. 19.
[196] See Moore, *Missouri Controversy*, pp. 122–3.
[197] Moore, *Missouri Controversy*, p. 177 (quoting Morgan Lewis).
[198] See Moore, *Missouri Controversy*, pp. 106–7, 151, 200–1; Morrison, *Slavery*, pp. 51–2.
[199] Moore, *Missouri Controversy*, p. 341.

would have long runs. For antislavery Northerners, the Missouri Compromise highlighted the importance of forming a sectional party that could become the national legislative majority necessary to abolish slavery.[200] Rufus King thought Missouri might provide a rallying point to break Jeffersonian strength in the North. Both he and other anti-Missouri Northerners regarded the central issue in the conflict as the balance of power in the Union, "whether 'Virginian' rule should be perpetrated, or the balance of power be righted in favor of the free states." "THIS QUESTION INVOLVES … THE FUTURE WEIGHT AND INFLUENCE OF THE FREE STATES," the *New York Daily Advertiser* trumpeted. "IF NOW LOST – IT IS LOST FOREVER."[201] Thirty-five years later, under even better demographic conditions, Abraham Lincoln would find a more persuasive appeal.

The Constitutional Order Modified: 1820–1860

In the years following the Missouri Compromise, sectional moderates faced increasing challenges. Northern population grew much faster than Southern population, and free states proved far easier to fashion out of free territories than anyone imagined. Attitudes toward human bondage evolved in ways that confounded the original expectations of New Englanders, Virginians, and South Carolinians alike. Sectionalism hardened. Southerners became less willing to consider emancipation. Northerners became more opposed to slavery. These developments left nineteenth-century unionists struggling to find means for preserving the constitutional commitment to bisectionalism when the free states had the population necessary to control the national government, a growing number of free-state citizens were committed to forming a free-state majority, and those citizens had the power necessary to block a formal constitutional amendment that might better secure the balance of sectional power.

New Demographics

Despite the three-fifths clause, the growth of slavery in the Lower South, the annexation of Texas, and the congressional failure to ban slavery in territories acquired after the Mexican War, every decade between 1820 and 1860 witnessed an increase in the relative population and political power of the North. Immigrants, Eric Foner notes, "demonstrated their preference for

---

[200] The Missouri Compromise also inspired more aggressive free-state efforts to repeal the three-fifths clause: Moore, *Missouri Controversy*, pp. 51, 58, 67.

[201] Moore, *Missouri Controversy*, pp. 75, 85.

life in a free labor society by refusing to settle in the South."[202] Virginia in 1790 had almost twice the population and representation of New York. By 1850, New York had nearly three times the population and representation of Virginia. Ohio, a territory in 1790, had more population and representation than any slave state in 1850. The framers thought Georgia would be a particularly populous state and Wisconsin a frigid wasteland. Less than a decade after achieving statehood, Wisconsin had a larger free population than Georgia. By the late 1850s, the Northern white population was more than double that of the Southern white population.[203] Southerners who hoped the Mexican War might increase proslavery political power were bitterly disappointed when New Mexico applied for statehood in 1850 with a proposed state constitution that outlawed slavery.[204] Slavery might have thrived in the Far West under the proper political conditions.[205] Still, Southerners at mid-century had no reason to believe that any new state would have a relatively enduring commitment to slavery. In his last speech, Calhoun complained that "there is not a single territory in progress in the Southern section, and no certainty that any additional [slave] State will be added during the decade."[206]

These trends changed the balance of power in the federal government. In 1790, 57 members of the House represented free states while 49 represented slave states. Thirty years later the respective numbers were 123 and 90, and by 1850 they were 147 and 90.[207] For a time, the approximately equal number of slave and free states partly compensated for increasing Northern control of the House of Representatives.[208] After California joined the Union in 1850, however, the Senate had six more representatives from free states than from slave states. These increases in free-state population and in the number of free states gave the North a substantial electoral college advantage. Antislavery coalitions could win presidential elections even when

[202] Eric Foner, *Free Soil, Free Labor, Free Men: The Ideology of the Republican Party before the Civil War* (Oxford University Press: London, 1970), p. 236. See *Congressional Globe*, 31st Cong., 1st Sess., App., p. 263 (Seward).

[203] Jesse T. Carpenter, *The South as a Conscious Minority: A Study in Political Thought* (University of South Carolina Press: Columbia, 1990), pp. 21–2.

[204] Mark J. Stegmaier, *Texas, New Mexico, and the Compromise of 1850: Boundary Dispute & Sectional Crisis* (Kent State University Press: Kent, 1996), p. 119.

[205] Jaffa, *House Divided*, p. 397; *Congressional Globe*, 31st Cong., 1st Sess., pp. 1697–8 (Thomas Clingman).

[206] *Congressional Globe*, 31st Cong., 1st Sess., p. 451. See David M. Potter, *The Impending Crisis: 1848–1861* (ed. Don E. Fehrenbacher) (Harper & Row: New York, 1976), p. 93.

[207] All statistics in this and the following paragraph are taken from Harold W. Stanley and Richard G. Niemi, *Vital Statistics on American Politics*, 2nd ed. (CQ Press: Washington, D.C., 1990), pp. 179–80.

[208] See Potter, *Impending Crisis*, p. 28.

they did not completely unite the North. Republicans after the Mexican War could control the executive branch despite losing Pennsylvania or any three states west of Ohio.

New Ideologies and Political Movements

Equally unanticipated developments in sectionalism further aggravated the divisive consequences of these unexpected population trends. The national trend toward emancipation that began during the late eighteenth century continued unabated north of Maryland as the Industrial Revolution increased the demand for wage labor. The ink was hardly dry on the Constitution, however, when liberalizing trends in much of the South halted abruptly. Increased international demand for cotton, concerns with maintaining local political hegemony, and an unwillingness to consider the consequences of living in a multiracial society combined to snuff out liberal sentiments among the plantation elite.

Proslavery in the South. The late eighteenth century marked the high-water mark for emancipatory trends in most slave states. By the early nineteenth century, Southern opponents of slavery were mournfully declaring: "We are in fact dead" with "no hope of reanimation."[209] Liberal manumission laws heralding the eventual extinction of slavery were repealed.[210] Liberalizing judicial doctrines were ignored or overruled.[211] Antislavery literature was burned, censored, and barred from the mails.[212] Antislavery societies were disbanded.[213] A strong effort to get Virginia to adopt a very, very gradual emancipation policy was swept aside by the state legislature in 1832.[214] Southern state legislatures that once inched toward abolition now spoke of "the evil and pernicious practice of freeing slaves."[215]

After ratification, Southern politicians and intellectuals began claiming with increasing frequency that slavery was a positive good. South Carolinians

---

[209] Klinkner and Smith, *Unsteady March,* p. 27. See Kolchin, *Slavery,* pp. 86–90.

[210] Kolchin, *Slavery,* pp. 89–90, 128; Robinson, *Slavery,* p. 49; Potter, *Impending Crisis,* p. 39; Smith, *Civic Ideals,* pp. 178–9, 254; Klinkner and Smith, *Unsteady March,* p. 27; Cooper, *Liberty and Slavery,* p. 98.

[211] See especially *State v. Mann,* 2 Dev. 263 (N.C. 1829). See also Wiecek, *Antislavery,* pp. 142–4.

[212] Michael Kent Curtis, *Free Speech, "The People's Darling Privilege": Struggles for the Freedom of Expression in American History* (Duke University Press: Durham, 2000), pp. 131–215, 271–99; Clement Eaton, *The Freedom-of-Thought Struggle in the Old South,* rev. ed. (Harper & Row: New York, 1964).

[213] Syndor, *Development,* p. 242.

[214] A. Freehling, *Drift,* pp. 122–69; W. Freehling, *Disunion,* pp. 181–9. The Virginia legislature did, however, declare that slavery was an "evil" and looked forward to the "final abolition" of that institution: A. Freehling, *Drift,* p. 164.

[215] Robinson, *Slavery,* p. 290 n.°.

in the First Congress vigorously defended their peculiar institution.[216] In the 1790s, several Southern notables gave lectures and issued pamphlets on the virtues of human bondage.[217] Representative Peter Early of Georgia informed Congress in 1806 that "a large majority of people in the Southern states do not consider slavery as an evil."[218] Southern representatives defended the morality of slavery in greater numbers during the Missouri Crisis.[219] Shortly after Virginia refused to move toward emancipation in 1832, Thomas Dew issued the first sustained American justification of black slavery.[220] John C. Calhoun publicly described slavery as "the most safe and stable basis for free institutions in the world."[221] By the 1850s, the joy of slavery was a staple of Southern rhetoric, particularly in the Lower South.[222]

Proslavery politics and economics moved in lockstep with proslavery ideology. By the 1850s, large slaveholders had solidified their hegemonic hold over Southern politics. Various malapportionment schemes ensured a privileged place for plantation owners in local legislatures. Slaveholding elites maintained the centrality of agriculture in Southern political economy by preventing important changes in common-law doctrines that facilitated industrialization in the North.[223] Some masters nevertheless explored how slaves might become craft and industrial workers, a practice that might have strengthened slavery in the Upper South and enabled human bondage to move westward more easily.[224] Southern laws criminalized moderate

---

[216] *Annals of Congress*, 1st Cong., 2nd Sess., pp. 1229, 1242–3 (James Jackson), 1503–14 (William Loughton Smith). See Newman, "Prelude to the Gag Rule," pp. 583–4; Joseph C. Burke, "The Proslavery Argument in the First Congress," 16 *Duquesne Review*, 3–4, 7–10 (1969); Fehrenbacher, *Slaveholding Republic*, p. 138.

[217] William Graham, "An Important Question Answered," reprinted in David W. Robson, "'An Important Question Answered': William Graham's Defense of Slavery in Post-Revolutionary Virginia," 37 *William and Mary Quarterly*, 3rd Ser., 644 (1980). See Cooper, *Liberty and Slavery*, p. 98.

[218] *Annals of Congress*, 9th Cong., 2nd Sess., p. 238. See Robinson, *Slavery*, p. 331; Cooper, *Liberty and Slavery*, p. 99. For Southern defenses of slavery as a positive good, see *Annals of Congress*, 15th Cong., 2nd Sess., pp. 1186–9, 1233–4; *Annals of Congress*, 16th Cong., 1st Sess., pp. 1324–7.

[219] *Annals of Congress*, 16th Cong., 1st Sess., pp. 173 (Walker), 226 (Macon), 266–75 (Smith), 1323–5 (Pinckney).

[220] Thomas R. Dew, *Review of the Debate [on the Abolition of Slavery] in the Virginia Legislature of 1831 and 1832* (T.W. White: Richmond, 1832). See W. Freehling, *Disunion*, pp. 190–3; Wiecek, *Antislavery*, pp. 147–8, 220.

[221] *Congressional Globe*, 25th Cong., 2nd Sess., App., pp. 61–2.

[222] See Potter, *Impending Crisis*, p. 383; Ronald T. Takaki, *A Pro-Slavery Crusade: The Agitation to Reopen the African Slave Trade* (Free Press: New York, 1971), pp. 19–22, 78–80, 86, 96–101; William J. Cooper, Jr., *The South and the Politics of Slavery, 1828–1856* (Louisiana State University Press: Baton Rouge, 1978), pp. 59–60.

[223] See Howard Schweber, *The Creation of American Common Law, 1850–1880: Technology, Politics, and the Construction of Citizenship* (Cambridge University Press: New York, 2004).

[224] See Takaki, *Pro-Slavery Crusade*, pp. 39–49.

antislavery sentiments of the type once routinely expressed by all prominent Southern moderates. Hinton Helper was chased out of the South for making white supremacist attacks on slavery.[225]

The prospects for eventual abolition were not entirely bleak during the 1850s. Slavery remained under significant political attack in the border states. In 1847, the Delaware legislature came within a vote of passing a bill that would eventually have freed all slaves in that state.[226] Proponents of conditional termination retained some influence on mid–nineteenth-century politics in the Upper South.[227] Still, by 1850, Virginians spoke of abandoning slavery through increased slave sales to the Lower South[228] rather than through manumission. No reason existed for thinking emancipation would take place farther south than Maryland, Kentucky, or Missouri without active federal efforts.[229]

Antislavery in the North. Slave-state hopes that commercial intercourse would increase free-state support for human bondage were partly realized during the early nineteenth century. Cotton Whigs in New England expressed no interest in emancipation and supported fugitive slave laws. Most free-state citizens wanted no part of an abolition movement that might encourage black migration northward. Senator William Allen of Ohio declared: "The people of the free States know that if they succeeded in obtaining emancipation at present, they must take the negroes." "As far as New York is concerned," Representative George Rathbun asserted, "should the refuse part of the population from Virginia reach our territory, we will carry them back to Virginia."[230] These same racist attitudes also underlay increased Northern opposition to slavery in the territories. Free-state citizens indifferent to emancipation did not want to compete with black labor. "Admit the slave," Representative Robert McClelland of Michigan stated, "and you expel the free laborer."[231] Charles Clarke of Michigan declared that "[e]verybody knows ... the existence of slavery in a Territory or State excludes, effectively excludes all white laboring men."[232]

[225] Curtis, *Free Speech*, pp. 271–88.

[226] See W. Freehling, *Disunion*, pp. 197–210.

[227] W. Freehling, *Disunion*, pp. 119–23, 181–96; A. Freehling, *Drift*, pp. 154–5, 158, 231–4, 248–9.

[228] W. Freehling, *Disunion*, pp. 418–23, 468–71, 554.

[229] Kolchin, *Slavery*, p. 179.

[230] *Congressional Globe*, 28th Cong., 2nd Sess., p. 343; *Congressional Globe*, 29th Cong., 2nd Sess., App., p. 180.

[231] *Congressional Globe*, 29th Cong., 2nd Sess., App., p. 392.

[232] *Congressional Globe*, 31st Cong., 1st Sess., App., p. 565. See *Congressional Globe*, 31st Cong., 1st Sess., p. 1701.

The ranks of Northerners who regarded slavery as a moral wrong swelled during the mid-nineteenth century. Between the Missouri Compromise and the Mexican War, antislavery advocates lost faith that slavery would gradually disappear as long as Virginia moderates controlled public policy. In 1820, John Quincy Adams privately noted what many Northerners were discovering: "In the abstract they admit that slavery is an evil,... [b]ut when probed to the quick upon it, they show at the bottom of their souls pride and vainglory in their condition of masterdom." [233] American abolitionists abandoned gradualism for immediatism during the 1830s, [234] at the same time that the last major emancipation effort in Virginia failed and Southerners began censoring antislavery speech. [235] If slavery was going to disappear, an increasing number of Northerners concluded, the federal government would have to take proactive steps to facilitate emancipation.

Most antislavery advocates concluded that slavery could be constitutionally abandoned only when the balance of sectional power shifted. A few radical abolitionists repudiated the Constitution, insisting that the text imposed too many unjust protections for slavery. [236] For most abolitionists and mainstream Northern opponents of slavery, the problem was not the Constitution but rather the proslavery officials interpreting it. Opponents of slavery could bring about emancipation, they argued, by taking advantage of Northern population superiority and wresting control of the national government from the slaveholding elite. Once control over national institutions was established, antislavery Northerners proposed, the national government could more actively pursue emancipation than most persons responsible for the Constitution of 1787 had thought necessary.

Members of the Liberty, Free-Soil, and Republican parties asserted that the Constitution's republican aspirations had been subverted by an undemocratic "Slave Power." This "aristocracy of slaveholders" [237] exercised a control

---

[233] J. Q. Adams, 5 *Memoirs*, p. 10.

[234] Wiecek, *Antislavery*, pp. 85, 151–5, 159–62, 167–71.

[235] See also Gerard N. Magliocca, "The Cherokee Removal and the Fourteenth Amendment," 53 *Duke Law Journal*, 875, 907–14 (1993) (noting how Native American removal soured antislavery advocates on colonization).

[236] Wendell Phillips, *The Constitution Is a Pro-Slavery Compact or, Extracts from the Madison Papers, Etc.* (American Anti-Slavery Society: New York, 1856); Henry David Thoreau, *The Portable Thoreau* (ed. Carl Bode) (Penguin: New York, 1975), p. 120. See Henry Mayer, *All on Fire: William Lloyd Garrison and the Abolition of Slavery* (St. Martin's Griffin: New York, 1998), pp. 65, 175, 312–28, 319, 339, 341, 368, 397–8, 531. Many radical abolitionists before 1860 hoped for disunion. See Stampp, *And the War Came*, pp. 247–8.

[237] Foner, *Free Soil*, p. 89. See *Congressional Globe*, 31st Cong., 1st Sess., App., pp. 473–4, 479 (Salmon Chase), 511 (David Wilmot). Samuel Portland Chase and Charles Dexter Cleveland, *Anti-Slavery Addresses of 1844 and 1845* (J.A. Bancroft: Philadelphia, 1867), pp. 96–7.

over national policy that was disproportionate to their actual numbers. Free-state politicians and intellectuals spoke of "a vast moneyed corporation, bound together by an indissoluble unity of interest, by a common sense of a common danger, counseling at all times for its common protection; wielding the whole power, and controlling the destiny of the nation." [238] Sectional politics was about whether that aristocratic minority or popular free-state majorities would govern. Antislavery advocates asserted that "the slaveholding states desire to secure for themselves an absolute ascendancy in the Federal councils, so that they can shape the legislation of the country." "The object of the South is manifest," Republicans claimed: "she is determined to rule this nation in all time to come." [239]

Lincoln and other advocates of free soil found majoritarianism a powerful rhetorical weapon for uniting Northerners against slaveholders. [240] Republican newspapers consistently asserted that slavery policies violated republican principles by allowing minority rule. "If our Government, for the sake of Slavery, is to be perpetually the representative of a minority," one journal declared, "it may continue republican in form, but the substance of its republicanism has departed." [241] William Seward declared that the central issue of the day was "whether a slaveholding class exclusively shall govern America." [242] Few aspects of public policy, antislavery advocates contended, escaped minority control in the slaveholding republic. Republicans "feared the effect of continued national rule by slaveholding interests on northern rights, on civil liberties, on desired economic measures and on the future of free white labor itself." [243] Southern efforts to censor antislavery speech in the House of Representatives and in slave states confirmed suspicions that slavery and republicanism were fundamentally at odds. The slave power, Benjamin Wade declared, was "an oligarchy" that "reigns and domineers over four fifth of the people of the South;... which gags the press; which restrains the liberty of speech." [244] Economic policy was also undemocratically dictated by the slaveholding minority. "[L]et us admit Texas," Joshua

---

[238] Wiecek, *Antislavery,* p. 211 (quoting Francis Jackson).

[239] Morrison, *Slavery,* pp. 150, 113.

[240] William E. Gienapp, "The Republican Party and the Slave Power," *New Perspectives on Race and Slavery in America: Essays in Honor of Kenneth Stampp* (ed. Robert H. Abzug and Stephen E. Maizish) (University Press of Kentucky: Lexington, 1986), p. 57.

[241] Gienapp, "Slave Power," p. 65 (quoting the *Cincinnati Commercial*).

[242] Seward, 4 *Works,* p. 274.

[243] See Larry Gara, "Slavery and the Slave Power: A Crucial Distinction," 15 *Civil War History,* 5, 6 (1969).

[244] *Congressional Globe,* 33rd Cong., 2nd Sess., App., p. 751. See *Congressional Globe,* 34th Cong., 1st Sess., App., p. 854 (Henry Wilson).

Giddings asserted, "and ... our tariff will then be held at the will of the Texian advocates of free trade."[245] These concerns made the antislavery crusade as much a jihad for white liberty as for black freedom. "Every free state man must feel that the Slave oligarchy must be crushed or his own freedom given up," Northern editorials warned.[246]

Northern opponents of slavery championed a general policy – variously described as "the absolute and unconditional divorce of the Government from slavery,"[247] "freedom national,"[248] "opposition to slavery within the constitution,"[249] and the "denationalization of slavery entirely"[250] – that required the federal government to take all steps toward emancipation short of direct interference with slavery in a state.[251] Free-state parties would ban slavery in all territories, refuse to admit slave states into the Union, forbid federal officials from recovering fugitive slaves, emancipate all slaves in the nation's capital, and abolish the interstate slave trade.[252] Many party members hoped an antislavery administration would also use the power of appointment and the post office to encourage local abolition movements within slave states. "We should be far from countenancing any legislative interference with Slavery in the States, which we regard as unconstitutional," a Republican paper opined, "but the Government may legitimately use its patronage and influence to encourage the growth of principles congenial with its own."[253]

Opposition to slavery in the territories was the centerpiece of antislavery party platforms. Northerners feared that introducing slavery in the West would cause the free states to "be bourne down by the influence of ... slaveholding aristocratic institutions."[254] "The Slave-Power," others declared, "showed the ultimate design of cutting the free states, with a line of slave

---

[245] *Congressional Globe*, 28th Cong., 1st Sess., App., p. 705.

[246] Morrison, *Slavery*, p. 166 (quoting the *Cincinnati Gazette*).

[247] Foner, *Free Soil*, p. 79; Chase and Cleveland, *Antislavery Addresses*, pp. 96, 100. See also Charles Sumner, *The Works of Charles Sumner*, vol. 2 (Lee & Shepard: Boston, 1870–1883), p. 284.

[248] Foner, *Free Soil*, p. 83; *Congressional Globe*, 31st Cong., 1st Sess., p. 474.

[249] Foner, *Free Soil*, p. 117; Edward Lillie Pierce, *Memoir and Letters of Charles Sumner*, vol. 3 (Roberts Bros.: Boston, 1893), p. 310.

[250] Wiecek, *Antislavery*, p. 216; Richard H. Sewell, *Ballots for Freedom: Antislavery Politics in the United States, 1837–1860* (Oxford University Press: New York, 1976), p. 285.

[251] Republicans did repeatedly insist that the national government had no power to regulate slavery directly in a state. Even the American Antislavery Society conceded that "each State, in which slavery exists, has, by the Constitution of the United States, the exclusive right to legislate in regard to its abolition in said State": Wiecek, *Antislavery*, p. 169 (quoting Proceedings of the Anti-Slavery Convention). Republican radicals in Congress made similar points: *Congressional Globe*, 31st Cong., 1st Sess., App., p. 268 (Seward); 34th Cong., 3rd Sess., p. 11 (John P. Hale).

[252] Foner, *Free Soil*, pp. 79–80, 83–4, 115–19; Wiecek, *Antislavery*, pp. 216–17.

[253] Foner, *Free Soil*, p. 122 (quoting the *National Era*).

[254] Morrison, *Slavery*, p. 57.

states to the Canada line, from all possible extension toward the great West and Mexico." Should slaveholders win this "open contest for supremacy," the South would gain "a majority in the Senate which would then become practically a House of Lords, with a veto on all legislation and with a claim to a larger share of the patronage of government."[255] Successfully implemented, however, territorial prohibitions promised to secure abolition by strangulation and political might. Republican proposals, Lincoln frequently noted, would "arrest the future speed of [slavery], and place it where the public mind shall rest in the belief that it is in the course of ultimate extinction."[256]

Each additional free state increased free-state power in the national government. The *New York Times* recognized that "the real contest was for political power."[257] William Seward boasted that the admission of additional free states in the 1850s ensured the triumph of antislavery interests in forthcoming political struggles.[258] "We will engage in competition for the virgin soil of freedom," he declared after the passage of the Kansas–Nebraska Act. "We will engage in competition for the virgin soil of Kansas, and God give the victory to the side which is stronger in numbers as it is in right."[259] No Republican felt obliged to gain Southern support for any antislavery measure. Antislavery advocates would triumph by outvoting the South. "The change can be now made," Seward advised fellow Northerners, "by the agency of the ballot box." Lincoln agreed that "peaceful ballots only, are necessary."[260]

This sectional strategy was constitutionally legitimate in the eyes of its devotees. The antislavery Constitution permitted any coalition, national or sectional, that established a legislative majority by constitutional means to determine public policy. William Seward condemned John C. Calhoun for maintaining "that the free States having already ... majorities of States, majorities of population, and majorities of both houses of Congress, shall concede to the slave States, being a minority in both, the unequal advantage of an equality." Such concessions were "subversive of the principle of democratic institutions," argued one antislavery congressman.[261] Northern political activists in the free states declared that Republicans would succeed

[255]　Morrison, *Slavery*, p. 169 (quoting John Murray Forbes and Cassius Marcellus Clay).

[256]　Abraham Lincoln, *The Collected Works of Abraham Lincoln*, vol. 2 (ed. Roy P. Basler) (Rutgers University Press: New Brunswick, 1953), p. 461.

[257]　Gienapp, "Slave Power," pp. 57–8 (quoting the *New York Times*, May 30, 1860); Seward, 4 *Works*, p. 274.

[258]　*Congressional Globe*, 35th Cong., 1st Sess., pp. 521, 1044, 1980. See Foner, *Free Soil*, pp. 222, 236.

[259]　*Congressional Globe*, 33rd Cong., 1st Sess., App., p. 769.

[260]　Seward, 4 *Works*, p. 237; Lincoln, 2 *Collected Works*, p. 454.

[261]　*Congressional Globe*, 31st Cong., 1st Sess., App., p. 263.

"by securing a majority in the Senate and in the House of Representatives, and voting you gentlemen of the South down."[262] Southern and Northern majorities were felt to be equally legitimate. "The slaveholders have ruled the American government for the last fifty years," Frederick Douglass proclaimed; "[l]et the anti-slavery party rule the nation for the next fifty years."[263]

New Foundations for Bisectionalism

Southern political leaders understood that their fundamental political problems resulted from population trends that were causing control over the national government to slip from their grasp. "The great and primary cause" of discontent in the slave states, Calhoun declared in his valedictory address to the Senate, was that "the equilibrium between the two sections, in the Government as it stood when the constitution was ratified ... has been destroyed." The senior senator from South Carolina maintained that, "as things now stand, the Southern states cannot remain in the Union" because "the North has acquired a decided ascendancy over every department of this government."[264] Disunionists pointed to Northern demographic superiority when justifying secession.[265] *De Bow's Review* warned Southern unionists in 1860 that the free states had the population necessary to exercise "permanent control of one branch of the federal government, and will, ... within the next four or five years, attain in the other a clear and working majority."[266]

Numerous proposals for increasing Southern political power circulated during the years between the Missouri Compromise and the Civil War. Southerners who championed Texas noted how acquisition would favorably adjust the balance of power. Senator Albert Brown declared: "Annex Texas ... and you give the South a degree of influence in the councils of a nation which will enable her to assert her rights with confidence and maintain them with independence."[267] Some viewed Caribbean and Central American nations as potential slave states. Jefferson Davis insisted such acquisitions were

[262] *Congressional Globe*, 33rd Cong., 2nd Sess., App., p. 238 (Henry Wilson). See Charles Sumner, "The Antislavery Enterprise: Its Necessity, Practicality, and Dignity; with Glances at the Special Duties of the North," 4 *Works of Sumner*, pp. 50–1.

[263] Frederick Douglass, *The Frederick Douglass Papers: Series One: Speeches, Debates, and Interviews*, vol. 3, 1855–63 (Yale University Press: New Haven, 1985), p. 365.

[264] John C. Calhoun, *The Works of John C. Calhoun*, vol. 4 (ed. Richard K. Cralle) (Appleton: New York, 1861), pp. 544, 576, 551.

[265] See George H. Reese, ed., *Proceedings of the Virginia State Convention of 1861*, vol. 1 (Virginia State Library: Richmond, 1965), p. 63.

[266] Robert W. Johannsen, *Lincoln, the South, and Slavery: The Political Dimension* (Louisiana State University Press: Baton Rouge, 1991), p. 123.

[267] Cooper, *The South*, p. 196.

vital means for "increas[ing] the number of slaveholding constituencies." [268] Overoptimistic Southern filibusters promised that acquiring Mexico would lead to twenty-five additional slave states.[269] Slaveholders did not have to go abroad to gain political power in the 1850s. Texas, under the treaty of annexation, could be broken up into as many as five states, all of which might have been represented by proslavery advocates. Dividing California in half might also have produced another slave state.[270] The international slave trade provided still another means for preserving the sectional balance of power. A massive influx of new slaves, each of whom counted for three fifths of a person when apportioning representation, would have significantly augmented proslavery influence in the national government. "It takes people to make States," Alexander Stephens pointed out, "and it requires people of the African race to make slave states." [271]

In the new constitutional politics of slavery, whoever controlled the West controlled the national government.[272] Jefferson Davis declared that so-called antislavery advocates were less concerned with slaves in the Western Territories than with "grasping for political power" and "weaken[ing] the political power of the Southern states ... to promote the industry of New England States." [273] Expansion was also vital, slaveholders believed, because human bondage would not survive politically or economically if denied access to the West. Robert Toombs informed a Georgia legislature considering secession that "we must expand or perish." [274] Finally, territorial bans on slavery insulted slave states.[275] Prohibiting slavery in territories strongly implied that slavery was a moral wrong that should be eradicated as soon as politically feasible. "If it is right to preclude or abolish slavery in a Territory," the

---

[268] *Congressional Globe*, 35th Cong., 2nd Sess., p. 347. See Robert E. May, *The Southern Dream of a Caribbean Empire, 1854–1861* (Louisiana State University Press: Baton Rouge, 1973), pp. 4–12, 36–9, 49–53, 57–8, 114–19, 132–4, 136–42, 148–51, 161–2, 169–76, 186–93, 232–3; Cooper, *Liberty and Slavery*, p. 219.

[269] Potter, *Impending Crisis*, pp. 466–7; May, *Southern Dream*, p. 150.

[270] See *Congressional Globe*, 31st Cong., 1st Sess., pp. 436–9; Stegmaier, *Texas*, pp. 95, 104–7, 146; Holman Hamilton, *Prologue to Conflict: The Crisis and Compromise of 1850* (Norton: New York, 1964), p. 50.

[271] Henry Cleveland, *Alexander Stephens in Public and Private* (National Publishing Company: Philadelphia, 1866), p. 646; Takaki, *Pro-Slavery Crusade*, pp. 1–2, 4–6, 25–7, 167.

[272] See Potter, *Impending Crisis*, p. 33; Morrison, *Slavery*, p. 6.

[273] *Congressional Globe*, 35th Cong., 1st Sess., p. 441; Morrison, *Slavery*, pp. 117–18.

[274] Robert Toombs, "Robert Toombs's Secession Speech, Tuesday Evening, November 13," *Secession Debated: Georgia's Showdown in 1860* (ed. William W. Freehling and Craig M. Simpson) (Oxford University Press: New York, 1992), p. 40. See *Congressional Globe*, 26th Cong., 1st Sess., App., p. 77.

[275] See *Congressional Globe*, 25th Cong., 2nd Sess., App., p. 558 (Preston).

South Carolina secession convention opined, "why should it be allowed to remain in the States?"[276]

Legal Protections for Slavery. Law was the first line of defense against Northern population advantages. "What bulwark of defense was stronger than the Constitution itself?" Senator Robert Strange of North Carolina asked in 1837.[277] Henry Clay declared, "the Constitution remains a perpetual and sure bulwark against all attacks upon the rights of the slaveholding States."[278] Northern population increases were constitutionally irrelevant when slaveholders rights were constitutionally guaranteed. Southern politicians and journalists declared that slave states "would freely and voluntarily, cooly and deliberately withdraw from the Confederation" should the national government violate Southern constitutional rights.[279]

Leading Southern politicians and government officials made numerous constitutional demands. In December 1837, John C. Calhoun insisted the Senate pass six resolutions supporting the constitutional rights of slaveholding states. The crucial resolutions declared that Congress had no power to abolish slavery in the District of Columbia, no power to abolish slavery in any territory, and no power to consider the morality of slavery when deciding whether to acquire additional territory.[280] The Nashville Convention of 1850 repeated Calhoun's claim that slavery could not constitutionally be banned in any territory.[281] The "Georgia Platform," adopted earlier that year, insisted that the Constitution imposed upon all representatives certain legal obligations, the violation of which would justify secession. "The American Union," that document proclaimed, is "secondary in importance ... to the rights and principles it was designed to perpetuate." Georgia would "resist even ... to a disruption of every tie which binds her to the Union, any action of Congress ... incompatible with the safety, domestic tranquility, the rights and honor of the slave-holding states."[282] In 1860, Jefferson Davis proposed resolutions committing Congress to passing a territorial slave code should one prove necessary.[283]

---

[276] Foner, *Free Soil*, p. 315.
[277] *Congressional Globe*, 25th Cong., 2nd Sess., p. 59.
[278] *Congressional Globe*, 25th Cong., 2nd Sess., App., p. 57.
[279] Cooper, *The South*, p. 64 (quoting Thomas Ritchie).
[280] *Congressional Globe*, 25th Cong., 2nd Sess., p. 55. See *Congressional Globe*, 29th Cong., 2nd Sess., p. 455 (1847).
[281] "Resolutions of the Nashville Convention," 1 *Documents of American History*, p. 325.
[282] "The Georgia Platform, 1850," 1 *Documents of American History*, pp. 323–4.
[283] *Congressional Globe*, 36th Cong., 1st Sess., pp. 658–9, 1937.

Dred Scott clinched the legal deal. Slaveholders interpreted that decision as demonstrating unequivocal support for Southern constitutional understandings. "The umpire selected as the referee in this controversy," Davis asserted, "has decided that neither Congress nor its agent, the territorial government, has the power to invade or impair the right of property within the limits of a Territory."[284] As interpreted by slaveholders, *Dred Scott* required Congress to pass a federal slave code when territories failed to respect Southern property rights.[285] Northern Democrats who insisted on waiting for further judicial clarification, slaveholders thought, were insufficiently mindful of their constitutional obligations. "If the Supreme Court have decided ... that slaves are property, and if the legislative authorities of the Territories have attempted to interfere," Andrew Johnson asked, "why not, like men, propose by legislative enactment by Congress, to protect slave property in the Territories?"[286]

Calhoun and his supporters thought constitutional fidelity and enlightened self-interest would induce free-state support for these constitutional demands. "If we stand fast," Calhoun declared, "all who agree with us from every quarter ... will ultimately rally around our principles and the Constitution." His resolutions would "create an awakening spirit in the country in favor of the Constitution."[287] "A strong moral impression," Strange agreed, "would thereby be made in our favor in the non-slaveholding states."[288] South Carolinians were confident that Northern industrialists did not want to disrupt Southern labor practices. "The North is as much interested in upholding the slaveholding States as the latter can be themselves," Calhoun maintained. "Annihilate the products of [slave] labor," he stated, "and what would become of the great shipping, navigating, commercial, and manufacturing interests of the non-slaveholding States?"[289]

This reliance on constitutional law repeatedly proved to be politically inadequate. Calhoun had no difficulty gaining Northern support for such staples of Jacksonian rhetoric as state control over domestic institutions; most antebellum free-state representatives needed little inducement to condemn

---

[284] *Congressional Globe*, 36th Cong., 1st Sess., p. 1941. See *Congressional Globe*, 36th Cong., 1st Sess., pp. 1966, 1968–9 (Judah Benjamin), 1970 (Thomas Clingman), 2150 (Jefferson Davis), 2235–7 (Benjamin), 2341 (John Crittenden).

[285] *Congressional Globe*, 36th Cong., 1st Sess., p. 1941.

[286] *Congressional Globe*, 36th Cong., 1st Sess., p. 1972. See *Congressional Globe*, 36th Cong., 1st Sess., p. 2122 (Jefferson Davis).

[287] *Congressional Globe*, 25th Cong., 2nd Sess., App., p. 61; *Congressional Globe*, 25th Cong., 2nd Sess., p. 59.

[288] *Congressional Globe*, 25th Cong., 2nd Sess., App., p. 63.

[289] *Congressional Globe*, 29th Cong., 2nd Sess., 467; Calhoun, 4 *Works*, pp. 385–6.

abolitionists and deny federal power to interfere with slavery within states.[290] On crucial specifics, however, the national legislature consistently balked. Most Northerners and many Southerners refused to support resolutions declaring that Congress had no power to ban slavery in the District of Columbia or in all territories. Substitute resolutions were passed declaring inexpedient any ban on slavery in the District and unconstitutional any ban on slavery in those territories where slavery had previously been permitted. A majority of senators from both slave and free states voted to table Calhoun's resolutions on national expansion.[291] No subsequent resolution expressing distinctive Southern constitutional understandings passed or even garnered near-unanimous slave-state support in the national legislature.

Calhoun could not rally the South because slaveholders did not regard "equality in the Union" as requiring full Northern acquiescence to all Southern constitutional demands. Southerners were willing to waive some claimed constitutional rights. In 1820 and for the next thirty years, slave-state representatives maintained that the Missouri Compromise was both unconstitutional and binding. The Nashville Convention of 1850 declared that Congress had no power to ban slavery in any territory but that the South would abide by a compromise extending the Missouri line to the Pacific.[292] Southerners, Reverdy Johnson of Maryland asserted, "were, for the sake of peace, even at the sacrifice of constitutional opinion and of feeling, willing to have [the Missouri Compromise line] extended throughout all our territory."[293] The "Georgia Platform" called on "the thirty-one" states to "yield somewhat, in the conflict of opinion and policy, to preserve Union." "In that spirit," Georgians declared, while they did "not wholly approve," they would "abide by" the Compromise of 1850 "as a permanent adjustment of this sectional controversy."[294]

Slaveholders recognized that constitutional law was a poor shield against constitutional majorities. Echoing James Madison, prominent Southerners declared: "Power ... is never restrained by written laws."[295] "I have no faith

[290] See *Congressional Globe,* 25th Cong., 2nd Sess., App., pp. 21–2 (Norvell, Mich.), 24–5 (Young, Ill.), 31 (James Buchanan).

[291] *Congressional Globe,* 25th Cong., 2nd Sess., p. 98.

[292] "Nashville Convention," p. 325. Calhoun had previously endorsed this proposal: *Congressional Globe,* 29th Cong., 2nd Sess., p. 454. See *Congressional Globe:* 31st Cong., 1st Sess., p. 201 (Thomas Clingman); 36th Cong., 1st Sess., p. 1962 (Clingman).

[293] Reverdy Johnson, *Remarks on Popular Sovereignty, as Maintained and Denied Respectively by Judge Douglas and Attorney-General Black* (Murphy: Baltimore, 1859), p. 33. See *Congressional Globe,* 33rd Cong., 1st Sess., App., pp. 408–15 (John Bell).

[294] "Georgia Platform," p. 324.

[295] *Congressional Globe,* 31st Cong., 1st Sess., App., p. 430. See Morrison, *Slavery,* p. 118.

in parchment," John Randolph confessed.[296] Few Southern politicians believed a free-state majority would faithfully respect the constitutional rights of slaveholders. A Northern majority, Thomas Clingman of North Carolina warned, would "find the power … to nullify the provision of the Constitution for the protection of fugitive slaves" and would declare that "there is nothing in the Constitution of the United States which obstructs or ought to obstruct the abolition of slavery, by Congress, in the States." [297]

Southerners wanted a political process that assured adequate protection for Southern rights and interests.[298] Henry Wise stated the fundamental Southern orientation toward antebellum politics when he asserted: "Whatever differences of opinion may exist among Virginians upon [slavery,] we are unanimous on one point, a positive determination that no one shall think or act for us." [299] When a constitutional politics was in place that could be trusted to secure slavery, Southerners played fast and loose with the constitutional law of slavery. The right to bring slaves into all territories was traded for other concessions that assured slaveholders political equality. The primary concern was "equality in the Union." [300] This equality required "a restoration of the Constitutional rights" but, more crucially, "a restoration of that equilibrium of political power which was originally incorporated into the government by the fathers of the republic." [301]

The Balance Rule. The balance rule in the Senate is the best-known means by which antebellum Americans sought to preserve bisectionalism. Jefferson Davis declared that sectional balance in the national legislature was crucial to the Union. "It is essential," he maintained,

> that neither section should have such power in Congress as would render them able to trample upon the rights of the other section of this Union. It would be a blessing, an essential means to preserve the Confederacy, that in one branch of Congress the North and in the other the South should have

---

[296] *Annals of Congress*, 18th Cong., 1st Sess., p. 2361. See *Congressional Globe*, 25th Cong., 2nd Sess., p. 59 (Preston).

[297] *Congressional Globe*, 31st Cong., 1st Sess., p. 203. See *Congressional Globe*, 31st Cong., 1st Sess., App., pp. 74–8. See also Fehrenbacher, *Slaveholding Republic*, p. 270; Morrison, *Slavery*, pp. 107, 210; Carpenter, *The South*, p. 141.

[298] See Cooper, *Liberty and Slavery*, p. 219.

[299] Cooper, *The South*, p. 61 (quoting Henry A. Wise).

[300] Howell Cobb, "Howell Cobb to the People of Georgia," *The Correspondence of Robert Toombs, Alexander H. Stephens, and Howell Cobb* (ed. Ulrich Bonnell Phillips) (Da Capo: New York, 1970), p. 514. See Morrison, *Slavery*, p. 255.

[301] Andrew Johnson, *The Papers of Andrew Johnson*, vol. 3 (ed. Roy P. Graf and Ralph W. Haskins) (University of Tennessee Press: Knoxville, 1972), p. 386. See Morrison, *Slavery*, p. 216.

a majority of representation.... [I]f legislation was restricted and balanced in the mode I have suggested, Congress would never be able to encroach upon the rights and institutions of any portion of the Union, nor could its acts ever meet with resistance from any part of it.[302]

Thomas Bayly of Virginia stressed "the importance of that balance to preserving the harmony of our system."[303] Contemporary commentators agree. According to Barry Weingast, "the *balance rule in the Senate*" was "the most important" institutional device for maintaining political equilibrium before the Civil War (emphasis in original).[304]

The debates over Texas cast doubt on claims that the balance rule actually protected the South before 1850. Only four slave-state representatives invoked that norm. "The balance of interests was gone; the safeguard of American property, of the American constitution, of the American union, vanished into thin air," Henry Wise of Virginia informed the House of Representatives, "unless, by [the annexation] treaty, the South could add more weight to her end of the lever."[305] Two Northern representatives employed the balance rule when opposing annexation. Senator W. Woodbridge of Michigan asserted that "the present resolutions" would "destroy the balance of power between the States, by the admission of a foreign territory."[306] Most slaveholders did not discuss the balance rule at all. Many regarded sectional equality in the Senate as having been previously abandoned. A. H. Sevier of Arkansas maintained that "the slaveholding and planting interest" were "greatly in the minority in both Houses of Congress."[307] Others conceded the South would inevitably become a permanent minority. "It is impossible to survey these vast regions across the map," George Dromgoole of Virginia declared, "and not perceive at a single glance, that in our future progress

[302] *Congressional Globe*, 31st Cong., 1st Sess., App., p. 150.
[303] *Congressional Globe*, 28th Cong., 2nd Sess., App., p. 126.
[304] Barry R. Weingast, "Political Stability and Civil War: Institutions, Commitment, and American Democracy," *Analytic Narratives* (ed. Robert H. Bates, Avner Greif, Margaret Levi, Jean-Laurent Rosenthal, and Barry R. Weingast) (Princeton University Press: Princeton, 1998), pp. 151–2. See Stegmaier, *Texas*, pp. 213–14.
[305] *Congressional Globe*, 27th Cong., 2nd Sess., p. 174. See *Congressional Globe*, 28th Cong., 2nd Sess., App., pp. 126 (Bayly), 233 (Merrick); *Congressional Globe*, 28th Cong., 2nd Sess., p. 281 (Morehead).
[306] *Congressional Globe*, 28th Cong., 2nd Sess., p. 361. See *Congressional Globe*, 28th Cong., 2nd Sess., App., p. 390 (Dayton). Representative Dean of Ohio would support annexation only if balanced by the admission of additional free states: *Congressional Globe*, 28th Cong., 2nd Sess., App., p. 103.
[307] *Congressional Globe*, 28th Cong., 1st Sess., App., p. 559 (Sevier). See *Congressional Globe*, 28th Cong., 2nd Sess., p. 279 (Morehead); *Congressional Globe*, 28th Cong., 2nd Sess., App., pp. 195 (Haralson), 201 (Cobb).

of population and admissions of States, our non-slaveholding brethren are destined to a certain and increasing ascendancy."[308]

Southerners rarely invoked the balance rule during the debates over the Compromise of 1850. Jefferson Davis and David Yulee of Florida were the only senators who raised concerns about sectional equality in the upper house of Congress when debating California statehood.[309] Henry Hilliard performed a solo when he championed the balance rule in the House of Representatives.[310] Slaveholders more commonly objected to the Taylor administration's effort to have Californians apply for admission as a free state before Congress had authorized a constitutional convention or empowered a territorial government. The ten Southern Democrats who jointly "protest[ed] against the bill admitting California as a state" made no mention of sectional equality in the Senate. They condemned "the unauthorized action of a portion of the inhabitants of California, by which an odious discrimination is made against the property of the fifteen slaveholding States of the Union."[311] Southern Whigs never mentioned the balance rule when debating territorial policy in the wake of the Mexican War. Convinced California would inevitably be free, President Taylor initiated the process by which that state joined the Union without ever having been a territory. Better to have additional free states, Whigs contended, than continued destructive debates over bans on slavery in places unfit for human bondage.[312] Prominent Whigs preferred partisan advantage to the balance rule. President Taylor's plan, Senator John Clayton of Delaware informed Senator John Crittenden of Kentucky, would enable "California and New Mexico" to "be admitted – free and Whig."[313]

Slaveholders did not sacrifice much when they abandoned even the pretense of sectional equality in the Senate in 1850. From 1820 to 1846, the Senate was not appreciably more proslavery than the House. From the Missouri Compromise until the Mexican War, no major proslavery measure passed in the Senate only to founder in the House. The House of Representatives was more enthusiastic about annexing Texas and Southern expansion than

---

[308] *Congressional Globe*, 28th Cong., 2nd Sess., App., p. 307. See *Congressional Globe*, 28th Cong., 1st Sess., p. 654 (Benton); *Congressional Globe*, 28th Cong., 1st Sess., App., p. 702 (Berrien); *Congressional Globe*, 28th Cong., 2nd Sess., App., pp. 94 (Bowlin), 200 (Cobb), 271 (Chappell), 287 (Ashley), 376 (Yancey).

[309] *Congressional Globe*, 31st Cong., 1st Sess., pp. 150, 1162, 1533.

[310] *Congressional Globe*, 31st Cong., 1st Sess., pp. 358–9.

[311] *Congressional Globe*, 31st Cong., 1st Sess., p. 1578.

[312] Michael F. Holt, *The Rise and Fall of the American Whig Party: Jacksonian Politics and the Onset of the Civil War* (Oxford University Press: New York, 1999), pp. 412, 437–8.

[313] Holt, *American Whig Party*, p. 438.

was the Senate. Both adopted gag rules. The Wilmot Proviso was the first antislavery measure that passed the House but not the Senate. The Senate became consistently more proslavery than the House only after 1850, when the balance rule was no longer in effect. Kansas statehood marked the first occasion when the House repeatedly defeated proslavery measures that passed the Senate.[314]

The balance rule could protect slave-state interests only to a very limited degree. A united South could only veto legislation.[315] Equilibrium in the Senate did not enable slaveholders to acquire new territories, repeal laws banning slavery in existing territories, or improve the rendition process. Armed only with the power to prevent new antislavery laws, slave states were powerless against demographic trends enabling free states to control the House of Representatives and, eventually, the presidency. A Northern coalition that controlled the one branch of the national legislature and the White House could make executive appointments and execute existing laws in ways that threatened Southern practices. The Senate could not compel an antislavery president to enforce fugitive slave laws or prevent postmasters from delivering abolition pamphlets throughout the South.[316]

Sectional politics in the South further undermined the balance rule. The balance rule empowered senators from the border states, all of whom had to vote with South Carolinians in order for this sectional veto to function. Such unity was a phantasm. Representatives from Missouri, Kentucky, Maryland, and Delaware "often viewed [state] interests and the welfare of the country through a different lens than the rest of the South."[317] Many antebellum slaveholders did not even consider Delaware to be a slave state.[318] Maryland was economically as linked to Pennsylvania as to Virginia. On issues as diverse as gag rules and California statehood, the pattern of border-state voting was closer to the pattern of Lower North voting than Lower South voting. Thomas Hart Benton, the longtime senator from Missouri, defended Western interests when those interests conflicted with Southern interests.[319] John

---

[314] Cooper, *Liberty and Slavery*, p. 261.

[315] See *Congressional Globe*, 28th Cong., 2nd Sess., App., p. 126 (Bayly).

[316] The balance rule did not even secure slave-state control over the Senate. If free-state majorities united, antislavery proposals would easily pass the House of Representatives, pass the Senate when a free-state vice-president broke ties, and be signed by a free-state president.

[317] Cooper, *Liberty and Slavery*, p. 169. The hated tariff passed the Senate because border-state senators defected; see Cooper, *Liberty and Slavery*, p. 150.

[318] See *Congressional Globe*, 25th Cong., 2nd Sess., App., p. 558 (Preston); *Congressional Globe*, 28th Cong., 1st Sess., App., p. 702 (Berrien); *Congressional Globe*, 28th Cong., 2nd Sess., App., p. 382. For a free-state representative who similarly classified Delaware as a free state, see *Congressional Globe*, 28th Cong., 2nd Sess., p. 324 (Dickinson).

[319] See Cooper, *Liberty and Slavery*, p. 279.

Clayton, the longtime senator from Delaware, supported the Wilmot Proviso.[320] Henry Clay was no John C. Calhoun.

Partisanship further vitiated the balance rule as a means of protecting slavery. The South was not a political monolith.[321] Slaveholders were divided by party, ideology, and region. Whigs and Democrats disputed the best means for protecting slavery, as did slaveholders from South Carolina and Louisiana. Most Southern Whigs opposed Southern Democrats on the annexation of Texas and other proposals for Southern expansion.[322] Upper South representatives overwhelmingly opposed Lower South calls to reopen the international slave trade.[323] A diverse and shifting coalition of Southerners opposed plans to divide Texas and California.[324] Many Virginians did not want to increase the number of persons of color or lower the value of border-state slaves. Many Texans and Californians did not want their territory divided for fear of economic loss and the possibility that free states would result. Even with the balance rule, Southerners needed numerous Northern political allies because of the weaknesses in Southern political coalitions.

National Parties. The Jacksonian party system and the Jacksonian Democratic Party were the primary means by which mid–nineteenth-century Americans preserved their original constitutional commitment to bisectionalism.[325] The persons most responsible for fashioning the second party system prevented sectional issues from dominating the political agenda by maintaining mass national parties that fostered cooperation between free- and slave-state politicians.[326] Martin Van Buren famously declared that, if the

---

[320] Holt, *American Whig Party*, p. 320.
[321] See especially W. Freehling, *Disunion*, pp. 13–36. See Cooper, *Liberty and Slavery*, p. vi ("there were also many Souths").
[322] May, *Southern Dream*, pp. 194–205. When Mississippians insisted that Texas be annexed to ensure "an equipoise of influence in the halls of congress" (Syndor, *Development*, p. 322), Calhoun, future Supreme Court justice John A. Campbell of Alabama, and other Southern extremists insisted that, because Mexico was "wholly unfit for a negro population, . . . all acquisition of Mexican territory results in an increase of the strength of the nonslaveholding states and a corresponding diminution of our own." John A. Campbell to John C. Calhoun, November 20, 1847, in *Fourth Annual Report of the Historical Manuscripts Commission: Correspondence of John C. Calhoun* (ed. J. Franklin Jameson) (Government Printing Office: Washington, D.C., 1900), p. 1140. See Waddy Thompson to John C. Calhoun, December 18, 1847, in *Fourth Annual Report*, p. 1152.
[323] Takaki, *Pro-Slavery Crusade*, pp. 103–33, 152–3.
[324] For Southern disunity on Texas, see Stegmaier, *Texas*, pp. 108, 136–7, 147, 219, 262–3, 298–300, 304, 309; William W. Freehling, *The Reintegration of American History: Slavery and the Civil War* (Oxford University Press: New York, 1994), pp. 158–75; Potter, *Impending Crisis*, pp. 396–401.
[325] See Morrison, *Slavery*, pp. 186–7.
[326] Michael Wallace, "Changing Concepts of Party in the United States: New York, 1815–1828," 74 *American Historical Review*, 453, 490 (1968).

old bisectional cleavages between Federalists and Republicans were "suppressed, [then] geographical differences founded on local instincts or what is worse, prejudices between free & slave holding states [would] inevitably take their place."[327] Only "a truly national party," Millard Fillmore declared thirty years later, reduced to a minimum "the constant and disturbing agitation of slavery."[328] The framers assumed Northerners controlling the Senate would have to compromise with Southerners controlling the House of Representatives in order to pass legislation. Jacksonians, by comparison, assumed ambitious Northerners would have to compromise with Southerners in order to enjoy the spoils of national office. Public policy under the Jacksonian regime was both republican and proslavery because politicians in the free states gained necessary Southern support for their nonslavery interests only by providing certain protections for slaveholders. Southern political divisions did not undermine human bondage as long as each slaveholding faction had Northern allies willing to support what some prominent slave-state citizens believed were adequate protections for their peculiar institution.

Antebellum Democrats and Whigs abandoned the antipartisan bias of the original Constitution. Most prominent antebellum politicians placed their political faith in a national party system.[329] Stephen Douglas began his first debate with Abraham Lincoln by celebrating "the Whig and Democratic parties" as "national and patriotic, advocating principles that were universal in their application."[330] A New Yorker declared, "the principles of a national party like the Constitution itself must be such as to embrace all, from the extreme North to the extreme South."[331] What democracies had to fear were not parties per se, these politicians felt, but sectional parties. The *Albany Argus* asserted:

> When men are governed by a common principle, which is fully indulged and equally operative in all parts of the country, the agency of party conduces to the public good. But the political opinions of some men, when actuated by feelings of a sectional character are directly the reverse. What is *party* in the one case, is *faction* in the other.[332] (emphasis in original)

---

[327] Wallace, "Changing Concepts of Party," p. 490 (quoting Martin Van Buren).

[328] Holt, *American Whig Party*, p. 911.

[329] Calhoun was the notable exception; see Cooper, *Liberty and Slavery*, pp. 199–200.

[330] Lincoln, 3 *Collected Works*, p. 1. Republicans, Douglas informed Congress, were "an exclusive sectional party against the organization of which we were so often warned by the fathers of the republic": *Congressional Globe*, 34th Cong., 1st Sess., App., p. 844.

[331] Morrison, *Slavery*, p. 136 (quoting John Floyd).

[332] Wallace, "Changing Concepts of Party," p. 490 n.145 (quoting the *Albany Argus*).

President Buchanan's inaugural address expressed his hope that "geographical parties, ... so much dreaded by the Father of his Country, [would] speedily become extinct."[333]

Slaveholders pledged allegiance to their party of choice as the best vehicle for preserving their human property. Southern Jacksonians spoke of "our Democratic friends from every section of the Union ... who ... would co-operate with us in our effort to maintain our equality in the Union." "[T]he Democratic party in every State of the Union," they boasted, "stands like a break water, resisting the onsweeping tide of fanaticism and folly."[334] Whigs aggressively asserted that they could better protect slavery than their Democratic rivals. "Two vigorous parties," Cooper details, "each claiming to be the paladin of the South, competed almost equally all across the south."[335]

National parties delivered slavery policies acceptable to the South when issues other than slavery excited and divided the latent Northern majority. The partisan solution to the problem of constitutional evil required free-state citizens to cast ballots on the basis of their ethnocultural identities, economic interests, or desire for patronage. These concerns badly divided the Northern electorate. Majorities in some free states favored Whig plans for national development; other free-state majorities preferred the more limited federal role championed by Andrew Jackson and his political followers. These divisions obliged free-state politicians seeking internal improvements or reduced tariffs to seek Southern votes when forging national majorities.[336] Slave-state politicians bargained over national economic development only with "a northern connection that ... accepted the southern interpretation and use of slavery related issues."[337] No Southern politician would strike a deal with Northerners unwilling to keep free-state hands off of slavery. James Hammond exaggerated only slightly when he claimed that, before the Civil War, slaveholders retained political power by "divid[ing] the North & govern[ing] it essentially."[338] The more accurate assertion is that national parties allowed slave-state politicians to take advantage of pre-existing political divisions within the free states.

That Democrats and Whigs were firmly established before the politics of slavery excited most Northern voters contributed significantly to the capacity

---

[333] James Buchanan, "Inaugural Address," *A Compilation of the Messages and Papers of the Presidents 1789–1897*, vol. 5 (ed. James Richardson) (Government Printing Office: Washington, D.C., 1897), p. 342.

[334] Morrison, *Slavery*, pp. 222, 185. See Cooper, *The South*, p. 259.

[335] Cooper, *Liberty and Slavery*, p. 195. See Klinkner and Smith, *Unsteady March*, p. 45.

[336] See Brown, "Missouri Crisis," pp. 58, 62, 69–71.

[337] Cooper, *Liberty and Slavery*, p. 197.

[338] Takaki, *Pro-Slavery Crusade*, p. 105 (quoting James Hammond). See *Congressional Globe*, 31st Cong., 1st Sess., App., pp. 473–4, 479 (Salmon Chase quoting John Randolph).

of the national party system to prevent slavery from disrupting the union. Free-state politicians who remained in bisectional coalitions enjoyed several advantages over sectional defectors. Political actors forming new parties had to combat established political allegiances. New York Free-Soilers lost elections when sympathetic voters "show[ed] their willingness to sacrifice the holy cause of crushed humanity on the polluted altar of party politics."[339] Thoreau complained about fellow citizens who would "postpone the question of freedom to the question of free trade."[340] Antislavery advocates had to build from scratch political organizations with the same capacity to turn out voters as existing Democratic and Whig machines. Ambitious politicians such as Abraham Lincoln were extremely reluctant to abandon parties with the proven capacity to win elections.[341]

The national party system infused support for slavery throughout the national government. No national office was immune to the partisan imperative to appease the South. Free-state representatives in both houses of Congress supported slaveholding demands when putting together national majorities on issues of greater concern to the North. The president supported Southern demands in order to secure needed electoral votes from slave states. The federal judiciary supported Southern demands because justices were nominated by a president indebted to the South and confirmed by a sectionally balanced Senate.[342] Congress provided a further boon to the South by placing five of the nine federal circuits entirely within slave states.

Expansion illustrated how partisanship compensated for internal differences between slaveholders. Democrats from the slaveholding states who "adopted expansion as their own flesh and blood"[343] could not rally slave-state Whigs but consistently gained support from free-state Jacksonians who as enthusiastically championed policies aimed at acquiring new territories.[344] Stephen Douglas promised to "make this an ocean-bound republic." James Buchanan celebrated expansion as facilitating "that spirit of progress, and that desire to roam abroad, and seek new homes, and new fields of enterprise, which characterized [Americans] above all other nations, ancient or

---

[339] Sewell, *Ballots for Freedom,* p. 18 (quoting Gerrit Smith).

[340] Thoreau, *The Portable Thoreau,* p. 115.

[341] David Herbert Donald, *Lincoln* (Simon & Schuster: New York, 1995), pp. 180–1.

[342] See Henry J. Abraham, *Justices, Presidents, and Senators: A History of the U. S. Supreme Court Appointments from Washington to Clinton,* rev. ed. (Rowman & Littlefield: Lanham, 1999), pp. 71–86; Cooper, *The South,* pp. 129–30, 237–8.

[343] Cooper, *Liberty and Slavery,* p. 215.

[344] Stephen A. Douglas, *The Letters of Stephen A. Douglas* (ed. Robert W. Johannsen) (University of Illinois Press: Urbana, 1961), pp. 119–20; May, *Southern Dream,* pp. 19–20, 23, 174–5, 178–80; Fehrenbacher, *Slaveholding Republic,* pp. 129–30; Morrison, *Slavery,* p. 138; Cooper, *The South,* p. 254.

modern, which have ever existed."[345] The desire for new territories was indifferent to direction. Northern Democrats cheerfully supported the annexation of Texas. As many Northern Democrats as Southerners endorsed Jefferson Davis's effort to acquire more of Mexico as a consequence of the Mexican War.[346] The Polk, Pierce, and Buchanan administrations resolved to acquire Cuba and additional Mexican land.[347] If these policies did not yield additional slave states, they would at least generate additional Democratic states. The more Democrats in Congress, the greater the support for expansion, gag rules, and whatever policies Southern Democrats thought best protected slavery.

The Modified Constitution in Action: 1820–1850
American politics during the thirty years after the Missouri Compromise demonstrated that national parties operating the political institutions established in 1787 could generate policies that satisfied Southern moderates even when the free states enjoyed substantial and increasing popular majorities. Whigs and Democrats nominated presidential candidates who appealed to voters throughout the United States. Jacksonians ensured bisectional support for party nominees by requiring a two-thirds vote in the party convention. Whigs nominated multiple regional candidates (1836), candidates from slave states (1832, 1844, 1848, 1852), and a candidate who was born in a slave state (1840). These presidential nominees and their campaign platforms downplayed slavery issues or championed policies that had strong support in both the free and slave states. Martin Van Buren and Henry Clay sidestepped the annexation of Texas. James Polk supported annexation and promised similar expansionist policies in the Northwest. Both party platforms in 1852 celebrated the compromise of 1850 as the final solution to the slavery problem.[348] Elections were vigorously contested in both the North and the South. The winning candidate in every presidential election between a Whig and a Democrat carried at least seven free states and seven slave states. No candidate from 1832 to 1852 gained a landslide in only one section. The elections of 1832, 1840, and 1852 were national landslides. The losing candidate (or slate of candidates) in 1836, 1844, and 1848 carried at least five slave states and five free states.

---

[345] *Congressional Globe*, 28th Cong., 2nd Sess., App., p. 68; Bruce Collins, "The Ideology of the Ante-bellum Northern Democrats," 11 *Journal of American Studies*, 103, 106 (1977) (quoting James Buchanan).
[346] Potter, *Impending Crisis*, p. 5. See Cooper, *Liberty and Slavery*, p. 215.
[347] See May, *Southern Dream*, pp. 19, 23, 40–5, 54–6, 58–9, 67–70, 155–60, 163–9.
[348] "Democratic Platform of 1852," *National Party Platforms*, vol. 1 (compiled by Donald Bruce Johnson) (University of Illinois Press: Urbana, 1956), p. 17; "Whig Platform of 1852," 1 *National Party Platforms*, p. 21.

The second party system fostered sectional cooperation throughout the national government. Presidents favored slaveholders when making cabinet and executive branch appointments. Free-state representatives supported slave-state representatives for leadership positions in the House of Representatives and the Senate. The presidential practice of appointing one Supreme Court justice from each circuit guaranteed a Southern majority on that tribunal. The Northern justices appointed to the Supreme Court after 1837 were on record as supporting the Fugitive Slave Act, the Compromise of 1850, and, after 1857, *Dred Scott*.[349] As of 1861, approximately twice as many Supreme Court justices, speakers of the House, presidents pro tem of the Senate, attorneys general, foreign ministers, and civil servants had come from slave states as had hailed from free states.[350]

This combination of representatives with Southern sensitivities, presidents with bisectional coalitions, and proslavery majorities on the federal bench explains "the slaveholding republic."[351] Every national institution was sensitive to Southern interests. Proslavery policies were handed down in numerous areas. Slavery flourished in the nation's capital[352] and was a central concern of foreign policy.[353] Congress refused to discuss abolitionist petitions.[354] The national executive ordered postmasters not to deliver abolitionist mailings.[355] Everybody condemned abolitionists.[356] Neither Congress nor the president responded to Southern laws banning free black seamen. The Supreme Court decided most important constitutional questions in favor of slaveholding interests.[357] *Prigg v. Pennsylvania*[358] held that Congress had the power to pass fugitive slave laws and that slaveholders could recapture fugitive slaves without official assistance. Every federal justice who adjudicated a fugitive slave case upheld the Fugitive Slave Acts of 1793 and 1850.[359] Northern and Southern legislatures banned the international slave trade, Northern

---

[349] *Dred Scott* probably reflects the overrepresentation of Southerners (5) on the Supreme Court in 1857: see Mark A. Graber, "The Nonmajoritarian Difficulty: Legislative Deference to the Judiciary," 7 *Studies in American Political Development*, 35, 65 (1993); Brown, "Missouri Crisis," p. 72.

[350] Fehrenbacher, *Sectional Crisis*, p. 46.

[351] See Fehrenbacher, *Slaveholding Republic*, p. 296.

[352] Fehrenbacher, *Slaveholding Republic*, pp. 75–7.

[353] Ward McAfee, "Introduction," *Slaveholding Republic*, p. xi; Fehrenbacher, *Slaveholding Republic*, pp. 91–117.

[354] Miller, *Arguing about Slavery*; Cooper, *The South*, pp. 92, 129–30.

[355] Curtis, *Free Speech*, pp. 155–81.

[356] Cooper, *The South*, p. 137.

[357] *Dred Scott*; *Ableman v. Booth*, 60 U.S. 506 (1859); *Strader v. Graham*, 51 U.S. 82 (1850); *Groves v. Slaughter*, 40 U.S. 449 (1840). But see *United States v. Libellants & Claimants of the Schooner Amistad*, 40 U.S. 518 (1841).

[358] 41 U.S. 539 (1842).

[359] Morris, *Free Men All*, pp. 67–8, 152–3, 178–9.

and Southern justices interpreted those bans broadly, and Northerners and Southerners in the executive branch did little to implement those laws and judicial decrees.[360] Free-soilers and abolitionists bitterly complained about how national parties practically guaranteed comprehensive protections for slavery by ensuring that slaveholders would be disproportionately represented in all governing institutions. Wendell Phillips cited the "unbroken practice of every department of the Government, judicial, legislative, and executive, and the acquiescence of the whole people" as conclusive proof that the Constitution was a proslavery compact.[361]

Partisanship trumped sectionalism during the debates over the annexation of Texas. Northern Whigs and Southern Democrats directly appealed to sectional interests. Jacob Collamer of Vermont declared: "It remains now for the vote ... to decide whether the constitution and the balance of power now in the hands of the free states shall be preserved."[362] R. Barnwell Rhett of South Carolina claimed annexation would be a slaveholding victory in the "great struggle for sectional power between the North and the South."[363] These appeals, however, failed to unite either the North or the South. Northern Jacksonians championed annexation as part of a broad expansionist policy. "I am anxious to go on and add State to State," Representative Ezra Dean of Ohio declared, "and it requires no great stretch of the imagination to anticipate not only the annexation of Texas and Oregon, but of every nation on this continent, from the polar regions of the north to its extreme Southern limits."[364] Southern Whigs, conversely, feared annexation would harm the nation and the South. Senator Archer of Virginia believed new slave territories in the West would encourage slaveholding migration that would reduce "the sphere of slavery, the number of slaveholding States, [and] the amount of slaveholding influence in the national councils."[365] Other Southern Whigs condemned Jacksonians for preferring a joint resolution passed by majorities in both houses to a treaty requiring a

---

[360] See Fehrenbacher, *Slaveholding Republic*, pp. 137, 151, 160–1, 169, 174–6, 203–4; Klinkner and Smith, *Unsteady March*, p. 30.

[361] Phillips, *Pro-Slavery Compact*, pp. 4–5. See Fehrenbacher, *Slaveholding Republic*, p. 13.

[362] *Congressional Globe*, 28th Cong., 2nd Sess., App., p. 406. See *Congressional Globe*, 28th Cong., 2nd Sess., App., pp. 316 (Marsh), 335 (Hudson), 342–3 (Giddings), 354 (Miller), 372 (McIlvain), 400 (Huntington).

[363] *Congressional Globe*, 28th Cong., 2nd Sess., App., p. 146. See *Congressional Globe*, 28th Cong., 2nd Sess., App., p. 89 (Yancey), 107 (Holmes), 170 (Payne), 233 (Merrick), 314 (Stephens).

[364] *Congressional Globe*, 28th Cong., 2nd Sess., App., p. 105. See *Congressional Globe*, 28th Cong., 2nd Sess., App., pp. 97 (Brown), 138–9 (Ellis), 212 (Seymour), 227 (Stone), 236 (Woodbury). Many Northern Democrats remarked that adding Texas would benefit free states: see *Congressional Globe*, 28th Cong., 2nd Sess., App., pp. 83 (Weller), 189 (Norris); *Congressional Globe*, 28th Cong., 1st Sess., App., p. 699 (Owen).

[365] *Congressional Globe*, 28th Cong., 1st Sess., App., p. 696.

two-thirds vote of the Senate. "I marvel more especially that a southern senator, representing one of the States which … are destined in all time to be numerically inferior in the councils of the nation," John Berrien of Georgia declared, "should be willing to abandon as unimportant this constitutional safeguard of the rights of a minority."[366] In the end, party proved a better predictor of the congressional vote on annexation than section.[367]

Partisanship also trumped sectionalism during the Mexican War. Whigs opposed the war and new territorial acquisitions,[368] while Jacksonians favored both.[369] Northern Whigs and Southern Jacksonians made sectional appeals. Senator Albert Greene of Rhode Island declared, "we have had enough of the introduction of any new slave-holding States from foreign territory."[370] Seaborn Jones of Georgia treated the House of Representatives to a lecture demonstrating that slavery "was positively ordained of God."[371] Southern Whigs and Northern Democrats forswore this sectional rhetoric. Free-state Jacksonians continued to support expansion in any direction. Representative Isaac Parrish of Ohio was "for acquiring … the greatest amount of territory that can honorably and justly be attained."[372] Southern Whigs continued to worry that expansion would drain slaves from existing slave states or that slavery would not flourish in the West.[373] Calhoun called Mexico "the forbidden fruit; the penalty of eating it would be to subject our institutions to political death."[374]

The specter of sectional politics was raised and temporarily exorcised when, in 1846, David Wilmot proposed banning slavery in all territory that might be acquired from Mexico.[375] The overwhelming majority of Northern representatives initially favored the proviso; virtually all representatives

---

[366] *Congressional Globe*, 28th Cong., 2nd Sess., App., p. 386. See *Congressional Globe*, 28th Cong., 2nd Sess., App., pp. 329 (Archer), 382 (Rives), 392 (Barrow); *Congressional Globe*, 28th Cong., 2nd Sess., p. 279 (Morehead).

[367] See Cooper, *Liberty and Slavery*, pp. 215–17; Cooper, *The South*, pp. 208–9, 212, 223, 228.

[368] See Morrison, *Slavery*, pp. 21–5, 72–3.

[369] See *Congressional Globe*, 31st Cong., 1st Sess., App., pp. 272–3 (Webster) (discussing voting patterns during the Mexican War); Morrison, *Slavery*, pp. 29, 31, 36, 81.

[370] *Congressional Globe*, 30th Cong., 1st Sess., App., p. 344. See *Congressional Globe*, 29th Cong., 2nd Sess., App., pp. 177 (Rathbun), 180 (Hunt), 343 (Wood), 364 (Rathbun), 369 (Hudson), 371 (Stewart).

[371] *Congressional Globe*, 29th Cong., 2nd Sess., App., p. 361. See *Congressional Globe*, 29th Cong., 2nd Sess., App., p. 376 (Brockenbrough, Fla.).

[372] *Congressional Globe*, 29th Cong., 2nd Sess., App., p. 342. See *Congressional Globe*, 29th Cong., 2nd Sess., App., pp. 210 (Breese), 321 (Strong).

[373] Cooper, *The South*, pp. 212, 228.

[374] *Congressional Globe*, 29th Cong., 2nd Sess., App., p. 324. See *Congressional Globe*, 30th Cong., 1st Sess., App., p. 274; *Congressional Globe*, 29th Cong., 2nd Sess., App., pp. 297–301 (Berrien), 313 (Reverdy Johnson), 433–7 (Pearce).

[375] *Congressional Globe*, 29th Cong., 1st Sess., App., p. 1217.

from slave states were opposed.[376] Party leaders quickly regrouped. Most Democrats agreed that the Wilmot Proviso should not interfere with the war effort or attempts to acquire territory; most Whigs agreed that the Wilmot Proviso would be irrelevant if they could prevent any territory from being acquired.[377]

The Treaty of Guadalupe Hildago presented a more serious threat to Jacksonian parties. The bisectional coalitions that disputed expansion were made possible by intrasectional disputes over the likely future of acquired territory. Northern Jacksonians who thought new territories more likely to attract free-state émigrés had united with Southern Jacksonians who thought new territories more likely to attract slave-state émigrés.[378] Northern Whigs who thought new territories conducive to slavery had joined with Southern Whigs who thought new territories inhospitable to human bondage.[379] Once territory was actually acquired, these grounds for partisan cooperation evaporated. Whigs could no longer unite by opposing all new territories. Democrats had to resolve differences over whether the West was to be a new empire for slavery.

Bisectionalism survived these initial tests. Compromise was achieved when Southern Whigs voted to admit California and Northern Jacksonians voted to organize the other territories acquired from the Mexican War without reference to slavery.[380] Convinced the Mexican Cession was destined to be free, Whig slaveholders helped Northerners defeat Southern Democratic proposals to divide California at the Missouri Compromise line. "If I had been a northern man, and desired to vote with reference to sectional advantage," Robert Toombs of Georgia declared, "I would have accepted the proposition to divide California, with the confident expectation of getting two non-slaveholding States instead of one."[381] Convinced the Mexican Cession was inhospitable to slavery (and far distant from their Northern constituents), Northern Democrats and a few conservative Whigs concluded that the Wilmot Proviso was an unnecessary sectional irritant. Daniel Webster spoke for free-state proponents of compromise when he declared, "slavery

---

[376] See Morrison, *Slavery*, pp. 45, 277; Cooper, *The South*, pp. 240–1.

[377] Holt, *American Whig Party*, pp. 252–8.

[378] Compare *Congressional Globe*, 28th Cong., 2nd Sess., App., p. 189 (Norris) with p. 89 (Yancey).

[379] Compare *Congressional Globe*, 31st Cong., 1st Sess., App., p. 266 (Seward) ("there is no climate uncongenial to slavery") with John A. Campbell to John C. Calhoun, November 20, 1847, in *Fourth Annual Report*, p. 1140. See Waddy Thompson to John C. Calhoun, December 18, 1847, in *Fourth Annual Report*, p. 1152.

[380] See Morrison, *Slavery*, pp. 63–4, 108–9; Cooper, *The South*, pp. 285, 301.

[381] *Congressional Globe*, 31st Cong., 1st Sess., p. 1775. See *Congressional Globe*, 31st Cong., 1st Sess., p. 1701 (Brooks).

[is] excluded from those territories by ... the law of nature – of physical geography."[382]

Slave-state majorities supported the Compromise of 1850. Southern Whigs, often running on unionist tickets, soundly thrashed Southern Democrats who questioned that settlement. Slave-state Democrats turned the tide in the next series of elections by claiming their party was the more committed to preserving the sectional status quo. Southern Jacksonians boasted that the Compromise of 1850 was "generally well received by the Democratic party in the free states ...; but [was] likely to lay the foundations of a serious division among the Whigs."[383] They ran campaigns highlighting how Northern Democrats, "our only friends in the North,"[384] had supported Southern claims in the territories. Howell Cobb declared that Democrats in the free states had "given practical evidence of their intention to stand ... by the Constitutional Union of their fathers – recognizing and enforcing all the rights guaranteed by that solemn compact to their brethren of the South."[385] Continued Northern Whig opposition to the Compromise of 1850 strained partisan ties in that coalition,[386] but in 1852 the bisectional Jacksonian Democrats seemed more united than ever.

The Constitutional Order Collapses: 1850–1860

Political blunders, irreconcilable differences, partisan dynamics, and constitutional malfunctions brought down the Jacksonian constitutional order. The political blunders and irreconcilable differences are well known.[387] Partisan dynamics and constitutional malfunctions, though less often discussed, played as important a role. The Jacksonian party system was weakened by forces that create partisan instability in all democracies. Political losers in antebellum America abandoned the issues that initially divided Whigs from Democrats for the same reason that politicians in two-party systems have always sought to reverse their political fortunes by injecting new concerns into electoral competition. Slavery became the issue of choice because Article II enabled free-state coalitions to capture the presidency

---

[382] *Congressional Globe*, 31st Cong., 1st Sess., App., p. 274. See *Congressional Globe*, 31st Cong., 1st Sess., App., p. 1408 (Henry Clay); Fehrenbacher, *Slaveholding Republic*, p. 271.

[383] Morrison, *Slavery*, p. 129.

[384] Cooper, *The South*, p. 288.

[385] Morrison, *Slavery*, p. 132. See Cooper, *The South*, pp. 254, 257, 320–1; Cooper, *Liberty and Slavery*, pp. 224, 236, 288.

[386] See Morrison, *Slavery*, pp. 131, 139; Cooper, *The South*, pp. 329–30, 335–7, 343.

[387] Potter, *Impending Crisis*; Fehrenbacher, *Dred Scott*; Morrison, *Slavery*; Holt, *American Whig Party*; W. Freehling, *Disunion*. What follows is extraordinarily indebted to these and other fine works on the origins of secession.

without winning any slave-state votes or popular majorities and because the processes for electing national officials in local elections prescribed by Article I privileged sectional appeals.

The Conventional Narrative. The Whig convention of 1852 put the first dent in the consensus of 1850. Bypassing Millard Fillmore, a united North aided by a few Virginians nominated Winfield Scott for the presidency. Scott's previous dalliances with the Wilmot Proviso made him the first candidate of a Jacksonian party with no appeal in the South. "I do not know of a single sentiment ever uttered by General Scott," Robert Toombs of Georgia informed fellow Southern Whigs, "that is in unison with my own or the convictions of the slaveholding States of this Union."[388] Scott's poor campaign skills weakened Whig appeal in the North.[389] The result was an electoral debacle. Whigs won no electoral votes south of the border states and very few in the North. This landslide loosened Whig allegiances in both sections. Northerners questioned whether the Whig Party was capable of winning national elections on a regular basis, while Southerners questioned whether slave-state candidates could politically survive their association with antislavery Northern Whigs eager to overturn the Compromise of 1850.

The Kansas–Nebraska Act ended the Whig run as a major national party and severely weakened the Democrats. Many Northerners were outraged by the explicit repeal of the Missouri Compromise. Prominent free-state Whigs abandoned their Southern connections to build free-state coalitions that promised to restore the ban on slavery in territories north of the 36° 30′ line. Northern Democrats who provided the crucial votes to pass the Kansas–Nebraska Act incurred substantial political costs. Most free-state Jacksonians who supported that measure were defeated in the 1854 midterm elections. Survivors were put on notice that further concessions to the South would make the Democrats a permanent minority in the North.

The forces that destroyed the national Whig Party paved the way for the eventual formation of the sectional Republican Party.[390] After 1856, Northern Democrats competed against candidates not constrained by a Southern connection. Rejecting any constitutional commitment to bisectionalism, Lincoln and his political allies openly championed free-state values and interests. Their aggressive sectionalism further limited free-state Jacksonians'

---

[388] *Congressional Globe*, 32nd Cong., 1st Sess., App., p. 820.

[389] Roy Nichols and Jeannette Nichols, "Election of 1852," *History of American Presidential Elections, 1789–1968*, vol. 2 (ed. Arthur M. Schlesinger, Jr.) (McGraw-Hill: New York, 1972), pp. 947–8.

[390] See William E. Gienapp, *The Origins of the Republican Party, 1852–1856* (Oxford University Press: New York, 1987).

capacity to accommodate slaveholders. Democrats had previously masked and excused their complicity with the slave power by highlighting ties between Northern and Southern Whigs. This strategy was no longer feasible when Republicans took the field as the main alternative to Jacksonians.

The collapse of the Whig Party, the weakening of Northern Jacksonians, and the rise of Republicans destroyed the Democrats' bisectional coalition for national expansion. In 1856, Democrats retained the Northern support necessary to carry a national election when the South unanimously supported James Buchanan. After 1854, however, Southern expansionists no longer had the free-state support necessary to compensate for Northern demographic advantages and slave-state defectors. During the 1850s, anti-expansionist slaveholders had the power to prevent Southern expansion. Lacking the Southern votes necessary to support new Southern territories,[391] Southerners could secure additional slave states only by legalizing slavery in existing Western Territories. Slaveholders united on the constitutional right to bring slaves to Kansas, but their Jacksonian free-state coalition partners increasingly preferred that slavery expand southward. Northern constituencies were far more willing to have Cuba join the Union as a slave state than Kansas.[392] Free-state Jacksonians who enthusiastically joined bisectional alliances committed to Manifest Destiny risked their political future when supporting slavery north of the Missouri Compromise line.

The debate over Kansas statehood severed ties between crucial members of the Jacksonian coalition. Northern Democrats barely survived the Kansas–Nebraska Act in part because popular sovereignty was consistent with Jacksonian norms and in part because many were convinced that the remaining territories north of the Missouri Compromise line were inhospitable to slavery.[393] When Southern representatives demanded that Kansas become a slave state, crucial free-state Jacksonians defected. Stephen Douglas appealed to deaf ears when he pointed out that his Northwest constituency would not tolerate the admission of Kansas under the Lecompton constitution. After the House of Representatives rejected Kansas statehood, outraged slaveholders demanded as a condition of union that Northern Jacksonians support a slave code for the territories. Most Northern Jacksonians, under too much pressure from Republicans, refused.

The 1860 national election ended the era of national parties as instruments for securing the constitutional commitment to bisectionalism. Southern Democrats, furious with Douglas over Lecompton, demanded that the

---

[391] During the late 1850s, a united South had the Northern votes necessary to acquire Cuba. See W. Freehling, *Reintegration*, p. 166; W. Freehling, *Reintegration*, pp. 159–60, 164–75, 209–10.

[392] See Morrison, *Slavery*, p. 222.

[393] See Part I, notes 160–163 and the relevant text.

party platform support territorial slave codes. They rejected a free-state compromise offer that would have left the decision to the Supreme Court. When slaveholders walked out of the Democratic national convention, each sectional wing of the former Jacksonian coalition nominated a candidate for the presidency. Whether a single Jacksonian could have triumphed is doubtful. Divided, the Democrats fell. After the election of a president who believed a free-state majority was constitutionally authorized to make antislavery policies without Southern consent, the Lower South seceded. When shots were fired at Fort Sumter, the Middle South followed.

Partisan Dynamics. Partisan dynamics hastened the collapse of the Jacksonian party system. Many problems that political elites faced during the 1850s were typical of aging coalitions.[394] Party systems are dynamic: they evolve, dealign, and realign. Old issues lose their power to mobilize voters; political insurgents raise new issues that crosscut existing political cleavages. Major events responsible for the Civil War were in part consequences of decisions made by politicians seeking to gain and retain office under changing political conditions. Antebellum politicians committed to bisectionalism had to cope with strains within the dominant Democratic coalition, efforts by dissident Whigs to alter the balance of power, and the normal ebbs and flows of political life. Majority coalitions were unstable. The balance of power within Andrew Jackson's cabinet changed dramatically during his first term.[395] Presidents Polk and Pierce struggled to do "equal justice" to every coalition partner, all of whom suspected they were being shortchanged.[396] Political losers sought to ride new issues to victory. Democrats abandoned Martin Van Buren in 1844 and turned to expansion to prevent a repeat of their 1840 defeat. When Whigs lost on the issues, they substituted personalities. The party nominee in 1848 took no position on expansion, the issue on which Whigs lost in 1844, or the national bank, the issue on which Whigs had lost in previous elections. Unexpected events also altered the balance of power between the major parties. The Petticoat Affair, the Panic of 1837, and the death of two Whig presidents while in office had short- and long-term consequences for the balance of partisan forces in antebellum America.

[394] James L. Sundquist, *Dynamics of the Party System: Alignment and Realignment of Political Parties in the United States,* rev. ed. (Brookings Institution: Washington, D.C., 1983); William H. Riker, *The Art of Political Manipulation* (Yale University Press: New Haven, 1996), pp. 1–9; E. E. Schattschneider, *The Semisovereign People: A Realist's View of Democracy in America* (Dryden: Hinsdale, 1975), pp. 61–75.

[395] See Donald B. Cole, *The Presidency of Andrew Jackson* (University Press of Kansas: Lawrence, 1993), pp. 83–95.

[396] Stephen Skowronek, *The Politics Presidents Make: Leadership from John Adams to George Bush* (Harvard University Press: Cambridge, 1993), p. 168. See Skowronek, *Politics,* pp. 155–96.

Tensions within an aging Jacksonian coalition help explain the Wilmot Proviso.[397] Northern supporters of Martin Van Buren were upset when their standard-bearer was cast aside during the Democratic convention of 1844. They were further alienated by administration patronage policies, by Polk's veto of an internal improvement bill, by the president's refusal to readjust Texas's boundaries, and by the administration's decision to compromise American claims to Oregon. By 1846, free-state Jacksonians were under heavy Whig assault for having little to show for their cooperation with the South. Vulnerable to Free-Soil charges of being stooges for the slave power, angry Northern Democrats proposed outlawing slavery in every territory captured from Mexico during the war. If Southern Jacksonians would not help develop the Northwest frontier, then Northern Jacksonians would limit slaveholding access to the Southern frontier.

The popularity of the Wilmot Proviso tempted all failing free-state candidates. Rather than campaign on the national issues that historically divided Whigs from Democrats, Northern politicians out of power could mute previous differences on national economic development and vigorously oppose slavery in the territories. Candidates from both parties adopted this approach after electoral defeats, but such strategies proved particularly congenial to free-state Whigs. Most Northern Whigs were more antislavery than most Northern Democrats. As Whigs lost confidence that they could win elections supporting national banking, tariffs, and internal improvements, many turned to sectionalism. Some immediately joined small antislavery parties.[398] Most initially responded by attempting to commit the national Whig Party to bans on slavery in the territories. Free-state Whigs demanded Winfield Scott be the party nominee in 1852 because defeats in recent elections had convinced them that they could gain office in the North only by attacking the Compromise of 1850. Whigs-turned-Republicans observed how other issues no longer had power to unseat incumbent Jacksonians. "We, the old whigs, have been entirely beaten out on the tariff question," Lincoln wrote in a letter urging supporters to concentrate on sectional appeals.[399]

These strategies alienated Southern Whigs and influenced Northern Jacksonians. The more that Northern Whigs attacked the Compromise of 1850, the more vulnerable Southern Whigs were to Jacksonian attacks. Robert Toombs declared: "We can never have peace and security with Seward, Greely and Co. in the ascendant in our national counsels, and we had better

---

[397] See Eric Foner, "The Wilmot Proviso Revisited," 56 *Journal of American History*, 262 (1969); Cooper, *Liberty and Slavery*, p. 217; Morrison, *Slavery*, pp. 42–3; Fehrenbacher, *Slaveholding Republic*, p. 267.

[398] See Holt, *American Whig Party*, pp. 156–7.

[399] Lincoln, 3 *Collected Works*, p. 487. See Cooper, *The South*, p. 269.

purchase them by the destruction of the Whig party than of the Union." [400]
Northern Jacksonians were forced to respond as Whigs increased their sectional rhetoric. Defeated nationally in 1848, local Democratic candidates responded by taking more antislavery stances in the North and more proslavery stances in the South.[401]

Kansas–Nebraska was a Jacksonian effort to preserve power, the second party system, and bisectionalism through national expansion and Western development. Increased emphasis on territorial policy was politically necessary because, by 1850, national economic policy was losing power to rally the faithful. George Bancroft thought expansion was replacing "the bank and the tariff" as "the dividing line between the parties." [402] In 1853, Douglas believed that Northern Whig demands for free soil had left the Democrats "in a distracted condition" that would require "all our wisdom, prudence, & energy to consolidate its power and perpetuate its principles." [403] Kansas–Nebraska promised a needed Jacksonian balm. Western development, Douglas reasonably thought, was the best way to combat free-state politicians who employed sectional issues to weaken the Democrats in the North. Just as Northerners had previously stomached some proslavery policies in order to obtain majorities for Jacksonian economic policies, so Jacksonian expansionists thought their constituents would consider popular sovereignty a small price to pay for opening up Kansas to settlement – given that Kansas was quite likely to become a free state in any event. Democrats had ridden expansion to victory in 1844 and 1852. Three times seemed a charm.

National expansion proved too good a Jacksonian issue. A clear national consensus emerged before Kansas–Nebraska. Americans favored territorial acquisition and development. When Whigs united on platforms dedicated to maintaining existing national boundaries, they lost elections in both the free and slave states. This consistent series of electoral defeats convinced anti-Jacksonians in the free states to substitute sectional attacks on slavery extension for bisectional attacks on national expansion. Northern Whigs abandoned their Southern allies in 1854 because sectional demands to make Kansas a free territory was their best strategy for vanquishing a bisectional Jacksonian coalition dedicated to popular sovereignty.

Kansas was another failed effort to gain partisan advantage. Buchanan short-circuited the normal process required for statehood in the hope of obtaining another reliable Democratic state. Territorial policy, he informed the territorial governor, was intended "to build up a great democratic party

[400] Craven, *Southern Nationalism*, p. 140.
[401] Holt, *American Whig Party*, p. 955.
[402] Morrison, *Slavery*, p. 31. See Holt, *American Whig Party*, p. 955; Cooper, *The South*, p. 224.
[403] Holt, *American Whig Party*, pp. 800–1 (quoting Stephen Douglas).

... composed of pro-slavery and free State democrats."[404] Presidential politics may explain his decision in the fall of 1857 to support the Lecompton constitution. That choice was unanimously hailed by Southern Democrats and vigorously supported by Democratic senators from the Lower North.[405] Assuming that this support represented more general opinion in those states, Buchanan had put together the minimum coalition for winning the 1860 national election. His support for making Kansas a slave state prevented any serious challenge to Democratic hegemony in the slave states and seemingly had sufficient support in Pennsylvania and Indiana to assure an electoral college majority. The differences between Buchanan and Douglas over Kansas were partly the differences between the political needs of a president from Pennsylvania and a senator from Illinois and partly the differences between the political needs of presidential aspirants from the Lower North and Northwest.

The normal vagaries of partisan politics helped destroy whatever life was left in the Democratic coalition after Lecompton. Republicans did not need slavery or sectional issues to defeat Buchanan in 1860. The main alternative to the Democrats was likely to triumph that year no matter what the nominal policy differences. An economic recession hit the North in 1857 and continued throughout the Buchanan years. Buchanan's administration was wracked by corruption, particularly in the War Department. Patronage fights sapped Jacksonian strength in several states. These three factors all inspired voters who had little interest in Kansas statehood or *Dred Scott* to cast crucial ballots for Lincoln.[406] Bisectionalism collapsed because, in 1860, Northern voters could punish the Democrats for economic, moral, and other failings *only* by supporting a sectional coalition whose promise to contain slavery may not have swayed that many free-state citizens.

Constitutional Malfunctions. Constitutional malfunctions further undermined the original and Jacksonian constitutional commitments to bisectionalism. Had population flowed southwestward as expected, every ruling

---

[404] Kenneth M. Stampp, *America in 1857: A Nation on the Brink* (Oxford University Press: New York, 1990), p. 175 (quoting Buchanan).

[405] See *Congressional Globe*, 35th Cong., 1st Sess., App., pp. 113–15 (Sen. William Bigler, Pa.); *Congressional Globe*, 35th Cong., 1st Sess., App., pp. 163–6 (Sen. Jesse D. Bright, Ind.); *Congressional Globe*, 35th Cong., 1st Sess., pp. 137–41 (Sen. Graham M. Fitch, Ind.). See also Stampp, *American in 1857*, pp. 303–5.

[406] For the political impact of that recession, see James L. Huston, *The Panic of 1857 and the Coming of the Civil War* (Louisiana State University Press: Baton Rouge, 1987). For the political impact of corruption and patronage issues, see Peter Knupfer, "James Buchanan, the Election of 1860, and the Demise of Jacksonian Politics," *James Buchanan and the Political Crisis of the 1850s* (ed. Michael J. Birkner) (Susquehanna University Press: Selinsgrove, 1996), pp. 160, 163–4.

majority would have included free- and slave-state representatives. Normal partisan dynamics might have influenced the composition but not the existence of bisectional coalitions. When population moved northwestward, institutions designed to promote bisectionalism began to foster sectional extremism. Constitutional rules practically guaranteed that the challenge to Jacksonian national parties would be sectional parties, not parties with different national constituencies. The electoral college and state elections for national legislators privileged sectional appeals and geographically cohesive minorities. The constitutional rules for staffing government and making policy influenced every crucial event leading up to secession. The normal dynamics of party competition explain why the Jacksonian party system was vulnerable to new issues. Article I explains why politicians out of power during the 1850s consistently chose sectional issues rather than different national issues on which to campaign. Article II explains why antislavery advocates relied on sectional parties to defeat bisectional parties. Free-state coalitions sought to gain majorities or pluralities in most free states rather than gain popular national majorities, because the former is the constitutionally prescribed strategy for winning control of the national executive.

Normal partisan instabilities could not disrupt the constitutional order when constitutional rules privileged bisectional coalitions. New Yorkers upset with the Southern nationalists who controlled the presidency from 1808 until 1824 could form an alliance with Southern Old Republicans and Southwestern entrepreneurs, but not with Indianans and Northwestern farmers. Northern politicians campaigning against slavery in existing territories could do so only by opposing the acquisition and development of any new territory. No free-state politician interested in forming national majorities could take antislavery positions on all the sectional issues of the day. Population changes expanded Northern coalitional choices. "No new slave states, no new slave territories" became a viable political option when immigration and emigration gave free states the latent power to control the national government. New Yorkers upset with Polk administration policies in 1846 could abandon Virginians for Indianans. Rather than compromise on slavery to present a united front on national economic policy, antislavery advocates repeatedly compromised on national economic policy to present a united front on slavery. "In the organization of the Republican party this question of Slavery was more important than any other," Lincoln declared. "The old question of the tariff ..., the question of the management of financial affairs, the question of the disposition of the public domain," he continued, "cannot even obtain a hearing." [407]

---

[407] Lincoln, 4 *Collected Works*, p. 14.

The electoral college proved an unexpected boon to free-state coalitions when population flowed northwestward. Article II grants victory to whatever coalition obtains majorities in most of the most populous states. After 1845, antislavery advocates could gain the presidency by appealing to the average Northern voter instead of to the average national voter. Proponents of free soil spoke about rallying the Northern majority, but their efforts were actually directed at rallying a majority of that majority. Sectional candidates playing by constitutional rules had no reason to seek a popular majority. In 1860, Republicans obtained 60 percent of the electoral vote with less than 40 percent of the popular vote. Lincoln could have won the election by carrying only eleven states with about a quarter of the popular vote. Republicans were a minority coalition whose victory was made possible by constitutional rules no other democracy adopts.

Article I provided similar benefits for free-state coalitions in the House of Representatives. All national legislators are constitutionally required to be elected within states and, after 1842, were statutorily required to be elected in single-member districts within states.[408] As was the case with the presidency, constitutional rules enabled free-state coalitions to control the lower house of Congress by appealing to the average Northern voter. Republicans interested in forming legislative majorities were not compelled to seek any slave-state votes or to obtain a popular majority. By 1860, a free-state coalition could control the House of Representatives after winning no elections in the slave states and losing more than a fifth of all free-state districts. By so inflating support for antislavery candidates, Article I partly compensated for the three-fifths clause.

Throughout the antebellum United States, local elections privileged candidates who promised to take uncompromising stands on slavery. Candidates for the national legislature from both the free and slave states appealed to voters by pledging to secure sectional interests. As one commentator observed in 1860, "it is easy in the North to gain power by denouncing slavery's existence in the South, and as easy in the South to win favor by denouncing its northern opponents."[409] Individual extremists may have represented the majority in their districts, but single-member districts inflated their numbers in the House of Representatives with respect to the general population. The approximately 40 percent of Americans who voted for Stephen Douglas or John Bell in 1860 could be fairly represented in Congress only if they were majorities in 40 percent of all congressional districts. When 60 percent of the voters in most Southern congressional districts favored aggressively

---

[408] 5 U.S. Stat. 491 (1842).
[409] Morrison, *Slavery,* p. 1.

expanding slavery and 60 percent of the voters in most Northern congressional districts favored placing slavery on the path of "ultimate extinction," the legislative power of the sizable bloc of centrist voters was substantially diminished.

Constitutional rules frequently facilitated the election of free-state congressmen who held more extreme antislavery views than the average voter in their state or district. The constitutional requirement that state legislatures choose senators enabled Free-Soil minorities who held the balance of power in many Northern states to trade votes on all local issues to the major party that supported their preferred Senate candidate. This bargain was quite attractive. Most state legislators were more concerned with local matters than national politics. Few free-state politicians confronted an equally committed proslavery minority that would withdraw from any coalition that made deals with Free-Soilers. Salmon Chase, Charles Sumner, and Benjamin Wade were among the antislavery advocates who gained national office through such arrangements.[410] Similar considerations influenced House elections in the North. When single-issue antislavery advocates held the balance of power in a congressional district, one or both parties frequently increased their antislavery advocacy in order to gain majorities for their economic programs. Northerners more concerned with the tariff than slavery may have made proslavery bargains to form national majorities, but they made antislavery bargains to form local majorities.[411]

Article I created different pressures for increasing sectionalism in Southern elections. George Troup observed how slave-state parties spent their energies "cutting one another's throats in the controversy as to which of the two belongs the higher degree of abolitionism."[412] When one party introduced a new proslavery demand, all Southern politicians were under great pressure to support and extend that demand. "Any suggestion of trimming by a party or of less than all-out effort would cause terrible political damage," Cooper declares, "because the party would find itself in the docket accused of violating its compact with the South, of failing to protect vigorously and at all costs southern interests."[413] Unless they could be tainted with secession, as was the case in 1850 and 1851,[414] Southern politicians almost never lost elections by making too extreme a defense of slavery.

Sectionalism fed on sectionalism. As Southern politicians bid to demonstrate they were the best protectors of slavery, the risk always existed that

[410] Sewell, *Ballots for Freedom*, pp. 180, 210, 221.
[411] Sewell, *Ballots for Freedom*, pp. 167–9.
[412] Cooper, *The South*, p. 148.
[413] Cooper, *Liberty and Slavery*, p. 183.
[414] W. Freehling, *Disunion*, pp. 523–8.

conversation would turn from policies fairly easy for Northern majorities to stomach (gag rules) to policies far more controversial in the North (abandonment of the Missouri Compromise). Free-state politicians willing to accommodate slave-state politicians instantly became electorally vulnerable. "Northern Whigs," Cooper notes, "consistently denounced Northern Democrats for bowing to southern demands."[415] The louder the cry "slave power" from the North, the more Southern parties competed over which coalition was most committed to human bondage.[416] The more provocative the demand generated by the politics of slavery in the South, the more Northern politicians competed to prove their independence from the slave power. Border-state representatives aside, the Constitution placed few politicians in positions where they could resist sectional pressures.

Constitutional federalism further exacerbated sectional tensions. Not being responsible to national constituencies, state and local officials frequently adopted policies that strained relationships among national elites interested in compromise. Representatives in national coalitions passed strict fugitive slave laws and condemned filibustering in central America. State officials passed personal liberty laws in the North and supported private efforts to secure new slave territories in the South.[417] Federal justices confirmed by national majorities were far more accommodating on fugitive and foreign slave issues than state justices who owed their positions to local officials or electorates.[418] Had national majorities the sole power to determine fugitive slave policy, this sectional irritant would have been substantially alleviated.

Article 1 helped transform the Kansas–Nebraska Act from a debate between Democrats and Whigs to an imbroglio between the North and South.[419] The crucial turning point in the congressional debate occurred when Senator Thomas Dixon from Kentucky proposed amending the original bill to make the repeal of the Missouri Compromise bill explicit. Dixon did so because he was a politically vulnerable Whig from a state increasingly inclined to support Jacksonians.[420] Southern Democrats, not wanting to be outbid in the politics of slavery, made that demand their own.[421] Free-Soilers, wishing to make inroads into the Northern electorate, responded with an "Appeal to Independent Democrats," denouncing the Kansas bill

---

[415] Cooper, *The South*, p. 281.

[416] Cooper, *Liberty and Slavery*, p. 183.

[417] See Morris, *Free Men All*; Gavin B. Henderson, "Southern Designs on Cuba, 1854–1857 and Some European Opinions," 5 *Journal of Southern History*, 371 (1939).

[418] Morris, *Free Men All*, pp. 67–9, 152–3, 174–5, 178–9, 187–8.

[419] The best accounts of this transformation are W. Freehling, *Disunion*, pp. 536–65, and Michael F. Holt, *American Whig Party*, pp. 804–35.

[420] See Cooper, *The South*, pp. 349–50.

[421] See Cooper, *The South*, p. 346.

as a sellout to the slave power. Northern Whigs, in order to prevent defections to Free-Soil coalitions, began attacking Kansas–Nebraska as a Southern rather than a Jacksonian measure.[422] Slave-state Whigs who were initially inclined to oppose Kansas–Nebraska as another ill-fated Democratic effort at expansion[423] could not politically withhold support once opposition was tainted with abolitionism.[424] Increased Southern Whig support for Kansas–Nebraska further increased Northern perceptions that the bill was motivated by the slave power. As Northern Whigs increased anti-Southern rhetoric, Southern Whigs became even more vulnerable to charges that they were allied with a party bent on destroying the South.[425] By the final debates, what began as a normal partisan struggle had evolved into a sectional crisis.

The constitutional pressures for sectionalism similarly aggravated conflict over Kansas statehood. Slave-state Democrats could not risk bisectionalism after annihilating the Whigs. During the late 1850s, "every political group opposed to the Democrats slashed at the dominant party with the politics of slavery." Democrats responded as they always had, by accusing their rivals of "betray[ing] the interests of the south," and "snip[ing] at the Democrats rather than join[ing] forces to present a united front to the new, determined enemy."[426] Slaveholders in this electoral environment who thought the Lecompton constitution fraudulent or the long-term prospects for slavery in Kansas dubious could not afford to compromise politically. Charles Conrad, a moderate Southern Whig, noted that "the clamor that has been raised" in favor of Kansas prevented "even ... those who were originally opposed to it" from making "any attempt to repeal it."[427] Many Democrats from the Northwest were as electorally vulnerable. Voting for Kansas statehood conceded the next election to Republicans. "We could never recover from it," the Jacksonian editor of the *Chicago Times* informed Stephen Douglas.[428] A constitution that mandated sectional elections compelled most politicians facing tough choices in 1857 to err on the side of sectionalism.

Millard Fillmore, the politician best positioned to promote sectional compromise,[429] was repeatedly a victim of Article II. The New Yorker would

---

[422] Holt, *American Whig Party*, p. 908.

[423] See Craven, *Southern Nationalism*, pp. 193–5, 201–3.

[424] Craven, *Southern Nationalism*, pp. 203–4. Some Southern Whigs did vote against the Kansas–Nebraska Act; see Cooper, *The South*, p. 354.

[425] See Cooper, *Liberty and Slavery*, pp. 241–7, 357–63, 373; Holt, *American Whig Party*, pp. 908–9; Craven, *Southern Nationalism*, p. 205.

[426] Cooper, *Liberty and Slavery*, pp. 258, 264. See Cooper, *The South*, p. 374.

[427] Holt, *American Whig Party*, p. 925.

[428] Stampp, *America in 1857*, p. 291 (quoting James W. Sheahan). See Craven, *Southern Nationalism*, p. 300.

[429] See Holt, *American Whig Party*, pp. 595–9, 630–2, 802, 914–16, 967, 973.

have been the Whig nominee in 1852 had the framers required presidential candidates to win a majority of the popular vote. He would have at least influenced the final result in 1856 had majority rule been adopted in 1787. His Whig-American campaign that year prevented any other candidate from winning a popular majority. Fillmore failed because he had to prevent candidates from gaining a majority of the electoral vote. Conservative Whigs could influence the election only by gaining a majority or plurality of votes in individual states. Fillmore had substantial support in many states but a majority in only one. His 22 percent of the popular vote earned him only 3 percent of the electoral college vote. The antebellum politician who vigorously championed reverence for the Constitution was done in by constitutional rules that few questioned.

The Whig-American failure in 1856 had serious political consequences. By throwing the election into the House of Representatives, Fillmore thought he could force Democrats and Republicans to moderate their sectional appeals.[430] Candidates forced to bargain with the remnants of the Whig Party, he predicted, would have to abandon making Kansas a slave state or forgo banning slavery in all territories.[431] Buchanan did not have to accommodate Fillmore, however, because his 45 percent of the popular vote garnered a more than constitutionally sufficient 59 percent of the electoral college vote. The fifteenth president supported Lecompton, antagonized Stephen Douglas, and accepted the most Southern interpretation of *Dred Scott* in part because his was a minority coalition beholden to bare Southern majorities. Buchanan had no ideological commitment to any position on slavery in the territories.[432] He risked a position unacceptable to Democrats in the Upper North and Northwest that almost certainly did not command majority support partly because the Constitution enabled a Jacksonian coalition to retain the presidency without support from those regions or from popular majorities.

Change the constitutional rules and electoral incentives change. Candidates who in 1857 had to appeal to the median national voter probably would have opposed Kansas statehood, favored some version of popular sovereignty in the territories, and interpreted *Dred Scott* narrowly. Such a coalition would have gained support from Northern Democrats and Southern moderates. Had the Constitution required runoff elections when no presidential candidate won a majority of the popular vote, relied on a proportional voting system to elect the House of Representatives, or – as called for in the original

---

[430] Holt, *American Whig Party,* p. 967.
[431] See Holt, *American Whig Party,* pp. 914–15.
[432] See Graber, "Non-Majoritarian Difficulty," pp. 48–9.

Virginia Plan – mandated that the House of Representatives select the Senate,[433] public policy after the Mexican War would probably have continued to be acceptable to crucial elites in both the free and slave states. Under the rules adopted in 1787, however, the political coalitions capable of preserving the antebellum constitutional commitment to bisectionalism were constitutionally incapable of influencing national elections.

Article II created a different artificial majority in 1860. Lincoln gained 60 percent of the electoral college vote with less than 40 percent of the popular vote. The electoral college inflated support for the other sectional candidate, John Breckenridge, who obtained 23 percent of the electoral college vote with only 18 percent of the popular vote. These electoral increments were taken entirely from Stephen Douglas, the only candidate who campaigned throughout the United States.[434] Douglas, with nearly 30 percent of the popular vote, managed only 4 percent of the electoral vote. Democrats (Douglas, Breckenridge) won a higher percentage of the popular vote in 1860 than 1856, but they lost because their vote was too widely distributed. Lincoln, by increasing Republican vote totals by 6 percent in the free states, increased that party's electoral college total by 61 percent.

Douglas and John Bell did not influence the outcome in 1860, even though they gained the support of the median voter who allegedly dictates results in democracies.[435] Their political platforms, acceptable to crucial elites in both sections, would have preserved the constitutional commitment to bisectionalism. Nevertheless, majorities in the North preferred free soil to popular sovereignty, and Southern majorities preferred slave codes to the more narrow reading of *Dred Scott* asserted before Lecompton. Acceptable second choices, under Article II, have no constitutional standing when a coalition with a minority of the popular vote gains a majority of the electoral college vote. Political centrists in antebellum American could not overcome the constitutional requirement that they gain majorities in many free and slave states. Compromise in the election system laid out in Article II risked "all prospects of [electoral] success." [436]

By privileging sectional appeals and inflating support for sectional candidates, the Constitution aggravated the antagonisms responsible for the Civil War. Candidates committed to bisectionalism were available. No state might have seceded had Stephen Douglas followed James Buchanan as president. Republicans could not have formed a free-state majority had Millard

---

[433] "The Virginia or Randolph Plan," 1 *Documents of American History*, p. 134.
[434] See Robert W. Johannsen, *The Frontier, the Union, and Stephen A. Douglas* (University of Illinois Press: Urbana, 1989), pp. 166–81, 198–205.
[435] See Anthony Downs, *An Economic Theory of Democracy* (Harper: New York, 1957).
[436] Morrison, *Slavery*, p. 246. See Morrison, *Slavery*, p. 250.

Fillmore been elected in 1852 or influenced the electoral choice in 1856. Both Douglas and Fillmore enjoyed sizable followings and occupied the center of American politics. Their problem was that the Constitution does not empower median national politicians. Minority coalitions playing by constitutional rules gained power in 1856 and 1860. The first, to maintain its Southern base, championed policies that destroyed the surviving national party. The second, to maintain its Northern base, championed policies that led to secession. Although differences between the free and slave states were theoretically reconcilable in 1860, they simply could not be reconciled under the rules laid down in 1787.

THE CONSTITUTION AND THE CIVIL WAR

Republican Remedies and Constitutional Failure

The Constitution caused the Civil War by failing to establish institutions that would facilitate the constitutional politics necessary for the national government to make policies acceptable to crucial elites in both sections of the country. Blaming Southern extremists or free-soilers for making unconstitutional demands misses the underlying structure of the original constitutional compromise. The persons responsible for the Constitution assumed that factions were a normal part of political life that could be combated only by well-designed constitutional institutions.[437] They expected that politicians in the free and slave states would pursue sectional interests. The fundamental protection for both slavery and national union, they believed, was a series of political institutions, later augmented by national parties, thought to ensure that national policy would enjoy bisectional support. Contested constitutional questions would be settled by compromise, because no section had the population necessary to make their factional constitutional vision the law of the land. These institutional foundations for bisectionalism collapsed during the mid-nineteenth century. As population moved northwestward, a constitution designed to prevent sectional politics fostered sectionalism. Abraham Lincoln became president in 1860 only when the constitutional rules expected to privilege Virginians inflated free-soil political strength far beyond free-soil political support.

Article II practically guaranteed that a sectional crisis would occur sooner rather than later. The electoral college permitted a free-state party to capture the White House by gaining bare majorities in most free states. Under a different system of voting, antislavery coalitions would have had to gain a

---

[437] Hamilton, Madison, and Jay, *Federalist Papers*, pp. 80–4.

majority of all votes. Republicans might have eventually succeeded, given population trends. Still, had the Constitution required a popular majority for the presidency, Northern sectionalists might not have won the presidency until 1880. Had another means been available or chosen for augmenting slave representation in presidential voting, free-state majorities might not have triumphed until the twentieth century.

The constitutional system for electing national officials further aggravated sectional crises by encouraging and artificially strengthening candidates and parties that made sectional appeals. Political coalitions gained control of the national government by obtaining majorities in particular states and election districts. Freed from the moderation imposed by a national electorate, politicians outside the border states rose to power by aggressively championing sectional interests. Lincoln and the Republican Party benefited from an electoral system that did not permit votes in South Carolina and Massachusetts to be combined. Northern doughfaces and Southern Whig unionists were consistently underrepresented because their support was dispersed throughout the United States. Had the United States adopted a proportional system of voting for Congress, a coalition of Southern Whigs and moderate Democrats might have maintained solid control of the national legislature for most of the nineteenth century. By mandating rules that promoted sectional extremism and inhibited cooperation between sectional moderates, Articles I and II are as much to blame for the secession crisis as the Wilmot Proviso, the Kansas–Nebraska Act, *Dred Scott,* and Lecompton.

Law and Politics

At first glance, antebellum disputes over constitutional law might have been avoided had the framers embodied their constitutional aspirations more explicitly in the constitutional text. No interpretive schism would have arisen had the Constitution established a fixed timetable for emancipation or constitutionalized Calhoun's concurrent majority. Express constitutional law would have clarified sectional obligations and possibly fostered a political culture more supportive of emancipation or bisectionalism. Constitutional declarations of rights, many framers believed, molded popular opinion. Madison wrote Jefferson that bills of rights are useful because "[t]he political truths declared in that solemn manner acquire by degrees the character of fundamental maxims of free Government, and as they become incorporated with the National Sentiment, counteract the impulses of interest and passion."[438] A clear constitutional call for abolition might have sustained the

---

[438] Madison, *Letters and Other Writings,* p. 426. See Rakove, *Original Meanings,* pp. 324, 335–6.

momentum toward emancipation that developed during the late eighteenth century. A constitution explicitly committed to bisectionalism might have better promoted future compromises.

Law mattered in antebellum America. Explicit agreements on constitutional law constrained popular politics. Northerners constantly grumbled about the overrepresentation of the South but proved willing to play by clear constitutional rules. The three-fifths clause, the most determined antislavery advocate confessed, could be repealed only by a constitutional amendment. Deep South slave traders similarly acknowledged that Congress had power to ban the international slave trade after 1808. These examples of constitutional fidelity suggest that if the original constitution (or early federal government) had provided such legal guarantees for slavery as the right to bring slaves into the territories, then Northern commitments to the rule of law might have trumped antislavery values. A well-designed "postnati" provision might have yielded a grudging commitment to eventual emancipation in the South.

Ratification difficulties, however, were one obstacle to these legal solutions. Obtaining a national consensus on a constitution that either set a timetable for emancipation or provided more explicit legal protection for slavery was impossible. South Carolinians would not have consented to any constitution committing the United States to abolition. The slender margin that Federalists eventually obtained in such free states as New York and Massachusetts[439] would have vanished had proponents of the Constitution been forced to defend provisions incorporated into the Confederate Constitution such as "[n]o ... law denying or impairing the right of property in negro slaves shall be passed," "the citizens of each State ... shall have the right of transit and sojourn in any State of this [Union], with their slaves," and "the inhabitants of the several ... States and Territories shall have the right to take to such Territory any slaves lawfully held by them."[440] Lack of a consensus in 1860 similarly foiled efforts to reach compromise on legal rules. The Crittenden proposal to extend the Missouri Compromise line to the Pacific[441] might have quelled secession,[442] but that measure lacked the support necessary to pass Congress (and probably would not have had the state support necessary to be ratified).[443]

---

[439] Cecil L. Eubanks, "New York: Federalism and the Political Economy of Union," *Ratifying the Constitution*; Michael Allen Gillespie, "Massachusetts: Creating Consensus," *Ratifying the Constitution*.

[440] "The Constitution of the Confederate States of America," 1 *Documents of American History*, pp. 379, 383.

[441] *Congressional Globe*, 36th Cong., 1st Sess., pp. 112–14.

[442] Stampp, *And the War Came*, p. 166; May, *Southern Dream*, pp. 226–32. But see Stampp, *And the War Came*, pp. 132–6.

[443] See Potter, *Impending Crisis*, pp. 532, 549; Stampp, *And the War Came*, pp. 132–57.

More important, whether the framers could have adopted constitutional specifics for all circumstances is doubtful. Legal settlements are vulnerable to future political and social developments. No evidence exists that the fugitive slave clause was intentionally vague. The framers did not foresee the issues that the rendition process presented after the 1820s. The three-fifths clause was based on erroneous population assumptions. Had slaveholders correctly anticipated demographic trends, they probably would have insisted on a better ratio. Measures that seemed proslavery became boons to antislavery forces. During the 1850s, Southerners cursed the slaveholders who in 1803 insisted that the Constitution plainly authorized national expansion.

Most important, undue emphasis on legal protections may weaken more fundamental political protections for contested practices. Southerners who insisted that persons had a constitutional right to bring slaves into the territories sometimes failed to appreciate that maintaining a sectional balance of power was more crucial to securing their constitutional understandings. If politically astute Southerners had supported internal improvements or Northern expansionist designs in Oregon, policies that freed no slaves, then Northern Democrats would not have introduced the Wilmot Proviso or supported that measure to nearly the same degree.[444] Many Northern Democrats complained that Southern efforts on behalf of Kansas–Nebraska and the Lecompton constitution sapped Northern support that could have been used to acquire Cuba.[445]

President Polk's decision to oppose an internal improvement bill cherished by Northwestern Jacksonians highlights the tension between legal and political protections for slavery. His veto superficially advanced slaveholding interests by narrowly construing federal power.[446] One common Southern objection to broad understandings of the interstate commerce clause was that such "latitarian" constitutional decisions provided precedents for national laws emancipating slaves.[447] Most Western Democrats, however, were quite willing to leave slavery alone as long as they received other benefits from their political association with slaveholders. Polk's veto strengthened a legal protection for slavery by weakening an alliance with Northerners willing to provide political support for the South, yet the legal precedent established by the veto was unnecessary. Justice Wayne's opinion in *Smith v.*

---

[444] Foner, "Wilmot Proviso"; Potter, *Impending Crisis*, pp. 24–6.
[445] Potter, *Impending Crisis*, p. 198; May, *Southern Dream*, pp. 36–7.
[446] James K. Polk, "Veto Message," 4 *Compilation of Messages*, pp. 610–26.
[447] See *Annals of Congress*, 18th Cong., 1st Sess., pp. 1307–8 (John Randolph); R. Kent Newmyer, "John Marshall, *McCulloch*, and the Southern States' Rights Tradition," 33 *John Marshall Law Review*, 875, 880–1 (2000).

Turner demonstrated that proslavery advocates who endorsed broad federal power over commerce could find constitutional reason for making exceptions for slaves and persons of color.[448] Abraham Lincoln's effort to overturn *Dred Scott* demonstrated that contested constitutional precedents would not constrain antislavery majorities in power. Viewing the antebellum polity through a prism of constitutional law, Polk and other Southern Jacksonians forgot that sound political allies were more vital than good legal doctrine.

The persons responsible for the Constitution did not propose comprehensive legal solutions for their problem of constitutional evil because they could not agree on much law and because they recognized the limits of law as a permanent solution. Law could not anticipate all future constitutional questions or political developments. Given an uncertain future, all the framers could do was create a constitutional politics that enabled Americans to resolve constitutional questions as they arose in ways that preserved the peace between the sections. The rhetoric of constitutional law that developed in the early nineteenth century subverted this constitutional project. Northern Republicans and Southern fire-eaters too often spoke as if a comprehensive agreement on constitutional law had been reached in the past, and both claimed that the other was violating the original constitutional bargain. The better view was that the framers bequeathed to their descendants a set of constitutional institutions they hoped would facilitate future bargaining over the constitutional status of slavery. Constitutional exegesis was supposed to resemble renegotiation as much as interpretation.

---

[448] *Smith v. Turner*, 48 U.S. 283, 426 (1849) (Wayne, concurring) (state laws barring free blacks do not violate the commerce clause). In *Groves v. Slaughter*, 40 U.S. 449, 510 (1841), such nationalists as Joseph Story and Wayne "concurred with the majority of the Court in opinion that the provision of the Constitution of the United States, which gives the regulation of commerce to Congress, did not interfere with the provision of the constitution of the state of Mississippi, which relates to the introduction of slaves as merchandise, or for sale."

PART THREE

Compromising with Evil

Abraham Lincoln dramatically changed his *public* challenge to the *Dred Scott* decision after being elected president. Lincoln as senatorial and presidential candidate condemned on moral, historical, and aspirational grounds the judicial ruling that the federal government lacked constitutional power to ban human bondage in the territories.[1] His speeches from 1856 until the spring of 1860 repeatedly asserted that slavery was evil, that the persons responsible for the Constitution recognized that slavery was evil, that those framers attempted to place slavery on "the course of ultimate extinction," and that Congress was constitutionally empowered to ban slavery in any territory where human bondage was not previously legal. Immediately after the election of 1860, he ceased making these public attacks on the Taney Court and the Democratic Party. The last public address Lincoln delivered before the Civil War that declared slavery to be a moral and constitutional evil was delivered on March 6, 1860.[2]

During the months immediately before the engagement at Fort Sumter, Lincoln treated the status of slavery in the territories as constitutionally open. "*May* Congress prohibit slavery in the territories?" his first inaugural address asked. "The Constitution does not expressly say." "*Must* Congress protect slavery in the territories?" Lincoln continued. "The Constitution does not expressly say."[3] This constitutional silence, Lincoln suggested, placed *Dred Scott* and the Republican platform of 1860 on equal political footing. Both proposed settlements to the constitutional status of slavery in the territories

---

[1]   See Abraham Lincoln, *The Collected Works of Abraham Lincoln*, vol. 2 (ed. Roy P. Basler) (Rutgers University Press: New Brunswick, 1953), pp. 238–9, 240, 244–5, 274, 400, 403–4, 492–3, 514–15; Lincoln, 3 *Collected Works*, pp. 18, 77–8, 87, 92–3, 117, 181, 254–5, 276, 306–8, 311, 398, 404, 414–15, 422, 466, 498, 523–53; Lincoln, 4 *Collected Works*, pp. 21–2.

[2]   Lincoln, 4 *Collected Works*, pp. 21–2.

[3]   Lincoln, 4 *Collected Works*, p. 267.

were potentially temporary, subject to repeal at "very short intervals" by a new administration.[4] The first inaugural informed Southerners who feared the consequences of Republican policies that "no administration, by any extreme of wickedness or folly, can very seriously injure the government in the short space of four years."[5] Americans who thought Republican policies constitutionally wrong were constitutionally free to reinstitute *Dred Scott* when they next controlled the national government.[6]

Lincoln's changed political status explains his changed political rhetoric. As a candidate, he had to convince free-state majorities that they should vest the Republican Party with the control over governing institutions necessary to prevent the extension of human bondage. His electoral task was to persuade Northerners that the Constitution was best interpreted as permitting federal bans on slavery in the territories. As the president, Lincoln had to convince slave-state majorities who believed the Constitution provided substantial federal protection for human bondage that free-state majorities were nevertheless constitutionally authorized to ban slavery in the territories. His governing task was to persuade Southerners that his administration's effort to prevent the extension of slavery was a *legitimate* political and constitutional policy. The election of 1860, Lincoln believed, provided him with a consensual basis for exercising that constitutional authority. The same shared commitments to majority rule, previous constitutional compromises, and valued constitutional relationships that obligated free-state citizens to acquiesce whenever Jacksonian constitutional majorities interpreted constitutional ambiguities as sanctioning proslavery policies, Lincoln argued, also obligated slave-state citizens to acquiesce whenever Republican constitutional majorities interpreted those constitutional ambiguities as sanctioning antislavery policies.

Constitutional authority in antebellum American was more deeply infected by constitutional evil than Lincoln acknowledged. Every argument Lincoln employed when claiming that an antislavery Northern majority was constitutionally authorized to resolve constitutional controversies either lacked adequate constitutional foundations or justified slaveholding claims that constitutional controversies could be constitutionally settled only by bisectional agreement. The slavery compromises Americans reached from 1787 to 1860 provided powerful precedents for a constitutional obligation to resolve sectional issues by compromise even when a free-state majority controlled the national government. When Lincoln insisted that the

---

[4] Lincoln, 4 *Collected Works*, p. 270.
[5] Lincoln, 4 *Collected Works*, p. 270.
[6] Lincoln, 4 *Collected Works*, p. 207.

Constitution established a majoritarian democracy, slaveholders pointed out that the antebellum constitutional order was better conceptualized as a consensus democracy in which the structure of governing institutions guaranteed that slaveholders would influence any settlement of a constitutional controversy. The contract metaphors Lincoln employed when justifying Republican power to challenge *Dred Scott* provided better support for claims that Southern consent to federal bans on slavery in the territories was conditioned on such policies having substantial support in both the free and slave states. When Lincoln invoked the constitutional relationship between the sections, slaveholders responded that the balance of sectional power was crucial to preserving that relationship.

Much contemporary commentary, by positing justice as the appropriate tiebreaker for resolving constitutional controversies, fails to acknowledge Lincoln's problem of constitutional authority. Governing officials, members of many interpretive schools proclaim, should accommodate no more injustice than is constitutionally necessary. In this common view, constitutional evil exists only when the text cannot be interpreted as sanctioning practices that are more just. Professor Philip Bobbitt maintains that the "United States Constitution require[s] decisions that rely on the individual moral sensibility when the modalities of argument clash."[7] It may not be "a bad characteristic for a[n] [originalist] constitutional theory," Justice Antonin Scalia agrees, that "the inevitable tendency of justices to think the law is what they would like it to be will ... cause most errors in judicial historiography to be made in the direction of projecting upon the age of 1789 current, modern values."[8] Rogers Smith goes further, insisting that constitutional authorities retain a prerogative power to do justice in cases where the constitutionally mandated result is clearly stupid or evil.[9]

This recourse to justice, however, provides neither a meaningful critique of *Dred Scott* nor a consensual basis for political authority. Appeals to consensual principles of justice rarely resolve constitutional questions. Constitutional controversies are politically salient only when rooted in underlying normative controversies. The claim "slavery is evil" did little constitutional

---

[7] Philip Bobbitt, *Constitutional Interpretation* (Blackwell: Oxford, 1991), p. 168. See Bobbitt, *Constitutional Interpretation*, pp. 157, 161, 163–4. See also Michael W. McConnell, "Free Exercise Revisionism and the Smith Decision," 57 *University of Chicago Law Review*, 1109, 1153 (1990); Edward B. Foley, "Interpretation and Philosophy: Dworkin's Constitution," 14 *Constitutional Commentary*, 151, 166 (1996).

[8] Antonin Scalia, "Originalism: The Lesser Evil," 57 *University of Cincinnati Law Review*, 849, 864 (1987).

[9] Rogers M. Smith, "The Inherent Deceptiveness of Constitutional Discourse: A Diagnosis and Prescription," *NOMOS XL: Integrity and Conscience* (ed. Ian Shapiro and Robert Adams) (New York University Press: New York, 1998), pp. 247–8.

work in 1860 because sectional disputes were rooted in differences over whether justice was served by preventing the extension of human bondage. Limited to cases where a moral consensus exists, arguments from justice work only in hindsight, resolving long-dead controversies while providing little guidance for the living. Justice-seeking constitutionalism at most provides consensual grounds for abandoning such statutory relics as laws that during the 1960s permitted the police to search the marital bedroom for contraception.[10] That approach to constitutional settlement had no value to Lincoln, who needed reasons why persons who disputed both his political and constitutional convictions should nevertheless have acknowledged his political and constitutional authority.

Lincoln invoked majoritarianism, consent, and fraternity when claiming constitutional authority to ban slavery in the territories. His first inaugural address asserted that majority rule was constitutionally appropriate for resolving constitutional issues not settled by previous agreement. Other speeches asserted that the free states had never consented to allow slavery in territories not covered by the Missouri Compromise and Compromise of 1850, while the slave states had consented to having constitutional controversies resolved by any coalition – sectional or bisectional – that gained constitutional control of the national government. The final paragraph of the first inaugural implores slaveholders not to forsake cherished constitutional relationships unless plain constitutional commands were violated.

These justifications of constitutional authority recognized two grounds for accommodating evil. Lincoln respected all previous constitutional compromises consented to by free-state representatives, whether these compromises were embodied in the Constitution or in legislation. He also accorded temporary respect to constitutional decisions made by coalitions in constitutional control of the national government. Lincoln insisted, however, that a free-state majority had no duty to accommodate any more slavery than plainly mandated by past settlements. Compromise, he maintained, was often a political necessity but was never a constitutional obligation.

The persons responsible for the American Constitution felt a more robust obligation to compromise. Faced with intractable disputes over human bondage, the framers and their Jacksonian descendants favored political institutions that generated policies satisfactory to elites in both the slave and free states. They understood that obtaining bisectional consent for major national initiatives was more vital for realizing essential constitutional aspirations than satisfying numerical majorities. Constitutional institutions were

---

[10] *Griswold v. Connecticut,* 381 U.S. 479 (1965).

designed to prevent sectional majorities from unilaterally making slavery policies. The original Constitution fostered compromise by establishing a bicameral legislature with one branch controlled by slave states and the other controlled by free states. The Jacksonian Constitution fostered compromise through national parties that required ambitious politicians from the South and North to cooperate in order to enjoy the spoils of national office. When these governmental and partisan institutions were functioning as expected, the national government could sanction antislavery policies only when prominent Southerners supported those measures.

Consent theory provides a related foundation for the constitutional obligation to compromise. In 1787, Americans consented to a constitution that all believed vested both slave and free states with a veto on national policy. If, as most Americans have historically insisted, the Constitution ought to be interpreted consistently with contract and consent theory – and if, as much present contract law maintains, persons consent only to the reasonably foreseeable consequences of their bargains – then the original constitutional contract was legally binding only as long as constitutional institutions functioned in ways consistent with the original constitutional commitment to bisectionalism. Consent theory vests no constitutional authority in a coalition unwilling to compromise that gains office when population shifts unforeseen by the original constitutional bargainers destroy the intended sectional balance of power. Lincoln's unwillingness to share power, to borrow a term from contemporary law, "frustrated" the constitutional contract, providing legal grounds for Southern secession.

Relational contract theory suggests similar grounds for preserving the sectional veto and recognizing a constitutional obligation to compromise. Relationships are maintained over time only when all crucial parties are reasonably satisfied with the consequences of mutual cooperation. Persons committed to preserving constitutional relationships must interpret existing rules in ways that all important parties find satisfactory. The crucial question is whether the benefits of the relationship are sufficient to maintain the willingness of each party to accommodate the other, even in circumstances where previously established rules may not necessarily require accommodation. The demand to play by rules not functioning as expected will, in practice if not in theory, end the relationship. In this view, Lincoln – if he wished to preserve the constitutional relationship between the sections – should have offered slaveholders something more than the increasingly unrealistic hope that Southerners might prove more successful in future national elections.

The best justification for constitutional compromises and maintaining constitutional relationships with proponents of evil is the belief that human beings are capable of recognizing and abandoning immoral practices when consistently exposed to morally superior ideals and social arrangements. Inspired by Enlightenment thought, many Americans of the late eighteenth century did not anticipate that they were establishing a permanent slaveholding republic. Decent persons, they believed, recognized or could be persuaded over time that slavery was a moral wrong that should not be tolerated any longer than necessary. Constitutional accommodations for human bondage were, they felt, justifiable means for guaranteeing that slaveholders would be exposed to sound attacks on their peculiar institution. The constitutional commitment to maintain union and the social peace was both an end in itself and the best way to guarantee the conditions under which citizens are most likely to abandon their evil practices. No firm promises were made, but most Northerners assumed that slavery would eventually wither on the republican vine.

This republican justification for compromising with evil provided Republicans with legitimate constitutional grounds for concluding that slaveholders had abandoned the original constitutional relationship between the sections. The Southern efforts after 1830 to prevent slavery from being subject to rational scrutiny broke faith with this vital constitutional commitment to republicanism. The pervasive censorship of antislavery advocacy undermined the foundation of the sectional veto on national policy. By attempting to close off all criticisms of slavery, Southern political actors were eliminating the main republican practice furthering emancipation: rational persuasion. Free-state officials who consented to a slaveholding republic were constitutionally authorized to ban slavery in the territories after 1860 because they had never consented to a slaveholding oligarchy.

This happy ending needs two qualifications. First, whether Southern antirepublican practices justified abandoning bisectionalism is contestable. Northerners who tolerated mobs freeing fugitive slaves and supported John Brown's terrorist attack on Harper's Ferry could hardly claim to have clean hands. Despite censorship, most Southerners were well aware of the major arguments against slavery. Given the costs and uncertainties of attempts to impose justice by force, the better constitutional alternative may have been to continue recognizing a constitutional obligation to compromise while working for emancipation within an imperfect marketplace of ideas. Second, Southern antirepublican practices provided constitutional justification for Northern abandonment of the Constitution of 1787, not for coercing Southern participation in a new constitutional order. The original Constitution was committed to a balance of sectional power. The new constitutional regime – contemplated by Lincoln's first inaugural address and realized through bloodshed – was majoritarian and rooted in a claimed commitment to human equality.[11]

MAJORITARIANISM AND CONSTITUTIONAL EVIL

Lincoln's Majoritarianism

Abraham Lincoln insisted that popular majorities were constitutionally authorized to resolve such constitutional controversies as the status of slavery in the territories. In many speeches, he acknowledged that Jacksonian majorities were constitutionally empowered to interpret the Constitution as prohibiting bans on slavery in American territories. His first inaugural insisted that majoritarian principles vested a sectional Republican majority with the same constitutional power to ban slavery in American territories. Lincoln assured Southerners that the principle of majority rule vested his coalition with no more authority than the Buchanan administration had enjoyed to settle forever the constitutional status of slavery. Citizens who thought *Dred Scott* should be the fundamental law of the land were reminded that a Jacksonian coalition victorious in 1865 would have the same constitutional authority to reverse Republican understandings as the victorious Republican coalition in 1861 had to reverse Jacksonian understandings.

Lincoln's first inaugural celebrated democratic majoritarianism. "A majority, held in restraint by constitutional checks, and limitations," that address declared, "is the only true sovereign of a free people." The virtues of majority rule were nearly self-evident to Lincoln. "Unanimity is impossible," the first inaugural stated; "the rule of a minority, as a permanent arrangement, is wholly inadmissible; so that rejecting the majority principle, anarchy, or despotism in some form, is all that is left."[12] Democratic majorities were specifically empowered, he argued, to resolve contested constitutional questions. Lincoln's maiden speech as president noted how "constitutional controversies ... divide" Americans "into majorities and minorities." "If a minority, in such case, will secede rather than acquiesce," he asserted, "they make a precedent which, in turn, will divide and ruin them; for a minority of their own will secede from them, whenever a majority refuses to be controlled by such minority."[13]

---

[11] See Garry Wills, *Lincoln at Gettysburg: The Words That Re-Made America* (Simon & Schuster: New York, 1992).

[12] Lincoln, 4 *Collected Works,* p. 268.

[13] Lincoln, 4 *Collected Works,* p. 267.

Lincoln's speeches before and after the first inaugural further defended and elaborated majority rule as the appropriate principle for resolving constitutional controversies. One month before taking office, the president-elect asserted:

> The question is, as to what the Constitution means – "What are the rights under the Constitution?" That is all. To decide that, who shall be the judge? Can you think of any other, than the voice of the people? If the majority does not control, the minority must – would that be right? Would that be just or generous? Assuredly not![14]

Lincoln later condemned the constitution of the Confederacy for exalting minority rights at the expense of majority power. "These politicians are subtle, and profound, on the rights of minorities," he observed, but "[t]hey are not partial to that power which made the Constitution, and speaks from the preamble, calling itself 'We, the People.'"[15]

Compromises with evil were appropriate, Lincoln felt, only when popular majorities favored compromise. Government actors were expected to be faithful when their electorate rejected accommodations for slavery. Lincoln offered majoritarian reasons when condemning the Kansas–Nebraska Act as "conceived in violence, passed in violence, maintained in violence, and … executed in violence." "[I]t could not have been passed at all," he stated, "but for the vote of many members, in violent disregard of the known will of their constituents." The Illinois Republican further observed that "the elections since, clearly demand its repeal, and this … demand is openly disregarded."[16] During the secession winter, Lincoln insisted that his democratic principles forbade abandoning constitutional commitments made during the presidential campaign. Sharing power with slaveholders and their doughface allies would, he said, "distinctly set the minority over the majority."[17]

Majoritarianism did legitimate substantial protection for slavery. Throughout his political life, Lincoln maintained that local majorities in any state could vote to legalize slavery[18] and outlaw negro citizenship.[19] He favored abolishing slavery in the District of Columbia only "on a vote of the majority of qualified voters."[20] More important, Lincoln thought popular majorities

---

[14] Lincoln, 4 *Collected Works*, p. 207.
[15] Lincoln, 4 *Collected Works*, pp. 436–7.
[16] Lincoln, 2 *Collected Works*, p. 421.
[17] Lincoln, 4 *Collected Works*, pp. 200–1. See Lincoln, 4 *Collected Works*, pp. 175–6, 259.
[18] Lincoln, 3 *Collected Works*, pp. 41, 116–17.
[19] Lincoln, 3 *Collected Works*, p. 179.
[20] Lincoln, 3 *Collected Works*, pp. 41–2. See Lincoln, 1 *Collected Works*, p. 75; Lincoln, 2 *Collected Works*, p. 22; Lincoln, 3 *Collected Works*, p. 96.

could protect slaveholding whenever the relevant constitutional provision was unclear or unsettled. The status of slavery in the West was the most prominent example of a matter on which Lincoln believed majoritarianism trumped what he believed to be the best interpretation of the Constitution. Although he repeatedly declared the decision wrong, Lincoln insisted that *Dred Scott* was good law while Jacksonians held office and would be good law again should a pro–*Dred Scott* coalition win a future national election. "The principle that the majority shall rule," Lincoln told an audience in Cincinnati, guaranteed proponents of *Dred Scott* "another chance in four years" to elect a president committed to their proslavery constitutional vision.[21]

Lincoln's democratic majoritarianism was nevertheless limited by his constitutionalism. Popular majorities were constitutionally authorized to make decisions only when the Constitution did not very plainly specify the appropriate rule. Constitutional commitments constrained majority rule substantially and procedurally. Clear constitutional commands forbade certain majorities from making particular policies. National majorities could not force states to outlaw or adopt slavery;[22] that was for local majorities to decide. Clear constitutional commands also authorized deviations from majority rule. The three-fifths rule was "manifestly unfair" and a "violat[ion] of the equality between American citizens," Lincoln felt. Nevertheless, he declared, "[i]t is in the constitution; and I do not, for that cause, or other cause, propose to destroy, or alter, or disregard the constitution."[23]

Whether Lincoln thought judicial decisions interpreting the Constitution were subject to majoritarian politics is more complicated. Responding to Jacksonian claims "that constitutional questions are to be decided by the Supreme Court," his first inaugural declared:

> if the policy of the government ... is to be irrevocably fixed by decisions of the Supreme Court, the instant they are made,... the people will have ceased, to be their own rulers, having, to that extent, practically resigned their government, into the hands of that eminent tribunal.[24]

Contemporary commentators treat this claim as the seminal expression of constitutional departmentalism, the view that elected officials may resolve constitutional questions as they see fit.[25] Closer reading suggests Lincoln did

---

[21] Lincoln, 4 *Collected Works*, p. 207. See Lincoln, 4 *Collected Works*, pp. 201, 259, 270–1.

[22] Lincoln, 4 *Collected Works*, pp. 5, 162, 258, 263, 270.

[23] Lincoln, 2 *Collected Works*, pp. 269, 246.

[24] Lincoln, 4 *Collected Works*, p. 268.

[25] See Larry D. Kramer, *The People Themselves: Popular Constitutionalism and Judicial Review* (Oxford University Press: New York, 2004), pp. 211–12; Herbert Wechsler, "The Courts and the Constitution," 65 *Columbia Law Review*, 1001, 1008 (1965).

not reject judicial authority to settle constitutional controversies. Instead, he advanced a vision of judicial supremacy that reconciled judicial power with democratic majoritarianism.

Before assuming the presidency, Lincoln had vigorously defended judicial supremacy. In an early speech in the Illinois state legislature, he asserted: "that the individuals composing our [state] Supreme Court have, in an official capacity, decided in favor of the constitutionality of the bank, would, in my mind, seem a sufficient answer to" the claim that the state bank was unconstitutional. The state judiciary was "the tribunal, by which and which alone, the constitutionality of the Bank can ever be settled."[26] His speech in Congress on internal improvements declared: "The constitutional question will probably never be better settled than it is, until it shall pass under judicial consideration."[27] In 1856, with specific reference to federal power over slavery, Lincoln argued that "[t]he Supreme Court of the United States is the tribunal to decide such questions, and we will submit to its decisions; and if you do also, there will be an end of the matter."[28]

The first inaugural and other speeches implied that courts retained the power to settle constitutional controversies. While Lincoln denied that "the policy of the government" could "be **irrevocably** fixed by the decisions of the Supreme Court, **the instant they are made**"(emphasis added),[29] he implicitly affirmed that "the policy of government could be irrevocably fixed by the decisions of the Supreme Court" **over time.** Republican elected officials retained the power to seek bans on slavery in the territories, Lincoln maintained, only because the rule of *Dred Scott* was not "fully settled."[30] An aberrant judicial decision could not forever resolve a constitutional issue. *Dred Scott* would have been good law had the issue "been before the court more than once" and "been affirmed and re-affirmed through a course of years." "[I]t ... might be ... factious, nay, even revolutionary, to not acquiesce in it as a precedent," Lincoln stated, had the Taney Court ruling "been made by the unanimous concurrence of the judges, without any apparent partisan bias, and in accordance with legal public expectation, and with the steady practice of the departments through our history."[31] *Dred*

---

[26] Lincoln, 1 *Collected Works,* pp. 62–3. See Lincoln, 1 *Collected Works,* pp. 69, 109, 112–13, 171, 237, 247–8.

[27] Lincoln, 1 *Collected Works,* p. 486.

[28] Lincoln, 2 *Collected Works,* p. 355.

[29] Lincoln, 4 *Collected Works,* p. 268.

[30] Lincoln, 2 *Collected Works,* pp. 400–1.

[31] Lincoln, 2 *Collected Works,* p. 401.

Scott did not, in his view, satisfy these conditions. The right to bring slaves into the territories was "not ... yet quite established [as] a settled doctrine for the country," Lincoln argued, because that judicial decision was "wanting in all these claims to public confidence." [32] Nevertheless, on the campaign trial, Lincoln never proposed substituting presidential authority for the judicial power to establish official constitutional meanings. Republican political efforts were directed at securing judicial change, at having *Dred Scott* "reversed if we can, and a new judicial rule established upon this subject." [33] "We think the *Dred Scott* decision is erroneous," Lincoln stated. "We know the court that made it, has often over-ruled its own decisions, and we shall do what we can to have it over-rule this." [34]

The sixteenth president never specified the precise conditions necessary for permanently settling constitutional controversies. He sometimes declared "a decided majority" could "accomplish the ... settlement" of constitutional debates over slavery. [35] Other speeches declared "constitutional questions ... fully settled" when judicial decisions were "affirmed and re-affirmed through a course of years." [36] These claims provide two judicial paths by which *Dred Scott* could become established constitutional law. Lincoln's reference to "apparent partisan bias" suggests Republican elected officials would be constitutionally obligated to respect a decision made by Republican judicial appointees protecting the right to bring slaves into the territories. Lincoln's reference to "a course of years" suggests that *Dred Scott* could become settled law if, as a result of a series of elections, popular majorities clearly authorized Jacksonian elected officials and justices to maintain the slaveholding republic. [37] Had *Dred Scott* been judicially reaffirmed after overwhelming Douglas victories in 1860 and 1864, those decisions might have settled forever the constitutional status of slavery in the territories.

The stakes in the election of 1860 highlighted the close practical connection between forging permanent majorities and securing the consistent reaffirmation of a judicial precedent. Republicans sought to control the elected branches of the national government in part to forestall the series of judicial decisions necessary to make *Dred Scott* permanent constitutional law. Lincoln would "prevent these things being done by either ***congresses***

---

[32] Lincoln, 2 *Collected Works,* p. 401.
[33] Lincoln, 3 *Collected Works,* p. 255.
[34] Lincoln, 2 *Collected Works,* pp. 400–1.
[35] Lincoln, 4 *Collected Works,* p. 2.
[36] Lincoln, 2 *Collected Works,* pp. 400–1.
[37] This was Herbert Wechsler's view. See Wechsler, "The Courts," pp. 1008–9.

or *courts*," he promised; "the people are the rightful masters of both congress, and courts," he asserted, "not to overthrow the constitution, but to overthrow the *men* who pervert it" (emphases in original).[38] Antebellum Americans from all sections of the United States anticipated that, if Republicans established a decided majority in the elected branches of government, then the Supreme Court would in time issue a steady stream of constitutional decisions elaborating moderate antislavery principles. "With a Northern Executive to nominate Judges, and a Northern Senate to confirm," Senator David Yulee asked with concern, "how long would it be before the Supreme Bench might be filled with judges imbued with Northern sentiments and bias, and instrumental to Northern purposes of aggression?"[39] To the extent judicial supremacy attached only to enduring judicial commitments, and to the extent that enduring judicial commitments were likely to reflect the constitutional vision of a dominant and stable political coalition, free- and slave-state politicians recognized that judicial supremacy was quite compatible with democratic majoritarianism.

Good reason exists for thinking Lincoln's precise attitudes toward the judiciary were instrumental, as were those of his political rivals. Attitudes toward the Supreme Court in 1861 were rooted in beliefs about the legitimacy of sectional majorities, not beliefs about the relative merits of justices and elected officials as constitutional authorities. Neither Jacksonians nor Republicans demonstrated any firm position on judicial authority that transcended *Dred Scott*. During the debates with Douglas, Lincoln noted that Jacksonians who vigorously attacked judicial power during the 1830s were now championing judicial supremacy.[40] Many Northern Whigs who celebrated judicial power during the 1830s suddenly discovered the virtues of Jeffersonian departmentalism during the late 1850s.[41] The possibility exists that Lincoln had abandoned previous commitments to judicial supremacy by his first inaugural or during the events leading up to *Ex parte Merryman*.[42] Yet whatever his exact position on judicial power in March 1861, Lincoln's understanding of constitutional authority was rooted in his commitment to the power of a free-state majority to resolve constitutional controversies. Judicial supremacy was at stake in 1861 because the federal courts had become the last bastion of slave-state power.

---

[38] Lincoln, 3 *Collected Works*, p. 435. See Lincoln, 3 *Collected Works*, pp. 421, 460.
[39] *Congressional Globe*, 31st Cong., 1st Sess., p. 1162.
[40] Lincoln, 3 *Collected Works*, pp. 27–8.
[41] See Charles Warren, *The Supreme Court in United States History*, vol. 2, rev. ed. (Little, Brown: Boston, 1947), pp. 213–14.
[42] 17 F. Cas. 144 (C.C.D. Md. 1861).

The Majoritarian Conception of Constitutional Evil

Lincoln's majoritarianism provides an attractive solution to the problem of constitutional evil. No one in 1861 could have proposed policies that Americans throughout the United States thought consistent with fundamental human rights. The best anyone could offer was a commitment to relying on fair political procedures when making slavery policy. Some political and constitutional evil is a necessary consequence of a pluralistic society. When people disagree over principles of justice, government must necessarily adopt a policy some people think morally wrong. Accommodations for evils are justified, therefore, when embedded in political processes recognized as intrinsically fair and as the best instrumental means for mitigating actual injustice.

Democratic majoritarianism seems a particularly appropriate theory of political authority for a polity wracked by problems of constitutional evil. Majority rule promotes self-government, which "maximizes the number of persons who can exercise self-determination in collective decisions." [43] More people are governed by the rules they think best in majoritarian regimes than under alternative political arrangements. Majoritarianism also promotes good government: Robert Dahl points out that "majority rule" is "more likely than any other to lead to correct decisions." [44] If we make the reasonable assumption that people are more likely, even infinitesimally more likely, to hold right than wrong opinions on any political question, then the policy preferred by the most people is most likely the right policy.

Majority rule has several characteristics that reduce the unavoidable incidence of constitutional evil in a heterogeneous society. Majority rule limits perceptions of constitutional evil. When majorities determine whether to ban slavery in the territories, for example, government makes the policy choice fewest persons think evil. Majority rule also reduces the actual incidence of constitutional evil. If citizens are capable of preferring justice to injustice, then the policy preferred by the majority is more likely to be just than the policy preferred by the minority. When people agree on majority rule, majoritarian solutions to political disputes do not add procedural insult to substantive injury.

Majority rule is not a perfect solution for problems of constitutional evil. Majoritarianism does not reduce constitutional evil when majoritarian preferences are far weaker than minority preferences. [45] Minority rule is a better

---

[43] Robert A. Dahl, *Democracy and Its Critics* (Yale University Press: New Haven, 1989), p. 138.

[44] Dahl, *Democracy and Its Critics*, p. 141.

[45] See Robert A. Dahl, *A Preface to Democratic Theory* (University of Chicago Press: Chicago, 1956), pp. 98–9.

vehicle for limiting constitutional evil in a society whose minority believes abolition a horrible evil and whose majority regards slavery only as an inefficient practice. Majority rule is often meaningless when citizens face more than two policy choices, none of which enjoys majoritarian support. Political scientists and economists recognize that certain axioms of democracy must be modified when public preferences cannot be rank ordered.[46]

Lincoln's claim that majoritarian principles justified Republican efforts to ban slavery in the territories nevertheless seems justified even when these problems with majority rule are acknowledged. Republicans believed slavery to be as evil as Southerners regarded abolition. Given this distribution of public preferences, majority rule was the procedure most likely to minimize public perceptions of constitutional evil. The antebellum debate over slavery did not exhibit those characteristics that render majoritarianism meaningless. Preferences in the debate over slavery *could* be rank ordered. Lincoln claimed power to reverse the result in *Dred Scott* only when Republicans enjoyed a "decided majority." Such a majority would presumably have been one sufficiently strong to avoid the cycling problems that create democratic instability. Rule by a Republican majority under these circumstances did seem the best procedural solution to the problems of constitutional evil associated with slavery.

Problems with Democratic Majoritarianism

What Popular Majority?

In 1860, the practical problem with this majoritarian defense of Republican power to reverse *Dred Scott* was that democratic majorities did not support antislavery policies. The congressional elections held that year revealed the general public's ambivalence about slavery and *Dred Scott*. Republicans picked up five Senate seats, but their total of 31 was one short of the majority needed to control a 64-seat Senate. Lincoln's party lost seven seats in the House of Representatives. Had the slave states not seceded, Republicans would have controlled only 106 of the 237 seats in the lower chamber of Congress. Northern Democrats recognized this limitation on Republican power. Stephen Douglas urged Southerners not to secede because Democrats still had sufficient power in the House of Representatives to defeat all antislavery proposals emanating from the administration.[47]

---

[46] The canonical work in this tradition is Kenneth J. Arrow, *Social Choice and Individual Values*, 2nd ed. (Yale University Press: New Haven, 1963).

[47] Stephen A. Douglas, *The Letters of Stephen A. Douglas* (ed. Robert W. Johannsen) (University of Illinois Press: Urbana, 1961), p. 501.

The Lincoln presidency presents another practical difficulty. Lincoln was a plurality president: he received only 39.8 percent of the votes cast in the 1860 presidential election. This is the lowest percentage received by any winning presidential candidate in American history. Lincoln did receive a clear majority of the electoral college. Contemporary democratic majoritarians, however, think the electoral college a constitutional stupidity.[48] History confirms the majoritarian failings of Article II. Eighteen presidential winners in national elections held between 1828 and 2004 failed to gain a clear majority of the popular vote. Three failed to gain more popular votes than their closest rival. The theory and practice of the electoral college may be justifiable,[49] but not as a means for furthering majority rule.

The Constitution when interpreted as an effort to establish majority rule consists almost entirely of anomalies. Lincoln condemned the three-fifths clause for giving "[t]he citizens of Slave States ... a political power in the general government beyond their single votes."[50] The Senate provides small states with political power not justified by their population.[51] Bicameralism, the separation of powers, and the presidential veto create a lawmaking process that consistently frustrates majority rule.[52] Reconciliation may be possible,[53] but these pervasive deviations from majority rule suggest that the Constitution in both 1787 and 1861 was more committed to an alternative form of democratic politics.

Majoritarianism and Democracy

The normative problem with majoritarian justifications for the Republican Party's power to ban slavery in the territories is that majority rule is neither an axiom of democratic theory nor the fundamental procedural commitment underlying the Constitution of 1787. The constitutional commitment

---

[48] See Akhil Reed Amar, "A Constitutional Accident Waiting to Happen," *Constitutional Stupidities, Constitutional Tragedies* (ed. William N. Eskridge, Jr., and Sanford Levinson) (New York University Press: New York, 1998), p. 15.

[49] See Keith E. Whittington, "The Electoral College: A Modest Contribution," *The Longest Night: Polemics and Perspectives on Election 2000* (ed. Arthur J. Jacobson and Michel Rosenfeld) (University of California Press: Berkeley, 2002); Judith Best, *The Case against Direct Election of the President* (Ithaca: Cornell University Press, 1975).

[50] Lincoln, 2 *Collected Works*, p. 246. See Lincoln, 2 *Collected Works*, pp. 269–70.

[51] See William N. Eskridge, Jr., "The One Senator, One Vote Clauses," *Constitutional Stupidities*; Suzanna Sherry, "Our Unconstitutional Senate," *Constitutional Stupidities*; Frances E. Lee and Bruce I. Oppenheimer, *Sizing Up the Senate: The Unequal Consequences of Equal Representation* (University of Chicago Press: Chicago, 1999).

[52] See generally Mark Tushnet, "The Whole Thing," *Constitutional Stupidities*.

[53] See e.g. John Hart Ely, *Democracy and Distrust: A Theory of Judicial Review* (Harvard University Press: Cambridge, 1980).

to democratic republicanism did not necessarily entail a constitutional commitment to democratic majoritarianism. Although Lincoln's first inaugural treats the alternative to majority rule as minority rule,[54] prominent democratic theorists disagree. Consensus democrats challenge the "flawed paradigm of majority rule."[55] They think the best governing processes maximize the number of persons who influence public policy rather than the number of persons who think the best policy was chosen. Arend Lijphart, the leading champion of consensus democracy, declares that "instead of being satisfied with narrow decision-making majorities," popular government should "aim at broad participation in government and broad agreement on the policies government should pursue."[56] A policy that virtually all citizens think reasonable, in this view, is more democratic than the policy slightly more than half the citizenry thinks best.

Proponents of consensus democracy insist that majority rule is more likely to exacerbate than resolve problems of constitutional evil. Majoritarianism, they maintain, is suited only for societies whose citizens agree on fundamental regime questions. Political losers tolerate their absolute lack of power because actual differences between ins and outs are relatively small.[57] When persons dispute more fundamental questions, majoritarian political institutions prove destructive to the regime. "In plural societies" where people are divided "into virtually separate subsocieties with their own political parties, interest groups, and media of communication," Lijphart asserts, "majority rule is not only undemocratic but also dangerous because minorities that are continually denied access to power will feel excluded and discriminated against and may lose their allegiance to the regime."[58] Empirical studies conclude that polities with permanent electoral losers suffer from injustice, coercion, and violence.

Consensus democracy does better than majority rule at reducing constitutional evil in pluralistic societies. Power-sharing arrangements limit the perception and incidence of injustice. Institutions that maximize the number of persons who must consent to governmental decisions minimize the number of persons who think governmental policies violate fundamental rights. Assuming persons have some capacity for making just choices, maximizing political participation will best facilitate reasonably just public policies. Broad

---

[54] Lincoln, 4 *Collected Works*, pp. 267–8.

[55] Andre Kaiser, "Types of Democracy: From Classical to New Institutionalism," 9 *Journal of Theoretical Politics*, 419, 429 (1997); Arend Lijphart, "Majority Rule in Theory and Practice: The Tenacity of a Flawed Paradigm," 43 *International Social Science Journal*, 483 (1991).

[56] Arend Lijphart, *Patterns of Democracy: Government Forms and Performance in Thirty-Six Countries* (Yale University Press: New Haven, 1999), p. 2.

[57] Lijphart, *Patterns of Democracy*, p. 32. See Lijphart, *Patterns of Democracy*, p. 46.

[58] Lijphart, *Patterns of Democracy*, pp. 32–3.

participation promotes political fairness. "To exclude the losing groups from participation in decision-making," Lijphart declares, "clearly violates the primary meaning of democracy."[59] Power-sharing arrangements are known to help prevent secession and civil war. Internal violence is less likely in consensus than in majoritarian regimes.[60]

The United States in 1787 and 1861 exhibited the social pluralism thought to require consensus democracy. Antebellum Americans lived in a polity divided "into virtually separate subsocieties with their own political parties, interest groups, and media of communication." Political groups and interests were geographically concentrated to an exceptional degree. No Republican influenced policy in South Carolina. No interest group fought to reestablish slavery in Massachusetts. The vast majority of citizens identified with their local community.[61] With the exception of a few elites, Americans learned about the world from a local, highly partisan press. Few national institutions fostered capacities to transcend local prejudices.

Prominent slaveholders and their Northern Jacksonian allies repeatedly insisted that the antebellum United States was a polity best governed by institutions presently associated with consensus democracy. "Without a balance of power such as will enable every interest to protect itself," Jefferson Davis declared, "the great purposes of this Union could never be preserved."[62] Stephen Douglas began and ended his debates with Lincoln by insisting that national coalitions govern the United States. He declared as "radically wrong" "any political creed … which cannot be proclaimed in every State, and in every section of th[e] Union."[63] "If such an organization as the Republican party should acquire complete possession of the federative government," Samuel Tilden asked, "what sort of system would it be?" His answer was: "to the people of the fifteen states it would be a foreign government."[64] As noted previously, rights were negotiable when slave-state representatives were parties to the negotiation. The Nashville Convention of 1850 declared

[59] Lijphart, *Patterns of Democracy,* p. 31 (quoting Arthur Lewis).

[60] Ian S. Lusick, Dan Miodownik, and Roy J. Eidelson, "Secession in Multicultural States: Does Sharing Power Prevent or Encourage It," 98 *American Political Science Review,* 209 (2004); Lijphart, *Patterns of Democracy,* pp. 260–1, 271.

[61] See Alexander Hamilton, James Madison, and John Jay, *The Federalist Papers* (New American Library: New York, 1961), p. 294.

[62] *Congressional Globe,* 31st Cong., 1st Sess., App., p. 150. See *Congressional Globe,* 31st Cong., 1st Sess., p. 1162 (speech of David Yulee); Robert Young Hayne, *An Oration. Delivered in the Independent or Congregational Church, Charleston* (A.E. Miller: Charleston, 1831), pp. 29–30; Jesse T. Carpenter, *The South as a Conscious Minority, 1789–1861: A Study in Political Thought* (University of South Carolina Press: Columbia, 1930), pp. 109–10.

[63] Stephen Douglas, "Seventh Joint Debate," *The Lincoln–Douglas Debates of 1858* (ed. Robert W. Johannsen) (Oxford University Press: New York, 1965), p. 288.

[64] Carpenter, *The South,* p. 125 (quoting Samuel Tilden).

that Southerners would forgo their constitutional right to bring slaves into certain Northern regions in return for "an equitable partition of the territories."[65] During the antebellum years, Southern proposals for constitutional reform would have countered Northern population increases by creating more consensual democratic institutions. Calhoun endorsed a concurrent majority that would "prevent any one interest or combination of interests from using the powers of government to aggrandize itself at the expense of others by taking the sense of each interest or portion of the community which may be unequally and injuriously affected by the action of the government separately through its own majority ... and to require the consent of each interest."[66] On the eve of the Civil War, Southern moderates offered numerous constitutional amendments that would have created an executive branch balanced between Northern and Southern interests. Proposals included requiring the presidency to be rotated between the sections or a multimembered presidency, with representatives from all sections each having veto power over the others.[67]

Lincoln and other antislavery Republicans excoriated institutions associated with consensus democracy. Lincoln described proposals aimed at ensuring a balance of sectional power in the executive branch of the national government as "open folly."[68] Opponents of slavery on the eve of the Civil War publicly favored sectional parties that would not be politically compelled to compromise with slaveholders. Lincoln declared that "the abolition of slavery in the territory of the United States can never be accomplished unless the North is united." Free-state citizens were urged to "form the United Party of the North."[69] "With the friends of Fremont," the future president asserted when campaigning in 1856, "it is an *expected necessity* ... to elect him, if at all, principally, by free state votes" (emphasis in original).[70]

The first inaugural address misleads contemporary readers by implying that a broad antebellum consensus existed on majority rule. Jacksonians preferred those slavery policies that commanded the broadest national support to those that any simple majority might think best. Democratic theory does not resolve this issue. Committed republicans then and now dispute the

---

[65] "Resolutions of the Nashville Convention," *Documents of American History*, vol. 1 (ed. Henry Steele Commager) (Appleton-Century-Crofts: New York, 1963), p. 325.

[66] John C. Calhoun, *A Disquisition on Government and Sections from the Discourse* (ed. C. Gordon Post) (Bobbs-Merrill: Indianapolis, 1953), p. 20.

[67] See *Congressional Globe*, 36th Cong., 2nd Sess., pp. 78 (speech of John W. Noell), 82–3 (speech of Andrew Johnson), 329 (speech of Robert Hunter); Carpenter, *The South*, pp. 96–7.

[68] Lincoln, 2 *Collected Works*, p. 354. See Lincoln, 3 *Collected Works*, p. 388; Lincoln, 2 *Collected Works*, p. 368.

[69] Lincoln, 2 *Collected Works*, p. 9.

[70] Lincoln, 2 *Collected Works*, p. 356.

merits of majority rule. Jeremy Waldron and Lincoln defend majoritarianism.[71] Arend Lijphart and Stephen Douglas favor consensual democracy.[72] Antebellum constitutional history is clearer. Both the Constitution created in 1787 and the Jacksonian Constitution support the claim that, when Lincoln took office, the United States was more committed to consensus than majoritarian democracy.

Majoritarianism and the Constitution

Majoritarianism was clearly not the central value underlying the Constitution of 1787. Scholars detail how the persons responsible for that constitutional order sought to stem an egalitarian tide that engulfed the nation during and immediately after the American Revolution.[73] Federalists believed republican government should secure a common good that was frequently opposed to what unrefined popular majorities preferred. They feared a factional politics that enabled government to do whatever most ordinary people thought best. The original Constitution was committed to democratic elitism reinforced by republican filters, to government by those best able to discern the public interest and protect fundamental rights. "All of the Federalists' desires to establish a strong and respectable nation in the world," Gordon Wood details, "depended upon the prerequisite maintenance of aristocratic politics."[74]

Determining whether the original constitutional commitment to republican elitism is more consistent with consensus or majoritarian democracy shoehorns an eighteenth-century political vision into categories created during the late twentieth century. The primary concern of many Federalists was to create a democratic republic that retained certain aristocratic virtues.[75] Federalist discussions of majoritarianism were far more concerned with how ordinary people should participate in politics than with differences between majoritarian and consensus orders. Nevertheless, the means Federalists used to implement aristocratic republicanism are far more consistent with consensus than majoritarian democracy. When sectional issues were explicitly on the table, the leading proponents of ratification made clear that constitutional institutions should strive for a broad consensus on acceptable policy.

---

[71] Jeremy Waldron, *Law and Disagreement* (Oxford University Press: New York, 1999), p. 109.

[72] Lijphart, *Patterns of Democracy*, especially pp. 301–8.

[73] See Gordon S. Wood, *The Radicalism of the American Revolution* (Knopf: New York, 1992); Stanley Elkins and Eric McKitrick, *The Age of Federalism: The Early American Republic, 1788–1800* (Oxford University Press: New York, 1993).

[74] Gordon S. Wood, *The Creation of the American Republic* (Norton: New York, 1969), p. 492.

[75] Wood, *Creation*, p. 517. See Wood, *Creation*, pp. 480, 485, 496, 508, 513.

The Constitution of 1787 adopted those institutional practices presently associated with the "federal-unitary dimension" of consensus democracy. Consensus democracies are characterized by federalism, bicameralism, hard-to-amend constitutions, judicial review, and independent central banks.[76] The original Constitution explicitly established the first three, implicitly established the fourth, and was immediately interpreted as sanctioning the fifth. The framers created or maintained independent state governments, a bicameral legislature with differently constituted houses, and a constitution that could be changed only by extraordinary majorities. Most persons in 1787 expected that courts would have the power to declare laws unconstitutional,[77] and that practice soon developed.[78] Congress gave the original constitutional order a perfect score on the federal-unitary dimension of consensus democracy by incorporating an independent central bank in 1791.

The constitutional order of 1787 also sought to secure several important institutional practices associated with the "executive-parties dimension" of consensus democracy. Consensus democracies are characterized by an "executive–legislative balance of power," "broad multiparty coalitions," "multiparty systems," "proportional representation," and "corporatist interest groups systems aimed at compromise and concentration."[79] The original Constitution explicitly established the first, was designed to secure the second and third, and devised alternatives to the fourth and fifth. The framers created an executive–legislative balance by providing that the president and members of Congress be elected separately. They thought a large republic would result in either a multiparty system or no party system. Most elections in 1787 took place in single-member districts, but those districts were thought large enough to prevent two-party competition from developing in most localities.[80] The large republic and large election districts were also thought sufficient to prevent either corporatism or interest-group politics.

The framers rejected virtually every institutional practice associated with majoritarian democracy. Contemporary majoritarian democracies are characterized by "united and centralized government," a "unicameral legislature,"

[76] Lijphart, *Patterns of Democracy*, pp. 2–3.

[77] See William E. Nelson, *Marbury v. Madison: The Origins and Legacy of Judicial Review* (University Press of Kansas: Lawrence, 2000), pp. 34–40; Maeva Marcus, "Judicial Review in the Early Republic," *Launching the "Extended Republic": The Federalist Era* (ed. Ronald Hoffman and Peter J. Albert) (University Press of Virginia: Charlottesville, 1996); Jack N. Rakove, "The Origins of Judicial Review: A Plea for New Contexts," 49 *Stanford Law Review*, 1031 (1997); Mark A. Graber, "The Problematic Establishment of Judicial Review," *The Supreme Court and American Politics: New Institutionalist Approaches* (ed. Howard Gillman and Cornell Clayton) (University Press of Kansas: Lawrence, 1999).

[78] See Nelson, *Marbury*, pp. 72–94.

[79] Lijphart, *Patterns of Democracy*, p. 2.

[80] See Hamilton, Madison, and Jay, *Federalist Papers*, pp. 81–2; Wood, *Creation*, pp. 504–5, 510–12.

"flexible constitutions that can be amended by simple majorities," "legislatures [that] have the final word on the constitutionality of their own legislation," "central banks that are dependent on the executive," "single-party majority cabinets," "executive–legislative relationships in which the executive is dominant," "two-party systems," "majoritarian electoral systems," and "pluralist interest group systems."[81] The Constitution of 1787 rejected united and centralized government, a unicameral legislature, an easy amendment process, and executive dominance. The persons responsible for the Constitution almost certainly rejected legislative supremacy. Federalists thought two-party competition, single-party cabinets, and interest-group politics undesirable. They were divided on national banking. The only accepted political practice at the time of the framing that is presently associated with majoritarian democracy is winner-take-all elections. Single-member districts, however, were neither constitutionally mandated in 1787[82] nor understood as distinctively majoritarian practices. The framers thought large electoral districts would prevent permanent majorities from forming.

Federalists did their constitutional best in 1787 to prevent the development of a two-party system, the practice central to majoritarian democracy. Most framers opposed all political parties. "Parties," they believed, "are the dangerous diseases of civil freedom."[83] Convinced that parties and factions could not be entirely eradicated, proponents of the Constitution sought to create the environment necessary for the multiparty system favored by consensus democrats. "Atticus" feared "two factions of nearly equal strength ... would either mutually destroy each other ... or the contest would terminate in the utter extinction of one, and the insolent triumph of the other." "Either event," he concluded, "would introduce a most insupportable tyranny. Hence the necessity of a third power sufficient to check both."[84] Madison championed the large republic as the best republican means for preventing two-party politics at the national level. "Extend the sphere" of government, he famously declared, "and you take in a greater variety of parties and interests."[85]

Proponents of the Constitution, moreover, repeatedly condemned simple majoritarianism. George Washington thought "a **bare** majority ... [was]

---

[81] Lijphart, *Patterns of Democracy*, pp. 2–3.

[82] Single-member districts for congressional elections were legislatively mandated in 1842, another example of the majoritarian tendencies of Jacksonian America; see 5 Stat. 491.

[83] Wood, *Creation*, p. 403 (quoting the *Charleston S.C. and American Gazette*). See "A Citizen of America", in *Friends of the Constitution: Writings of the "Other" Federalists, 1787–1788* (ed. Colleen A. Sheehan and Gary L. McDowell) (Liberty Fund: Indianapolis, 1998), p. 374.

[84] "Atticus", "Essays: I–IV," *Friends of the Constitution*, pp. 331, 335.

[85] Hamilton, Madison, and Jay, *Federalist Papers*, p. 83.

... to be deprecated" (emphasis in original).[86] Madison believed that "there is no maxim in my opinion which is more liable to be misapplied ... than the current one that the interest of the majority is the political standard of right and wrong."[87] Another Federalist complained of "faction, dissension, and consequent subjugation of the minority to the caprice and arbitrary decisions of the majority, who instead of consulting the interests of the whole community collectively attend to partial and local advantages."[88] Noah Webster agreed. "[P]ure democracy," he wrote, "proves both to be inconsistent with the peace of society, and the rights of freemen."[89] The persons responsible for the original Constitution were obsessed by the perceived need to prevent the tyranny of the majority, "democratic despotism,"[90] and "the licentiousness of the people."[91] The generation that ratified the Constitution redefined tyranny to include simple majoritarianism. Madison and Jefferson proclaimed that "an elective despotism is not the government we fought for." Federalists championed the separation of powers, a central practice in consensus democracy, as the best means for preventing simple majoritarian rule. "The concentrat[ion]" of "all the powers of government ... in the same hands," Madison and Jefferson agreed, "is precisely the definition of despotic government."[92]

In 1787, majority rule was revered as well as feared. Prominent framers agreed that majorities were entitled to rule. As Madison wrote, "the will of the majority [is] to be deemed the will of the whole."[93] Fisher Ames thought that "the people must be governed by a majority."[94] Other Federalists declared that "the minority must yield to the majority,"[95] and that

---

[86] George Washington, *George Washington: A Collection* (ed. W. B. Allen) (Liberty Classics: Indianapolis, 1988), p. 381.

[87] James Madison, *Letters and Other Writings of James Madison*, vol. 1 (R. Worthington: New York, 1884), pp. 250–1.

[88] Jonathan Elliot, ed., *The Debates in the Several State Conventions on the Adoption of the Federal Constitution as Recommended by the General Convention at Philadelphia in 1787*, vol. 3 (Lippincott: Philadelphia, 1836), p. 107. See Fisher Ames, "Speech," *Friends of the Constitution*, p. 199; Wood, *Creation*, p. 502.

[89] "A Citizen of America", in *Friends of the Constitution*, p. 378. See Wood, *Creation*, pp. 413, 609.

[90] Wood, *Creation*, p. 404.

[91] "Fabius" (John Dickinson), "The Letters: VII–IX," *Friends of the Constitution*, p. 487. See Sheehan and McDowell, "Introduction," *Friends of the Constitution*, p. 161.

[92] Hamilton, Madison, and Jay, *Federalist Papers*, pp. 310–11; Thomas Jefferson, *The Portable Thomas Jefferson* (ed. Merrill D. Peterson) (Penguin: New York, 1975), p. 164. See "Fabius" (John Dickinson), "The Letters: IV–VI," *Friends of the Constitution*, p. 219; Wood, *Creation*, pp. 447–553, 608.

[93] James Madison, *The Writings of James Madison*, vol. 9 (ed. Gaillard Hunt) (Putnam's: New York, 1910), p. 570.

[94] Ames, "Speech," *Friends of the Constitution*, p. 197.

[95] "Civis" (David Ramsey), "An Address to the Freemen of South Carolina on the Subject of the Federal Constitution," *Friends of the Constitution*, p. 450.

"in a free government every man binds himself to obey the public voice, or the opinions of a majority."[96] Persons who endorsed the social contract, the *Providence Gazette* maintained, agreed "[t]o submit to the form of government agreed upon by the majority."[97]

Federalists resolved their ambivalence about popular majorities by devising a "republican remedy for the diseases most incident to republican government."[98] Their constitutional order promoted rule by deliberative, nonpartisan, and national majorities. The persons responsible for the Constitution of 1787 established those government institutions they believed secured the best persons for national office and allowed those persons to deliberate on the common good.[99] "Nothing but the real weight of character," James Wilson declared, "can give a man real influence over a large district."[100] Noah Webster thought that senators with long terms of office would "gradually lose their partiality, generalize their views, and consider themselves as acting for the whole confederacy."[101] Constitutional institutions were designed to ensure that no single coalition would control all political powers. Gordon Wood notes that the framers sought to "prevent[] ... various social interests from incorporating themselves too firmly in the government."[102] Washington's decision to include both Hamilton and Jefferson in his first cabinet reflected the framing desire that all influential political factions find a place in the executive branch.

Sectional majorities were regarded as the worst form of faction. Washington's Farewell Address proclaimed a "matter of serious concern, that any ground should have been furnished for characterizing parties by *Geographical* discrimination: *Northern* and *Southern; Atlantic* and *Western*" (emphases in original).[103] As we have seen, constitutional institutions were designed to guarantee broad national support for any national policy related to slavery or to any other divisive issue. Had the Constitution of 1787 been

[96] "A Citizen of America", in *Friends of the Constitution*, p. 396. See "A Citizen of America", in *Friends of the Constitution*, p. 374; "One of Four Thousand", in *Friends of the Constitution*, p. 317.

[97] Wood, *Creation*, p. 284. See "A Countryman" (Roger Sherman), "The Letters: I–II," *Friends of the Constitution*, p. 263; "America" (Noah Webster), "Essay," *Friends of the Constitution*, p. 177; Wood, *Creation*, p. 412 (quoting the *Boston Independent Chronicle*).

[98] Hamilton, Madison, and Jay, *Federalist Papers*, p. 84.

[99] See Ames, "Speech," *Friends of the Constitution*, p. 200; Herbert J. Storing, "The 'Other' Federalist Papers: A Preliminary Sketch," *Friends of the Constitution*, p. xli.

[100] James Wilson, "Speech," *Friends of the Constitution*, p. 204.

[101] "A Citizen of America" (Noah Webster), "An Examination into the Leading Principles of the Federal Constitution," *Friends of the Constitution*, p. 383. See "A Citizen of the United States", in *Friends of the Constitution*, p. 384.

[102] Wood, *Creation*, p. 606.

[103] George Washington, "Farewell Address," *George Washington*, p. 517.

functioning as expected, no policy vigorously opposed by any section could ever become law.[104] Politicians in both the free and slave states would be obliged to compromise in order to gain the support necessary to pass measures of value to their constituents.

Federalists advanced a consensual notion of constitutional change. Ratification and amendment required bisectional support. The Constitution, "State Soldier" declared, was in "the interest of more than seven of the northern states, since we know it will require more than the consent of that number to set it in motion." Bare majorities could not dictate the constitutional future. Constitutional amendments needed the same bisectional consensus necessary for ratification. Referring to Article V, "State Soldier" claimed "the same causes which establishes must remain to support it."[105] Contemporary commentators recognize the bisectional aspiration underlying Article V. As Martin Diamond notes, "the real aim and practical effect of the complicated amending procedure was not at all to give power to minorities, but to ensure that passage of an amendment would require a ***nationally*** distributed majority" (emphasis in original).[106] The framers left "all legal power in the hands of ordinary majorities so long as they [were] national majorities."[107]

Evolving Constitutional Understandings

The original constitutional attempt to empower a republican aristocracy was largely abandoned within a decade. Constitutional forms proved to be mere parchment barriers, unable to hold back more popular democratic tides.[108] The feared two-party system began forming during the Washington administration, championed to a significant degree by the formerly antiparty stalwart James Madison.[109] The election of 1800 and the passage of the Twelfth Amendment furthered the majoritarian revolution in American politics.[110] By the 1840s, politics was structured by the most vigorous two-party system ever seen in the world. The more successful of the two parties, the Jacksonian Democrats, celebrated majority rule in both theory and practice, though majorities consisted only of white men.

---

[104] See Part II, notes 54–70 and the relevant text.

[105] "State Soldier", "Essays: I, II, V," *Friends of the Constitution*, p. 130.

[106] Martin Diamond, "Democracy and The Federalist: A Reconsideration of the Framers' Intent," 53 *American Political Science Review*, 52, 57 (1959).

[107] Diamond, "Democracy and The Federalist," p. 58.

[108] Wood, *Radicalism*, p. 369. See Bruce Ackerman, *We the People: Foundations* (Harvard University Press: Cambridge, 1991), p. 70.

[109] See Sidney M. Milkis, *Political Parties and Constitutional Government: Remaking American Democracy* (Johns Hopkins University Press: Baltimore, 1999), pp. 3–4.

[110] Bruce Ackerman, *The Failure of the Founding Fathers: Jefferson, Marshall, and the Rise of Presidential Democracy* (Harvard University Press: Cambridge, 2005).

Nevertheless, the Republican Party was not a majority coalition of the type the Jacksonian constitutional order authorized to resolve constitutional controversies concerning slavery. Jacksonians were not constitutionally committed to letting simple majorities of white males resolve all contested constitutional questions. The second American party system fostered majority rule only on issues directly concerned with national economic development. Jacksonian political organizers formed bisectional majorities on such issues as the national bank, internal improvements, and the tariff to prevent sectional majorities from forming on slavery issues. Both Democratic and Whig party leaders believed that "national parties and slavery agitation were mutually exclusive."[111] Martin Van Buren, the major architect of the second party system, asserted that if the old bisectional cleavages between Federalists and Democratic-Republicans were not revived, destructive "prejudices between free and slave-holding states [would] inevitably result."[112]

Two changes in the American political order were necessary to provide constitutional sanction for Republican efforts to overturn *Dred Scott*. First, simple majorities had to be acknowledged as being constitutionally authorized to resolve all constitutional controversies. Second, sectional majorities had to be understood as having the same constitutional standing as bisectional majorities. In this new constitutional universe, political parties that took uncompromising stands on slavery in the territories would be as legitimate as the Jacksonian parties that took uncompromising stands on the national bank. These constitutional transformations had not occurred before Lincoln took office. Free-state citizens who in 1828 rejected the original Constitution's antagonism to political parties could elect Lincoln in 1860 only by rejecting the Jacksonian Constitution's antagonism to sectional parties.

After the Civil War, Republicans constitutionalized their hostility both to slavery and to the political order they thought provided too many accommodations for slaveholders. The Constitution of 1868 embodied the prewar Republican commitment to democratic majoritarianism. The persons responsible for the original constitutional order sought to prevent popular majorities from violating fundamental rights by establishing institutions that would promote a broad consensus on the public good. The persons responsible for the post–Civil War constitution sought to protect fundamental rights by empowering national Northern majorities to act whenever local Southern majorities violated constitutional guarantees. The first sections of the Thirteenth, Fourteenth, and Fifteenth amendments outlawed human bondage

---

[111] John M. McFaul, "Expediency vs. Morality: Jacksonian Politics and Slavery," 62 *Journal of American History*, 24, 27 (1975).

[112] Robert V. Remini, *Martin Van Buren and the Making of the Democratic Party* (Columbia University Press: New York, 1959), p. 131.

and provided important constitutional protections to free blacks. The last sections of each amendment entrusted majorities in the national legislature with primary responsibility for enforcing those guarantees.[113] No effort was made to provide every geographical section or interest group with a de facto veto on national race policy. The united coalition of Northern states that won the Civil War was constitutionally authorized to determine how best to eradicate slavery and ensure that free blacks were treated as equal citizens. Compromise with (former) slaveholders was no longer necessary in constitutional practice or theory. William Nelson correctly notes: "The Fourteenth Amendment was understood less as a legal instrument to be elaborated in the courts than as a peace treaty to be administered by Congress in order to secure the fruits of the North's victory in the Civil War."[114] Decided majorities, in 1868 and 2006, have the constitutional authority to resolve constitutional controversies as they think best whenever they gain constitutional control of all three branches of the national government. But not in 1861.

CONTRACT, CONSENT, AND CONSTITUTIONAL EVIL

Contract and consent theory provide a simpler solution to the problem of constitutional evil that might justify Lincoln's authority to reverse *Dred Scott*. Slaveholders at the constitutional convention bargained for the electoral college, proportional representation in the House of Representatives, and the counting of slaves as three fifths of a person for representation purposes. Republicans were prepared to honor these constitutional agreements. Opponents of slavery who accepted the Constitution, Lincoln insisted, were morally, legally, and politically obligated by their consent to respect these clearly understood constitutional protections for human bondage. Southern framers, however, had not obtained or even bargained for an explicit constitutional guarantee that slave states would always have the political power necessary to defeat any antislavery settlement of contested constitutional questions. Slave-state representatives had consented to the provisions for staffing the national government laid out in Articles I, II, and III. A free-state coalition that gained control of the national government consistently with those rules, therefore, had no obligation to compromise or obtain Southern support when resolving constitutional issues not covered by previous constitutional agreements.

---

[113] See William E. Nelson, *The Fourteenth Amendment: From Political Principle to Judicial Doctrine* (Harvard University Press: Cambridge, 1988), p. 122; Mark A. Graber, "The Constitution as a Whole: A Partial Political Science Perspective," 33 *University of Richmond Law Review*, 343, 364–9 (1999).

[114] Nelson, *The Fourteenth Amendment*, pp. 110–11.

Contract law is a useful vehicle for exploring whether slaveholders who consented to the Constitution also consented to granting sectional majorities in control of the national government the power to resolve constitutional controversies. Antebellum Americans from Madison to Lincoln commonly analogized constitutions to various agreements and insisted that constitutions be interpreted as contracts. Much of contract law and theory lays down rules and principles for determining what duties persons assume when they consent to particular bargains. Legal theorists and common-law judges have considered at great length the problems associated with omitted terms and unforeseen circumstances. Both issues confronted antebellum constitutionalists. Most important, many contracts present problems of constitutional evil in miniature. People bind themselves to perform disagreeable acts in order to bind others to act justly. Hence examining the role and limits of compromise in contract law may yield useful insights into the role and limit of compromise in constitutional law.

As "consent" is determined by the two most prominent approaches to contract law, slaveholders did not consent to be ruled by a free-state coalition. Classical theory insists that parties have a legal duty to perform only clearly agreed-upon obligations. Lincoln could not lawfully ban slavery in the West, in this view, because the Constitution omitted provisions authorizing federal power over slavery in the territories or authorizing the national government to settle constitutional controversies. Neoclassical theory insists parties are not legally bound by the terms of their agreements when, because of mutually unanticipated developments, adhering to the letter of their bargain destroys the value of the bargain. If neither the free nor slave states in 1787 anticipated that a sectional majority could gain control of the national government, then slave-state citizens did not contractually consent to allowing a free-state majority to settle constitutional controversies.

The antebellum Constitution, interpreted consistently with neoclassical theory, obliged free-state coalitions to share power with slaveholders. Leading contemporary authorities on contract law regard bargains as legally binding only when the mutual assumptions underlying the agreement remain valid. When two parties agree on the sales price for a cow that both believe is sterile and the animal turns out not to be sterile, courts following neoclassical principles have ruled that no legal obligation results, even when no contractual provision refers to the cow's fertility.[115] The cow's sterility is a crucial condition underlying the bargain. To the extent constitutions should be interpreted as contracts and all parties to the constitutional contract in 1787

---

[115] *Sherwood v. Walker*, 33 N.W. 919 (Mich. 1887). See *Krell v. Henry*, 2 K.B. 740 (1903).

assumed that constitutional institutions would guarantee a balance of sectional power, then the Constitution was legally binding only as long as that balance of sectional power was maintained. Constitutional authority was premised on constitutional controversies being settled in ways that enjoyed substantial support in both the free and slave states. Free-state coalitions not compelled to compromise with the South as a matter of political necessity, frustration of contract law suggests, were compelled to share power with slaveholders as a condition for maintaining political legitimacy.

Contract is a metaphor and an analogy, not a fully accurate description of the Constitution. Obvious differences exist between legally enforceable bargains and constitutional agreements. The most obvious is that constitutions bind all persons to the political order, not merely those citizens who explicitly consent to constitutional authority.[116] Nevertheless, the differences between contracts and constitutions are not as great as sometimes supposed, particularly when the paradigm of a contract is the bargain necessary to create a multinational corporation rather than the agreement to sell a watch. The contract metaphor is an especially useful vehicle for highlighting how most constitutions are compromises, not declarations of shared values or blueprints of the good society. Just as parties to a contract cooperate so that each may better secure individual interests and values, so the only aspiration that parties to constitutional contracts may have in common is the belief that they are better-off in than out of their constitutional relationship. Constitutional theories attuned to the contractual elements of constitutionalism accommodate the conflicting values that motivate citizens to form constitutional relationships and do not maximize any particular conception of the constitutional good. At the very least, the focus on contracts highlights how constitutional relationships are often between persons who have very different values, interests, and beliefs about justice. Those relationships are jeopardized when practical differences are ignored in pursuit of highly abstracted commonalities.

Lincoln on Constitutional Contracts and Constitutional Evil

Lincoln frequently employed contractual metaphors when discussing sectional issues. The future president referred to "our federal compact."[117] He described constitutions as "bargains."[118] The national government could not interfere with slavery in the states, he argued, because Americans had agreed

---

[116] See Christopher L. Eisgruber, "The Fourteenth Amendment's Constitution," 69 *University of Southern California Law Review*, 47, 57–8 (1995).

[117] Lincoln, 2 *Collected Works*, p. 231.

[118] Lincoln, 1 *Collected Works*, p. 126; Lincoln, 3 *Collected Works*, p. 422.

that the national government would have no power to do so. "I am standing up to our bargain," Lincoln declared in 1858, "for [slavery's] maintenance where it lawfully exists."[119] Continued adherence to the three-fifths clause and fugitive slave laws followed from promises that free-state representatives, states, or citizens had voluntarily given. These proslavery accommodations were "in the bond" Americans made with each other.[120]

Lincoln's majoritarian commitments were tempered by this felt obligation to maintain past compromises embodied in the constitutional text and in extraordinary legislation. Certain statutory bargains on slavery, he felt, had transcended their legislative origins and gained the same "sacred" status as past constitutional bargains.[121] The Missouri Compromise was a "contract made between North and South" that both parties were honor bound to maintain.[122] The resolution annexing Texas was a "sacred contract" binding free-state representatives to support additional slave states in appropriate circumstances.[123] The Compromise of 1850 was a similar agreement. The principle of that compromise, Lincoln declared, "was the system of equivalents":[124] "The North gained two measures and the South three."[125]

Free-state citizens had obligations to support slavery in new territories when and only when such forbearance had been bargained for. Republicans were constitutionally free to propose banning slavery in all territories acquired after 1820 because free-state representatives had never bargained away their right to support free soil in those regions. "The North," Lincoln asserted,

> secured that portion of the Louisiana purchase north of 36.30 to freedom, by giving the South what they demanded as an equivalent therefor, namely, Missouri. We got it fairly and honestly, by paying for it: then what reason was there in endeavoring to make the stipulation upon which we purchased it apply as a principle to other and all future territories?... There was no show of sense in endeavoring to make this bargain apply to any future territory acquired by the United States.[126]

Lincoln would allow slavery in territories outside the Louisiana Purchase if slave states would provide free states with an acceptable quid pro quo. Opposing human bondage in Kansas and Nebraska, he declared: "ask us not to

---

[119] Lincoln, 3 *Collected Works*, pp. 77–8.
[120] Lincoln, 2 *Collected Works*, p. 246. See Lincoln, 3 *Collected Works*, p. 453.
[121] See Lincoln, 3 *Collected Works*, p. 488; Lincoln, 2 *Collected Works*, pp. 230, 236, 252, 258, 285.
[122] Lincoln, 2 *Collected Works*, p. 238.
[123] Lincoln, 3 *Collected Works*, p. 125.
[124] Lincoln, 2 *Collected Works*, p. 259.
[125] Lincoln, 2 *Collected Works*, p. 238.
[126] Lincoln, 2 *Collected Works*, p. 238.

repeat, for nothing, what you paid for in the first instance. If you wish the thing again, pay again."[127] Consistent with this call for negotiation, Lincoln declared his willingness to support slavery in additional territories should the South "pay again." "The North consented to th[e] provision" organizing the New Mexico and Utah territories without reference to slavery, he declared,

> not because they considered it right in itself; but because they were com-
> pensated – paid for it. They, at the same time, got California into the Union
> as a free State .... They also got the area of slavery somewhat narrowed
> in the settlement of the boundary of Texas. Also, they got the slave trade
> abolished in the District of Columbia. For all these desirable objects the
> North could afford to yield something; and they did yield to the South the
> Utah and New Mexico provision .... Now can it be pretended that the
> *principle* of this arrangement requires us to permit the same provision to
> be applied to Nebraska, *without any equivalent at all?* Give us another
> free State; press the boundary of Texas still further back, give us another
> step toward the destruction of slavery in the District, and you present us a
> similar case.[128] (emphases in original)

Maintaining past bargains on slavery was crucial for future sectional accommodation. When Southerners and their Northern sympathizers abrogated the Missouri Compromise without compensation, Northerners opposed to slavery lost the trust necessary to negotiate further. Lack of consideration explains why – while insisting the Republican Party uphold previous protections for slavery that had been paid for by antislavery concessions – Lincoln favored repealing the Kansas–Nebraska Act for offering uncompensated boons to the South. Restoring the Missouri Compromise was vital, Lincoln declared. Otherwise, "we shall have repudiated – discarded from the councils of the nation – the SPIRIT of COMPROMISE; for who after this will ever trust in a national compromise?" Lincoln would bargain further on slavery only when assured that previous and future agreements would be kept. Were the Missouri Compromise line restored, Lincoln continued, "[w]e therefore reinstate the spirit of concession and compromise – that spirit which has never failed us in past perils, and which may be safely trusted for all the future."[129]

Expectations about future events not explicitly embodied in constitutional provisions were not part of constitutional contracts. Lincoln's analysis of the slave trade concluded that present policy makers had no obligations to act

---

[127] Lincoln, 2 *Collected Works*, p. 259.
[128] Lincoln, 2 *Collected Works*, p. 259.
[129] Lincoln, 2 *Collected Works*, p. 272.

consistently with predictions made by those responsible for the original Constitution. "[T]he framers of th[e] Constitution did expect that the African Slave-Trade would be abolished at the end of twenty years," one speech declared. Nevertheless, Lincoln continued, "while they so expected, they gave nothing for that expectation, and they put no provision in the Constitution requiring it should be so abolished."[130] As Lincoln elsewhere commented, "they made no bargain about it."[131] In the absence of particular constitutional sanction, future generations were free to decide whether to ban imported slaves. Had the national government permitted the international slave trade after 1808, disappointed Northerners could not claim that the constitutional contract was violated. "There is absolutely nothing in [the Constitution] about" what was to be done when the twenty-year period came to an end, he informed the people of Cincinnati – "only the expectation of the framers of the Constitution that the Slave-trade would be abolished at the end of that time."[132]

Lincoln's interpretation of the constitutional moratorium on banning the international slave trade explains why he never recognized a constitutional commitment to bisectionalism or a constitutional obligation to share power with slaveholders. If the original constitutional compact did not incorporate general expectations that the slave trade would be banned after twenty years, then that agreement also did not incorporate general expectations that constitutional institutions would never yield antislavery policies without Southern consent. Extratextual expectations about who would control the national government or the status of the slave trade after 1808 were not part of the constitutional bargain. That the Rutledges, Pinckneys, and other slaveholders made a worse constitutional bargain than they realized no more justified altering the duties they voluntarily assumed under the constitutional agreement of 1787 than the mere disappointment of any party to a contract provides legal grounds for changing their voluntarily undertaken obligations. The constitution Southerners bargained for required that slavery policy be made by a House of Representatives elected by population (augmented by slave population), a Senate in which every state had an equal vote, an executive chosen by the electoral college, and a judiciary whose members were nominated by the president and confirmed by the Senate. Whenever Republicans gained control of these institutions, the constitutional compact both authorized that free-state majority to make public policy and bound

[130] Lincoln, 3 *Collected Works*, p. 448.
[131] Lincoln, 3 *Collected Works*, p. 422.
[132] Lincoln, 3 *Collected Works*, p. 448.

Southerners to accept antislavery answers to contested constitutional questions for as long as that antislavery majority held constitutional control of the national government. Lincoln accepted as binding the proslavery answers to constitutional controversies made when Southerners controlled the national government. Turnabout was fair constitutional play.

After winning the presidency, Lincoln frequently rejected proposed constitutional compromises. "No one who has sworn to support the Constitution," he stated, "can conscientiously vote for what he understands to be an unconstitutional measure, however expedient he may think it."[133] The sixteenth president was "inflexible on the territorial question."[134] "I am for no compromise," he informed Seward, "which *assists* or *permits* the extension of the institution on soil owned by the nation."[135] In January 1861, Lincoln bluntly declared: "I will suffer death before I will consent or will advise my friends to consent to any concession or compromise which looks like buying the privilege of taking possession of this government to which we have a constitutional right."[136] These refusals to compromise, however, exercised Northern rights under the constitutional contract without denying the validity of previous constitutional compromises. Past constitutional agreements, Lincoln felt, entitled persons who held national office to act on their best understanding of the Constitution. Compromises were appropriate only when government was divided. Lincoln's message on the need to supply Fort Sumter declared: "No compromise, by public servants, could, in this case, be a cure; not that compromises are not often proper, but that no popular government can long survive a marked precedent, that those who carry an election, can only save the government from immediate destruction, by giving up the main point, upon which the people gave the election."[137]

Constitutional aspirations mattered to Lincoln, but not as legal authority. Lincoln's first inaugural address declared that persons have a constitutional obligation to obey decisions made by constitutional authorities unless those decisions are plainly inconsistent with constitutional text and practice. When deciding how to resolve constitutional controversies, however, Lincoln thought constitutional authorities should consult both the letter and spirit of the law. He believed that national officials should interpret the Constitution as permitting bans on slavery in the territories partly because

---

[133] Lincoln, 3 *Collected Works*, p. 531.
[134] Lincoln, 4 *Collected Works*, p. 154. See Lincoln, 4 *Collected Works*, pp. 152–3.
[135] Lincoln, 4 *Collected Works*, p. 183.
[136] Lincoln, 4 *Collected Works*, pp. 175–6.
[137] Lincoln, 4 *Collected Works*, p. 440.

the persons responsible for the Constitution were committed to the ultimate extinction of human bondage. Unnecessary constitutional protections for slavery, Lincoln argued, "destroy[ed] the principles that is the charter of our liberties, the Declaration of Independence."[138] Still, Lincoln did not think his authority to ban slavery in the territories rested on his interpretation of constitutional aspirations. *Dred Scott* and the Republican Party platform were constitutionally legitimate because Chief Justice Taney and Lincoln held office by constitutional right and because the policies they advanced were consistent with previous constitutional agreements. Although he believed that governing officials *should* be guided by the spirit of the constitutional contract, Lincoln also held that they were actually bound only by the letter of that agreement.

The Contractual Conception of Constitutional Evil

Lincoln's use of contract metaphors provides a second possible solution to the problem of constitutional evil. Constitutional evil is justifiable, in this view, when embedded in the greater goods associated with voluntary agreement. Consent theorists proclaim that "people are generally the best judges of what's in their own best interests" and think that people are treated as moral beings only when they "are entitled to make their own choices."[139] A world in which disputes over justice are resolved by uncoerced compromises is a world in which generally prevailing notions of justice are accommodated to the greatest degree possible. Few people live in what they regard as a utopia. Most live in what they think is a better world when people, through constitutional contracts, induce others to respect what they believe are just principles by agreeing to accommodate some perceived evil. Consent to political practices thought to be mistaken, stupid, or evil is justified as the best means for obtaining support for political practices thought to be correct, wise, or just.

The contractual understanding of constitutional evil acknowledges that constitutions are "made for people of fundamentally differing views."[140] Disagreement runs deep. Citizens dispute what policies are best as well as the best procedures for resolving disputes about public policies. Large heterogeneous societies are particularly vulnerable to intractable conflicts. "The more numerous the people who have to act together," Joseph Carens

---

[138] Lincoln, 3 *Collected Works*, p. 300.
[139] Don Herzog, *Happy Slaves: A Critique of Consent Theory* (University of Chicago Press: Chicago, 1989), p. 222.
[140] *Lochner v. New York*, 198 U.S. 45, 76 (1905) (Holmes, dissenting).

observes, "the greater the likelihood of conflict among the goods people seek and disagreement about the relative priorities that should be attached to different goods."[141] Turning to more abstracted principles of moral philosophy or democratic theory rarely reduces pervasive disagreement.[142] Citizens who agree that liberty and democracy are desirable do not support constitutional provisions that authorize the government to promote liberty and democracy when they know that bitter controversies exist over what constitutes and promotes liberty and democracy.[143]

Persons in the "circumstances of politics"[144] often agree only that each is better-off making an agreement to cooperate than having all parties acting as they individually think best.[145] Persons accept binding obligations to promote values and interests they believe foolish or pernicious in order to induce other persons to create binding obligations to promote more cherished concerns.[146] These compromises frequently entail sacrificing strongly held principles. All parties must agree to make the concessions on interest and fundamental value "necessary to avoid war and achieve peace without coercion."[147] "In a democratic society," Arthur Kuflik notes, "very little is accomplished that does not bear the marks of concession and accommodation."[148]

Contract limits the perception and incidence of constitutional evil. People acquiesce in lesser evils for promises to abandon or reduce greater evils. If people have some capacity for moral judgment, then justice is served by allowing persons to trade promises to accommodate some injustice for promises to secure goods that are more vital. Constitutional contracts minimize the number of persons forced to accommodate evil against their will. Consenting parties do so with a clear conscience, believing they have secured as much justice as is possible in their society. Just as private contracts are considered good means of "enhanc[ing] allocative efficiency,"[149] so bargains

---

[141] Joseph H. Carens, "Compromise in Politics," *NOMOS XXI: Compromise in Ethics, Law and Politics* (ed. J. Roland Pennock and John W. Chapman) (New York University Press: New York, 1979), p. 126.

[142] See Herzog, *Happy Slaves*, p. 145.

[143] Mark A. Graber, "Conscience, Constitutionalism, and Consensus: A Comment on Constitutional Stupidities and Evils," *NOMOS XXXIX: Integrity and Conscience* (ed. Ian Shapiro) (New York University Press: New York, 1997), p. 326.

[144] Waldron, *Law and Disagreement*, p. 7.

[145] See Alex Kozinski and Harry Susman, "Original Mean[der]ings," 49 *Stanford Law Review*, 1583, 1597 (1997).

[146] See Michel Rosenfeld, "Contract and Justice: The Relation between Contract Law and Social Contract Theory," 70 *Iowa Law Review*, 769, 790, 792–3, 856 (1985).

[147] Theodore M. Benditt, "Compromising Interests and Principles," *NOMOS XXI: Compromise*, p. 32.

[148] Arthur Kuflik, "Morality and Compromise," *NOMOS XXI: Compromise*, p. 41.

[149] Rosenfeld, "Contract and Justice," p. 847.

may be the best means individuals have for maximizing justice in societies marked by deep disagreement over fundamental values. Constitutional compromises also reduce violence and promote political stability.[150] Social unrest is less likely when people negotiate fundamental decision rules. Political actors consent to constitutional provisions they think mistaken or evil when they prefer a stable polity committed to inferior norms over risking the public peace in an effort to secure what they perceive are better rules.

Constitutional contracts may ameliorate an accommodated evil or promote other goods. Lincoln thought free-state citizens bound by the Missouri Compromise and Compromise of 1850 because Northerners received valuable antislavery consideration for their proslavery concessions. The constitutional bargain of 1787 enabled Northerners to secure greater national power over commerce and all (white) Americans to enjoy the benefits associated with a strong national state. Accommodation of slavery was perceived as necessary because those responsible for the Constitution were convinced that violent wars would break out should Americans not agree on a national constitution. Given deep Southern intransigence and the general sense that immediate abolition would produce social chaos, constitutional bargainers agreed to disagree on slavery in order to promote the goods associated with a strong commercial policy.

The Constitution as a Contract

Lincoln invoked values far more rooted in American constitutionalism than majoritarianism when he employed contract metaphors. The persons responsible for the Constitution maintained that "all power in just free governments is derived from compact,"[151] that constitutions were actual social contracts or compacts,[152] and that political authority was ultimately grounded in the actual consent of the citizenry.[153] Madison constantly referred to the "constitutional compact of the United States."[154] Hamilton regarded the Constitution as "the compact made between the society at large and each

---

[150] See Benditt, "Compromising Interests and Principles," *NOMOS XXI: Compromise*, p. 32.

[151] Andrew C. McLaughlin, "Social Compact and Constitutional Construction," 5 *American Historical Review*, 467, 484 (1900) (quoting James Madison).

[152] See Elizabeth Kelley Bauer, *Commentaries on the Constitution, 1790–1860* (Columbia University Press: New York, 1952), pp. 213, 254, 308; McLaughlin, "Social Compact," pp. 467, 482; Anita L. Allen, "Social Contract Theory in American Case Law," 51 *Florida Law Review*, 1, 38–9 (1999).

[153] Wood, *Creation*, p. 602. See Elliot, 4 *Debates*, p. 9 (statement of James Iredell); Elliot, 4 *Debates*, p. 10 (statement of Mr. McLaine); Hamilton, Madison, and Jay, *Federalist Papers*, p. 294.

[154] Madison, 4 *Writings*, pp. 390–1; McLaughlin, "Social Compact," p. 484.

individual."[155] George Washington thought the Constitution "the last great experiment for promoting human happiness by reasonable compact."[156]

The framers recognized that the Constitution of 1787 was better conceptualized as a compromise than as an expression of shared values. Too many different interests had to be accommodated for the Constitution to reflect any single, coherent philosophy. Benjamin Franklin observed how every provision had to be negotiated, given the wide diversity of opinions and interests represented at the constitutional convention. He described the bargaining as resembling "a game of dice with many players 'their ideas so different, their prejudices so strong and so various, and their particular interests, independent of the general, seeming so opposite, that not a move can be made that is not contested.' "[157] This diversity of interest guaranteed that the final constitution would more resemble a negotiable instrument than a work of political theory. As Federalists reminded their contemporaries, "a faultless plan was not to be expected."[158] *Federalist* 37 bluntly declared that the Constitution did not resemble "that artificial structure and regular symmetry which an abstract view of the subject might lead an ingenious theorist to bestow on a Constitution planned in his closet or in his imagination."[159] George Washington defended the Constitution as "the best that could be attained at the time."[160]

Slavery was the most important matter on which principled arrangements proved impossible. Proponents and opponents of human bondage in 1787 realized that agreement had to be reached about national power over slavery in order to reach and maintain more pressing agreements about national security and commercial power. "Publius" gave up trying to find any coherent justification for treating slaves as three fifths of a person; he simply pronounced the relevant constitutional provision one of many "compromising expedient[s] of the Constitution."[161] Three fifths was the rule – rather than zero, one, four sevenths, or two thirds – because that was the compromise agreed upon.

All major participants in the antebellum disputes over slavery employed the contract metaphor. Chief Justice Taney in *Prigg v. Pennsylvania* declared that, "by the national compact, this right of property is recognized as an

---

[155] Alexander Hamilton, *The Works of Alexander Hamilton* (ed. John C. Hamilton) (John P. Trow: New York, 1850), p. 322. See McLaughlin, "Social Compact," p. 478.
[156] Washington, *George Washington*, p. 537.
[157] Wood, *Creation*, p. 584 (quoting Benjamin Franklin).
[158] Hamilton, Madison, and Jay, *Federalist Papers*, p. 225.
[159] Hamilton, Madison, and Jay, *Federalist Papers*, p. 230.
[160] Washington, *Washington*, p. 370.
[161] Hamilton, Madison, and Jay, *Federalist Papers*, p. 339.

existing right in every state of the Union."[162] Justice McLean's *Prigg* opinion noted that Southerners "viewed" slavery "as a cherished right, incorporated into the social compact."[163] Both wings of the abolitionist movement regarded the Constitution as a contract. Lysander Spooner labored to demonstrate that slavery violated the "constitutional contract."[164] The best-known work of anticonstitutional abolitionism is Wendell Phillips's *The Constitution Is a Pro-Slavery Compact.*[165]

Contemporary Americans of all political persuasions still regard the Constitution as a social contract or compact. The plurality opinion in *Planned Parenthood v. Casey* asserts: "Our Constitution is a covenant running from the first generation of Americans to us."[166] "[T]he Constitution," Keith Whittington states, "is also an actual contract, an agreement among diverse parties, with real or separate interests."[167] Akhil Amar declares: "The ratifications themselves formed the basic social compact by which formerly distinct sovereign Peoples, each acting in convention, agreed to reconstitute themselves into one common sovereignty."[168] Social contract theory lives in state constitutionalism. The present constitution of Connecticut begins with the words: "All men when they form a social compact . . . ."[169] The constitution of New Hampshire, the highest court in that state asserted in 1983, "originates in a social compact."[170]

Americans who analogize the Constitution to a contract further insist that the Constitution be interpreted as a contract. Madison's first major speech on constitutional interpretation invoked the contract metaphor. "In

---

[162] *Prigg v. Pennsylvania*, 41 U.S. 539, 628, 633 (Taney, concurring).

[163] *Prigg* at 660 (McLean, dissenting).

[164] Lysander Spooner, "The Unconstitutionality of Slavery," 28 *Pacific Law Review*, 1015, 1054 (1997 [1845]).

[165] Wendell Phillips, *The Constitution Is a Pro-Slavery Compact or, Extracts from the Madison Papers, Etc.* (American Anti-Slavery Society: New York, 1856).

[166] *Planned Parenthood v. Casey*, 505 U.S. 833, 901 (1992) (opinion of O'Connor, Kennedy, and Souter).

[167] Keith E. Whittington, *Constitutional Interpretation: Textual Meaning, Original Intent, and Judicial Review* (University Press of Kansas: Lawrence, 1999), p. 149. See Neals-Erik William Delker, "The House Three-Fifths Rule: Majority Rule, the Framers' Intent, and the Judiciary Roles," 100 *Dickinson Law Review*, 341, 344–5 (1996); Kirk A. Kennedy, "Reaffirming the Natural Law Jurisprudence of Justice Clarence Thomas," 9 *Regent University Law Review*, 33, 47 (1997).

[168] Akhil Reed Amar, "Of Sovereignty and Federalism," 96 *Yale Law Journal*, 1425, 1460 (1987). See W. Burlette Cater, "Can This Culture Be Saved? Another Affirmative Action Baby Reflects on Religious Freedom," 95 *Columbia Law Review*, 473, 498 n.75 (1995); Frank H. Easterbrook, "Textualism and the Dead Hand," 66 *George Washington University Law Review*, 1119 (1998).

[169] See Allen, "Social Contract," p. 5 n.16; M. Kate Curran, "Illegal Aliens, the Social Compact and the Connecticut Constitution," 13 *Bridgeport Law Review*, 331 (1993).

[170] *State v. Brousseau*, 470 A.2d 869, 877 (N.H. 1983).

controverted cases," he declared, "the meaning of the parties to the instrument ... is the proper guide."[171] Common-law contract reasoning provided the framework for much constitutional interpretation during and immediately after ratification.[172] Contract plays a crucial role in contemporary originalist thought. "The fundamental theory of political legitimacy in the United States," Frank Easterbrook declares, "is contrarian, and contrarian views imply originalist, if not necessarily textualist, interpretation by the judicial branch."[173] Randy Barnett does "not view the Constitution as a contract in a literal sense" but thinks "the constitution of the United States is a *written* document and it is *writtenness* that makes relevant contract law theory pertaining to those contracts that are also in writing."[174]

Cracks in the Constitutional Contract

The most obvious problem with attempts to analogize constitutions to contracts is that constitutions do not meet important conditions for legally enforceable bargains. Few Americans have consented to the Constitution in the ways that provide binding consent to contracts. Many persons, most notably persons of color, did not give even give tacit consent to the constitutional contract.[175] The substance of the constitutional contract is also troubling. Contract law does not permit persons to create binding obligations to violate the rights of third persons.[176] If slavery is inconsistent with natural law,[177] then no constitutional contract supporting human bondage is valid.

These difficult theoretical problems with the contract metaphor were not the source of Lincoln's political troubles in 1861. The first inaugural did not have to convince Southerners that they had consented to the Constitution or that contracts authorizing slavery were valid. While one wing of the abolitionist movement condemned the Constitution as a "covenant with death," most slaveholders pledged allegiance to the Constitution, properly

---

[171] 1 *Annals of Congress*, 1946 (1789).

[172] See H. Jefferson Powell, "The Original Understanding of Original Intent," 98 *Harvard Law Review*, 885, 894–6, 930–4 (1985).

[173] Easterbrook, "Textualism," p. 1121.

[174] Randy E. Barnett, "An Originalism for Nonoriginalists," 45 *Loyola Law Review*, 611, 629 (1999).

[175] See Jerome McCristal Culp, Jr., "Toward a Black Legal Scholarship: Race and Original Understandings," 1991 *Duke Law Journal*, 39, 74 (1991).

[176] See A. John Simmons, "Tacit Consent and Political Obligation," 5 *Philosophy and Public Affairs*, 274, 276 (1976).

[177] See *Osborn v. Nicholson*, 80 U.S. 654, 663 (1871) (Chase, dissenting); Rosenfeld, "Contract and Justice," p. 797.

interpreted. Slave-state citizens claimed they were committed to the original constitutional bargain and regarded that bargain as a form of contract.
The crucial questions that divided most antebellum Americans concerned
how the constitutional contract should be interpreted, not the contract
metaphor itself. Lincoln's practical problem with the contract metaphor
in 1861 was that nineteenth-century contract law did not support claims that
slaveholders had consented to having free-state majorities resolve constitutional controversies.

The Constitution as a Classical Contract

Lincoln and his contemporaries employed some version of classical contract
theory when interpreting voluntary agreements. Persons who made contracts, most lawyers at the time of the first inaugural believed, consented
to be bound by the objective meaning of contractual provisions at the time
the agreement was formed. Contractual obligations were determined by the
language of the bargain, not by the subjective understandings of the parties.
Learned Hand declared in *Hotchkiss v. National City Bank of New York*:

> A contract has, strictly speaking, nothing to do with the personal, or individ-
> ual, intent of the parties. A contract is an obligation attached by the mere
> force of law to certain acts of the parties, usually words, which ordinarily
> accompany and represent a known intent. If, however, it were proved by
> twenty bishops that either party, when he used the words, intended some-
> thing else than the usual meaning which the law imposes upon them, he
> would still be held, unless there were some mutual mistake, or something
> else of the sort.[178]

Lincoln relied on these principles when insisting that the explicit constitutional moratorium on federal laws banning the international slave trade
incorporated no implicit legal obligation to prohibit that commerce after
twenty years. When parties omit crucial terms or use vague language, classical contract theory maintains, no legal obligation results. Samuel Williston
insisted that contractual language had to be "so definite in its terms ... that
the promises and performances to be rendered by each party are reasonably
certain."[179] Courts, the conventional analysis goes, "do not 'make contracts'

---

[178] *Hotchkiss v. National City Bank of New York*, 200 F. 287, 293 (S.D. N.Y. 1911).
[179] American Law Institute, *Restatement of the Law of Contracts*, vol. 1 (American Law Institute:
St. Paul, 1932), p. 40. See Richard E. Speidel, "*Restatement Second*: Omitted Terms and Contract Method," 67 *Cornell Law Review*, 785, 787–8 (1982); Juliet P. Kostritsky, "When Should
Contract Law Supply a Liability Rule or Term?: Framing a Principle of Unification for Contracts," 32 *Arizona State Law Journal*, 1283, 1290–1 (2000).

for the parties."[180] No legal authority may create legally binding obligations when the parties by omission or imprecision fail to do so.[181] Parties consent only to express contractual terms.

This classical demand for explicit textual promises meant that Lincoln could not successfully impute slaveholding consent to Republican policies that prevented the extension of slavery. Lincoln's first inaugural conceded that federal power in the territories was an omitted term. The Constitution, he stated, did not "expressly say" whether Congress could forbid human bondage in the West. If that federal power was not specified, then classical contract law provides no basis for constitutional authority. Slaveholders consented only to have Congress exercise such powers as the power to regulate interstate commerce, a power plainly vested in that body by the constitutional text. The parties in 1787, according to classical contract law, failed to create any legal rule concerning federal power over slavery in the territories.

Lincoln would fare no better by claiming that slaveholders consented to having the national government settle constitutional controversies. The precise location of constitutional authority is another omitted term. Article III empowers the federal judiciary to adjudicate cases "arising under this Constitution." This language does not plainly authorize courts to settle constitutional disputes or to supply provisions omitted from the original constitutional bargain. Many commentators think Article III was understood in 1787 as vesting courts only with the power to strike down government actions that clearly violated the Constitution.[182]

The constitutional contract also omits any provision concerning independent state authority to resolve constitutional controversies. The supremacy clause obligates state officials to obey the Constitution but says nothing about adherence to constitutional interpretations promulgated by national officials. The Constitution interpreted as a classical contract neither affirms nor denies the Jeffersonian claim that, "as in all other cases of compact among parties having no common judge, each party has an equal right to judge for itself."[183] The parties to the constitutional bargain may have expected that some combination of national institutions would have the power to settle constitutional controversies, just as they expected that constitutional controversies would

---

[180] Speidel, "Omitted Terms," p. 788. See e.g. *Chicago & N.W.R. Co. v. Chicago Packaging Fuel Co.*, 195 F.2d 647 (7th Cir. 1952).

[181] See Melvin Aron Eisenberg, "The Emergence of Dynamic Contract Law," 88 *California Law Review*, 1743, 1794–96 (2000).

[182] Kramer, *The People Themselves*; Sylvia Snowiss, *Judicial Review and the Law of the Constitution* (Yale University Press: New Haven, 1990).

[183] Jefferson, *The Portable Jefferson*, p. 281.

be settled by bisectional coalitions. Nevertheless, the same classical principles that Lincoln could invoke when rejecting claims that bisectionalism was part of the constitutional bargain prevented him from asserting that Southerners consented in 1787 to having constitutional controversies resolved by a sectional majority controlling all three branches of the national government. Neither expectation was expressly incorporated into the Constitution.

This problem with ambiguity and omitted terms highlights the general problem with using classical theory when interpreting constitutions. Classical contract theory presumes that parties cover all exigencies.[184] Constitutions rarely fit this model. Such agreements "are inherently incomplete" because of "the inability to foresee all the possible contingencies."[185] Frequently, as was the case in 1787, potentially disruptive debates are finessed by decisions to employ vague phrases and leave crucial constitutional issues unsettled. "Mindful of life's exigencies, a limited ability to peer into the future, the inadequacies of language, and other factors," A. E. Dick Howard notes, "framers may well accept, even welcome, some degree of indeterminacy in a constitution."[186] Prominent Federalists recognized that omitted terms were a constitutional problem. Madison noted that it "was foreseen at the birth of the Constitution, that difficulties and differences of opinion might occasionally arise in expounding terms & phrases necessarily used in such a charter ... [a]nd that it might require a regular course of practice to liquidate & settle the meaning of some of them."[187] Ratification exacerbated the problems with interpreting the Constitution as a classical contract. Because the Constitution could be ratified only "as an all-or-nothing proposition," a high probability exists that such provisions as the necessary and proper clause had no generally agreed-upon meaning in 1787.[188]

These inevitable confusions about constitutional meaning at the time of ratification collapse constitutional authority when constitutions are interpreted as classical contracts. If legal authority depends on "the promises and performances to be rendered by each party [being] reasonably certain,"

[184] Rosenfeld, "Contract and Justice," p. 845. See Ian R. McNeil, *The New Social Contract: An Inquiry into Modern Contractual Relations* (Yale University Press: New Haven, 1980), pp. 15–16.

[185] Jonathan Rodden and Susan Rose-Ackerman, "Does Federalism Preserve Markets?" 83 *Virginia Law Review*, 1521 (1997).

[186] A. E. Dick Howard, "The Indeterminacy of Constitutions," 31 *Wake Forest Law Review*, 383, 396 (1996). See Cass R. Sunstein, *Designing Democracy: What Constitutions Do* (Oxford University Press: New York, 2001), pp. 57–60, 66.

[187] James Madison, *The Writings of James Madison*, vol. 8 (ed. Gaillard Hunt) (Putnam's: New York, 1908), p. 450. See Gary Rosen, *American Compact: James Madison and the Problem of the Founding* (University Press of Kansas: Lawrence, 1999), pp. 156, 161–2, 164.

[188] Kozinski and Susman, "Original Mean[der]ings," p. 1597. See Jack N. Rakove, *Original Meanings: Politics and Ideas in the Making of the Constitution* (Knopf: New York, 1996), p. 96.

then the Constitution was never a legally binding instrument. The numerous constitutional debates in the First Congress over the staffing of the federal government and federal powers[189] highlight how even the persons responsible for the original constitutional text did not agree on basic constitutional meanings. Constitutional theory needs, and neoclassical theory provides, principles that impute consent to terms not explicitly agreed upon when a bargain was made.

The Constitution as a Neoclassical Contract

Persons who make contracts, most lawyers at the turn of the twenty-first century believe, consent to be in a legally binding agreement. When the general outline of the contract is clear and the parties clearly wished to create a legally enforceable bargain,[190] legal authorities relying on neoclassical principles often enforce obligations not expressly stated in the text. "[I]t is enough that there is a core of common meaning sufficient to determine their preferences with reasonable certainty," the most recent *Restatement of Contracts* declares.[191] When terms are omitted in a legally binding contract, "a term which is reasonable in the circumstances is supplied by the court."[192]

Neoclassical theorists would not regard the omission of provisions specifying the exact location of constitutional authority as fatal to the constitutional contract. The framers intended to create binding obligations, they would argue, even though the precise content of many obligations was not determined. Although the Constitution made no express commitment to having the federal government resolve constitutional controversies, national institutions were designed to ensure constitutional settlements would be compromises that had substantial support in both the free and slave states. Interpreting the Constitution as vesting the national government with the power to resolve constitutional controversies was, in light of the underlying purposes of Articles I, II, and III, "reasonable in the circumstances" anticipated by the framers.

When determining what is "reasonable in the circumstances," neoclassical theory begins with the basic purposes underlying the bargain. Crucial

---

[189]   See David P. Currie, *The Constituton in Congress: The Federalist Period 1787–1801* (University of Chicago Press: Chicago, 1997), pp. 7–122.

[190]   See Speidel, "Omitted Terms," p. 790.

[191]   American Law Institute, *Restatement of the Law Second, Contracts 2d* (student edition), vol. 1 (American Law Institute: St. Paul, 1981), pp. 59, 92. See American Law Institute, 1 *Restatement*, p. 81; Speidel, "Omitted Terms," pp. 790–1.

[192]   American Law Institute, 2 *Restatement*, p. 204. See Larry A. DiMatteo, "Equity's Modification of Contract: An Analysis of the Twentieth Century's Equitable Reformation of Contract Law," 33 *New England Law Review*, 265, 281–2 (1999).

assumptions are treated as central to the contract, even when they are not made explicit. Parties are not bound even by express contractual language when unexpected events create a dramatic imbalance in contract benefits and burdens.[193] The *Restatement* declares:

> Where, after a contract is made, a party's principal purpose is substantially frustrated without his fault by the occurrence of an event the non-occurrence of which was a basic assumption on which the contract was made, his remaining duties to render performance are discharged.[194]

"Frustration" of contract occurs when the mistake goes to the heart of the contract, to the very reason why the party accepted the bargained-for exchange. "The transaction would make little sense" had the parties planned for the event, and "the frustration must be so severe that it is not fairly to be regarded as within the rules that he assumed under the contract."[195] As the *Restatement* concludes, "relief is only appropriate where a mistake of both parties has such a material effect on the agreed exchange of performances as to upset the very basis for the contracting," making "the resulting imbalance in the agreed exchange ... so severe that [the affected party] cannot fairly be required to carry it out."[196]

If consent is limited to the foreseeable consequences of an agreement, then slaveholders did not consent to having constitutional silences and ambiguities interpreted by a free-state majority. Vital constitutional institutions were structured on the basis of a mutual assumption that proved false. Articles I, II, and III made sense and had value only if the framers were right that population trends in the United States would permanently guarantee a balance of sectional power. Thus, from the perspective of neoclassical theory, slaveholders consented to be governed by institutions that made sectional accommodation a political necessity, not by institutions that in practice often made sectional compromise political suicide. It was not "reasonable" after Lincoln's election to impute slaveholding consent to institutions that all thought would facilitate compromise when those institutions in practice had fostered extremism.

---

193 See E. Allan Farnsworth, *Changing Your Mind: The Law of Regretted Decisions* (Yale University Press: New Haven, 1998), p. 25; Hans Smit, "Frustration of Contract: A Comparative Attempt at Consolidation," 58 *Columbia Law Review*, 287 (1958).

194 American Law Institute, 2 *Restatement*, pp. 334–5. Sections 152 and 261 set out nearly identical rules for mistake and impracticability: American Law Institute, 1 *Restatement*, p. 385; American Law Institute, 2 *Restatement*, p. 313. See John P. Dawson, "Judicial Revision of Frustrated Contracts: The United States," 64 *Boston University Law Review*, 1, 3 (1984).

195 American Law Institute, 2 *Restatement*, p. 335.

196 American Law Institute, 1 *Restatement*, p. 388.

Dred Scott was a sound application of the version of neoclassical theory –
adopted in many European countries, approved by many American legal
commentators, and followed by occasional American judicial decisions[197] –
that authorizes courts to reformulate frustrated agreements. The Dutch
legal code declares, "the judge may modify the effects of a contract ... on
the basis of unforeseen circumstances which are of such a nature that the
co-contracting party, according to criteria of reasonableness and equity, may
not expect that the contract be maintained in an unmodified form."[198] The
Restatement provides that "the court may grant relief on such terms as justice requires which may include supply[ing] a term."[199] Recognizing a right
to bring slaves into the territories was arguably consistent with the "criteria
of reasonableness and equity" after "unforeseen circumstances" frustrated
the means originally expected to guarantee the constitutional commitment
to bisectionalism. The framers attempted to ensure that constitutional authorities made those policies that would garner substantial support in both
the slave and free states. *Dred Scott* satisfied that condition far better than
the Republican platform of 1860. Northern Democrats could tolerate the
right to bring slaves into all territories as long as that policy was announced
by justices. No sizable slave-state constituency supported any Republican
proposal on slavery.

Dred Scott was also a reasonable application of the neoclassical commitment to good-faith bargaining. The *Restatement* proclaims, "every contract
imposes upon each party a duty of good faith and fair dealing in its performance and in its enforcement."[200] Good faith and fair dealing "may
require more than honesty" and "extends to dealing which is candid but
unfair."[201] The commentary gives as an example "taking advantage of the
necessitous circumstances of the other party to extort a modification of a
contract."[202] The Jacksonian effort to facilitate judicial policy making promoted fair dealing on slavery by guaranteeing that all settlements of constitutional controversies continued to be approved by national institutions with
free-state (the Congress) and slave-state (the Supreme Court) majorities.
Republican proposals failed to exhibit this good faith. Lincoln's commitment to implementing antislavery policies without Southern consent took

---

[197] See Smit, "Frustration," p. 307.
[198] Jan M. Van Dunne, "Narrative Coherence and Its Function in Judicial Decision Making and
Legislation," 44 *American Journal of Comparative Law*, 463, 478 (1996).
[199] American Law Institute, 1 *Restatement*, pp. 419–20. See American Law Institute, 1 *Restatement*, pp. 382–3; American Law Institute, 2 *Restatement*, pp. 312, 356–7.
[200] American Law Institute, 2 *Restatement*, p. 99.
[201] American Law Institute, 2 *Restatement*, pp. 100, 102.
[202] American Law Institute, 2 *Restatement*, p. 102.

advantage of slave-state political weaknesses in ways frowned upon by neo-classical theory.

Lincoln had no satisfactory response to these justifications for *Dred Scott*. Pointing out that American courts typically discharge all contractual obligations when frustration occurs[203] concedes that all constitutional authority vanished when unforeseen population changes enabled a free-state coalition to gain control of the presidency. Noting how classical theory rejects any unexpressed constitutional commitment to bisectionalism entails rejecting any unexpressed constitutional commitment to having the national government resolve constitutional controversies. Abandoning contract and consent altogether would leave Lincoln with majoritarianism and all the previously noted difficulties with that justification for overturning *Dred Scott*.

Frustration of Constitution

Good reasons warrant importing frustration into constitutional theory even if, as some prominent commentators think, frustration should rarely be recognized in contract law.[204] One important difference between constitutions and contracts is that only the former bind nonsignatories or future generations. Parties to ordinary contracts may gamble on the future, but constitutions are binding only to the extent rules and institutions secure equitable benefits across generations. Future generations do not assume the risk that their ancestors made inaccurate assumptions about the future. When unanticipated events dramatically alter the burdens and benefits of constitutional cooperation, either the constitution must be adjusted in a manner analogous to the ways European courts reformulate contracts or the constitution can no longer be considered legally binding.

Frustration of constitution has strong practical grounds. Governments have the capacity to force persons to honor bad contracts, even when strict liability destroys vital personal interests. No peaceful means exist for forcing large groups of people to live with constitutional settlements that no longer serve vital interests. Unless constitutional understandings are reformulated, either by reinterpreting existing constitutional understandings or by creating new ones, bad constitutional bargains will result in coercion, secession, or civil war. Even if Lincoln was right that slaveholders consented to rule by a sectional majority in 1787, the first inaugural gave their descendants no good reason why they should continue honoring that constitutional bargain.

---

[203] See American Law Institute, 2 *Restatement*, p. 311.

[204] See e.g. Nicholas Weiskopf, "Frustration of Contractual Purpose – Doctrine or Myth," 70 *St. John's Law Review*, 239, 265 (1996).

Frustration of constitution is a new description for a perennial problem. Long-term contracts and enduring constitutions must cope with unforeseen circumstances. American political development has witnessed substantial social changes, almost none of which were anticipated in 1787. Industrialization, new broadcast technologies, national expansion, and northwestward population movements all created constitutional problems unforeseen by the framers. Each destabilized inherited constitutional settlements, forcing political elites to make informal constitutional adjustments. Preserving the status quo has not been a constitutional option. A constitutional order that lacks radio, television, and the Internet differs from a constitutional order where those media flourish, no matter how those media are regulated. A constitutional order in which sectional equilibrium is guaranteed by constitutional institutions differs from one in which sectional equilibrium is maintained by national political parties. Both differ from a regime in which a sectional majority has the latent power to gain control of the national government.

Constitutional texts and practices mediate, but do not determine, responses to political changes. Pre-existing constitutional norms rule out some alternatives. Complete government control of radio and television, for example, is inconsistent with basic First Amendment principles. Granting South Carolina veto power over any antislavery policy was inconsistent with original understandings that Southern moderates would control the national government. Still, several paths are often constitutionally plausible. History and text do not clarify whether television is more analogous to a newspaper or the town green. American constitutional practice from 1787 to 1860 did not clarify whether the Constitution merely boosted Southern political power or was committed to a sectional veto on national policy. Having assumed that the electoral procedures mandated by the Constitution would maintain a balance of sectional power, the framers did not consider the constitutional consequences of a free-state coalition gaining control over the entire national government. When we rank order their commitments to republicanism and the sectional veto,[205] the commitments are theirs but the priorities are ours.

Bargaining over the terms of constitutional cooperation does not end when constitutions are ratified. Constitutions must consistently be interpreted in ways that satisfy those crucial elites whose support is needed for the maintenance of the political order. When circumstances change, parties to a constitutional bargain must make the constitutional adjustments necessary to preserve beneficial cooperation. The resulting negotiation will inevitably

---

[205] See Walter F. Murphy, "An Ordering of Constitutional Values," 53 *University of Southern California Law Review*, 703 (1980).

change both the nature and the precise degree of protection given to perceived constitutional evils. Parties to constitutional agreements, Lincoln recognized at the end of the first inaugural, do not really debate their inherited legal obligations. The fundamental question Americans faced in 1861 was whether, in the face of demographic changes and pervasive disagreements about justice, previous constitutional relationships were worth maintaining.

These constitutional relationships require less thinking about venerable ancestors and more talking to ordinary neighbors. The latter must be negotiated with, not the dead. Constitutions are means for inducing the heterogeneous living to perform certain tasks, secure certain interests, and protect certain rights. Individuals make commitments, formulate opinions about justice, and have aspirations. Two or more persons are necessary to make a contract, a compromise, or a constitution.

CONSTITUTIONAL RELATIONSHIPS AND
CONSTITUTIONAL EVIL

The conclusion to Lincoln's first inaugural suggests that preserving constitutional relationships might provide an alternative to contract and majoritarianism as an approach to the problem of constitutional evil. The last paragraph offers a poetic appeal for national unity:

> I am loath to close. We are not enemies, but friends. We must not be enemies. Though passion may have strained it must not break our bonds of affection. The mystic chords of memory, stretching from every battlefield and patriot grave to every living heart and hearthstone all over this broad land, will yet swell the chorus of the Union, when again touched, as surely they will be, by the better angels of our nature.[206]

Abandoning majoritarianism and consent, this passage implores citizens of the United States not to forsake cherished constitutional relationships. The Constitution is not simply a collection of rules designed to govern the behavior of persons otherwise strangers to each other, Lincoln suggests, but a repository of shared political life. The colonists had earlier invoked this common national identity when justifying separation from Great Britain. The Declaration of Independence describes Americans as "one people." The English were charged with being "deaf to the voice of justice and of consanguinity."[207] The first inaugural insists that Americans remained "friends."

---

[206] Lincoln, 4 *Collected Works*, p. 271.
[207] Jefferson, *The Portable Jefferson*, pp. 235, 239.

The free states, Lincoln maintained, were not guilty of the wrongs that justified the colonial decision in 1776 to "dissolve the political bands" between them and their former "British brethren." [208]

The most fundamental constitutional question before the American polity in 1861 concerned what Lincoln referred to as "our bonds of affection." Majorities in both the free and slave states believed that most citizens in the other section were committed to unjust, unconstitutional, and illegitimate policies. The political order under these conditions of pervasive dispute could survive only if crucial elites in at least one section concluded that the benefits of union justified living with what they believed was substantial constitutional evil. This was less a question of constitutional law than a question about the nature and value of the constitutional relationships between the free and slave states.

The Constitution as a Relational Contract

Relational Contracts

Relational contract theory may help guide investigations of the extent to which the constitutional ties between Americans justified compromises that accommodate more evil than constitutionally necessary. Relational contract theorists focus on what parties must do to maintain ongoing legal relationships. The perspective is that of parties deciding whether to continue cooperating rather than a court deciding the legal rights of the parties after cooperation has broken down. With respect to 1861, relational contract theory focuses on whether and how the constitutional relationships between the sections could have been maintained and not on whether Lincoln had the authority to impose a ban on slavery as a matter of law.

Relational contract theory regards consent to a contract as consent to being in a particular kind of relationship. Omitted terms are common. Persons making long-term commitments rarely spell out rules that govern all contingencies. Parties to relational contracts see "the relation as an ongoing integration of behavior" that will "grow and vary with events in a largely unforeseeable future." [209] The possibility of frustration is taken for granted. Parties adopt tentative processes for resolving future disagreements, which are then subject to revision in light of subsequent events. "Future planning of such substantive issues will occur through the structures and processes

---

[208] Jefferson, *The Portable Jefferson*, pp. 235, 239.
[209] Paul J. Gudel, "Relational Contract Theory and the Concept of Exchange," 46 *Buffalo Law Review*, 763, 765 (1998) (quoting Ian McNeil).

being established at the beginning," Ian McNeil observes, but "even those must be subject to future change."[210] Aware that their relationship is likely to develop in ways unanticipated at any particular time, parties to a relational contract rarely worry about allocating the risk for unforeseen changes. People intending to cooperate for the foreseeable future "wait to see if anything bad does happen" and then "deal with the problem with the whole range of community processes available for hard times."[211] Stewart Macauley observes that "businessmen may welcome a measure of vagueness in the obligations they assume so they may negotiate matters in light of the actual circumstances."[212]

Relational contracts are interpreted consistently with the ties uniting persons engaged in ongoing cooperation. Duties are inferred from "the reality of the parties' developed relation."[213] Parties "consent to a relation" and to be "bound by the norms of the relation" rather than to explicit legal terms.[214] Provisions in relational contracts are understood in light of this commitment to maintaining mutually beneficial cooperation. Specific agreements are important parts of that relationship. Parties to personal or business relationships do not lightly cast aside previously given promises.[215] Still, the relationship transcends the particular terms of past bargains.[216] When – for reasons not related to a desire to end the relationship – parties cannot beneficially carry out their end of the agreement, obligations are adjusted to ensure that the benefits from cooperation continue flowing. The distinction between legitimate and illegitimate breaches is more pragmatic than legal. Persons in long-term relationships determine for themselves whether their partners are facing unanticipated problems or are seeking unjust benefits. Eric Posner observes: "Courts are not very good at deterring opportunistic behavior in contractual relationships, but parties are." This, he declares, explains "why so much contractual behavior depends on reputation, ethnic and family connections, and other elements of nonlegal regulation, and not on carefully written and detailed contracts enforced by disinterested courts."[217]

---

[210] McNeil, *New Social Contract,* pp. 24–5. See McNeil, *New Social Contract,* pp. 27, 31; Stewart Macauley, "Non-Contractual Relations in Business: A Preliminary Study," 28 *American Sociological Review,* 55, 58, 60, 64 (1963).

[211] McNeil, *New Social Contract,* p. 20. See McNeil, *New Social Contract,* pp. 27, 31.

[212] Macauley, "Non-Contractual Relations," p. 64.

[213] Gudel, "Relational Contract Theory," p. 769. See McNeil, *New Social Contract,* pp. 49–50.

[214] Gudel, "Relational Contract Theory," p. 784. See McNeil, *New Social Contract,* pp. 50, 66.

[215] See Macauley, "Non-Contractual Relations," p. 63.

[216] McNeil, *New Social Contract,* p. 86.

[217] Eric A. Posner, "A Theory of Contract under Conditions of Radical Judicial Error," 94 *Northwestern University Law Review,* 749, 758 (2000).

Parties committed to ongoing legal relationships do not demand the letter of the law be observed no matter what. Macauley's seminal study of contract practice found that "[d]isputes are frequently settled without reference to contract or potential or actual legal sanctions."[218] Accommodation is appropriate when parties have a stake in future interactions that is greater than the benefit they might receive from demanding their pound of flesh in any particular instance. "Parties do not wish," Jack Beerman points out, "to drive their trading partners out of business because of the potential benefits of future trading and good will."[219] Modifications when unforeseen circumstances occur are aimed at maintaining mutually beneficial cooperation in the future. Rather than focus on the past, parties ask: "Do I think conditions will continue to exist whereby each of us will desire to and be able to depend on the other?"[220] Insisting on one's legal rights reflects beliefs that continued cooperation under new circumstances is not desirable.[221] "You don't read legalistic contract clauses at each other," a businessperson surveyed by Macauley declared, "if you ever want to do business again."[222]

Relational contract theory is particularly concerned with "limiting unilateral power in contractual relations."[223] Ongoing cooperative arrangements rely on a "norm of mutuality." This precept does not require "equality,... but some kind of evenhandedness."[224] When one party gains the legal power to dictate the future to the other, cooperative relations fall apart, no matter what the terms of the initial bargain. As McNeil points out, "contractual solidarity cannot survive in the face of perceptions that one side constantly gets too good a deal." Cooperation in such circumstances is maintained only by "external force."[225] "Flexibility" is required for maintaining long-standing relationships of any sort. Relational contracts survive only when the consequences of vague provisions, omitted terms, and unforeseen changes are negotiable so that cooperation remains mutually beneficial.[226]

---

[218] Macauley, "Non-Contractual Relations," p. 61.

[219] Jack Beerman, "Contract Law as a System of Values," 67 *Boston University Law Review*, 553, 566 (1987). See Macauley, "Non-Contractual Relations," p. 63; Posner, "A Theory of Contract," pp. 760–1.

[220] McNeil, *New Social Contract*, p. 92.

[221] Leon Trakman, "Winner Take Some: Loss Sharing and Commercial Impracticability," 69 *Minnesota Law Review*, 471, 471 n.3 (1985). See McNeil, *New Social Contract*, p. 86.

[222] Macauley, "Non-Contractual Relations," p. 65. See McNeil, *New Social Contract*, p. 61.

[223] Gudel, "Relational Contracts Theory," pp. 785–6.

[224] McNeil, *New Social Contract*, p. 44. See McNeil, *New Social Contract*, pp. 57, 92.

[225] McNeil, *New Social Contract*, p. 45.

[226] McNeil, *New Social Contract*, p. 57.

Relational Constitutions

Constitutions are easily analogized to relational contracts.[227] Consent to constitutions is attenuated,[228] cooperation is "expected to continue indefinitely,"[229] terms are omitted, and the nature of the bargain evolves over time in both formal and informal ways. The life of ongoing contracts is quite similar to the life of ongoing constitutional orders.

> [I]n the long term events are so hard to predict, that parties will not be able to allocate future obligations and payments in a way that maximizes the value of their contract. They will have to anticipate renegotiation as the future reveals itself.[230]

Crucial interpretive questions depend less on what was agreed upon at the time of formation than on the nature of the ongoing relationship. Parties determine whether continued cooperation is worthwhile and, if so, what is necessary to preserve their contractual or constitutional relationships.

The Constitution of 1787 was a relational contract intended to form a political order that benefited Americans from all sections. Providing a tentative framework for ongoing cooperation between the states was far more important to the framers than the precise legal terms of that cooperation. The most fundamental constitutional aspiration was for a strong national union. The first fourteen *Federalist Papers* discuss "[t]he utility of the UNION to your political prosperity." Americans would enjoy the blessings of liberty, other Federalists agreed, only if the United States remained one country. George Washington's only public argument in favor of ratification insisted that catastrophic disunion was the only alternative to confederation. "A Candid solution of a single question ... does," he declared, "decide the dispute, namely is it best for the States to unite, or not to unite."[231]

The "more perfect union" promised by the preamble strengthened pre-existing bonds between (white) Americans of all sections. Leading proponents of the American Revolution advanced a "conception of Americans as a distinct people, chosen to serve the Protestant God's emancipating purposes."[232] Race, culture, and divine destiny combined to promote national

---

[227] McNeil, *New Social Contract*, p. 124 n.39.

[228] See Gudel, "Relational Contract Theory," pp. 774, 783–4.

[229] McNeil, *New Social Contract*, p. 66. See *McCulloch v. Maryland*, 17 U.S. 316, 415 (1819).

[230] Posner, "A Theory of Contract," p. 751.

[231] Washington, *Washington*, p. 372. See Washington, *Washington*, pp. 378–9, 384.

[232] Rogers M. Smith, *Civic Ideals: Conflicting Visions of Citizenship in U.S. History* (Yale University Press: New Haven, 1997), p. 75. This paragraph borrows shamelessly from Smith's pathbreaking study of civic identity. See especially Smith, *Civic Ideals*, pp. 72–7, 120–3.

unity. Thomas Jefferson and J. Hector de Crevecoeur insisted that Americans were "one people," "a new race of men" who should live together in a distinctive nation with a distinctive national mission.[233] John Jay declared: "Providence has been pleased to give this one connected country to one united people – a people descended from the same ancestors, speaking the same language, professing the same religion, [and] attached to the same principles of government."[234]

This "one united people" could create and maintain a constitutional union only if all parties recognized that the need for ongoing cooperation entailed a need for ongoing compromise. "The spirit of accommodation," Washington informed correspondents, "was the basis of the present constitution."[235] The first president anticipated virtually every element of relational contract theory when reminding Gouverneur Morris that, regardless of the provisions contained in agreements with foreign nations, cooperation would continue only as long as all parties were better off cooperating. Washington understood that,

> unless treaties are mutually beneficial to the Parties, it is in vain to hope for a continuance of them beyond the moment when the one which concerns itself to be over-reached is in a situation to break off the connexion. And I believe it is among nations as with individuals, the party taking advantage of the distresses of another will lose infinitely more in the opinion of mankind and in subsequent events than he will gain by the strike of the moment.[236]

The same spirit of accommodation was required domestically to prevent "the ruin of the goodly fabric we have been creating." During constitutional debates over political economy and foreign policy, Washington demanded of his bickering cabinet that there "be liberal allowances, mutual forebearings, and temporising yieldings on *all sides*" (emphasis in original).[237]

The crucial compromises facilitating American constitutional relationships concerned the balance of sectional power. Not willing to have pervasive disputes over slavery prevent other cooperative endeavors, unable to agree on specific rules governing present disputes, and aware that new issues would

---

[233] Jefferson, *The Portable Jefferson*, p. 235; J. Hector St. John de Crevecoeur, *Letters from an American Farmer and Sketches of 18th-Century America* (ed. Albert E. Stone) (Penguin: New York, 1981), p. 70.

[234] Hamilton, Madison, and Jay, *Federalist Papers*, p. 38.

[235] Washington, *Washington*, p. 540.

[236] Washington, *Washington*, p. 557.

[237] Washington, *Washington*, pp. 578–9.

arise in the future, the persons responsible for the Constitution agreed on a process that they thought would consistently generate compromises most Americans could tolerate. As with provisions in other relational contracts, both the law of slavery and the processes for resolving sectional conflict evolved over time in ways not fully anticipated by constitutional framers. When unforeseen population changes prevented the House of Representatives from becoming a bastion of slave-state power, Southerners proved quite comfortable with institutional alternatives. National parties that competed for Southern votes proved one expedient for preserving constitutional relationships; so did having decisions made by a Supreme Court whose majority hailed from slave states.

Particular rules governing slavery were secondary to the process by which those rules were made. Southerners in 1820, 1850, and at other times proved willing to negotiate the level of constitutional and legal protections for slavery when slave-state representatives held crucial seats at the bargaining table. Constitutional relationships between the sections survived and deepened as long as each section could veto hostile legislation in order to ensure compromises whenever constitutional controversies divided slaveholders and free-soilers. Consistent with the "norm of mutuality," mainstream Whigs and Democrats cherished national parties and other practices that prevented any one section from dictating policy to the other. The precise manifestations of the sectional veto were negotiable. The veto was not.

If the Constitution was a compromise aimed primarily at establishing and maintaining political relationships between people who disagreed about slavery, then relational contract theory suggests that governing officials, when interpreting constitutional silences and ambiguities, should have sought the compromises most likely to maintain political relationships between people who disagreed about slavery. Free-state citizens could not read legal provisions at the South if they wished to preserve their common political order. Rather, as is the case for all relational contracts, the party that benefited from unanticipated events had to modify the terms of agreement to ensure ongoing mutually beneficial cooperation. Relationships formed by past compromises with evil could be maintained only by present compromises with evil.

Many new accommodations for slavery might have at least temporarily prevented secession. Free-state restraint was one possibility. Crucial Northern elites could have preserved union by refraining from banning slavery in the territories or from adopting any other antislavery policy that did not have substantial Southern support. An alternative was for Northern elites to combine

strong commitments to judicial supremacy with an equally strong commitment to preserving the 5-4 Southern majority on the Supreme Court. This
institutional arrangement might have ensured that all national policies were
vetted by at least one institution controlled by Southern moderates. The
Constitution might have been amended to prevent simple majorities from
making policies objectionable to the slave states. Better yet, given the electoral incentives for representatives from both the slave and free states to take
increasingly strong sectional positions,[238] constitutional amendments might
have been passed providing a more explicit sectional veto. Sectional control
of the national government might have been forestalled for at least a decade
or two by a constitutional amendment requiring the winning candidate for
the presidency to gain a majority of the popular vote.

None of these accommodations would have preserved the Constitution
of 1787 in pristine form. Abraham Lincoln and Jefferson Davis could no
more restore the original Constitution than they could eliminate political
parties, the Louisiana Purchase, or trains. Americans in 1861 were deciding
whether to continue an ongoing constitutional relationship – not what could
be done to freeze that relationship in its past form. Confederate-state majorities staked out their position: constitutional relationships were not worth
maintaining as long as free-state majorities had the power to impose antislavery constitutional understandings on the South. The question Lincoln faced
was whether free-state citizens should maintain the sectional veto in some
form as the price for union when that veto would be exercised to provide
more protection for slavery than constitutionally necessary or originally anticipated. The constitutional answer to this question depended on whether
the best justification for entering a constitutional relationship with evil in
1787 justified preserving that relationship in 1861.

The Constitutional Case for Abandoning the Constitution of 1787

"No Union with Slaveholders"

The Garrisonian wing of the abolition movement rejected existing constitutional relationships with slaveholders on the ground that such bonds should
never have been forged. William Lloyd Garrison and Wendell Phillips insisted that no person had any obligation to respect even the clearest constitutional commitment to slavery. The Constitution was "a covenant with death

---

[238] See Part II, notes 409–428 and the relevant text.

and an agreement with hell."[239] Maintaining the founders' compromises with evil in 1861 was a greater wrong than the compromises themselves, many radical abolitionists thought, given that slavery was clearly not dying from natural causes. If Northern secession would not free slaves, at least a free-state confederacy would not provide assistance for slaveholders and would cleanse the North of its political responsibility for slavery.[240] "The people must cease to hold slaves … though it cost them their existence as a people,"[241] Henry David Thoreau proclaimed. "No Union with Slaveholders" ran the banner on *The Emancipator*.[242]

Garrisonians did not offer constitutional reasons for their willingness to abandon the Constitution. They recognized that the Constitution of 1787 could be justified only if forging a constitutional relationship with slaveholders was justified. The most radical wing of the antislavery movement rejected the Constitution on that ground. "I am not for SLAVERY and UNION," Garrison declared; "this is the issue we make before the country and the world."[243] He and his followers condemned "the compromising spirit and the compromising Constitution." That a more antislavery constitutionalism was theoretically possible did not provide grounds for constitutional faith. Garrison pointed out to antislavery constitutionalists that "such construction is not to be tolerated *against the wishes of either party*" (emphasis in original).[244] He recognized that union with slaveholders meant honoring specific constitutional protections for slavery and resolving constitutional controversies about slavery in ways consistent with slaveholding interests. A constitution interpreted by slaveholders, he felt, was no better than a constitution that explicitly protected slaveholding.

Republicans rejected this criticism of the original Constitution. They thought free-state citizens in 1787 had good reason for providing various constitutional protections for slavery. Lincoln and his followers also accepted later bargains over human bondage, such as the Missouri Compromise. Pledged to honor inherited constitutional commitments to accommodate slavery, Republicans had to explain why the sound justifications for

---

[239] Henry Mayer, *All on Fire: William Lloyd Garrison and the Abolition of Slavery* (St. Martin's Griffin: New York, 1998), p. 531. For other Garrisonian attacks on the Constitution, see Mayer, *All on Fire*, pp. 65, 175, 312–28, 339, 341, 368, 397–8; Henry David Thoreau, *The Portable Thoreau* (ed. Carl Bode) (Penguin: New York, 1975), p. 120.

[240] Mayer, *All on Fire*, pp. 452–3, 469–70.

[241] Thoreau, *The Portable Thoreau*, p. 114.

[242] Mayer, *All on Fire*, p. 328.

[243] Mayer, *All on Fire*, p. 397.

[244] Mayer, *All on Fire*, p. 326.

compromising with slaveholders in 1787 did not justify ongoing compromises with slaveholders in 1861.

No Union with Permanent Slaveholders

Lincoln's frequent assertion that the framers assumed slavery was on the path of "ultimate extinction"[245] suggests a constitutional basis for rejecting constitutional relationships with slaveholders committed to maintaining their peculiar institution. If Northern agreement to constitutional arrangements was premised on beliefs that slavery would eventually be abolished,[246] then that justification for accommodating some temporary constitutional protections for slavery did not justify enduring and increasing constitutional protections for human bondage. The sectional veto, in this view, ensured that slave states would determine how slavery was abandoned but was not designed to vest the South with the power to make slavery permanent.

Constitutional arguments based on the assumption that slavery was on the road to extinction provide a relatively painless solution to the problem of constitutional evil. Persons may accept a constitution that they believe protects some constitutional evil as long as the evil is temporary. Temporary accommodations are particularly justified when more radical surgery will result in greater evils or when citizens genuinely do not know how best to eliminate the evil. Lincoln frequently declared that immediate emancipation presented intractable political problems. "When it is said that the institution exists; and that it is very difficult to get rid of it, in any satisfactory way," he proclaimed during the debates with Douglas, "I can understand and appreciate the saying." "If all earthly power were given me, I should not know what to do, as to the existing institution," Lincoln admitted.[247] The best that antislavery framers and citizens could accomplish were measures preventing that constitutional evil from becoming further entrenched, leaving to future generations the problem of eradication.

This belief that slavery in existing states could not have been immediately abandoned but would eventually wither largely dissolves the problem of constitutional evil. Problems of constitutional evil result when people who share the same civic space disagree sharply over the justice of prominent political practices. Lincoln saw no such disagreements when he looked to the founding. His speeches maintained that those responsible for the original Constitution agreed that all persons had certain natural rights, agreed that

---

[245] See e.g. Lincoln, 3 *Collected Works*, p. 18.
[246] See Mayer, *All on Fire*, p. 368.
[247] Lincoln, 3 *Collected Works*, p. 255.

slavery violated those natural rights, agreed that slavery had to be temporarily accommodated, and agreed that slavery should eventually be abolished. At most, Americans in 1787 disagreed moderately over the precise
timing and best means for freeing slaves. These disagreements were easily
resolved because, while all agreed that slavery was an evil, Americans also
agreed that morally decent persons might dispute how to abandon that practice without causing economic disruption in the South (and black migration
northward).

Republicans and Free-Soilers insisted that Southerners broke faith with
the Constitution when they employed their sectional veto as a vehicle for
expanding slavery. For Lincoln, the crucial commitment underlying the
constitutional relationship between the sections was the federal consensus,
the national commitment not to interfere with slavery in existing states.
This norm reflected what Republicans believed was the more general consensus in 1787 that slavery was an evil that should not be expanded. Past
compromises were thought consistent with this norm. Such measures as
the Louisiana Purchase, the annexation of Texas, and the Compromise of
1850 permitted slavery only where slavery was previously legal (or where
no one thought slavery would flourish) and were purchased by antislavery
concessions. What was new were nonnegotiable Southern demands to le
galize slavery in territories where slavery had previously been illegal. Such
efforts to entrench human bondage belied the antislavery impulse Republicans claimed was vital to the original Constitution, the federal consensus,
and past constitutional compromises.

History does not support Lincoln's antislavery constitutionalism. The persons responsible for the American Constitution were far more concerned
that controversies over slavery be settled peaceably than that they be resolved in favor of liberty. Whether and when slavery would die out was contested during the drafting and ratification process. Virginia slaveowners did
believe that human bondage would gradually be abandoned. Northerners
had good reason to think that if Virginians abandoned slavery then that practice was doomed. Representatives from the Deep South, however, firmly
insisted that human bondage was a relatively enduring institution.[248] South
Carolinians publicly claimed that New Englanders would eventually celebrate a proslavery regime. Given public awareness that South Carolina had
no desire to abandon human bondage, the original constitutional relationship between the sections cannot be said to rest on a common assumption
that slavery was on the path to ultimate extinction.

---

[248] See Part II, notes 108–110 and the relevant text.

The gradual extinction of slavery was also not an assumption central to free-state acceptance of the original constitutional bargain. Some free-state citizens defended the more proslavery features of the Constitution as temporary accommodations for a moribund practice.[249] Other Northerners declared that slavery was strictly the business of the slave states.[250] Most had more important priorities than emancipation. New Englanders willingly endorsed additional protections for slavery in return for concessions to Northern commercial interests. This compromise and the relative dearth of debate over slavery in most free-state ratification conventions suggest that few free-state citizens thought their constitutional relationships with slave-state citizens were conditioned on slavery being soon abolished, however many citizens may have hoped for such a possibility.

No Union with Antirepublican Slaveholders

Republicanism provides better constitutional grounds for abandoning the constitutional relationships between the sections, the sectional veto, and any duty to compromise with slaveholders. The original Constitution promised a republican solution to the problem of constitutional evil. Compromises with slaveholders were justified when embedded in republican institutions that, by promoting free inquiry, are the best human means for identifying and eventually curing injustice. Slave-state citizens did not make a constitutional commitment to emancipation, but they did make a constitutional commitment to republicanism. Republicans had constitutional reasons for rejecting the sectional veto after slave-state representatives violated their pledge to place the fate of slavery in republican hands.

During the 1850s, Republicans frequently proclaimed that the slave states had abandoned the Constitution's republican commitments. The proslavery demand that Kansas become a slave state – despite a clear popular majority favoring a free-state constitution – was only the most flagrant demonstration of antirepublican sentiment in the South. The South, antislavery advocates believed, had become an oligarchy whose slaveholding aristocrats threatened Northern political freedoms.[251] "Will they be satisfied if the Territories be unconditionally surrendered to them?" Lincoln's famed Cooper Institute address asked. "We know they will not." "[W]hat will convince them?" the future president continued. "This, and this only; cease to call slavery *wrong,* and join them in calling it *right*" (emphasis in original).[252]

---

[249] See Part II, note 90 and the relevant text.
[250] See Part II, notes 122–124 and the relevant text.
[251] See Part II, notes 243–246 and the relevant text.
[252] Lincoln, 3 *Collected Works,* p. 547.

Antislavery advocates in 1860 had reason to fear Southern efforts to prohibit "all declarations that slavery is wrong, whether made in politics, in
presses, in pulpits, or in private."[253] In the wake of the Nat Turner revolt
and Upper South feints toward conditional termination, many slaveholders
claimed "a perfect right to suppress ... injurious writings."[254] "Free speech,"
a rare Southern abolitionist noted, "is considered as treason against slavery."[255] Natives and visitors who spoke out against slavery were subject to
mob violence.[256] Postmasters would not permit the mails to be used for
antislavery tracts.[257] Maryland employed criminal libel law in an effort to
silence the young William Lloyd Garrison.[258] Most slave states passed legislation criminalizing antislavery speech. The Virginia statute required jail
terms for "any member of an abolition or antislavery society ... who shall
come into this state, and shall here maintain, by speaking or writing, that
the owners of slaves have no property in the same, or advocate or advise
the abolition of slavery."[259] Some state courts interpreted these provisions
narrowly,[260] but a North Carolina tribunal sentenced a Wesleyan minister
to prison for circulating a pamphlet suggesting that slavery was inconsistent with the Ten Commandments.[261] Although these laws were nominally

---

[253] Lincoln, 3 *Collected Works*, p. 548. The leading studies on repression against antislavery advocacy are Clement Eaton, *The Freedom-of-Thought Struggle in the Old South*, rev. ed. (Harper:
New York, 1964), and Michael Kent Curtis, *Free Speech, "The People's Darling Privilege":
Struggles for the Freedom of Expression in American History* (Duke University Press: Durham,
2000), pp. 117–299.

[254] Alison Goodyear Freehling, *Drift toward Dissolution: The Virginia Slavery Debate of 1831–32*
(Louisiana State University Press: Baton Rouge, 1982), p. 198 (quoting "Appomattox"). But see
A. Freehling, *Drift*, pp. 198–200 (noting sharp disagreement in Virginia over proposed bans on
antislavery agitation).

[255] Hinton Rowan Helper, *The Impending Crisis of the South: How to Meet It* (ed. George M.
Frederickson) (Harvard University Press: Cambridge, 1968), p. 409.

[256] Michael Kent Curtis, "The 1859 Crisis over Hinton Helper's Book, *The Impending Crisis*: Free
Speech, Slavery, and Some Light on the Meaning of the First Section of the Fourteenth Amendment," 68 *Chicago-Kent Law Review*, 1113, 1131, 1137–8, 1143 (1993); Michael Kent Curtis,
"The Curious History of Attempts to Suppress Antislavery Speech, Press, and Petition in 1835–
37," 89 *Northwestern University Law Review*, 785, 801, 817 (1995).

[257] Curtis, "Curious History," pp. 817–36.

[258] Mayer, *All on Fire*, pp. 53, 84–93.

[259] Curtis, "1859 Crisis," p. 1134 (quoting "An Act to Suppress the Circulation of Incendiary Publications," ch. 66, 1836 Va. Acts 44–5). North Carolina outlawed any work "the evident tendency
thereof is to cause slaves to become discontented with the bondage in which they are held ...
and free negroes to be dissatisfied with their social condition." Curtis, "1859 Crisis," p. 1164
(quoting 1854 "Act to Prevent Circulation of Seditious Publications," N.C. Rev. Code, ch. 34,
p. 16). That act was later amended to make the first offense punishable by death. Curtis, "1859
Crisis," p. 1167 (discussing 1869 N.C. Sess. Laws, ch. 23, p. 39 (1860)).

[260] See Curtis, "1859 Crisis," pp. 1135–6.

[261] Curtis, "1859 Crisis," p. 1136.

aimed at preventing slave revolts, state courts ruled illegal antislavery speech not directed at persons of color. The result of these official and unofficial measures was a complete "quarantine [on] antislavery expression" in the South.[262]

These Southern practices breached the Constitution's republican norms. South Carolina may not have made a constitutional commitment to gradual emancipation, but the Deep South and other slave states made a constitutional commitment to those republican political arrangements that opponents of slavery thought would eventually yield antislavery majorities in the slave states. Republican party activists had no legitimate constitutional complaint when majorities in the South continued to support slavery. Nevertheless, maintaining a sectional balance of power was justified only when Southern politics met republican standards. Slave states breached their constitutional commitments when they attempted to deny the power of republican majorities in the territories to pass a free-state constitution and when they prevented antislavery republican majorities from forming in their states by depriving residents of their republican right to criticize slavery and their republican duty to consider criticisms of slavery.

Republicanism and Constitutional Evil. Antebellum Americans thought government by "reflection and choice"[263] guaranteed the eventual triumph of wisdom and justice. Benjamin Franklin believed that, "when Truth and Error have fair play, the former is always an over match for the latter."[264] Variations on this Miltonic theme[265] became a cliché of American political thought.[266] John Adams declared, "if the press is stopped and the people kept in Ignorance we had much better have the first magistrate and Senators hereditary."[267] Similar declarations were made at the turn of the nineteenth century. "Truth is great, and will prevail, if left to herself," Tunis Workman proclaimed in the first treatise on expression rights published in the United States.[268] "If there be any among us who would wish to dissolve this Union or

[262] Curtis, "1859 Crisis," p. 1137.

[263] Hamilton, Madison, and Jay, *Federalist Papers*, p. 33.

[264] Benjamin Franklin, "An Apology for Printers," *Freedom of the Press from Zenger to Jefferson: Early American Libertarian Theories* (ed. Leonard W. Levy) (Bobbs-Merrill: Indianapolis, 1966), p. 5.

[265] John Milton, "Areopagitica," *The Works of John Milton*, vol. 4 (ed. Frank Allen Patterson) (Columbia University Press: New York, 1931), p. 347 ("that [Truth] and Falshood grapple; who ever knew the Truth to the wors, and a free and open encounter").

[266] See Leonard W. Levy, *Emergence of a Free Press* (Oxford University Press: New York, 1985), p. 184.

[267] Levy, *Emergence*, p. 200.

[268] Tunis Workman, *A Treatise Concerning Political Enquiry and the Liberty of the Press* (George Forman: New York, 1800), p. 174.

to change its republican form," Jefferson's first inaugural asserted, "let them stand undisturbed as monuments of the safety with which error of opinion may be tolerated where reason is left free to combat it."[269]

The leading opponents of slavery in antebellum America enthusiastically endorsed the republican connection between free speech and justice. Most were pacifists committed to moral suasion as the preferred means for achieving emancipation.[270] Benjamin Lundy believed "all that is wanting to ensure the ultimate triumph of liberty" was antislavery speech that would "draw the attention of his countrymen toward this subject, and ... induce them to THINK more about it."[271] William Lloyd Garrison supposed that "inquiry will induce conviction – conviction will lead to action – action will demand union – and then will follow victory." All prominent abolitionists were confident that the constitutional commitment to republicanism would eventually generate a public opinion committed to the abolition of slavery. "As slavery cannot exist with free discussion," Francis Jackson stated, "so neither can liberty breathe without it."[272] "Give us fair-play, secure to us the right of discussion, the freedom of speech," Hinton Helper declared, "and we will settle the difficulty at the ballot box, not on the battleground – by force of reason, not force of arms."[273]

This commitment to republicanism justifies the 1787 decision to accommodate slavery. Persons may form constitutional relationships with proponents of evil practices when those evil practices are subject to constant republican scrutiny. The original design of constitutional institutions privileged Southern positions, but the commitment to republicanism ensured that Southerners would influence policy only after being exposed to what many Americans believed were compelling arguments against permanently maintaining slavery. Slavery could survive in a republican polity only as long as proponents of human bondage could make persuasive arguments that justice required continued accommodation for their peculiar institution. If the framers were right, those arguments would become more difficult and less persuasive over time. Emancipation would take place because bisectional majorities could never be convinced that slavery was good and, through discussion, those majorities would discover the best means for securing human freedom.

---

[269] Jefferson, *The Portable Jefferson*, p. 292.

[270] See Aileen S. Kraditor, *Means and Ends in American Abolitionism: Garrison and His Critics on Strategy and Tactics, 1834–1850* (Pantheon: New York, 1969).

[271] Amy Reynolds, "William Lloyd Garrison, Benjamin Lundy and Criminal Libel: The Abolitionists' Plea for Press Freedom," 6 *Communication Law and Policy*, 577, 586 (2001).

[272] Mayer, *All on Fire*, pp. 126, 208. See Mayer, *All on Fire*, pp. 64, 262–4, 397, 423, 504.

[273] Helper, *The Impending Crisis*, p. 149. See Curtis, *Free Speech*, p. 1.

When Lincoln took office, he no longer had reason to believe that persons in the South were exercising their republican prerogative to maintain slavery. Southern restrictions on antislavery advocacy were destroying the moral capacities that best justified the original decision to protect human bondage. The sectional veto was republican only when slave-state citizens had the opportunity to evaluate the arguments for and against slavery. By 1860, this constitutional assumption was no more realistic than the assumption that population would flow southward. Fewer and fewer Southerners heard antislavery arguments. Fewer and fewer Southerners were politically free to express even moderate antislavery sentiments. Lincoln, recognizing that the constitutional relationship between the sections was no longer fostering either republicanism or liberty, took the steps necessary to forge a constitutional order committed to "a new birth of freedom," a majoritarian government "for the people, by the people, and of the people."

Violence was a legitimate means for bringing about this new regime. Lincoln justified the Civil War as "teaching men that what they cannot take by election, neither can they take it by a war." "Bullets," he declared, are alternatives to "ballots" only against those who refuse to be ruled by ballots.[274] Slave-state regimes could not complain that they would be governed by "accident and force." Their restrictive policies had already abandoned government by "reflection and choice." A government committed to reason may use military force against those who would perpetuate republican injustices by suppressing republican speech.

Republicanism and Republicans. Before commencing ritual celebrations of Lincoln, however, Americans should remember that the Republican commitment to republicanism evaporated almost immediately after the first inaugural. The majoritarian principles that Lincoln insisted were appropriate for resolving constitutional controversies over slavery in the territories were not deemed appropriate for resolving constitutional controversies over secession and the Civil War.[275] Lincoln administration officials arrested sixteen Maryland legislators in an effort to prevent that state from adopting a secession ordinance.[276] Martial law and summary arrests played crucial roles when state elections were held in Maryland, Kentucky, and

---

[274] Lincoln, 4 *Collected Works*, p. 439.

[275] Two excellent accounts of civil liberties during the secession crisis and the Civil War are J. G. Randall, *Constitutional Problems under Lincoln*, rev. ed. (University of Illinois Press: Urbana, 1951), and Mark E. Neely, Jr., *The Fate of Liberty: Abraham Lincoln and Civil Liberties* (Oxford University Press: New York, 1991); see also Curtis, *Free Speech*, pp. 300–56.

[276] Neely, *The Fate of Liberty*, pp. 14–18.

Missouri.[277] Federal troops frequently prevented voters opposed to the Civil War from casting ballots in other close elections. "[T]hose merely suspected of hostilities to the Republican party," Richard Bensel documents, "were often physically ejected from the polling place."[278] Several copperhead presses were temporarily shut down when they too vigorously challenged wartime policies.

These repressive measures were not legitimate responses to local practices that violated the constitutional commitment to republicanism. Bullets were not necessary to secure the integrity of ballots in free-state localities whose citizens opposed Republican Party policies. Persons were relatively free to take antislavery positions in the border states. In 1860, Delaware was on the verge of emancipation, and the subject was under serious debate in Maryland. Radical abolitionists, as always, risked formal and informal sanctions wherever they peddled their ideas. Still, border-state citizens at the time of Lincoln's first inaugural were far freer to champion abolition than they were to advocate secession or oppose the Civil War.

Both Republican and Southern repression were more the norm than the exception in nineteenth-century America. The antebellum United States was not a republican paradise, even when republicanism was limited to white men. John Roche accurately describes that polity as "an open society dotted with closed enclaves" where "one could generally settle with his co-believers in safety and comfort and exercise the right of oppression."[279] Political and religious dissenters often ran afoul of criminal libel and blasphemy laws,[280] Mormons were persecuted wherever they fled.[281] Elections were determined by which side better plied voters with alcohol, stuffed the ballot box, and intimidated rival partisans.[282] Perhaps Southern restrictions on abolitionist speech were different in degree than analogous repressive behavior throughout the United States, but such censorship does not seem

---

[277] Forrest McDonald, *States' Rights and the Union: Imperium in Imperio, 1776–1876* (University Press of Kansas: Lawrence, 2000), p. 201.

[278] Richard Franklin Bensel, *The American Ballot Box in the Mid-Nineteenth Century* (Cambridge University Press: New York, 2004), p. 217. See McDonald, *States' Rights and the Union*, p. 201.

[279] John P. Roche, "American Liberty: An Examination of the 'Tradition' of Freedom," *Aspects of Liberty* (ed. Milton R. Konvitz and Clinton Rossiter) (Cornell University Press: Ithaca, 1958), p. 137. See Levy, *Emergence*, p. 16.

[280] See Norman L. Rosenberg, *Protecting the Best Men: An Interpretive History of the Law of Libel* (University of North Carolina Press: Chapel Hill, 1986), pp. 56–152; Leonard William Levy, *Blasphemy: Verbal Offense against the Sacred. From Moses to Salman Rushdie* (Knopf: New York, 1993), pp. 400–23.

[281] See Sarah Barringer Gordon, *The Mormon Question: Polygamy and Constitutional Conflict in Nineteenth Century America* (University of North Carolina Press: Chapel Hill, 2002).

[282] See Bensel, *The American Ballot Box*.

different in kind. Very few public policies in antebellum America pass contemporary republican standards.

Public policy throughout the United States at the time Lincoln was elected probably passed republican muster by nineteenth-century standards. The marketplace of ideas in both the free and slave states was not entirely dysfunctional. Most Southerners were aware of the main antislavery arguments. Speech was free on the main sectional issues of the day. Slave-state Whigs vigorously opposed Southern expansion and openly challenged Jacksonian justifications of the Kansas–Nebraska Act.[283] The only change the Civil War guaranteed was that many young men who had only peripheral responsibility for slavery would die. Abraham Lincoln is justly acclaimed as the hero of the post–Civil War Constitution, but the better defender of the old constitutional order was probably John Bell – the most obscure major candidate running for the presidency in 1860.

[283] See Michael F. Holt, *The Rise and Fall of the American Whig Party: Jacksonian Politics and the Onset of the Civil War* (Oxford University Press: New York, 1999), pp. 177–8, 814, 820–1, 851, 854.

Voting for John Bell

American constitutionalists vote overwhelmingly for Abraham Lincoln whenever the presidential campaign of 1860 is refought in the contemporary academy. Lawyers, political scientists, and historians agree that Lincoln was "one of the unreconstructed Constitution's most able interpreters."[1] The sixteenth president is considered a "secular saint" who "teaches us both why we should be faithful to the Constitution and what fidelity is,"[2] "a model for the role of political authority generally,"[3] "our greatest teacher of what it means to be an American,"[4] and the "most awesome of American political icons."[5] The first inaugural address is sacred text in the American civil religion. Lincoln's speech has been called "a masterpiece of constitutional analysis" that "should be studied and taught ... as a classic of carefully reasoned legal analysis of the text, structure, and internal logic of the Constitution."[6] The few contemporary commentators who do not vote for Lincoln cast their ballots for Lysander Spooner[7] or Frederick Douglass,[8] political actors whose constitutional politics were even more antislavery than those of the sixteenth president. One looks in vain for any contemporary commentary suggesting that one of the other three contestants for the presidency in 1860 – Stephen

---

[1] Christopher L. Eisgruber, "The Fourteenth Amendment's Constitution," 69 *University of Southern California Law Review*, 47, 74 (1995).

[2] William Michael Treanor, "Learning from Lincoln," 65 *Fordham Law Review*, 1781 (1997).

[3] Robert A. Burt, *The Constitution in Conflict* (Harvard University Press: Cambridge, 1992), p. 77.

[4] Christopher L. Eisgruber, *Constitutional Self-Government* (Harvard University Press: Cambridge, 2001), p. 102.

[5] Walter Berns, *Making Patriots* (University of Chicago Press: Chicago, 2001), p. 18.

[6] Vesan Kesavan and Michael Stokes Paulsen, "Is West Virginia Unconstitutional?" 90 *California Law Review*, 291, 301–10 (2002).

[7] Randy E. Barnett, "Was Slavery Unconstitutional before the Thirteenth Amendment: Lysander Spooner's Theory of Interpretation," 28 *Pacific Law Journal*, 977 (1997).

[8] Sanford Levinson, *Constitutional Faith* (Princeton University Press: Princeton, 1988), p. 192.

Douglas, John Bell, or John Breckinridge – provides a better model than Lincoln for constitutionalists in the twenty-first century.[9]

Conventional wisdom proclaims that Lincoln was right on all the crucial constitutional issues facing the electorate in 1860. He correctly regarded the Constitution as being committed to the containment and eventual eradication of slavery.[10] He correctly condemned *Dred Scott*.[11] He correctly insisted that the Constitution vested sectional majorities with the power to reverse *Dred Scott*.[12] Upon taking office, Lincoln correctly declared secession unconstitutional.[13] He correctly resisted secession by military force,[14] although some of his presidential measures during the Civil War were constitutionally dubious.[15]

These tributes ignore how Lincoln consistently misperceived the dynamics of antebellum constitutional politics. He incorrectly maintained that territories where slavery was permitted would be inevitably settled by citizens from slave states.[16] He incorrectly insisted that the slave states would not secede should a Republican be elected president.[17] Having assured Northerners that votes for antislavery candidates would not disrupt national unity,

---

[9] Historians writing before the civil rights movement often voted for Stephen Douglas; see George Fort Milton, *The Eve of Conflict: Stephen A. Douglas and the Needless War* (Houghton Mifflin: Boston, 1934).

[10] See Clarence Thomas, "Toward a 'Plain Reading' of the Constitution – The Declaration of Independence in Constitutional Interpretation," 1987 *Howard Law Journal*, 691, 692–6 (1987); Cass R. Sunstein, *Designing Democracy: What Constitutions Do* (Oxford University Press: New York, 2001), pp. 204–5.

[11] See Part I, notes 6–20 and the relevant text.

[12] Michael Stokes Paulsen, "The Most Dangerous Branch: Executive Power to Say What the Law Is," 83 *Georgetown Law Journal*, 217 (1994); Edwin Meese III, "Putting the Federal Judiciary Back on the Constitutional Track," 14 *Georgia State University Law Review*, 781 (1998); Keith E. Whittington, "Extrajudicial Constitutional Interpretation: Three Objections and Responses," 80 *North Carolina Law Review*, 773, 843–7 (2002); Daniel Farber, *Lincoln's Constitution* (University of Chicago Press: Chicago, 2003), pp. 187–8; Larry Alexander and Frederick Schauer, "On Extrajudicial Constitutional Interpretation," 110 *Harvard Law Review*, 1359, 1381 (1997).

[13] Cass R. Sunstein, "Constitutionalism and Secession," 58 *University of Chicago Law Review*, 633, 633–4 (1991); Farber, *Lincoln's Constitution*, pp. 3, 81–91.

[14] Farber, *Lincoln's Constitution*, pp. 3, 112–14; Berns, *Making Patriots*, pp. 4–5, 87–8; Eisgruber, *Constitutional Self-Government*, p. 104.

[15] See Mark E. Neely, Jr., *The Fate of Liberty: Abraham Lincoln and Civil Liberties* (Oxford University Press: New York, 1991); Sanford Levinson, "Was the Emancipation Proclamation Constitutional? Do We/Should We Care What the Answer Is?" 2001 *University of Illinois Law Review*, 1135 (2001); *Ex parte Milligan*, 71 U.S. 2 (1866). For a particularly good analysis, see Farber, *Lincoln's Constitution*.

[16] Abraham Lincoln, *The Collected Works of Abraham Lincoln*, vol. 3 (ed. Roy P. Basler) (Rutgers University Press: New Brunswick, 1953), pp. 483, 485–6, 499.

[17] Lincoln, 2 *Collected Works*, p. 355.

Lincoln incorrectly claimed an electoral mandate to reverse the result in *Dred Scott* no matter what the political consequences.

More significantly, Lincoln misconstrued the fundamental principles underlying the antebellum constitutional order. He incorrectly asserted that those responsible for the Constitution of 1787 placed slavery on "the course of ultimate extinction."[18] He incorrectly insisted that *Dred Scott* had no plausible constitutional basis.[19] He incorrectly invoked a constitutional commitment to majority rule when justifying Republican attempts to ban slavery in all territories without any significant Southern support.[20] He incorrectly asserted that a Republican victory in 1860 would restore the constitutional status quo.[21] Upon taking office, Lincoln incorrectly insisted that maintaining national union justified the Civil War.[22]

Contemporary scholars wishing to support the presidential candidate in 1860 who was most likely to have preserved the original constitutional order and the constitutional peace might first turn to Stephen Douglas. Douglas better comprehended antebellum constitutional politics than Lincoln. He correctly realized that most Kansas settlers would hail from free states, even though slavery was legal during the territorial phase.[23] He correctly predicted that the slave states would secede should Republicans win the 1860 election.[24] Douglas also better understood the Constitution of 1787 than did Lincoln. He correctly recognized that the original constitutional order was more committed to consensus than majority rule on sectional issues.[25] Douglas rightly regarded *Dred Scott* as a centrist decision because he correctly anticipated that many Northerners would tolerate slavery in the territories as long as that policy was announced by Jacksonian justices rather than by Jacksonian elected officials.[26]

A contemporary vote for Douglas is nevertheless problematic, even when his virulent racism is discounted. A vote for Douglas is not a vote to keep the

---

[18] Lincoln, 2 *Collected Works*, p. 461. See Part II, notes 54–84 and the relevant text.

[19] Lincoln, 2 *Collected Works*, p. 401. See Part I, notes 83–385 and the relevant text.

[20] Lincoln, 4 *Collected Works*, pp. 267–8. See Part III, notes 73–74 and the relevant text.

[21] Lincoln, 4 *Collected Works*, pp. 21–2. See Part III, notes 111–112 and the relevant text.

[22] Lincoln, 5 *Collected Works*, pp. 388–9. See Sanford Levinson, *Written in Stone: Public Monuments in Changing Societies* (Duke University Press: Durham, 1998), p. 60.

[23] Stephen A. Douglas, *The Letters of Stephen A. Douglas* (ed. Robert W. Johannsen) (University of Illinois Press: Urbana, 1961), pp. 182, 289. See Part I, notes 160–164 and the relevant text.

[24] Douglas, *Letters of Douglas*, p. 440.

[25] *Congressional Globe*, 34th Cong., 1st Sess., App., p. 844 (speech of Stephen Douglas). See Part III, notes 63–64 and the relevant text.

[26] Bernard Schwartz, *A History of the Supreme Court* (Oxford University Press: New York, 1993), p. 124 (quoting Stephen Douglas). See Part I, notes 165–167 and the relevant text.

peace. The Illinois Democrat championed Manifest Destiny throughout his career.[27] Had he been elected president in 1860, the United States would most likely have found an excuse to invade Mexico or purchase Cuba.[28] When the decision is between the candidate who would fight a war for the eventual purpose of ending slavery and the candidate who would fight a war for the immediate purpose of expanding slavery, the decision for Lincoln is clear.

A too-easy way to mitigate the less attractive side of Douglas is to imagine a "Stephen Douglas" shorn of his racist and expansionist sentiments. Such a "Douglas" perhaps defended *Dred Scott* only because he believed maintaining the Constitution of 1787 as interpreted by the Taney Court was essential to preserving the peace. The problem with positing imaginary candidates is that all elections present the problem of constitutional evil in miniature. In order to form political parties large enough to win multiple offices, citizens must join with others whose views on many issues they find abhorrent. "Successful American parties," political scientists point out, "must be coalitions of enemies."[29] The partisan imperative requires voters to take candidates as they come, warts and all. When deciding between competing visions of the antebellum constitutional order, modern voters' choices should be limited to those candidates who were capable of gaining substantial support in 1860. This rules out such candidates as Frederick Douglass and a hypothetical Northern Jacksonian opposed to expansion.[30] Fortunately for the sake of the ensuing argument, antebellum voters unwilling to risk the peace between the states were not compelled to risk war in Central America. American politics on the eve of the Civil War generated a major candidate who, while far more tolerant of slavery and racism than Lincoln, was more opposed to expansion than Douglas.

John Bell was the stealth candidate in the 1860 presidential election, particularly when that election is refought in the contemporary academy. Bell ran "on a platform of having no platform other than 'the Constitution of the Country, the Union of the States, and the Enforcement of the Laws,' " and he had no issues other than preventing disunion.[31] Bell was a prominent

---

[27] See Robert W. Johannsen, "Introduction," *Letters of Douglas*, p. xxv; Douglas, *Letters of Douglas*, pp. 119–20.

[28] See Harry V. Jaffa, *Crisis of the House Divided: An Interpretation of the Issues in the Lincoln–Douglas Debates* (Doubleday: Garden City, 1955), pp. 99–101, 407–8.

[29] Gary Miller and Norman Schofield, "Activists and Partisan Realignment in the United States," 97 *American Political Science Review*, 245, 249 (2003).

[30] Every Northern Jacksonian who gained some support for the Democratic presidential nomination after 1844 was an ardent expansionist.

[31] Don E. Fehrenbacher, *The Dred Scott Case: Its Significance in American Law and Politics* (Oxford University Press: New York, 1978), p. 536; David Potter, *The Impending Crisis: 1848–1861*

border-state Whig who for thirty years led the Southern Whig fight against national expansion. He opposed the annexation of Texas and the Mexican War. He sought to minimize the amount of territory acquired from Mexico after that war. He spoke out against the Buchanan administration's efforts to purchase Cuba.[32] Bell was the candidate for the presidency in 1860 who made the greatest effort to prevent the following year's war between the seceding and nonseceding states.[33] A vote for Bell was a vote for a racist candidate with no commitment to bringing about the ultimate extinction of slavery,[34] but also a vote against risking foreign or domestic war.[35]

LINCOLN VERSUS BELL

The most difficult and important constitutional question Americans face today is the choice between politicians inspired by Abraham Lincoln and those inspired by John Bell – between candidates committed to pursuing constitutional justice and candidates committed to preserving the constitutional peace. Such commitments to justice and peace are not mutually exclusive. "Justice-seeking" constitutionalists recognize that prudence is a constitutional virtue. Christopher Eisgruber points out that "constitutional adjudication involves a complex mix of moral principle and institutional strategy."[36] Constitutionalists who are committed to social peace pursue justice. The crucial difference lies in the way the constitutional relationship between justice and social peace is conceptualized. Lincoln voters of the past and of the present believe constitutional controversies should eventually be settled justly or consistently with the Constitution's vision of justice. Bell voters believe contested constitutional questions should be settled peacefully. Lincoln voters are prudent when restraint is necessary to realize fundamental constitutional commitments to justice. Bell voters pursue justice when doing so is consistent with the fundamental constitutional commitment to preserving the political regime.

(Harper & Row: New York, 1976), p. 417; Joseph Howard Parks, *John Bell of Tennessee* (Louisiana State University Press: Baton Rouge, 1950), pp. 339–88.

[32] Parks, *John Bell*, pp. 205, 217, 220–3, 225, 332–5; *Congressional Globe*, 30th Cong., 1st Sess., App., pp. 189–201 (speech of John Bell); *Congressional Globe*, 35th Cong., 2nd Sess., pp. 1340–5 (speech of John Bell). Bell consistently voted against the gag rules enacted during the 1830s: Parks, *John Bell*, pp. 172–3.

[33] Parks, *John Bell*, pp. 389–403.

[34] See Parks, *John Bell*, pp. 309, 361. He favored colonization, opposed the Kansas–Nebraska Act, opposed the Lecompton constitution, and gave at most tepid support to the *Dred Scott* decision: Parks, *John Bell*, pp. 290–301, 326–9, 344.

[35] See Parks, *John Bell*, p. 394.

[36] Eisgruber, *Constitutional Self-Government*, p. 9.

The choice between Lincoln and Bell was easier when many Americans believed that slavery was not that bad a practice,[37] that human bondage was on the road to extinction,[38] or that persons of color lacked the capacity to be equal citizens.[39] Today, Bell voters reject these racist and historically dubious claims yet still consider supporting a racist, proslavery candidate. The question is whether constitutional theory provides reasons for preferring John Bell to Abraham Lincoln even when we acknowledge that slavery was a horrible evil,[40] that no one can say with any certainty what the fate of slavery would have been had the Civil War not been fought, and that persons of color have both the capacity and the right to be equal citizens.

As prospective Bell voters acknowledge slavery to be a gross violation of human rights, prospective Lincoln voters must acknowledge that virtue might not have triumphed in 1865. Whether the Union would win the war and free slaves in the wake of that victory was not foreseen with confidence in 1860. Might has historically demonstrated only the most limited tendency to make right.[41] James McPherson, one of our foremost historians of the Civil War, maintained: "Northern victory and southern defeat in the war cannot be understood apart from the contingency that hung over every campaign, every battle, every election, every decision during the war."[42] During the summer of 1864, Lincoln thought a Democratic victory quite likely in that fall's national election.[43] A Confederate military victory would almost certainly

---

[37] See Ulrich B. Phillips, *American Negro Slavery: A Survey of the Supply, Employment and Control of Negro Labor as Determined by the Plantation Regime* (Appleton: New York, 1918).

[38] See Chas. W. Ramsdell, "The Natural Limits of Slavery Expansion," 16 *Mississippi Valley Historical Review,* 151, 171 (1929); J. G. Randall, *Lincoln the President: Springfield to Gettysburg,* vol. 1 (Dodd, Mead: New York, 1945), p. 127.

[39] See generally Randall Kennedy, "Reconstruction and the Politics of Scholarship," 98 *Yale Law Journal,* 521, 523–5 (1989) (summarizing scholarship on Reconstruction before 1950).

[40] Stanley M. Elkins, *Slavery: A Problem in American Institutional and Intellectual Life* (Grosset & Dunlop: New York, 1959), pp. 9–17.

[41] Democratic regimes do tend to triumph when in combat with more autocratic regimes. See David A. Lake, "Powerful Pacifists, Democratic States and War," 86 *American Political Science Review,* 24 (1992); Dan Reiter and Allan C. Stam III, "Democracy, War Initiation, and Victory," 92 *American Political Science Review,* 377 (1998). This democratic success is at most a mere tendency, not a guarantee. Moreover, democracies may be more successful militarily because "democratic states choose conflicts in which they are especially likely to prevail." Christopher F. Gelpi and Michael Griesdorf, "Winners or Losers? Democracies in International Crisis, 1918–1994," 95 *American Political Science Review,* 633, 646 (2001). No reason exists for thinking that a "republic" that treated persons of color as second-class citizens was likely to triumph in combat with a "republic" that treated persons of color as slaves.

[42] James M. McPherson, *Battle Cry of Freedom: The Civil War Era* (Oxford University Press: New York, 1988), p. 858.

[43] See McPherson, *Battle Cry of Freedom,* p. 857.

have inspired slaveholders to expand southward. A McClellan presidency might have led to reunion on terms more favorable to slavery than the prewar Constitution. These plausible alternatives remind citizens who contemplate risking the constitutional peace in order to achieve constitutional justice to take seriously the possibility that they will achieve neither peace nor justice.

The Constitution of Today's Lincoln Voters

Lincoln's constitution commits Americans to work together for justice. The "more perfect union" envisioned by the preamble is a good political order. "The job of American constitutional theory," Eisgruber declares, "is to describe how Americans should conceive and inhabit their institutions so that they can govern themselves on the basis of their own best judgments about justice."[44] Abraham Lincoln believed Americans were constitutionally committed to the eventual abolition of slavery. Today, Lincolnians insist the Constitution commits Americans to liberal egalitarianism,[45] libertarianism,[46] populism,[47] deliberative democracy,[48] or the rule of law.[49]

This commitment to justice transcends differences between various schools of constitutional interpretation. Leading aspirationalists regard the Constitution as "the embodiment of our public morality."[50] "A constitution," one natural law theorist declares, "is simply political philosophy written down."[51] Constitutionalists who scorn such efforts to integrate moral theory and constitutional law nevertheless root their preferred approach to constitutional interpretation in a theory of justice. "Laws can still bind in conscience," a prominent originalist declares, "if the constitution that governs their making, application, and enforcement contains adequate procedures to assure that restrictions imposed on nonconsenting persons are just."

---

[44] Eisgruber, *Constitutional Self-Government,* p. 207. See Sotirios A. Barber, *On What the Constitution Means* (Johns Hopkins University Press: Baltimore, 1984), p. 60.

[45] Ronald Dworkin, *Taking Rights Seriously* (Harvard University Press: Cambridge, 1978).

[46] Randy E. Barnett, *Restoring the Lost Constitution: The Presumption of Liberty* (Princeton University Press: Princeton, 2003).

[47] Mark V. Tushnet, *Taking the Constitution Away from the Courts* (Princeton University Press: Princeton, 1999).

[48] Cass R. Sunstein, *Democracy and the Problem of Free Speech* (Free Press: New York, 1993).

[49] Antonin Scalia, *A Matter of Interpretation* (Princeton University Press: Princeton, 1998).

[50] Owen M. Fiss, "Two Models of Adjudication," *How Does the Constitution Secure Rights?* (ed. Robert A. Goldwin and William A. Schambra) (American Enterprise Institute: Washington, D.C., 1985), p. 49.

[51] Michael S. Moore, "A Natural Law Theory of Interpretation," 58 *University of Southern California Law Review,* 279, 394 (1985).

In the Lincolnian view, interpretation is how controversies over official constitutional meanings should be settled.[52] Lincoln determined the constitutional status of slavery by examining constitutional provisions in light of their original meaning, historical development, and underlying moral principles. Contemporary Lincolnians determine the constitutional status of abortion and affirmative action by relying on the same legal logics. Constitutional authorities resolve constitutional disputes by examining which side is making the best legal argument. Whether persons had a constitutional right to bring slaves into the territories or whether they have a constitutional right to terminate pregnancies depends entirely on the weight of the constitutional evidence.

Constitutional institutions, Lincoln and his followers believe, foster justice by their nature and effects. Some constitutional processes embody an underlying constitutional vision of procedural justice. Abraham Lincoln asserted that the constitutional rules for staffing the federal government evinced the fundamental constitutional commitment to democratic majoritarianism. Other constitutional practices are means for securing constitutional commitments to substantive justice. Madison believed that freedom of religion would best be secured by a large republic with large election districts.[53] Granting justices the power to declare laws unconstitutional, contemporary commentators insist, provides the best institutional protection for constitutional liberties.[54]

Constitutional norms and institutions are thought to mitigate the selfishness endemic to ordinary democratic politics. Bereft of constitutional guidance, political actors are prone to pursue self-interest in ways that violate the rights of others. Madison worried about factions "who are united and actuated by some common impulse of passion, or of interest, adverse to the rights of other citizens, or to the permanent and aggregate interests of the community."[55] Contemporary commentators worry about "public officials" who "serve their own institutional or personal self-interest at the expense of their constituents."[56] Constitutionalism breaks the spirit of faction by fostering deliberation about public ends, providing higher norms for guiding public opinion, and establishing institutions capable of acting on constitutional

---

[52] See especially Owen M. Fiss, "Objectivity and Interpretation," 34 *Stanford Law Review*, 739 (1982).

[53] Alexander Hamilton, James Madison, and John Jay, *The Federalist Papers* (New American Library: New York, 1961), p. 84.

[54] See James E. Fleming, "Constructing the Substantive Constitution," 72 *Texas Law Review*, 211 (1993); Eisgruber, *Constitutional Self-Government*, pp. 3–5, 7, 57–64, 78, 207.

[55] Hamilton, Madison, and Jay, *Federalist Papers*, p. 78.

[56] Eisgruber, *Constitutional Self-Government*, p. 168.

principle. Constitutional arguments are "good faith effort[s] to transcend
partisan, short-term goals and produce a long-term impartial assessment of
what is good for the country."[57] Abraham Lincoln believed the Constitution
infused Americans with a commitment to ending slavery that transcended
self-interested politics. Contemporary proponents of process jurisprudence
regard the Supreme Court as a "forum of principle."[58] "While other political institutions have pandered to the American people's baser selves," they
declare, "the Court has frequently had backbone enough to stand up for the
people's values."[59]

These interpretive logics and institutional arrangements ensure that constitutional controversies are resolved consistently with constitutional principle. Constitutions may initially be compromises between persons committed
to different visions of justice, but constitutional authorities have no obligation to resolve the constitutional controversies that arise after ratification in
ways that accommodate those crucial actors whose support was necessary
for the creation of the regime. Lincoln urged Americans to "be diverted by
none of those sophisticated contrivances such as groping for some middle
ground between the right and the wrong."[60] His Constitution was committed to democratic majoritarianism and the eventual abolition of slavery,
even though many antebellum Americans championed consensus democracy and human bondage. Contemporary Lincolnians assert constitutional
commitments to the right to die, sexual privacy, and color-blind policies that
are an anathema to many of their fellow citizens. Prominent law profes-
sors elaborate "secret"[61] or "lost"[62] constitutions that bind all Americans,
even those who think the underlying principles constitutionally mistaken or
morally obtuse.

Constitutional evil, stupidity, and tragedy are consequences of human imperfection. The Constitution is flawed because Americans have never been
fully capable of realizing or living up to constitutional principle. Some accommodations for evil were necessary at the creation. The Constitution
provided certain oblique protections for slavery because too many citizens
were not prepared to honor the constitutional aspiration for human freedom
and dignity. Other constitutional evils result from ongoing needs to temper

---

[57] Eisgruber, *Constitutional Self-Government*, p. 41.
[58] See Ronald M. Dworkin, "The Forum of Principle," 56 *New York University Law Review*, 469 (1981).
[59] Eisgruber, *Constitutional Self-Government*, p. 210.
[60] Lincoln, 4 *Collected Works*, p. 29.
[61] George P. Fletcher, *Our Secret Constitution: How Lincoln Redefined American Democracy* (Oxford University Press: New York, 2001).
[62] Barnett, *Restoring the Lost Constitution*.

justice with prudence. Lincoln would abolish slavery only when a clear consensus existed for the eventual emancipation anticipated by the Constitution. These constraints on constitutional justice seeking remain in force. Some proponents of gay marriage believe that this constitutional right to matrimony should not be judicially vindicated until the general public is more supportive.[63]

Constitutional evil is nevertheless limited to legal rules believed to be inconsistent with the general principles of justice animating the Constitution. Constitutionalists speak of "embedded mistake[s] ... whose meaning is unjust but which meaning and specific authority cannot be denied."[64] Persons have constitutional obligations to follow the letter of evil constitutional rules, but those rules have no broader spirit. "Though such a mistake may still have authority," Randy Barnett writes, "it does not provide the basis ... for interpreting by extension other provisions in an unjust manner."[65] Nothing in the Constitution requires future generations to accommodate an iota more evil than was initially clearly bargained for. The three-fifths clause and related constitutional provisions provide no support for the broader claim that a united coalition of slave-state representatives had the constitutional power to veto hostile legislation. A Senate in which all states are granted an equal vote does not justify any other departure from one person–one vote.[66]

Constitutional theory helps limit and eventually eradicate constitutional evil. In cases of constitutional doubt, constitutional interpreters make the constitutional order "the best it can be."[67] Following Lysander Spooner, the responsibility of constitutional authorities is to ascertain "the most *just and beneficial* intentions, which the words of the instrument, taken as a whole, can fairly be made to express or imply" (emphasis in original).[68] Withholding judgment is a constitutional possibility when the best constitutional norms cannot be successfully implemented.[69] Nevertheless, constitutional authorities must never advance inferior constitutional understandings merely to

---

[63] Andrew Koppelman, *The Gay Rights Question in Contemporary American Law* (University of Chicago Press: Chicago, 2002), pp. 141–54; Sunstein, *Designing Democracy*, p. 193.

[64] Barnett, "Was Slavery Unconstitutional," p. 1011. See Dworkin, *Taking Rights Seriously*, p. 121.

[65] Barnett, "Was Slavery Unconstitutional," p. 1011. See Dworkin, *Taking Rights Seriously*, p. 121; Barber, *What the Constitution Means*, p. 195; Eisgruber, *Constitutional Self-Government*, pp. 125–6.

[66] See *Reynolds v. Sims*, 377 U.S. 533, 572–5 (1964).

[67] Ronald Dworkin, *Law's Empire* (Harvard University Press: Cambridge, 1986), p. 379; Barnett, "Was Slavery Unconstitutional," p. 1011.

[68] Lysander Spooner, "The Unconstitutionality of Slavery," 28 *Pacific Law Journal*, 1015, 1034 (1997); Barnett, "Was Slavery Unconstitutional," p. 1011.

[69] See Alexander M. Bickel, "Foreword: The Passive Virtues," 75 *Harvard Law Review*, 40, 43–9, 75 (1961).

preserve the constitutional peace.[70] For Lincolnians, *Dred Scott* reminds Americans that severe injustice is the likely consequence of mistaken constitutional theories. The Taney Court, in this view, protected slavery and racism more than constitutionally necessary because the justices failed to grasp or apply correctly fundamental principles of constitutional justice. Had the justices been better constitutionalists, they would have held that free persons of color were American citizens and that slavery could constitutionally be banned in American territories.

The Lincolnian constitutional sensibility was expressed well by the bicentennial exhibit "Miracle in Philadelphia," discussed at the conclusion of Sanford Levinson's marvelous *Constitutional Faith*.[71] Visitors to the exhibit were presented with the original constitutional text and asked, "Will You Sign This Constitution?"[72] Persons signed in private as individuals. The exhibit did not permit discussion or debate over the reasons citizens had for approving or rejecting the Constitution of 1787. Professor Levinson writes that he signed in "memory of Frederick Douglass and his willingness to embrace the Constitution."[73] Perhaps the next person in line signed in memory of Roger Taney and his willingness to embrace the Constitution. Nothing in the exhibit required them to reconcile their understandings. Persons who signed in memory of Frederick Douglass were not asked to consider whether, depending on the results in the next series of elections, they had just consented to be ruled by or been authorized to rule over persons who signed the constitutional text in memory of Roger Taney. Those who signed in memory of Frederick Douglass were not asked whether they were constitutionally authorized to take military action against those who signed in memory of Roger Taney should the latter reject rule by the former.

The Constitution of Today's Bell Voters

John Bell's Constitution commits Americans to work together peacefully. The more perfect union envisioned by the preamble is one that better facilitates cooperation between persons who lack a common vision of the good society. Good constitutions preserve the social peace by establishing institutions and rules that privilege the policies most citizens find acceptable. John Bell believed Americans were constitutionally committed to institutions and

---

[70] See Bickel, "Passive Virtues," pp. 48–9, 51, 74; *Korematsu v. United States*, 323 U.S. 214, 244–8 (1944) (Jackson, dissenting).

[71] Levinson, *Constitutional Faith*, pp. 180–94.

[72] Levinson, *Constitutional Faith*, p. 180.

[73] Levinson, *Constitutional Faith*, p. 192.

rules that prevented disputes over slavery from interfering with the military and economic benefits of national union. His successors might think that Americans are constitutionally committed to institutions and rules that prevent disputes over abortion from interfering with the benefits of a fully staffed federal judiciary.

Bell voters regard constitutional theories based entirely on aspirations to justice as legally fruitless and politically offensive. Constitutional interpretation practiced properly, they feel, has only a limited tendency to privilege just answers to constitutional controversies. Rarely do clear, correct answers exist to such concerns as the constitutional status of slavery in the territories or the conditions under which affirmative action is consistent with equal protection. The Lincolnian tendency to distinguish between the party of constitutional principle and the party of self-interest disdainfully ignores how constitutional controversies are almost always rooted in disputes over justice. Self-interest does not explain why so many Southerners who did not own slaves died at Gettysburg or why so many opponents of *Roe* have been arrested for blockading abortion clinics. Calling on constitutional authorities to pursue justice when resolving constitutional controversies insults proponents of the disfavored position without making an argument for the favored position.

Constitutional theory is about how political regimes are maintained as well as about how they are improved or perfected. Lincoln's constitutional perfectionalism was limited to persuading Americans that the United States would be a more just society if the Constitution were interpreted as being committed to emancipation. John Bell's adequate constitutionalism more realistically engaged the problem of preserving a political order wracked by disputes over slavery. Bell championed national parties and the Crittenden Compromise because those institutions and rules promised to maintain sectional peace. He recognized that the American polity could be improved only when purported progressive policies accommodated those crucial elites whose support was needed to sustain the social order.

Bell voters consider negotiation the appropriate means for settling constitutional controversies. Bell championed the Crittenden Compromise because crucial elites were willing to support extending the Missouri Compromise line to the Pacific Ocean. Traditional constitutional exegesis plays a role in the bargaining process by which official constitutional meanings are established. What matters, however, is whom constitutional arguments persuade, not whether the arguments meet some apolitical criteria for soundness. Whether persons had a constitutional right to bring slaves into the territories depended on what plausible constitutional understanding would have best secured a bisectional consensus. For Bell voters, no person, section, or political interest may unilaterally impose a solution to a problem of constitutional evil, no matter how strongly they believe the weight of constitutional evidence favors their position.

Constitutional institutions foster social peace by privileging policies that most citizens will tolerate. The fundamental protection in 1789 against national laws emancipating all slaves or nationalizing human bondage was the constitutional requirement that national policies be passed by a Senate expected to be biased toward free-state concerns *and* by a House of Representatives expected to be biased toward slave-state concerns. The fundamental protection for slavery in 1850 was a national party system that required successful coalitions to compete for Southern votes. Bell and Douglas both supported continued judicial policy making on slavery in 1857 because they recognized that the Taney Court was likely to make slavery policies acceptable to the most people in the different sections of the United States.

Constitutional norms and institutions mitigate the zealotry endemic to ordinary democratic politics. Bereft of constitutional guidance, political actors are prone to pursue visions of justice that threaten the fundamental interests of other citizens. Madison knew that social peace was shattered as often by proponents of the true religion on crusades as by the avaricious coveting their neighbors' goods.[74] Constitutionalism prevents the politics of justice from destabilizing political regimes by providing unambiguous protections for some crucial interests likely to be insufficiently accommodated by ordinary politics and also by establishing institutions that privilege the policy choices that satisfy most powerful political actors. Judicial review is constitutionally desirable under this system because justices often reach centrist decisions on matters that badly divide national legislatures. Taney Court justices rejected sectional understandings that would have limited federal power to recapture fugitive slaves and eradicate the international slave trade. The contemporary court has been more successful than Congress at finding a middle ground on abortion and affirmative action.[75]

When constitutional institutions are functioning normally, citizens need not concern themselves with regime maintenance. Political actors in stable constitutional orders are free to interpret constitutional provisions consistently with their best understandings of justice. The structure of governing institutions ensures that public policies on most matters are acceptable to crucial political elites. The Jacksonian party system guaranteed that no

---

[74] Hamilton, Madison, and Jay, *Federalist Papers*, p. 84.
[75] See e.g. *Grutter v. Bollinger*, 539 U.S. 306, 326 (2003); *Gratz v. Bollinger*, 539 U.S. 244 (2003); *Planned Parenthood of Southeastern Pa. v. Casey*, 505 U.S. 833 (1992).

measure hostile to Southern interests could become law. The present process by which Supreme Court justices are selected guarantees that members of the Nazi Party will not gain control of the federal courts. By placing strong institutional barriers against proposals that might disrupt national union, good constitutions foster the conditions necessary for constructive dialogues about the good society. Rather than superimpose a vision of justice on a politics of interests, constitutions may function best by sufficiently protecting interests so that ordinary politics may be about justice. Peaceful advocacy of extremist policies does more to educate than threaten democracies when outlandish proposals will not become law unless most citizens are persuaded.

Constitutions are nevertheless imperfect vehicles for preserving the social peace. The persons responsible for their framing and ratification make mistakes. Even the best-designed constitution is capable of systemically generating outcomes that too many people find unacceptable. In these circumstances, citizens in constitutional relationships must accommodate more evil than originally anticipated. New means must be found for further empowering the wicked. When the original constitutional protections for slavery failed, John Bell and his political allies turned to political parties and judicial review as expedients for preserving the constitutional commitment to bisectionalism. These practices, in turn, provided additional protections for slavery. Such guarantees were justified only to the extent that preserving the constitutional relationship between the sections was justified.

Constitutional evil, stupidity, and tragedy are consequences of human diversity. Citizens of heterogeneous polities secure their fundamental interests and values in part by cooperating with others seeking to secure different interests and values. The constitutional bargains they strike are deficient from perspectives offered by any coherent theory of justice. Such settlements are rooted only in a common commitment that differences will not prevent mutually beneficial cooperation, and they are justified if maintaining a regime is better than secession and possible civil war.

Dred Scott teaches Americans that secession, civil war, or other political disasters result when constitutions generate answers to fundamental political and constitutional questions that prove unacceptable to crucial political actors. The Taney Court's decision in 1857 did not cause the Civil War by declaring that Congress could not ban slavery in the territories and that former slaves could not become American citizens, no matter how morally wrong and constitutionally egregious that ruling was. Enough Americans accepted either those constitutional rules or the procedures by which those rules were made to prevent further disruption to an endangered constitutional order. Secession and civil war occurred when existing constitutional rules permitted a sectional coalition to take power, a coalition committed to making slavery policies that were unacceptable to a geographically concentrated minority whose support was necessary for maintaining the antebellum constitutional order. Lincoln failed the Constitution by forgetting that his obligation to adopt a plausible interpretation of the Constitution that best preserved the social peace was constitutionally higher than his obligation to adopt a plausible interpretation of the Constitution that best promoted justice.

The lessons drawn from *Dred Scott* remain vibrant. The case might teach Americans that persons responsible for creating and maintaining new constitutions in heterogeneous societies cannot be Lincolnians. Leaders must ordinarily concentrate on preserving the social peace through agreement on rules and procedures that promise to generate social policies acceptable to crucial political actors for the foreseeable future. The regime maintenance function of constitutions is particularly important in many Eastern European, Middle Eastern, Asian, and African countries whose populations include distinctive subcultures that occupy distinctive territories. Finding grounds on which these people can live together – not implementing some vision of justice – is the fundamental constitutional task.[76]

Contemporary citizens of the United States enjoy greater freedom to indulge in Lincolnian quests for constitutional justice than persons in many other nations. The United States today has a majoritarian constitutional order and a social order likely to sustain majority rule.[77] Divisions between the two parties that regularly contest elections are relatively small, and most minorities are geographically dispersed. A very high probability exists that crucial political elites will find acceptable whatever policies present constitutional institutions yield. Many citizens are upset when the Supreme Court strikes down bans on abortion or declares affirmative action policies constitutional. Nevertheless, no one riots in the streets or moves toward secession, even when they think the justices have unconstitutionally determined the winner of a close presidential election.[78] As long as constitutional institutions yield policies that protect vital interests, citizens are free to use all constitutional means to make the Constitution "the best it can be."

Whether Americans should consistently insist on the best plausible understanding of the Constitution is open to question. Broader consensus on

---

[76] See Robert A. Dahl, *Democracy and Its Critics* (Yale University Press: New Haven, 1989), pp. 254–5; Benjamin Reilly, *Democracy in Divided Societies: Electoral Engineering for Conflict Management* (Cambridge University Press: New York, 2001).

[77] See Arend Lijphart, *Patterns of Democracy: Government Forms and Performance in Thirty-Six Countries* (Yale University Press: New Haven, 1999), pp. 31–3.

[78] Dworkin, *Law's Empire*, pp. 256–7.

what is acceptable might improve politics in the United States. Recent tendencies toward political polarization have produced gridlock, a decline of comity in the elected branches, and a substantial reduction in trust among the general population – all of which are having harmful political consequences.[79] Given the swarm of constitutionalists already advancing the best plausible interpretation of the Constitution, constitutional thinkers might rather spend some energy fashioning the most broadly acceptable plausible interpretation of the Constitution. These political visions might include constitutional protection for civil unions but not gay marriage, substantially increased procedural safeguards for capitally sentenced defendants, and a heavily regulated regime of legal abortion.

The constitution exhibit at the Bicentennial celebration seriously misrepresents the process by which constitutions are created and maintained. Persons do not sign constitutions in private. Constitutions begin as agreements and endure only as long as crucial political actors continue to reach temporary agreements when confronted with constitutional controversies. The communal nature of constitutional life would have been better captured by placing visitors to the Bicentennial celebration in rooms of thirty and then asking the collective whether to ratify. Participants in this setting would have negotiated their constitutional relationships. Citizens signing this constitution would acknowledge that under certain conditions they were consenting to a constitution as understood by other citizens. No one could sign the constitution in memory of Frederick Douglass unless they knew that such an interpretation was acceptable to most people in the room.

CONSTITUTIONAL JUSTICE OR CONSTITUTIONAL PEACE

Lincoln and contemporary Lincoln voters promise Americans a "justice-seeking" constitutionalism.[80] The Constitution in their hands is an "instrument of justice,"[81] which if interpreted correctly will provide citizens with "a blueprint of the good society,"[82] a robust democracy, and the rule of law. Although certain constitutional compromises are necessary to create and

---

[79] See e.g. Jon R. Bond and Richard Fleisher, eds., *Polarized Politics: Congress and the President in a Partisan Era* (CQ Press: Washington, D.C., 2000); Sarah A. Binder, *Stalemate: Causes and Consequences of Legislative Gridlock* (Brookings Institution: Washington, D.C., 2003); Eric M. Uslaner, *The Decline of Comity in Congress* (University of Michigan Press: Ann Arbor, 1994).

[80] See Lawrence G. Sager, "Justice in Plain Clothes: Reflections on the Thinness of Constitutional Law," 88 *Northwestern University Law Review*, 410, 416 (1993).

[81] Sotirios A. Barber, "Whither Moral Realism in Constitutional Theory? A Reply to Professor McConnell," 64 *Chicago-Kent Law Review*, 111, 127 (1988).

[82] Moore, "Natural Law," p. 394.

maintain a constitutional union, constitutional theory serves to mitigate these constitutional evils, stupidities, and tragedies to the extent interpretively feasible. Constitutional controversies are resolved consistently with what interpreters believe will make the United States a more just society. Duly constituted constitutional authorities, contemporary Lincoln voters proclaim, must at times pursue constitutional justice at the cost of the constitutional peace. Lincoln was right to fight the Civil War, they argue, because he was right about the best interpretation of the antebellum Constitution.

Today's Bell voters question these constitutional priorities. They see constitutions primarily as vehicles for preserving the peace among persons who have very different visions of the good society, a robust democracy, and the rule of law. Constitutions promote justice, they argue, by establishing political institutions and norms that help maintain political regimes beset by problems of severe political disagreement. Peace, they maintain, is intrinsically more just than war. When most people are rational and morally decent, choices made in conditions of peace are likely to promote justice in the long run. Lincoln was wrong to fight the Civil War, Bell voters believe, even if he was right about the best interpretation of the Constitution, because just causes are better realized by persuasion than by force. Had different battlefield accidents occurred, they warn, Lincoln's military choice might have entrenched human bondage in the South and enabled an independent Confederacy to enslave Central America.

Whether preserving the peace would have promoted justice in 1860 is questionable. Southern repression of antislavery speech violated the constitutional commitment to republican procedures for making slavery policy. Slave-state citizens unfamiliar with the constitutional and moral arguments against human bondage lacked the capacities necessary to make just choices on such issues as the constitutional status of slavery in the territories. Still, the marketplace of ideas was not entirely dysfunctional when Lincoln took office. Most slave-owners and slave-state citizens had some exposure to the basic arguments against slavery. Lively debates over emancipation were taking place in crucial border states. The good society under these imperfect conditions might have been better realized by the candidate of constitutional peace than by the candidate of constitutional justice. A vote for John Bell was a vote to accommodate more evil than constitutionally necessary in order to maintain constitutional conversations, however truncated, that over time *might* have realized a more just society.

The case for John Bell is stronger when we move from 1860 to 2006, from domestic policy to international affairs. Adversaries for the remainder of human history will have the capacity to inflict catastrophic damage on each other whenever they are unable to resolve disputes over justice peaceably. Peace will come to the Middle East and other troubled regions only when crucial political actors on all sides are willing to accept policies they regard as violating basic human rights and sacrificing important interests. The last best hope of mankind is that the conditions of an initially unjust settlement will suffice to bring about a better world over time. Contemporary constitutionalists who prefer fighting to the death in the name of justice will likely rid the world of human depravity only by ridding the world of human beings.

Index

CPSIA information can be obtained
at www.ICGtesting.com
Printed in the USA
LVHW010927191221
706635LV00004B/130